THE
COUNTRY HOUSEWIFE'S
FAMILY COMPANION

In memory of
ANDREW AGNEW,
1914–1996
Gentleman and farmer.

THE
COUNTRY HOUSEWIFE'S
Family Companion

WILLIAM ELLIS

With an introduction
by
MALCOLM THICK

PROSPECT BOOKS
2000

This edition published in Great Britain by Prospect Books in 2000 at Allaleigh House, Blackawton, Totnes, Devon TQ9 7DL.

The Country Housewife's Family Companion was first published in 1750 for James Hodges, London and B. Collins, Salisbury. This is a full transcript of the text.

British Library Cataloguing in Publication Data:
A catalogue entry for this book is available from the British Library.

ISBN 1 903018 005

Typeset and designed by Tom Jaine.

Printed and bound in Great Britain by the Cromwell Press, Trowbridge, Wiltshire.

CONTENTS

Introduction   7

The
Country Housewife's Family Companion

Frontispiece   28

Title Page   29

Preface   31

Introduction   33

Part I   41

Part II   248

Table of Contents   464

Glossary   481

Frontispiece from Richard Bradley, *The Country Housewife and Lady's Director*, 6th edition, 1736 (facsimile, Prospect Books, 1980). The contrast between this depiction of the rural idyll, and that shown in the frontispiece to William Ellis (below, page 28) is discussed in the Introduction.

Introduction

William Ellis was born in the 1680s. Little is known of his early life. He had sufficient schooling to write many books but the absence of classical allusions in his works suggests a basic education in a village school, or as an apprentice, rather than that of a gentleman. He was related to the Sherard brothers, both distinguished botanists. From stray comments in his books we learn that, prior to taking up farming, he was for a while an Exciseman. An uncle was a London brewer: Ellis was his executor and spent some time himself as a brewer in London. He may have been apprenticed to his uncle, carrying on the trade after he died.[1]

Often called 'William Ellis of Little Gaddesden' because in his books he firmly associates himself with this Hertfordshire village, Ellis probably started farming there in 1717 and so had long experience of country living by the time *The Country Housewife* was written. Gaddesden parish was then about thirty miles from London, close enough to feel the pull of the London food markets. Situated 'high up on a wooded spur of the Chilterns', the parish was at the edge of a plateau falling away gradually to the south-east with varying soils of clay, gravel and chalk, and little natural water. When *The Country Housewife* was written, all but 120 acres of cultivated land had been enclosed. At that time, Little Gaddesden had one long street of houses, most of them with vegetable or flower gardens. This pleasant rural scene was peopled by a fair number of poor landless labourers and itinerant beggars, whose plight enclosure had worsened, as well as farmers such as Ellis. Most of Ellis' children had grown up and left the farm; in 1748 one

---

[1] Pehr Kalm, *Kalm's account of his visit to England on his way to America in 1748*, trans Joseph Lucas, 1892, pp. 192, 195; Blanche Henrey, *British Horticultural and Botanical Literature before 1800*, vol II, pp. 65–7. Please note that footnote references have not been made to *The Country Housewife* itself.

son and a daughter lived with him. The farm had been purchased with his second wife's money and he dissipated much of the rest of her wealth on 'early experiments in husbandry'. She 'grieved so much' over the losses that she 'had not been able to recover herself' despite his partial return to prosperity by the time *The Country Housewife* was published.[1]

We are fortunate that the Swedish botanist, Pehr Kalm visited Little Gaddesden in 1748 specifically to meet Ellis, whose reputation as a writer had spread to Europe. He spent three weeks in the village and left an account of rural life there as well as much information about Ellis. Moreover, Ellis put a good deal about his life and work in his own books, *The Country Housewife* being a notable example.[2]

What sort of man was Ellis? In 1748, in his sixties, he claimed to have been generally healthy all his life apart from occasional attacks of gout. Kalm thought him mercenary and secretive. Some of his neighbours regarded him as eccentric because of the time he spent writing, and gullible for believing all the stories they told him. I think both Kalm and the neighbours witnessed Ellis' talent as a journalist – he was ever willing to listen and he coaxed information from people, giving little in return so as not to disturb the flow.[3] He was a good businessman, employing a number of ways of making money. He kept meticulous accounts and a detailed diary: on many occasions in *The Country Housewife* he tells us the precise date on which he sold some grain, visited an inn or killed a pig. Oh! that his papers had survived. Ellis' suspicions of rural

---

[1] When he died he still had substantial mortgages on his land. *Hertfordshire Archives*, D/Els M137; Vicars Bell, *Little Gaddesden*, 1959, pp. 1–2; Kalm, pp. 191–2. See also Vicars Bell, *To Meet Mr Ellis*, 1956, for further information on the village and the man.

[2] Kalm, pp. 188–342.

[3] Kalm, pp. 104, 196–7. Like many a journalist, Ellis sometimes misinterpreted what he hurriedly extracted from his interviewees. Kalm complained that Ellis wrote that Laplanders were not plagued with scurvy because they ate salt fish whereas Kalm had told him the salt in their diet was a principal *cause* of scurvy.

shopkeepers, warnings against shady dealers generally and remarks on rural thieves portray him as somewhat cagey and cautious. He was, however, an honest dealer himself, paying his day labourers in cash each night and settling other bills promptly.[1]

William Ellis is chiefly remembered as a writer. With the re-issues, anonymous works, and other confusions of eighteenth century publishing it is difficult to be certain of his exact output but I believe he wrote eleven books.

Apart from *The Country Housewife* and a book on brewing, all were agricultural works, many dealing with the husbandry of his own area. Starting in 1731, he produced a stream of books until his death in 1759. An edited collection of his farming works was published in 1772. Ellis wrote the type of book needed at the time, 'practical advice on routine operations and information on specific techniques or farm animals'. He was described as, 'probably the most widely read farming author in 1750' and, although his posthumous reputation was for many years not high, he is now recognized as a knowledgeable writer on agricultural matters. He was keen to promote new farming methods but was careful to cost them so that farmers could assess their economic worth. Pehr Kalm said of him in 1748 (before he had met him), 'Mr Ellis was a man who had a great reputation for his Practique...in Rural Economy, but still more for his many writings on the same Art, which latterly he published yearly'.[2]

Ellis' reputation as a writer suffered after his death because he wrote too much, too fast. His publisher demanded a steady stream of text and, when writing part-works such as *The Modern Husbandman*, he might have to supply up to 40,000 words a month. In effect, he was an agricultural journalist. When stuck for copy he improvised. In *The Modern Husbandman* for

---

[1] Kalm, p. 191.
[2] George Fussell, *More Old English Farming Books*, Aberdeen, 1978, pp. 11–12; Rothamsted Experimental Station, *Library Catalogue*, 1940, p. 53; Kalm, p. 187.

January 1744 for instance, correspondence between a gentleman and Ellis over the purchase of a plough is inserted verbatim, including a copy of the bill of exchange for £3 3s received in payment. A later critic condemned 'all those random and ridiculous details which have so disgraced his page'.[1]

Ellis also filled out his text (*The Country Housewife* included) with anecdotes of country life – although these tales may have been of interest to his readers who could identify with the situations described, and they are certainly of interest to us. Later critics were unsympathetic. The anonymous editor of his works in 1772 made sure that 'all his gypsies, wenches, thieves, rogues, &c., are discarded, and his old woman's tales which filled a page but diminished its value, are thrown aside'.[2]

Ellis the writer was not appreciated by his fellow villagers. One in 1748 told Pehr Kalm that, 'if Mr Ellis did not make more profit out of sitting and scribbling books, and selling the manuscripts to the publishers, than he realized from his farming, he would soon have to go and beg – for Mr Ellis mostly sits at home in his room and writes books, and goes sometimes a whole week without going out into his ploughed lands or meadows to look after the work, but mostly trusts his servants, and son who is still a boy.'[3] Here was another reason for Ellis' falling reputation – he wrote about farming but neglected his own farm. Kalm was shocked when, on arriving at Little Gaddesden, he went in search of Ellis in the fields and asked a farmer, 'Who is the owner of this field, which to a great extent stands under water, and is so ill cultivated?' and, 'Who works on the enclosure away there where the moss has so excessively got the upper hand?' The answer to both questions was, 'Mr Ellis'.[4] Other gentlemen visited the farm and were similarly disappointed.

[1] Ellis, *Modern Husbandman*, January, 1744, pp. 99–100; Ellis, *Husbandry, Abridged and Methodized,* 1772, Preface by the Editor.
[2] *Ellis' Husbandry, Abridged,* 1772, Preface.
[3] Kalm, p. 188.
[4] Kalm, p. 187.

Ellis was, however, much more than a prolific writer and indifferent farmer. The popularity of his early works caused gentlemen to write and ask advice, encouraged by the practical nature of his books. Ellis wrote back and also took to touring the country providing advice on the ground. He alludes at one point to his 'four years travels through several Counties in England',[1] and his knowledge of farming, brewing and food in many parts of England and Wales bears witness to the extent of his travels and his journalistic zeal for gathering information.

The books and the travel publicized his other money-making activities. He was an agricultural seedsman, selling seeds of the improving grasses, fodder crops and new strains of grain he wrote about. Ellis relates an anecdote about a gentleman's pig, heard when he was 'delivering to him some of my profitable Ladyfinger natural grass-seed, Tyne Grass-seed and Honeysuckle grass-seed'. Like other seedsmen of the time, he sold seeds with a page of 'directions for their management' thrust into each packet.[2] He had a nursery of local varieties of apple, pear , cherry, damson and elder trees for sale; he delivered ornamental fowls – 'Tame Pheasants, Guinea Hens, and Poland Dunghill Fowls'; he hawked a number of secret recipes, a new type of compound manure, a way to keep rats from granaries; and he sold a variety of new or improved agricultural implements. On pages 379 to 382 is a section headed '*ADVERTISEMENT*' which is probably a copy of a handbill distributed by Ellis to help sell his wares.

The agricultural implements elicited a good deal of interest at the time but were later dismissed as failures. On his own farm, he did not use the implements he so vigorously advertised, or even keep a full set for display (he told Kalm they would be stolen); having them made to order by local craftsmen. Indeed, Ellis used none of the improvements he

[1] Ellis, *London and Country Brewer*, 1759, p. 249.
[2] Malcolm Thick, 'Garden Seeds in England before the late Eighteenth Century: II, The Trade in Seeds to 1760', *Agricultural History Review*, vol 38, 1990, p. 115.

advocated in print on his own farm. We can only speculate whether his domestic economy was run in accordance with *The Country Housewife*. When the famous four-wheeled seed drill Ellis invented was demonstrated, it worked so badly that Kalm remarked acidly, 'Had man for all time past not been able to sow in a better manner than was done here to-day, mankind would long before have died of hunger.'[1] Ellis' drill was the latest in a number of attempts in England since 1600 to mechanize seed-sowing; later inventors benefited from his and earlier work.[2]

Ellis was, in short, an entrepreneur. Not content, or not cut out to be an ordinary farmer, he turned a lively mind to many ways of making money. His businesslike manner affronted Kalm, a gentleman and scholar who did not regard knowledge as a marketable commodity. He was shocked when, on taking his leave in April 1748, Ellis gave him a list of secret recipes he was prepared to divulge only for money and then tried to sell him a fourteen-day escorted tour of the south of England with instruction on 'English Rural Economy' in return for the keep of himself and his horse, 'with twelve to fourteen guineas into the bargain'.[3]

The loss of reputation after his death recalls a similar fate which befell the earlier writer on botany, agriculture and domestic economy Richard Bradley. I feel that the same prejudices may have been responsible. Both were working amongst gentlemen and writing books of interest to them but they were not themselves gentlemen, tainted by the need to make money from their ideas. Later readers did not make allowances for this when reading books hastily put together with the immediacy of journalism rather than careful scholarship.

The Country Housewife's Family Companion is not primarily a cookery book. It is a manual of country living, intended for

[1] Kalm, pp. 189–91, 231–2.
[2] Malcolm Thick, *The Neat House Gardens*, Totnes, 1998, pp. 70–73.
[3] Kalm, p. 342.

the wives of husbandmen, yeomen and country gentlemen. The comprehensive title page lists the topics covered, summing up the scope of the book succinctly as 'Suitable directions for whatever relates to the management and good oeconomy of the domestick concerns of a country life.' Recipes and methods of cooking form a sizeable part, but only a part, of a book with a great deal to say on the management of farmyard animals (pigs and fowls), preserving meat and vegetables, bread-making, malting, brewing and strong liquors of various sorts, management of the dairy, medicines both for humans and animals, warnings about country thieves and dishonest traders, hints on running a frugal household, advertisements for other works penned by Ellis, and a fascinating collection of anecdotes which defy categorization. Safe to say that nothing quite like it had been published in England before. Richard Bradley's *Country Housewife*[1] is more narrowly concerned with food, cookery and preserving, without the broad sweep of topics covered by Ellis. One has to look much further back to find comparisons: Markham's *English Housewife* of 1615 has the same comprehensive feel, especially when read as part of his compendium, 'The Way to Get Wealth'.[2] The same author's handsome 1616 edition of the *Maison Rustique*[3] contains a good deal on country households but little cookery, whilst Thomas Tusser's *Five Hundred points of Good Husbandry*, 1573,[4] covers all aspects of country household management, albeit in much less depth than Ellis. Tusser went through many editions, including one in 1744 only a few years before Ellis' book. If sixteenth-century doggerel had a ready market at the time, maybe Ellis (or, more likely, his publisher) saw a demand for a more up-to-date and detailed work.

[1] Richard Bradley, *The Country Housewife and Lady's Director*, intr. Caroline Davidson, 1980.
[2] Gervase Markham, *The Way to Get Wealth*, 1623.
[3] Charles Estienne and Jean Liebault, trans Richard Surflet, *Maison Rustique, or the Country Farm*, 1616.
[4] Thomas Tussser, *Five Hundred Points of Good Husbandry*, 1573.

The charm of *The Country Housewife* is that it has little organization: Ellis frequently digresses in order to relate a choice anecdote or even, one suspects, just to fill out the pages. The book's idiosyncrasies are apparent from the start. The title page announces the start of *The Country Housewife's Family Companion*, and the introduction echoes the title whereas the headings of the first and second parts and of the preface are to *The Country Family's Profitable Director*.

The book is in two parts of roughly equal length although part one is not described as such. No evidence has been found that they were issued separately but the work does not read as if planned as one volume from the start. Some topics – meal, grain and bread-making, the dairy, as well as a miscellany of recipes – occur in both parts. Others – poultry, harvest food and pickled pork, bacon and ham, preserving vegetables and fruit, veal production, pig keeping, cures for cows, brewing and malting – occur only once. The medicine and dairy sections are sketchy in the first part, much fuller in the second. The first part ends with a piece praising Scroop Egerton, the late Duke of Bridgewater, and reads like a conclusion. I suspect Ellis was pressed by his publisher for a work on rural household management and he quickly gathered together the information to hand and produced the first part. The publisher (then, as now, hard taskmasters) said the book was too slim and did not cover everything fully. Ellis did more research, pestered his maid, farm servants, neighbours, friends, visitors, correspondents and casual acquaintances for information, lifted more material from books and, pressed for a finished manuscript, he grafted the new material on to the existing text as a second part. The result, rushed and unpolished, is all the more interesting to the historian of rural life.

His publisher may have commissioned the frontispiece as an ironic comment on the book. Unlike other cookery books, here is no flattering portrait of the author, nor an immaculate kitchen with fashionably dressed servants, simply a tranquil farmyard scene.[1] It echoes the frontispiece to Richard Bradley's *Country Housewife* of 1736, but his scene is full of people engaged in country pursuits with a glimpse into a busy dairy whereas at the front of Ellis' book, one person milks a cow in a farmyard flanked by down-at-heel buildings and a battered paling fence. The scene recalls Pehr Kalm's impression of Ellis' farm – not worthy of so important a writer.[2]

Ellis was no cook. All his recipes came from others and he did not touch a pot or pan himself. He gained a good deal of information close to home: his maid is frequently cited as a source for recipes and the poor girl must have been fed up with his questioning. Friends and neighbours provided most of his recipes; occasional help came from gentry households but he relied most heavily on the wives of husbandmen and yeomen, who, he also hoped, would be the bulk of his readership. Many recipes are introduced as 'The Hertfordshire way…' and this makes the book of interest to local historians. But Ellis also gathered recipes on his travels, asking for details of dishes he ate at inns. On 13th June 1749, 'baiting at the Cat-Inn at East-Grinstead', he watched the cook-maid make Sussex pond pudding and noted the recipe. He obtained a good deal of information on the use of oatmeal from Cheshire and Lancashire visitors to fairs and markets in his locality. The scattering of Welsh recipes throughout the book was mostly derived from passing drovers or migrant workers, although a London correspondent passed on the Welsh way of preparing hogs-puddings from his wife, 'being what she practised when she lived with her Aunt in Wales'. Letters containing recipes were sometimes inserted straight into the text: a worthy gentleman wrote from London about baked pears in 1735, and a grateful young man, whom Ellis recommended as bailiff to a Devon estate, wrote from Plympton with a number of local recipes.

[1] For example: Edward Kidder, *Receipts of Pastry and Cookery*, c. 1720; Martha Bradley, *The British Housewife*, 1756; E. Smith, *The Compleat Housewife*, 1753.
[2] Kalm, p. 187.

As was common amongst cookery writers at the time, Ellis also took recipes from published sources. Many suspected borrowings are unacknowledged, but the characteristic opening word 'Take', which he does not use for recipes written in his own words, indicate a printed source. Not that Ellis was bashful about plagiarism, he freely admits to copying from other books. His reading was, however, quite narrow and almost entirely of very old cookery books, described by him as 'ancient authors'. in the main, he took recipes from works published in the seventeenth century: Gervase Markham, John Murrell, William Rabisha, Kenelm Digby, John Houghton as well as the more recent *Country Housewife* of Richard Bradley. Either he looked at the old books because they had the traditional, country recipes he sought or, more likely, these were the works he found in a local gentleman's library to which he had access (that of the Duke of Bridgewater perhaps?)[1]

As to the recipes themselves, this is the best book of the period to look for plain country fare, the everyday food of labourers, husbandmen and yeomen. Although he had lived in London and must have made frequent journeys there on business, Ellis ignores all fashionable food. There are no ragoûts or fricassées here, nothing *à la creme*, no bisques, not a salad, and butter the only sauce. Meat recipes are principally for the pig (pickled or cured), for offal, and for cheap ways of extending scarce resources. There is no plain, simple cookery of large joints. Puddings, both savoury and sweet, abound. Ellis explained that 'Pudding is so necessary a part of an Englishman's food, that it and beef are accounted the victuals they most love'. Black-, white- and hogs-puddings were by-products of killing a pig.

---

[1] The books he made use of were probably: Gervase Markham, *The English Housewife*, 1615; John Murrell, *Murrel's Two Books of Cookerie and Carving*, 1638; William Rabisha, *The Whole Body of Cookery Dissected*, 1661; Sir Kenelm Digby, *The Closet of the Eminently Learned Sir Kenelm Digby, Kt, Opened*, 1669; John Houghton, *A Collection for Improvement of Husbandry and Trade*, 1692; Richard Bradley, *op.cit.*

Ellis was also very fond of apple pies, accounting them 'some of the cheapest and most agreeable food a farmer's family can make use of', and filling pages with a poem by Leonard Welstead (1688–1747) in their praise. Apple pasties could be pocketed and eaten by farmers and their servants in the fields. Ellis had his maid make them every week or ten days 'from August to all the time when my hoarded apples last'. Pease soup, broth, gruels, frumenty, porridge, possets and suchlike wet and stodgy foods reflect a diet which in some ways had changed little in centuries.

The common thread running through the recipes is economy. 'Cheap' is the word most frequently encountered in the recipe headings. The apple pies were, 'a main part of a prudent, frugal farmer's family-food'; pancakes were 'one of the cheapest and most serviceable dishes of a farmer's family in particular'; potatoes were of use 'to save much consumption of eggs, meat, and bread'. Frugal housewives were singled out for praise. Mindful that some of his readers were richer than others, some dishes have plain recipes for the poor and variants with added cream, meat, fruit or sugar for the gentry.

Over thirty pages are devoted to victualling harvest workers in Hertfordshire, an important part of a country housewife's year. Bringing in the harvest was vital to the prosperity of corn-growing counties like Hertfordshire and extra labour was employed. At harvest, good workers found themselves, for a short period, much in demand. Ellis explained, 'In this county we hire harvest-men long before harvest, by way of security, that we may not be at a loss for them when we most want them; and give each man thirty or six and thirty shillings for his month's service, besides victualling and lodging them in the house all that time, for then they are ready early and late to do our work'.[1] In providing for these men, 'she that can do

---

[1] *Agrarian History of England and Wales*, 1989, ed. G.E. Mingay, vol. VI, p. 677; Kalm, (p. 191), said that the normal rate for day-labourers at Little Gaddesden outside harvest was 8d to 10d a day, say 20 shillings a month.

it cheapest, and most satisfactory, is the best housewife'. Ellis advised laying in a good store of root and green vegetables, a stock of suet for puddings, and fattening up a beast to slaughter for meat – a broken-mouthed ewe, a Welsh runt, or a 20–30 stone hog. He favoured the hog, and went into great detail on how to kill and preserve one in hot weather as well as the culinary uses of every part of the animal, and the art of making bacon and sausages.

The knack of harvest victualling was to have the men content with the variety, quality and amount of food, thus ensuring that they worked hard, whilst not spending too lavishly. During the wheat harvest they worked from four in the morning until eight at night, eating five times a day and subsisting on a diet of apple pie, cheese, bread, milk-porridge, hashed meat, boiled meat with vegetables, plum pudding, and cake, washed down with small and strong beer. Dinner at one o'clock was taken in the fields and was not to be late lest the men left off work to wait for it. Strong ale and cheese in the early evening kept their spirits up and spiced loaf or seed-cake provided variety at supper.

Ellis begins both the first and second parts of his book with discussions of bread grains, meal and flour. He tackles the subject from the viewpoint of a farmer, with opening paragraphs on the main types of wheat sown in England. Although these sections contain a fair number of bread recipes from books, neighbours and his own household, here, as in other parts of the book, it is household economy that concerns him most. He discusses whether a farmer should use his own wheat for bread or, if it is top quality, sell it and buy in the grade of meal appropriate to his family circumstances. Mixtures of barley and wheat (maslin) and other grains and pulses in bread-making are considered, balancing economy and palatability. The example of the careful way a labourer's wife made best use of a bushel of barley, or a yeoman's household subsisted on barley-bread are calculated to encourage frugality. Ellis covers the storage of meal to prevent its decay or infestation, how to make and keep yeast, and how not to be cheated by millers. The first sections on bread touches on oatmeal and much more space is devoted to this food in the second part, including recipes from Cheshire and Lancashire. Ellis met men and women from Manchester at local fairs and was told that they lived largely on oatcakes. He also questioned Pehr Kalm on the diet of Scandinavians, learning that the 'bread' of Laplanders was dried fish, that some Norwegians made bread from ground bark and that Swedes made do with flour of ground buck-bean and marsh-trefoil root.[1]

Apart from potatoes and dried peas, Ellis does not bother much with recipes for vegetables, contenting himself with describing ways of preserving roots, greens such as cabbages and beans, onions and garlic. Pease soup, porridge or pudding he regarded as cheap and filling meals and potatoes were also recommended as meat substitutes. They were becoming more popular in southern England at this time: in the north they were already a staple and Ellis remarks that 'At Manchester, a great Market in Lancashire, Potatoes stand in many Sacks as well as Oatemeal for publick Sale'. Advice is also provided on preserving a wide variety of fruit and producing syrups from fruit juices. Although Ellis is addressing a country audience, not bothering with the delicate vegetables produced for London tables, he brings out the importance of preserving fruit and vegetables in season, to provide variety throughout the year.

The dairy was, from earliest times, the domain of the farmer's wife, deriving its name from the Middle English 'dey', a serving maid, and 'erie', her place of work.[1] After an unsatisfactory attempt to cover the topic in part one, Ellis does give a full description of dairying in the second part of the book. But there is more here than dairying, he has much to say on

[1] Kalm, pp. 194–5.

improved grasses and fodder crops for cattle, including an advertisement for his own seed business. We learn about specialities in other many parts of the country: correspondents write about Devonshire clotted cream and a dairymaid reveals Somerset dairying methods. Cheese making in Somerset, Cheshire, Wales, Gloucestershire and Shropshire are described, largely thanks to talkative dairymaids, and Ellis also mentions a mixed ewes-milk and cows-milk cheese made in the Vale of Glamorgan. Cheese, durable and portable, was a major item of commerce for many areas. Butter too was a valuable commodity. Dairies near London sold it fresh but those further afield salted it in pots or barrels for sale, and country people did the same with butter for use at home. Ellis met a grazier from Towcester in Northamptonshire on the road who told him he sold butter to London the year round.

The section on veal calf production was included in the book by Ellis because this part of a farm was supervised by the farmer's wife. It was a by-product of dairying which, Ellis claimed, might be sometimes more profitable than butter or cheese. He himself sold his calves at Leighton Buzzard to specialist calf-rearers who prepared them for the London markets (the pull of London's demand is evident here as in many aspects of Hertfordshire husbandry). The descriptions of cramming calves and bleeding them to produce the white flesh demanded by London customers are not pleasant reading but they do further remind us that, by the mid-eighteenth century, many farmers near the capital tailored their production to the whims of consumers and thereby made a good living.[2]

Ellis gives advice on other farmyard activities such as pig keeping, poultry, and eggs. They had traditionally been tasks for the country housewife, producing food for the family, or at most pin money for wives and daughters. By the middle of

[1] Robin Weir and Caroline Liddell, *Recipes from the Dairy*, 1998, p. 9.
[2] The price of veal increased significantly the closer one got to London at this time. *Ag. Hist. Eng. & Wales*, vol. VI, 1989, pp. 193–4, 228.

the eighteenth century, however, such was the demand from London for eggs, fowls, milk and cheese, as well the butter and veal mentioned above, that these by-occupations had economic importance, especially in counties like Hertfordshire near to the capital. Ellis notes that Hertfordshire 'Dunghill Fowls' and their eggs were highly esteemed in London 'insomuch that the very cryers of eggs about London Streets take particular care to make the word Hertfordshire be well known'. The money to be made from poultry was recognized by Hertfordshire farmers, who let their wives have all the profit, but only to buy 'what we call common or trivial necessaries in the house, as sugar, plumbs, spices, salt, oatmeal &c. &c.' These 'trivial' items form part of many of Ellis' recipes and were luxuries which lifted an otherwise monotonous diet. Ellis recognized that some poultry keeping had become big business, no longer the province of wives. Turkeys and geese were kept in large flocks in East Anglia, great droves being driven to London for sale to poulterers.

Brewing was another occupation once largely the preserve of the housewife but increasingly becoming a business controlled by men. In London the alewives had given way to big brewers: in 1750 Sir William Calvert's brewery produced 56,000 barrels a year and Truman's sold 46,000 barrels. In the country however, a large number of alehouses still brewed their own beer and nationally sixty per cent of beer was still brewed at home in the 1750s. Ellis devotes only a few pages to brewing in *The Country Housewife*, readers wanting more probably noticed the advertisements in the text for his book on the subject.[1]

So far as we know, Ellis had no medical training, but as head of a rural household he had to have some knowledge of medicine to keep himself and family well. He draws on this knowledge to provide many of the prescriptions in the book, sometimes telling us of specific ills he has cured. The medical

[1] *Ag. Hist. Eng. & Wales,* vol. VI, 1989, pp. 1510.

sections provide an insight into the social history of medicine in Hertfordshire and remind us that life was hard at a time when so many ailments were likely to lead to death.

In his usual disordered fashion, Ellis imposed no system on the sections on medicine. In the first part of the book, a passage headed 'Of cheap, approved, and experienced medicines and remedies for divers diseases incident to human bodies' gives out after seventeen pages with some sensational tales of poisoning. The more modest heading 'Diseases and medicines' in part two opens a more substantial section of over fifty pages. One has the impression that here, as elsewhere, Ellis knew he had to cover this topic but he made a start with little research and had to come back to it. (The first medical section is largely composed of letters to Ellis from various gentlemen with advice and prescriptions.) In the end however, he covered much ground, giving advice on the most troublesome diseases of his time, notably ague, consumption, diabetes, scurvy, smallpox, gout, dropsy, jaundice, King's evil, measles, palsey, rheumatism, digestive disorders, swellings and skin diseases. Sprains, cuts and wounds, hazards of hard labour and crude tools are dealt with, as well as ailments of damp, cold, dirty living with a poor diet: lice, worms and other parasites, sore eyes, sore throats, coughs, indigestion, cramp, chilblains, chaps, toothache and general aches and pains.

Ellis obtained his cures from many sources. He looked for some of his medicines in books . He made however, only about twenty references to books and those he identified were con-temporary, unlike the cookery books he used. Several times he referred to 'Dr Quincy', consulting his *Pharmacopoeia officinalis* of 1749.[1] He also used Thomas Dover's *The ancient physicians legacy* of 1733[2] and publications of the celebrated

[1]John Quincy, *Pharmacopoeia officinalis & extemporanea: or, a compleat English dispensatory,* 1722.
[2] Thomas Dover, *The ancient physician's legacy to his country, being what he has collected in forty-nine years practice,* 1733.

Low Countries physician Herman Boerhaave.[3] As might be expected, the prescriptions from these sources usually meant a trip to the apothecary for mercury, sulphur, turpentine, 'bark' (quinine) and the like.

Most of Ellis' medical advice came from his friends and acquaintances. Margaret Pelling has shown that medicine was of concern to all classes in early modern England and that, especially in towns, recipes for cures circulated freely, often across class boundaries. There were many more men and women engaged full- or part-time in medicine than the university-educated doctors or formally apprenticed apothecaries, a situation reflected in Ellis' book.[4]

About forty of his cures were provided by the gentry, a reflection of Ellis' contact with gentlemen in the course of his business: for example a cure for consumption provided by a Derbyshire gentleman. The 'Gentleman Traveller' who regulated his system with flower of brimstone was probably encountered in a London coffee shop or booksellers. Most medical advice from the gentry was obtained locally: a local gentlemen had a cure for gout (an affliction of the affluent), whilst a lucky man treated for the gravel 'by a Lord in Hertfordshire with a seven-year old bottle of perry, voided almost a handfull of small stones'.

The diseases on which the gentry advised: colic, gout, indigestion and loss of appetite, piles and pimples, reflected no doubt the problems which particularly concerned them but they were by no means indifferent to the illnesses of the poor. Ellis extolled 'The character of a Lord's great and unparallel'd charity'. This local magnate, possibly the late Duke of Bridgewater,[3] 'although he was not bred a physician, extends his charity in a very uncommon manner; for he not only visits

---

[1] Possibly, H. Boerhaave, *Treatise on the Powers of Medicines*, 1740.
[2] Margaret Pelling, *The Common Lot*, 1998. (Especially the introduction.)
[3] Kalm, p. 221. John, 2nd Duke of Bridgewater died, a young bachelor, in February 1748.

the sick in the most contagious illness, but supplies them with medicines at his own cost'.

Some remedies originated from local medical professionals. Doctors like Dr Woodhouse, or Mr Goodwyn, a 'country apothecary', both of Berkhamstead, performed cures about which Ellis got to hear. Such lofty professionals were, as Margaret Pelling found, often willing to help the poor for little or nothing.[1] Ellis told of a 'poor widow and chair-woman' living near him who 'applying herself to a physician, he out of charity bid her stamp the leaves of plantane and nettles together, and take a tea-cup of their juice' to stop her spitting blood. One wonders if this was a country remedy suitable to her means whereas a higher-class patient would have been provided with something made up by an apothecary. In another instance a girl in Little Gaddesden, whose arm would not stop bleeding from a wound, 'cried mightily as she stood at the door of her mother's house' until 'a Hempstead surgeon, coming accidently by' advised applying hogs' dung to the wound. Ellis is ambivalent about doctors, giving them credit for successful cures but finding other cases where their treatment did not work, or where they despaired of a cure and effective treatment was eventually provided by a neighbour or 'country housewife'. Many of the prescriptions in the book originated from 'country housewives' by which Ellis meant women skilled in medicine. They had cures for minor and serious illnesses, mostly using herbs, vegetables and other homely ingredients – butter, treacle, honey, beer or pepper. Whilst some may have been no more then neighbours handing on the wisdom they themselves had been taught, some were called 'doctresses' by Ellis and clearly were highly regarded locally. Not all unlicensed local practitioners were women, Ellis heard of a cure for the itch provided by an exciseman of Ivinghoe 'who also acted as a surgeon'. One enterprising yeoman's wife, Mrs Sibley of Water-End, produced a herbal tonic said to

[1] Pelling, p. 1.

cure a range of diseases, sold at 18d. a quart and Ellis was a sales-agent for a friend, 'a most ingenious chymist', who produced a healing balsam at one shilling a sealed bottle. Ellis may have obtained one of his favourite prescriptions, a fearsome concoction of water and mercury, from this same friend.

Beggars were surprisingly skilled at medicine and Ellis talked to a number of them about remedies for the diseases to which they were prone – lice, skin diseases such as the itch, and rheumatism. A case of 'scald-head' which defeated a local physician was cured by a passing beggar woman, as was a young man crippled with rheumatism. The recurrence of medical advice offered by passing beggars leads one to speculate that they may have made a living from it.

The medicines suggested by Ellis are, as one would expect, predominantly either herbal or composed of ingredients available in a farm kitchen. Camomile, elder, rue, lavender, nettles, chickweed and sweet cicely from garden and hedgerow; mutton fat, honey, butter, vinegar, milk, eggs, ashes, hogs dung and the like; as well as groceries obtainable locally: tobacco, sugar, strong spirits, figs, prunes or pepper. Relatively few cures needed recourse to an apothecary for drugs or chemicals. Whilst there is often a touching faith in the power of homely ingredients to tackle serious illnesses such as consumption or diabetes, very few instances of magic or sympathetic medicine are included in the book.

For many readers the attraction of this book will not be the culinary or social history found therein but the many eccentricities it contains. The advertisements for Ellis' other books, his implements, seeds, and other merchandise; his warnings about thieves and rural shopkeepers; the obituary of his late landlord; a digression on the food of Scandinavians; letters from friends and acquaintances; the very details of his own household; the tales and anecdotes of country life with which these pages are filled. They may have exasperated a later editor, but they contribute mightily to our own pleasure.

Ellis was discursive but never dull. It might also be claimed that, by virtue of listening to friends and neighbours, rather than merely his betters, he succeeded in capturing for us a portrait of the daily diet of a section of society rarely centre-stage. Recovering the foundations of English cookery has never been easy. Food and cookery has ever seemed a trickle-down affair: the lowly aping the grand. Ellis redresses the balance, his recipes betraying a style of rude vigour and considerable bulk, if not refinement.

Malcolm Thick,
Harwell, January 2000.

Publisher's Note

This is a transcript of the original printed text. It reproduces the spelling and punctuation, as well as the typographical conventions. The exceptions are the use of the long 's' and the capitalization of nouns in the body of the text. Here, modern habits have been adopted save in the following instances. The printer often used capital letters at the beginning of direct or reported speech and direct quotation from printed books, rather than quotation marks. This convention has been preserved. Ellis uses the colon as the equivalent of a full-stop: the word following the colon is capitalized. This convention is also retained. Finally, the original capitalization of headings and sub-headings has been reproduced.

As to orthography, a very few corrections have been made (in square brackets), and there is a small number of [*sic*] messages where misunderstanding may arise.

The index or table of contents (mysteriously lacking the letter N) has been reproduced, but the page references are to the present edition.

For comparison's sake, the original text occupied 389 pages and the table of contents 19 pages. The pages measured 190mm high by 120mm wide. This present edition has 433 pages of text, with the contents occupying 16 pages. The page area is 234mm high by 156mm wide.

Thanks are due to Barbara Chesmore for supplying a useful book for the preparation of this edition; also to Alan Davidson for his copy of the original.

THE
COUNTRY HOUSEWIFE's
Family Companion:
OR
PROFITABLE DIRECTIONS for whatever relates to the Management and good Œconomy
OF THE
Domeſtick Concerns of a Country Life,
According to the
PRESENT PRACTICE of the Country Gentleman's, the Yeoman's, the Farmer's, &c. Wives, in the Counties of *Hertford, Bucks,* and other Parts of *England:*
SHEWING
How great SAVINGS may be made in Houſekeeping:
And wherein, among many others,
The following HEADS are particularly treated of and explained:

I. The Preſervation and Improvement of Wheat, Barley, Rye, Oats, and other Meals; with Directions for making ſeveral Sorts of Bread, Cakes, Puddings, Pies, &c.

II. Frugal Management of Meats, Fruits, Roots, and all Sorts of Herbs; beſt Methods of Cookery; and a cheap Way to make Soups, Sauces, Gruels, &c.

III. Directions for the Farm Yard; with the beſt Method of increaſing and fatning all Sorts of Poultry, as Turkies, Geeſe, Ducks, Fowls, &c.

IV. The beſt Way to breed and fatten Hogs; ſundry curious and cheap Methods of preparing Hogs Meat; Directions for curing Bacon, Brawn, pickled Pork, Hams, &c. with the Management of Sows and Pigs.

V. The beſt Method of making Butter and Cheeſe, with ſeveral curious Particulars containing the whole Management of the Dairy.

VI. The ſeveral Ways of making good Malt; with Directions for brewing good Beer, Ale, &c.

With Variety of CURIOUS MATTERS,

Wherein are contained frugal Methods for victualling Harveſt-men, Ways to deſtroy all Sorts of Vermine, the beſt Manner of ſuckling and fattening Calves, Preſcriptions for curing all Sorts of Diſtempers in Cattle, with Variety of curious Receits for Pickling, Preſerving, Diſtilling, &c.

The Whole founded on near thirty Years Experience by
W. ELLIS, *Farmer, at* Little Gaddeſden, *near* Hempſted, Hertfords.

LONDON:
Printed for JAMES HODGES, at the *Looking-glaſs,* facing *St. Magnus* Church, *London-Bridge;* and B. COLLINS, Bookſeller, at *Saliſbury.* 1750.

PREFACE

Country Family's Profitable Director.

THE great losses that have accrued to country families, by a wrong management of their household affairs, has partly induced me to send into the world the following treatise. Woeful experience has shewn this to be true in innumerable instances: The art therefore of saving the penny, and making money go the farthest, I have here endeavoured to make known, by publishing great numbers of serviceable matters, as they have been really practised in the most provident country families, and some of them in my own. The preservation of wheat, barley, and oat meals, meats, roots, fruits, herbs, &c. from the damage of insects, and if infected how to be cured; the making of many sorts of bread, cakes, pies, puddings, tarts; the cooking of many dishes of meat, soups, sauces, gruels, furmity, barley-broth, white-pot, and rice-milk; the best method of curing bacon, brawn, pickled pork, hams, tongues, hung-beef, sausages, by the latest and newest ways, and many other kitchen viands; brewing malt liquors, distilling, pickling, making cordials, teas, coffee, chocolate, natural and artificial, verjuice, vinegars; the management of sows and pigs, cows, and fowls of several sorts; a butter and cheese dairy after an uncommon manner, much better that what is commonly practised; the present way of victualling harvest-men, and maintaining farmers servants the rest of the year; the subtil ways, whereby servants have robbed their masters, laid open, that others may prevent the like; a receit thought to be the best that ever was

*published for curing the cows of the murrain distemper, with an
account of the famous effects of a quicksilver water, which
although as innocent to take as small beer or spring water, yet will
cure the pox, King's evil, leprosy, scald-head, itch, scurvy, and
mange in beasts; so that all persons, of what sex or age soever, ought
to drink of this water, with an account how a man in my
neighbourhood was thereby cured of an old ulcerated King's-evil
in his throat, and another elsewhere of a rivetted pox, when he
was so weak as not to be able to go through a salivation, have been
twice pox'd but cured before; the history of two noblemen, who
were excellent œconomists; how several men, women, and
children, have been poisoned, and some cured by eating poisonous
roots, herbs, and insects; with many receits of plain, cheap,
experienced medicines, and the cures they have made in country
families, with many other most serviceable matters, by which poor
families, and those that live at some distance from a town, may
become their own physician and surgeon, and probably many lives
thereby saved, as well as chargeable bills prevented: These and
many other most serviceable things I humbly offer to the publick,
hoping they will be candidly received, as my endeavours are truly
designed for my country's welfare, who am (with my best wishes
for their success) their sincerely devoted servant,*

WILLIAM ELLIS,

Author of The Practical Farmer, The Chiltern and Vale Farmer,
The Modern Husbandman, The London and Country
Brewer, The Supplement to Mr. *Trowell's* Book of
Husbandry and Gardening, *and* The Shepherd's Sure
Guide.

A N

INTRODUCTION

T O

The Country Housewife.

TO write a serviceable book of country houswifery, requires an author who lives amongst its practice; for without such an opportunity, it is not to be supposed it can be done to much purpose, because of the many branches of action depending on the same, both in the house and out-houses, garden, orchard, and field. And although that part of it, of securing (by the care and vigilance of our country housewife and her servants) a gentleman's, a yeoman's, and a farmer's property from the ravage of pilfering persons, has escaped the notice of almost all authors, yet I think it a matter of that consequence as deserves more than ordinary regard: For to what purpose is it for persons to study, labour, and be at a great expence to get crops of corn, hay, and fruit, to breed and fatten cattle, and endeavour by a hundred ways to promote their interest, and at the same time suffer themselves to be pilfer'd and cheated at home. I am therefore led to enlarge upon that instructive proverbial sentence, *Happy is he who by other mens harms learns to beware*, by giving my reader an account of several impositions that have really happened to gentlemen, yeomen, and farmers, by servants, pilfering neighbours, and others.

A captain of a man of war in Queen *Anne's* time, having acquired an estate of about 14000*l.* laid part of it out in purchasing houses and lands; one purchase whereof he made in *Buckinghamshire*, in buying a large farm of 300 acres of land, which he kept in his own hands, and a number of servants accordingly: Now this gentleman being a batchelor, he confided in his chief servant-maid to manage his houshold affairs; and as he kept a considerable number of cows, and made large quantities of butter for a *London* market, he ordered this his maid to make cheese for his servants of all skim mi[l]k, and this she did when she could not well help it, but when she had an opportunity she threw into the skim milk, new milk or cream; but although she did this contrary to her master's order, yet in the main I think the captain lost nothing by it, for when the cheese was made with all skim milk, the servants gave much of it away to dogs, and some they put into the hog-tub, and otherwise wasted it.

Another piece of bad management is of a yeoman's wife, who by her imprudence occasioned her husband much damage: The farm of about seventy pounds a year being his own, he did his part with much care and labour; but his wife was so indolent as to suffer a thievish neighbour now and then to harangue her itching ears with a gossip's story in defaming of another's reputation, and while her back was turned, and nobody present, they would catch up something or other; or if she went but up stairs, or out of the house, they would take a piece of pickled pork out of the pot, or cut off a slice of bacon, if in their reach, and the same by her cheese, bread, *&c.* Besides which, this yeoman's wife, thus blind to her husband's interest, kept a maid-servant, who was both a drunkard and thief, as well as possess'd of other faults, insomuch that she would carry out bread, cheese, and other provisions, and give them away to a neighbouring gin-seller, where she now and then got intoxicated, when to colour her drunkenness, she would hold her hand to her cheek, and complain of an excessive fit of the tooth-ach, in order for a pretext to lie down on the bed, and recover her senses: Thus she went on for some time, till at last her master saw through the imposition, and had her turn'd away: However, these and some other pieces of bad œconomy brought the yeoman's farm under a heavy mortgage, and so it remains at this day.

A lady now living, who kept seven or eight maid-servants, refused to hire any in her own neighbourhood, but had them from distant parts, because she thereby thought her goods the better secured from imbezzlement, as well knowing that there are many thefts committed by servants through the enticements of wicked parents or neighbours; many instances of which I could send into the world, but I hope these few hints will suffice to the intelligent: Supposing then, that a vigilant regard is duly observed by our country housewife, in securing her household and other goods from waste and the rapine of domestic and other thieves, I proceed now to farther advise her.

First to lay her money out to the best advantage in the buying of provisions not of her own produce, always remembering she cannot well lay out her money worse than buying her sugar, plumbs, candles, cheese, cloth, &c. at petty chandlers shops. I have known a pound of treacle sold at such a shop in the country at the rate of 4d. *per* pound, when in *London* I have bought it for about five farthings, taking half a hundred weight together; for this is what I am seldom without, as it saves sugar in pies, lessens the consumption of malt, and is of great service in curing colds in man or beast. Much also of the same bad housewifery may persons be guilty of, to a great loss, in buying tea, coffee, spice, and many other things, at such shops, and especially where the chalk is made use of, for then many buyers dare hardly find fault. Thus there are many parcels of whey butter or second butter sold for prime butter, bad running tallow candles sold for good ones, nasty dripping fat (which is often bought by the necessitous or ill housewife) for pure fat, *West-India* coffee for right *Turkey* coffee, though it is cheaper by one shilling or more in a pound. Oatmeal and salt are commonly sold at these petty shops by a wooden measure, from half a pint to several other quantities, and thus retail'd, to the prejudice of the poor buyer, who hereby comes off with scanty measure.

The next thing I have to advise our country housewife to, is to keep one or more pair of scales by her, in readiness to weigh the goods she buys. A person of my acquaintance paid for half a pound of hops at a chandler's shop in the country, and when at home (on weighing the same) found a full ounce wanting, upon which he upbraided the seller, who for excuse said their wooden scale was foul by weighing flour in it, which caused the mistake. Again, where any shopkeeper asks extravagantly more than the commodity is worth, I would not deal with such a one; and it is for this very reason that I have known some miss nearer shops, to go three miles farther in the country for buying their linen-cloth, because the shopkeeper was at a word in asking a reasonable price, and therefore a fool or an infant may be safely sent to such a market. And the advantage of this way of dealing is manifest in the character given by a taylor, who being ask'd where cloth for a coat might be bought at the lowest price, answer'd, at such a Quaker's shop, for that he will not ask above two pence in five shillings more than he will take. Some of our churchmen having since taken this hint, and to prevent the Quakers monopolizing of custom, have fell into the same way of dealing.

It is also very ill housewifery to buy bacon or pickled pork at shops (as is done by thousands) where there is a conveniency to prevent it, by feeding swine at home. Thus to keep the most serviceable victuals of all others at home, is to command in a great degree the butcher's shop; for if servants can't live upon a piece of bacon or pickled pork, and a pudding or apple dumplins for dinners and suppers, let them fast I say: It is what I observe for most part of the year, or else I think I should not get much by farming.

The brewing of beer at home, where conveniency will allow it, and keeping it to a right age, is certainly good housewifery. For to buy it abroad, and thereby pay excise, is extravagant management indeed; or to drink new beer, is not acting the saving part, because it quenches not drought like older, neither is it so wholsome.

The baking of bread at home, where it can be conveniently done, for a large family, will certainly pay much better than to buy it of bakers; for as home-baked bread may be made closer and heartier than theirs, it will last the longer in the stomach, and thus go farther than sale bread. But this is not all the inconvenience attending the buying of goods at petty shops; for where the shopkeeper is of the gossiping sort, they have a cow's tongue (as we call it in the country) a smooth side and a rough side: Such persons will get all the intelligence they can of your affairs, and if they are prejudiced against you, they will make an ill use of it, to your disadvantage; which is what I have known done to the woeful experience of several. Therefore take care, not to give your children or servants an opportunity of being corrupted by buying things at such a shop. If any shopkeeper should slander or backbite me unjustly, they may be assured (if I sent farther for my goods) I would not deal with them: And if all persons would observe to do the same, we should prevent that infinite number of inconveniencies which have happened for want of such precautions.

The keeping of servants at home must redound to their masters and mistresses profit, for according to their management they may be made either serviceable or unserviceable. I never knew a farmer thrive that let his servants stay long, or lie out at nights, to go to common dancing or drinking bouts, &c. which are the bane of youth; nor who let them lie too long in bed, or stand idle for want of appointing them work in due time. Remember that the eye of the master or mistress forwards business, and to rise at five is the way to thrive.

The burning of wood comes next under my notice, and with good reason, for by burning green wood instead of dry wood there is near a double waste made. I have known an indiscreet family, that used to lay a whole bound five-foot long faggot on at once, and thus a long fire devour'd as much wood again as was necessary. The same yeoman, who has about twenty inclosed fields besides a wood, for want of providing a stock of wood in the felling season, has been forced to sell a fruit-bearing large standard cherry-tree for fewel. Bad husbandry with a witness!

The keeping of salves and other remedies in the house, so as to have them always in readiness, is of such importance in gentlemen's, yeomen's, and farmer's families, that none should be without them, by reason of the many accidents that a country family is more liable to than most others: For here are horses, cows, hogs and dogs, besides the many cutting and pointed instruments of husbandry that must be unavoidably made use of. These and other remedies being ready at hand, may probably save the expence of large doctors bills, and perhaps lives.

The same in respect of preventing and curing sickness, which is of such consequence in a country family, that none that can afford it ought to be without brandy, cordial waters, or strong beer or ale, and other hearty liquors, oils, verjuice, and a hundred others of such kind of necessaries, for commanding their uses at any time; for in many country places, some of these can't be had for love nor money, nor a doctor be procured without sending several miles for one. This piece of good housewifery in many of the abler sort of good women is happily experienced, not only by their own families, but also by many of their poor neighbours, who are unable to provide such cordial remedies: And it is certainly one of the best of charities, for women of ability to distill cordial waters at home, to keep balsams by them, and to furnish their closet with such remedies as may relieve the necessitous poor people, who perhaps might lose their lives if not thus timely assisted with such charitable means. Instances of which sort of benevolence are well known to us at *Gaddesden*, by the noble actions of two gentlewomen now living near us; the one for giving an expensive liquor to penurious persons, and thereby curing many of their agues; the other for distributing of cordial waters to the sick, visiting them, and giving cloaths to some, according to her ability: Most worthy of the example and imitation of all those whose conveniency enables them to do the like. But for a farther description of a right country house-wife, I shall subjoin the following account, as published by a doctor of divinity amongst his works, in dispraise and praise of women, *viz.*

"What (says he) is more shameful than to see a woman in idleness, and with what pretext can she cover her sloth? If she has nothing to do for herself, has she nothing to do for the poor? Let her read in the last chapter of *Proverbs* the occupations of a compleat woman. She was without doubt a person of quality, since *Solomon* who gives her description, represents her husband in the rank of senators and princes of the earth: But did she do as the dames of our days, who pass all the morning in sleeping and dressing, the rest of the day to receive and pay visits, and all the night at play, at ball, at comedy, at feasts, and all other diversions that they can invent; who are provoked they can enjoy no more, and who regard labour as a thing unworthy of their rank, and proper only for low conditions; who employ all their industry and all their application to invent new modes, to search new pleasures, to overcome the deformity of nature by artificial beauties, to consume their substance in foolish expences, rather than conserve it by wise œconomy; who leave to servants the care of their houses and the conduct of their affairs, who have no concern on them of bringing up their children in piety, nor to keep their servants in their duty; who take no account of what passes in their family, and who are nevertheless curious of knowing all that happens in that of their neighbours, to make it a subject of entertainment and matter of diversion in company!

"This was not the life of that generous woman who was the model of her sex; she made no such bad use of her time; and had not such an ill opinion of labour; they saw her always in exercise and in action; she arose before the sun, to give her maidens work, and to teach them herself; she work'd on linen and woollen, and judged not that application unworthy of her study or the nobleness of her birth; she knew all the secrets of œconomy and government; there was nothing better managed than her house, nor nothing better regulated than her person; she had a very great care in the education of her children, and of the fidelity of her servants; as her estate was justly acquired, it was very usefully employed; she made a wise distribution of it in favour of those who had need, and she had no poor about her that escaped her knowledge and her charity; she comforted one and assisted another, she made one agree with the other, and composed all the differences which were bred between them; her husband, who had a perfect confidence in her, reposed himself intirely on her care of his domestick affairs, whilst he was employed in the most important negotiations of the state.

"You will perhaps say, that this woman is no other than in the idea of the wiseman, and that there are none of this sort in the world; but you will find a great number before the tribunal of *Jesus Christ*, who will condemn the lazy idle life that you lead, by the example of an acting and laborious one that they led: If there be any guilty of sloth, pretend not to justify yours by theirs."

COUNTRY Family's Profitable Director:

According to the Present Practice of the Country Gentleman's, *the* Yeoman's, *the* Farmer's, *the* Labourer's *Wives, and Others, of the Counties of* Hertford, Bucks, *and other Parts of* England.

Of the several Sorts of Wheat usually sown in England *for making Bread.*

HERE are various sorts of wheats sown in *England*, for making bread with their meals: As the White, the Red, and the Yellow Lamas sorts, that are justly accounted the best of wheats: The Dame, the Pirky, and the White-Cone, are likewise very valuable wheats: But the West-Country Grey, and Blue-Ball wheats, or what they call, in some other countries, the Dugdale or Bold-Rivet, and French wheats, are deemed the coarsest of all others. Now most of these are sown in *Hertfordshire*; and although the Bearded Blue and Grey Ball wheats are of the cheapest and coarser sorts, yet their meals are much made use of by the common baker, as well as private families, in the city of *Wells*, and in many other places of the

West; and in lesser quantities elsewhere: Which leads me to make observations on their different meals, and bread made of them in several parts of *England*.

Why some Gentlemen, Yeomen, and Farmers grind their own Wheat for their Family Uses.—THERE are many gentlemen, yeomen, and farmers, who occupy arable land, that think they have a great opportunity to save the penny, in the management of their offald wheat: For that these, if their farms are of the larger sort, must make what we in *Hertfordshire* call peggings, in large quantities, being what comes from the underline or blighted, or other wheat ears, most of which contain in them very thin little kernels, that will easily part from their chaff; and it is chiefly such ears that break off from their straw in threshing: And then it also is, that in making use of the knee fan, and wheat ridder sieve, these ears are fanned and sifted to the top of the wheat kernels; from whence they are taken off by the hand, and reserved till a good parcel are got together for being threshed over again; and the produce is that which we (when clean'd) call peggings, and are what we grind alone, or in a mixture with a better sort. Thus many yeomen and farmers eat the worser bread, as butchers and poulterers do their staler and worser meats, and by so doing sell the largest and best wheat at market; for he who mixes such small kernels with bigger stands the chance of losing a groat or six-pence in a bushel. It is true, that such underline small kernels make more bran and less flower than better wheat does; yet this is thought by some to be the lesser evil: Others are of a contrary opinion, and therefore I shall shew

Why Others refuse to grind their own Wheat, and buy Meal for their Family Uses.—THERE are several reasons to be assigned for this. *First,* it is the practice of some farmers to refuse grinding their own wheat, for buying what we call middling, which is a wheat meal, between the finest and the coarsest sorts; because, say they, we will not grind the worst wheat for our family, but the worst and best shall be sold together; and for so doing some will put a peck of peggings or thin offald wheat in the middle of a five bushel sack of good market wheat: Others, contrary to this, when they fling their threshed wheat out of its chaff, many light kernels fall short, which is a lean offald corn; these, when discharged of the seeds of weeds, they mix with larger body'd wheat, and sell all together. By this means they avoid grinding their lean worst corn, that seldom produces more than three bushels of meal from five bushels of such wheat, and instead thereof buy a coarse meal called randan, which is a third and the worst sort that millers separate. The first and finest meal that is grinded in *Hertfordshire*, called houshold, is all or most of it sold in *London*; so that little else is sold at our country shops but middling and randan meals. In the next place I am to inform my reader, that sometimes a bushel of our best wheat has weighed sixty or more pounds; and I and many others have sold five bushels of such wheat for as much money as five bushels of randan meal has cost: Whereas, if we grind our own good wheat, five bushels of the best sort generally make four bushels and an half, or more, of meal, and the bran we reckon pays for grinding. But notwithstanding this, some gentlemen, yeomen, and farmers, think it most to their interest to have five bushels of this randan wheat meal, which they buy at the same market they sell their wheat at, and bring it home by the return of their waggon or cart; for that, in so doing, they know they are out of the danger of being imposed on by any dishonest miller, in whose power it may be to return a due weight of flower, and yet bite the farmer, it being possible for such a miller to take out some of the finest and heartiest flower, and put coarse in its place; or to grind bad wheat, and keep the better sort. The same in other shapes; he may, if he is not an honest man, greatly damage that gentleman, yeoman, or farmer, who constantly grinds all the wheat he uses at his mill. It is a common computation, that in the cleaning of five and twenty bushels of wheat, there will be a bushel or more of offald thin kernels separated from the larger body'd sort, which, as I said, is by some yeomen and farmers mix'd amongst four and twenty bushels of the better wheat, because they think that in this quantity the bushel of offald will not be easily perceived by the buyer. However, it is my opinion, that where one yeoman or farmer sells all his wheat and buys meal, there are six that grind what they use for their families. For my own part, I must own I have sold my wheat and bought meal; but as I now grind my wheat grist with a reputable eminent miller, at *Oak-Mill*, near *Hempstead*, I am satisfied of his fair-dealing, and think myself so well used to have five bushels of wheat ground for only one shilling charge, that I grind all, and buy none. Yet I know a great farmer living near *Redbourne*, in *Hertfordshire*, that thinks it better œconomy to sell all his best wheat by itself, and his worst wheat by itself, and buys a sack of meal every week for his twenty in family. By all which a person may perceive, whether it best answers his interest, to sell all his wheat and buy all his flower, or grind his own wheat for his family uses.

How a private Family may preserve their whole Wheat sweet in Sacks for some Time.—I KNEW a little farmer, that kept only two horses at plow and cart, who preserved his threshed wheat in sacks, sweet and sound, a year together, in a chamber, for taking the advantage of a rising market; and to do this, he would once in a summer screen all this his sack wheat, to get the dust out of it; for it is the dust that heats the grain, while it stands thus undisturbed, causing it to ferment, and breed either the wevil, maggot, or mite, or else a mustiness and stink in it. Wherefore if whole wheat or wheat meal is dry, it is better kept in sacks, in a chamber, than near a fire-side, because the fire draws out its moisture, and sours it: Nor ought they to be kept in damp places, for here they will be apt to matt and cake, and spoil. The best way therefore, as I said, is to keep both wheat and flower in a chamber, at all times of the year: If in sacks, a thick stick should remain thrust down in the middle of it, with the mouth of the sack left open. And in case you mistrust the wheat or flower to suffer, tie up the sack's mouth, turn it topsy-turvy, and the removal will much contribute to the keeping of it sweet; for by such turning the wheat or flower lies in a looser body than it did before, as the position of their particles becomes thus altered; so it prevents in a great degree their heating, fermenting, and spoiling, and the surer, if such a sack of wheat or flower is thus turned once every two or three weeks: for it has been proved, that when a sack of wheat or flower has received a little damage, by standing too near a fire, or in a chamber too long undisturbed, that by now and then turning the sack topsy-turvy, it has recovered it. One set a sack of flower too near a fire, and was forced to give it to the hogs.—Or take this serviceable account in the following manner, *viz.* This subject affects mostly three sorts of country housewives; the yeomens, the farmers, and the labouring-mens wives: The two first, because it sometimes happens, that the yeoman and farmer are obliged to house their wheat in a damp condition; and as housekeeping requires a constant supply of bread, there is no waiting twelve months, or half twelve months, till such wheat gets dry in a stack, cock, or mow: So the labouring-man's family, who get part of their bread in leased wheat, requires likewise a present supply.—In which case, it concerns these three sorts of housewives to dry a sack of wheat more or less with the greatest expedition; and that it may be so done, such wheat should be placed by the fire-side, by setting a sack of it at a convenient distance from it. If it is a brick or other damp floor, the sack should stand four, six, or more inches above ground, on a stool or otherwise, if the place will admit of it, that it may get the sooner dry. This done, thrust a stick down the middle of the sack, of the length and thickness of a common broomstick, which let remain, turning it about twice or more in a week, for giving air to the wheat, and preventing its heating and musting, always keeping the mouth of the sack open. And that this piece of good housewifery may be performed the more effectual, my advice is, that every time our housewife bakes, and as soon as the bread is drawn, she take the stick out of the sack, and heat it in the oven, and when it is hot, that she thrust it down again into the middle of the sack, as before. This is done to draw the moisture of the wheat to the stick, for contributing to its quicker drying. And I add, that so much stress is laid on this way of drying a sack of wheat, that in damp seasons, it is, by some farmers, practised in order to obtain the greater price for it at market. But then they take care to shoot all the wheat out of the sack on the floor before-hand, to mix it all alike, lest that part, which stood next the fire, be dryer than the rest.

How to preserve Wheat-Meal sweet in Sacks.—THIS I shall shew by the case of a widow, who constantly bought her wheat-meal of a miller, and being few in family, asked him, How she should keep it dry and sweet, in the sack he brought it in, till she used it? To this the miller answered—Let it stand in a dry place, and turn the sack bottom upwards now and then, and he would engage it would keep sound many months.—Accordingly, I know that this widow and other *Hertfordshire* housewives observe to do the same; for that it keeps the meal from lying so close as to cake, heat, or breed mites, because by such transposition it has a little removal, and lies higher and hollower than it did before. And for a further security of this advantage, make use of the broomstick, as I have before directed, for by such alteration both whole wheat and wheat-meal may be much longer preserved sweet and sound, than if it stood in sacks without being managed in this manner.

How Wheat-Meal by various Means becomes damaged by Insects.—THERE are great quantities of bad meals sold at shops, occasioned by several means. *First,* By the nasty stinking wevil, which is a dark brown coloured insect, about the bigness of a large flea, and is mostly bred in damp wheats, or gets into heaps of dry sound wheat from contiguous infected lofts or grainaries; for these sort of vermin are travellers, and as they stale or dung, or both, amongst the kernels of wheat, they heat it, and thereby increase their breed in infinite numbers, especially in summer time; so that such wevilly wheat is really of a very unwholsome nature, and gives the bread, made of its meal, an ill taste, where they have been in vast numbers, notwithstanding what the miller does in sifting the wheat before it is grinded, to get them out. And what is more, such damp wheat, or infected wheat, is very apt to breed the mite in the meal. *Secondly*, In some old lofts and grainaries, that are boarded on all their sides, small worms are bred in wheat, hoarded at a cheap time in the same, and kept two, three, or more years against a rising market.—I know a yeoman, whose wheat was so infected with these insects in 1744, that he pulled down all his beechen side-boards, and put up new oaken ones in their room, as believing the first occasioned the breed of these vermin, which greatly increased, and would in time have eaten up all the kernels. But by doing this, and screening the wheat, he got most of them out. And what was somewhat strange, the wheat when first laid in here was thoroughly dry; so that this increase must be owing either to some worms, lodged in the crevices, bred perhaps from some former damp wheat, or else from the corrupt rottenness of the boards. *Thirdly*, Meal is frequently damaged by long keeping, for by this the mite is very apt to breed, and when once they have bred in it, they mightily increase in a little time; insomuch that they have been often seen to swarm in the meal, and even on the outside of the sacks. *Fourthly*, Meal is damaged when it comes from wheat that grew amongst the weeds of crow-garlick, mellilot, and much mayweed, *&c.* for these are of a most stinking nature, and grow in many inclosed Chiltern-fields, in such abundance, as makes some farmers despair of ever clearing their ground of them. All which is wrote, to give our country housewife warning to examine well the meal or flower before she buys it; and in this case it is necessary for her to employ her seeing, feeling, and tasting, the better to prevent those impositions, which the unwary and ignorant buyer is frequently brought under.

How to know good from bad Meals.—As there are great quantities of wheat-meals infected by mites, *&c.* and yet are sold out of mills, storehouses, and shops, both by wholesale and retail; it concerns our country housewife to make a nice inspection before she buys her meal. Therefore in the first place, by her sight, she may, perhaps, discover two sorts of damage in it; the mites, and a mixture of pollard. If by mites, they are to be perceived by their stirring the meal; for these creatures, although so small, as hardly to be seen by the naked eye, yet when they are in great numbers, they will move the top part of the meal, and when they swarm, if the flower is dented by the fingers, they will presently level it.—*Secondly,* For a confirmation of this, she may, by feeling, be the more sensible of the coarseness or fineness of the flower or meal, and thereby be able to make the truer estimation of its value; for if it is very mity, it will feel coarse, because the bodies of these insects are larger than the particles of fine meal. The same if pollard or the smallest of bran is amongst it.—A miller that brought a sack of sale-meal to a country shop, as soon as the woman opened it, and had seen and felt it, said, What have you brought me pollard instead of flower? No, says the miller, but if it is too coarse now, I will bring you finer next time to make amends.—Which leads me to observe, that as the whiter wheat is now generally sown, the smallest pollard is not so soon perceived in its meal, as that of the red or yellow Lamas, or brown pirky wheat, because, the whiter the skin, the less its bran is discovered in its flower. *Thirdly,* The damage of wheat-meal may be sometimes best found out by smelling it. Whools, or wevils, or maggots, may be screened and sifted from the flower, and good may be mixt with bad to lessen the taste and smell of them; but when such meal is tried by a nice observing nose, it may be discovered before it is bought. The same when mites are got into meal, and cannot be perceived by the eye nor felt by the finger, yet the nose may decide the matter; for if mites have done the flower some damage, it will smell disagreeably frousy, and be worth the less. So when flower is tainted by nasty stinking weeds that grew amongst its wheat, it is better known by smelling than by either seeing or feeling.

How a common Baker, living within four Miles of London, *improved his best Wheat-Meal.*—As I said, red Lamas is accounted the most ancient best sort of wheat in *England*, by producing a meal and price exceeding all others, for its whiteness, fineness, and palatableness; but it is apt to grind tougher than either white, or pirky, or Dugdale, or other wheats. Now as Dugdale wheat grinds shortest, and produces a sweet but coarse flower, and as it always sells for sixpence more or less in a bushel than Lamas wheat, a great common baker, living about four miles out of *London*, generally took this method to increase his profit, and yet made his Lamas wheat-flower rather better than worse. He usually bought five sacks of meal at a time, four of Lamas and one of Dugdale, which he mixed, and they agreed so well together, that the customer could not perceive any difference between a loaf of bread made with all Lamas wheat flower, and that made with a mixture of Dugdale wheat flower. But the chief benefit of such a mixture lies in this; that a loaf of bread made with these meals will keep moist two days or more, longer than if it was made with intire Lamas wheat meal. And therefore not only this baker, but many others in *London* and elsewhere follow this practice; not altogether beause they get something by the lower price of the Dugdale meal, but because it adds a sweet pleasant moisture to the loaf of bread, and thereby much lessens the stale harshness that in hot weather especially is apt to bring the finer Lamas flower loaf under. And now I am writing on Dugdale or bold Rivet wheat, I have farther to add, that it is thought by some farmers true husbandry to sow an acre or more of this sort of wheat wholly for their family uses, that they may be the better enabled to sell the more Lamas or other dearer wheats, as thinking this coarse sort good enough for themselves; and also because this is a greater yielder than any other wheat, will withstand blights when others suffer by them, and be fit to grind with Lamas wheat, in case a wet harvest happens, and it is housed damp.

 The Nature of grown Wheat, and how it comes to be such.— WHAT we call grown wheat, in *Hertfordshire*, is that which is damaged in the field by extraordinary wet weather: That is to say, when wheat is almost ripe and ready to reap, the straw and ears being then in their greatest magnitude, are by long rains apt to bend, and sometimes fall flat to the ground; then it commonly is, that for want of a free air and sun the kernels grow and sprout before the wheat is fit to be reaped. *Secondly*, It also sometimes happens, after the wheat is reaped, and lies to dry on the ground, for being bound up in sheaves, that rains fall for several days together, and cause the kernels to grow in the ear. *Lastly*, It has likewise been many times the case, almost throughout *England*, to have such a wet harvest, that though the wheat was bound up full dry in sheaves, and stood erect in shocks, yet rains have fell so heavy, and continued so long, that the kernels have grown in the ear. Now if wheat is grown by any of these three ways, the flower is damaged, and will never be so good as that produced from wheat which was never sprouted in the ear, because all bread, cake, and pye-crust, made of it, will be of a pudding consistence, if a peculiar art is not employed in the curing of it. This has been frequently experienced, in such a degree, that the bread has spread about in the oven pancake like, and the knife that cut the loaf, has brought away with it a sort of batter-crumb, that stuck to it, and was of a sweetish but fulsome taste. Hence it is that mealmen refuse to buy such grown wheat if they can get better, or if they do buy it, it must be at sixpence or a shilling a bushel less than dryer sounder wheat sells for. In short, if wheat is once grown and sprouted in the ear, whether it be got into the barn or mow dry or not dry, the flower of it will never make a right palatable stiff loaf, if it is kneaded in the common way with only yeast, warm water, and salt. And what seems very surprising to me is, that no author that I ever yet read or heard of, has so much as touched on this important article, although in some wet harvests it affects almost all the people of the nation; for that the bread, the cake, the pudding, the pye, and several other things, made of such grown wheat-meal, gives them little or more a disagreeable taste. But this I do not so much wonder at, if books of this nature are wrote in a *London* chamber; for then, in course, their authors must be deprived of that necessary country knowledge, as is requisite for enabling them to write those full and genuine instructions, which are perfectly wanted to assist a country housewife, in carrying on a true œconomy in managing her domestic affairs in the cheapest and most housewifely manner, for her family's greater advantage. But to return to my subject of grown wheat, I shall, for preventing the ill effects of it, propose the following remedies, *viz.*

How to cure damaged grown Wheat-Meal.—THIS may be done in a great degree, if any of these three ways are rightly put in practice. The first is, that instead of making use of warm water to knead this grown meal with, as the common way is, it should be mixed with it scalding hot; for by using it in such a degree of heat, the liquor astringes the flower, binds the dough, and tends very much towards making it into a stiff loaf, cake, pudding, pye, *&c.* Hence it is that the true house-wife, to make her raised paste at any time, always mixes a scalding or very hot water with her flower, to make it stiff enough to become a standing crust. But if skim or new milk was scalded, or rather boiled, and made use of instead of water, it would bind the grown wheat-meal, and make its loaf of bread lighter and whiter. You should also observe, that in this case of making use of scalding water or milk to knead the dough, you do not mix your yeast with it; if you do, it will scald the yeast, and prevent its fermenting and raising the dough. Therefore after you have sprinkled over your salt on the flower, then mix your scalding water or milk with it, and your yeast with water only warm. This done, knead all together into a pretty stiff dough, and after it has lain some time to ferment and rise, mould it into loaves, and bake them three hours. *Secondly*, Such grown wheat-meal is helped by mixing a peck of barley-meal with three of that, and made into a dough with scalding or warm water, or with milk, yeast, and salt, as aforesaid; for that such barley-meal, being of a dry short nature, will be serviceable in binding the grown wheat-meal, and preventing in some degree its baking into a clammy spreading condition. *Lastly*, such grown wheat-meal is cured in the surest manner of all other ways, by dissolving some allum in very hot water, and mixing the liquor with it by itself, without the yeast, and when they are a little mixed, then stir your yeast into some warm water, and incorporate this also with the flower; then knead all well together, and mould it into loaves, &c. for baking; but observe that in this last case, no salt must be made use of, because the allum will fully supply it. One or more of these directions may be of great service to those who are ignorant of them, and who consume much bread in their large families; when wheat has sprouted in the ear by great and long rains, as it did in 1716. A wet season (as I am informed) that caused laid wheat, in many places, to throw out sprouts as long as a child's finger; nor was standing wheat then free of this calamity, for most of it sprouted little or much, and so it has done in several years since, though in a lesser degree. Also observe, that although I mention scalding water to be made use of in stiffening the meal of grown wheat; the water, or milk, or whey, should be first boiled, and then put over and mixed with the meal while it is scalding hot, because boiling improves it, always remembering to work and knead this sort of dough stiff; for by so doing, the loaves will stand the firmer and tighter in the oven.

The Practice of a Hertfordshire *Housewife for improving the Meal of grown Wheat.*—THIS is practised both by rich and poor, as a good piece of housewifery, when wheat kernels have much sprouted in the field by too much moisture; for then, if the meal is used alone, it makes a clammy, lumpy, pudding sort of bread, that is very apt to spread in the oven, insomuch that when a loaf of such bread has been made and baked by an ignorant lazy housewife, it has been so soft as to become almost fit to be eaten with a spoon. Now to prevent this, our *Hertfordshire* good housewife, whether rich or poor, commonly endeavours to mix some meal of the last year's dry sound wheat, with such meal of grown wheat; and they always find that such management very much helps to cure the grown wheat-meal.

Meals made use of in some of the Northern Counties.—HERE they make vast consumptions of oatmeal, having but little wheat growing in these parts, and with this they make cakes that supply bread, by mixing oatmeal with water and a little salt, which they let stand together twenty or more hours, and then knead it into a dough or batter, and bake it like pancakes on a stone that has a fire under it; and when they have prepared a good parcel, they lay them on racks to dry, for in this manner they become hard, and will keep hard, sweet, and sound a long time. At the great and popular town of *Manchester*, their sacks of oatmeal stand for sale in their market, as our sacks of wheat do at *Hempstead*, and some other of the Southern markets. And so attached are many of their people to the eating of oatcake or brown bread, that when they come up with their waggons of wheat and cheese to *Hempstead* market, they bring their own coarse heavy bread, to prevent their being forced to eat our *Hertfordshire* wheaten bread, saying—They do not like such a corky, bitter sort;—for you must know that in these Northern Counties, their yeast is mostly saved from strong mild ale, and not from strong hopped beer. The same gust have the more Northern people for their oatmeal-cake-bread, which most of them like to that degree, as to slight wheaten bread.—In some parts of *Yorkshire* they eat a blackish rye bread, and when the rye is got in wettish, to improve its flower, they heat a brick and put it amongst the dough before it is made into loaves, in order to draw out the ill quality of it, and so prevent the rowing of it; here they employ leaven in common to make their bread, and as their kneading-tub has always part of this leavened dough sticking to it, it contributes towards leavening and fermenting the next dough.—Others in the county of *York* make an oatmeal dough with fine oatmeal-water, yeast and salt, as we do wheaten bread, and broil or bake it.—Others mix wheat flower with a little salt and butter-milk, and thus make a good cake broiled on a gridiron; and tho' perhaps a little sourish, yet it eats well.

Of the Nature and Uses of good and bad YEAST or BARM, *as it relates to baking of Bread.*

YEAST or barm is an ingredient so necessary, that without it neither brewing nor baking can be rightly performed. In the first, 'tis true, yeast may be made use of to poison human bodies, when too much of it (as is too commonly practised) is beat, ding'd or whip'd into ale or beer, for a week together, in cold weather, to work it, and to make it so strong as to save one or two bushels of malt in eight; as I have amply made appear in my treatise on brewing, intitled, *The London and Country Brewer*, sold by Mr. *Astley*, bookseller, at the *Rose* in *Pater-noster-Row, London.* But in baking there is so little a quantity of yeast employed (being mixed with much water to make bread with) that it is cured by the heat of the oven, which divests it of any ill quality it may naturally have in it. Yet there are many curious persons so nice in this point, that they endeavour to have their bread made with as little yeast in it as possible.

How to make a little Yeast go a great Way in making Bread, and how to make Grounds of Barrels supply Yeast.— Wheat flower, coarse sugar and salt are great promoters of fermentation, insomuch that if these three ingredients, in a proper quantity, are mixed with a little yeast, it will raise a brisk fermentation fit to mix with water and flower, and make a dough for bread, instead of all good solid yeast. And so will the same composition do, if mixed with only grounds of barrels, provided the grounds are thick and sweet. Thus if stale yeast is mixed with only sugar and hot water, and set near a fire, in about half an hour it will ferment and be like new yeast.

A second Account of making Grounds of Barrels serve for baking Bread, instead of good Yeast, in cold Weather.—IF grounds of barrels, or bottoms of strong or small beer vessels, are upon necessity to be made use of, for want of good yeast, to make bread; our country housewife may mix some sugar, salt, and flower with them, and then set the mixture within the heat of the fire (especially if ale grounds are made use of) and it will rise and ferment, and the sooner if you mix some warm wort or beer with them, provided the grounds are not sour, or otherways decayed. And thus poor thin yeast may be also made to ferment and bake with, instead of good yeast. Others put brandy and sugar to grounds of barrels or decayed yeast, and it will cause it to ferment quickly.

A Method practised by a frugal Housewife to keep her Yeast sweet and sound against baking time, in hot Weather.—THIS foresighted frugal housewife, if she brewed in hot weather, would, when her drink had done working, and the yeast settled, pour off the thin or liquid part, and reserve only the thick part, which she would dry in the sun and air, and then, after mixing some salt with it, would make it into rolers a foot long, and thus keep it sweet and sound a month or more together.

A second Way to preserve Yeast sweet and sound in hot Weather.—In summer time I knew a frugal housewife plaister a board over with thick yeast, and let it dry on, which being kept in a dry place, was preserved a long while sweet; and when wanted, she scraped some off. This, mixed with warm water, would ferment into a serviceable yeast; but if it was backward in fermenting, she added some salt and sugar to the warm water.

How to preserve Yeast with cold Water.—THERE is a way to preserve yeast sweet some time, if you put cold water on it; but then the yeast should be thick and solid, and after the water has stood on it three or four days, it should be poured off, and fresh added. This is one way to preserve yeast sweet; but then it is apt to waste the spirit of it, and make it the less lively. Others put sugar, salt, flower and brandy to it, for causing a fermentation.

How to preserve Yeast sweet in a Pitcher.—THIS is practised by many of our country housewives, who after their strong or small drink has fully done working, and the yeast settled in the tub or pan that receives it from the vessel, will pour off the thin beer part, and put the solid part into a pitcher, which if tied over with the skin of a hog's flair or bladder, and kept in a cool place, may be preserved sweet, for making bread with the same, a month or more.

How to preserve Yeast in Bottles.—THIS is done by pu[t]ting solid yeast into a stone or glass bottle, that has a wider mouth than common bottles have; then cork the bottle, and put it into a cool cellar, or more securely, into a ditch, pond, or river; and the coldness of the cellar or water will prevent its fermenting, and preserve it sweet a long time. So that a housewife need not be at a loss for yeast to bake with, if she will but get one or more of these bottles, and thus save her yeast from one baking to another. And observe, that whenever she puts such a bottle of yeast into a ditch, pond, river, or well, she should be sure to place it as near as she can to the shady side of it. For this reason a well is a better conservatory than a cellar, ditch, pond, or river, because the bottle of yeast is here entirely kept in the shade, and in the greatest coolness. Others will put yeast into a stone bottle, and keep it in a hole in the ground, as the best way of all others.

How an old Woman, that kept a public House in Hertfordshire*, made it her common Practice to increase the Quantity of her Yeast.*—THIS woman generally brewed once a week throughout the year, and not only sold her own yeast, but would buy that made by her private neighbours, in order to adulterate both for profit sake. And to do it in a manner that could not be easily perceived nor discovered, she mixed flower and the grounds of barrels with her good yeast, and sold it for four-pence a quart, to bake and brew with.

Of the Cheapness and Dearness of Yeast or Barm.—THE want of yeast, in many parts of *England*, obliges many persons to desist from baking their own bread, to their loss; and this even in some towns, where in warm weather it is cheaply and easily had for three-pence or four-pence a quart, and yet in hard and long frosts it is sometimes sold for six-pence, a shilling, two shillings, and I have known it sold for two shillings and six-pence a quart, in the great frost of 1740. Which is enough, I should think, to put our housewives upon a prevention of such an extravagant expence, which they may do, if they will but observe what I have written of saving yeast before-hand.

How a Tradesman in Hertfordshire *brewed ten Bushels of Pale Malt in the Hard Frost of* 1740*, chiefly for making an extraordinary Profit of the Yeast produced from the same.*—THIS fact was performed in the hard frost, 1740; which occasioned yeast to sell at the before-mentioned prices in many country towns within forty miles of *London*. And it was the extraordinary price of two shillings per quart, that yeast sold for in the months of *January* and *February*, that tempted an acquaintance of mine, then living at *Barkhamstead St. Peter*, in *Hertfordshire*, to brew ten bushels of pale leisure-dried malt, which by his care and skill produced him ten gallons of yeast, which he sold at two shillings per quart, and thus made four pounds of the bare yeast; for he was an excellent private brewer (not one of them that regard a serviceable secret like a Tale of *Tom Thumb*) who made a trial first to prove its effect, and as he found it, judged it. This person was noted for having a most silky, fine, palatable ale generally by him, of which, though a tradesman, he was no niggard; and that his malt-drink might excell the common sort in goodness, he did not grudge the charge of buying three pounds of hops, when others bought but two, because he boiled them only thirty minutes or less; but his wort he usually boiled longer, till it broke into particles as big as large lice: Or, to speak plainer, till the hops sunk, and the wort boiled curdled clear. Then it is, that such strong beer or ale (if the fermentation is rightly carried on) will yield a very large quantity of yeast.

To make a bitter Yeast fresh.— THERE are two or more ways of doing this; one is, as I said, by pouring cold water on it, and after its lying twenty-four, or more hours, it must be pour'd off, which may be easily done if the yeast is solid, for cold water will not mix with yeast like beer.—But the common bakers way is, to put long bran on a linen cloth, and your bitter yeast on that, which you are to wash out from the bran with hot water.—Or you may soak a birch broom in yeast, and though the yeast be bitter, the air will dry and freshen it against the next baking, when it may be washed in warm water.—— *N.B.* By the wash of the bran, the bitter part of the yeast lodges in it, and thus makes the wheat-meal go the further in making bread.

Good neighbours Yeast.—I CALL this good neighbours yeast, that is to say, where there is a good neighbourhood, when one brews, she lends her yeast to a neighbour for baking or brewing. And when the other brews, she does the same. Thus a good housewife need not be at much expence in buying yeast; as it is practised at a little innship called *Maintmore*, in *Bucks*, where there are about half a score houses, and where their neighbourhood so well agrees together, that this is their constant practice to lend one another yeast alternately. And thus they prevent their being at any extraordinary expence and trouble of buying it at a greater distance.

Of Leaven, and Leavened BREAD.

AS many are ignorant what leaven is, I shall in the first place give an account of it. And that it may be the more known, I shall here observe the method a days-man's (as we call them in *Hertfordshire*) or labourer's wife took to make and keep her leaven from one baking to another. Her family was a husband and five children, seven in all, which obliged her about every ten days end to bake one bushel of flower; and as her money was short, and yeast sometimes scarce and dear, she always took care to save a piece of her leavened dough, at each baking, about the bigness of her fist, and making a little hole in the middle of it with her finger, ram'd it full of salt, and in a ball shape she let it lie covered over with salt in her salt-box till the next baking; by which time it got dry and hard enough to break into crumbles, for mixing them with half a pint of yeast and warm water. This, when put into the middle of the flower, as it lay in a tub or kneading-trough, was stirred with some of the meal, and left to ferment and rise, which in warm weather it would do in an hour or two's time. Not that time is a true indication when it has fermented or risen enough; for to know this, she would look now and then, and when she saw the place cracked over where the leaven lay, she knew it was enough, and accordingly mixed the rest of the flower, and kneaded all into a moderate stiffness; for if it was kneaded too soft, the bread would be apt to spread in the oven, be light, and crumble; and if too stiff kneaded, it may be baked till it is too close, heavy, and hard.

How to make Leaven and leavened Bread for a private Family.—LEAVEN, as I said, is a piece of dough saved from the last leavened dough, and preserved with salt, as before mentioned, and is thus chiefly prepared for saveing yeast; for by this means half the usual quantity of yeast suffices, and yet causes the bread to eat pleasanter, to be hollower, and is wholsomer than if the dough was made with all yeast. On which accounts the *French* and other foreigners commonly make their bread with some leaven in it: For which purpose, the leavened piece should be kept dry enough to be broke small into salt warm water, well stirred about, till all is dissolved and thoroughly mixed. Then drain it through a sieve, to keep back any grouty part. This being done, make a large hole in the middle part of the flower, and pour into it this liquid leaven, which you are to incorporate so well, as to make this part of a hasty-pudding consistence; then cover with dry meal, and let all lie together all night to ferment and rise. Next morning add some yeast with some more warm water, and sprinkle salt over the whole parcel of flower according to discretion, which mix and knead together till the whole is made into a stiffish dough, and moulded into loaves; always remembering, with a pocket meat fork, or something else, to prick holes in the top part of each loaf, for this lets out the air when the bread begins to be hot in the oven, that otherwise would cause the upper crust to be puffed up and crack.

An Account given this Author by a —— Woman, who, when she was single, lived with a Country common Baker, that made use of the Spunge, otherwise Leaven, and employed Allum in making his Bread.—THIS woman says, that her master, who was a common baker just set up, used to bake four bushels of flower at a time, twice every week and always (both in summer and winter) saved a piece of his leavened dough about the bigness of a man's two fists, in which he put as much salt as would fill an egg-shell when the salt was wrapt up in this dough, he kept it cover'd all over in salt against he wanted it, and generally made use of that leaven which was about a week old; for she says, that he thought it better at that age than used sooner. Then, when he wanted it, he dissolved it with two ounces of allum in warm water, and with this liquid he mixed a pint of yeast, which he put into a cavity or hollow made in the meal, and covered all with dry meal; here it lay fermenting an hour or two, and when enough, he kneaded the whole quantity of meal, with what more warm water was necessary, into loaves, and baked them.—Allum, she says, saves salt, for by using it in this quantity, the baker employed no more salt in two bushels of meal than what was contained in the leaven. She says also, that allum saves yeast, because it helps to hollow the bread, yet binds and keeps the dough from spreading too much, and adds a whiter colour to the bread, than if salt was made use of in its stead. She further says, that she has heard that some great bakers have laid their spunge overnight; when this is done, the leaven must be put the deeper into the meal. [However, it is objected by some, that where allum is made use of, it brings on a staleness of the loaf of bread sooner than if yeast was made use of in its stead; makes it eat harsh, and causes it to crumble more than ordinary.] And that 'tis true her master thus made use of allum; she says, she has weighed it several times for this purpose. And why I am the more particular in my account of it is, because I never met with any common baker, but what denied he ever made use of allum in making his bread. This common baker began at first with baking only eight bushels of wheat-meal a week; but since is become a baker of great trade.

A Cheshire *Servant Maid's Account of her making leavened Bread.*—SHE told me in *November* 1746, that in the part of *Cheshire* where she had lived they eat barley-bread, or bread made with half rye and half wheat-meal, which they there call mobbum bread; but in other parts of *Cheshire*, towards *Manchester*, she says, they eat sour cake, that is to say, oatcake-bread. Her way to make barley or mobbum bread was to save a salted piece of leavened dough against next baking, and then crumble it into warm water, with which she mixed her flower, and made it just into a dough over night, and let it lie till next morning, when she kneaded it for good. She said, they make use of no yeast, unless they think the leaven not strong enough to ferment the dough of itself,—but to make leaven the first time, knead a piece of dough with salt, as long as it will take up any, then hang it up, or leave it covered in salt; and to make it better, you may add a little yeast to the dough, or instead thereof some grounds of ale, or an egg. The staler the leaven the closer will be the bread, and the sooner sour, and if the dough is not well kneaded, it will be streaky.

Of making common Wheaten-Bread for a private Family in Hertfordshire.

THE common way of making wheaten bread for a private family in *Hertfordshire*, is done by heating water a little more than lukewarm in summer, but hotter in winter, and as a bushel of flower or meal lies in the kneading-kiver, or trough, or tub, our country housewife sprinkles a handful of salt over it, and stirs it in; then she mixes a pint of yeast with some of the flower, and lets it lie a little while to rise; next she lades her warm water over the whole mass, and kneads away. Others mix the yeast with the hot water, and pour it over the flower, and then knead all into a dough moderately stiff; and as they begin this when the fuel is put into the oven, they get the bread ready against it is hot, which will be in about an hour's time; and to know when it is enough, there are many ovens that have a little stone fixed in the brick work, at the farthest end, opposite the oven's mouth, which when cold is of a blackish colour, but when it appears whitish, it is a mark or indication for knowing the oven is hot enough. Others regard the sparkles of the fire that fly up, on rubbing the bottom of the oven. If these then spread briskly about, they reckon the oven is hot enough to be swept, and the loaves put in and stopt up. The good housewife also observes not to heat her water too hot, knowing that if she does, it will cause the bread to be too heavy and close. Others, for this purpose, boil their water, or skim milk, or whey, and let it cool till it is a little more than blood-warm, as believing this adds to the goodness of the bread. But the common baker says, That country women do not understand making and baking bread in the best manner, because they generally, on putting their yeast, salt, and water to the meal, mix all together as fast as possible, and after letting the dough lie but little (as some of the worse housewives do) they mould it into loaves, and directly put it into the oven, without giving the dough its due time to ferment, swell, and rise: But the good housewife makes her dough ready before she begins to light the fire in the oven, that it may have the longer time to lie before it is moulded into loaves.

To make Bread with a Mixture of Wheat and Barley Meal, so as to make it answer the greatest Advantage of a Family.

GRIND of each a like quantity together (though some mix half a bushel of wheat with a bushel of barley) because these for this purpose are better grinded together than alone, by reason the barley being thus mixed with the wheat, is grinded the finer; for if the barley, which is the bigger-bodied corn, was to be grinded by itself, they seldom grind it very fine; but when incorporated with wheat, the miller knows it is for family use, and will grind it accordingly. Now to make the best use of this mixed flower, take skim milk, warm it, then add yeast to it, and mix this and the meal together, in the usual manner of making of dough with all wheat-meal, water, and yeast; but milk with yeast makes these meals into what we call a lively dough, that causes the bread to be hollower, sweeter, and whiter, than if water is only mixed with the yeast. Again, yeast is often times bitterish; when so, the bitterness is much lessened by the help of skim milk, for if only water with yeast was employed to make this barley and wheat mixture, the bread would be apt to be heavy and rough tasted, and bitter yeast has a predominant disagreeable taste. Thus, with these two Meals, a good sort of houshold-bread may be made.

How a Yeoman's Wife made a Barley Bread, with which she brought up her Family in Hertfordshire.—THIS yeoman lived about three miles from me, was owner of a farm that employed five horses, and brought up his numerous family with bread made of all barley-meal, which being of a shorter nature than wheat-meal, his wife usually mixed new milk with some warm water, in order the better to hold this short meal together, make the bread appear whiter, eat the sweeter, and keep the longer; for if skim milk was made use of; the dough would require the more squeezing and kneading, and keep the less time from souring; and because barley-meal is of such a short nature, there must be the more yeast or leaven (or both) mixed with it, to make it into a right dough. This woman also, in making her pye-crust, made it of barley-meal and wheat-meal mixed together, because she thought this mixture made shorter and better crust, than if all wheat-meal was made use of.

What chiefly occasions Bread to crumble, and what helps very much to prevent it.—IT is well known to our right country housewives, that if the meal is over-watered, or over-yeasted, the bread will crumble too much; but when the dough is made of a right mixture of these three ingredients, and is kneaded till it is hollow and stiffish, it is then work'd right; if otherwise, there is often what we call sluts-pennies among the bread, that will appear and eat like kernels: Or there will be little lumps of dry flower, both which are occasioned merely by wrong management, and causes the bread to be offensive both to the palate and stomach.

How in making Bread its Loaves are prevented from crumbling.—A WOMAN that came out of *Staffordshire*, to live near me in *Buckinghamshire*, said, She knew a common baker in her country that always made use of cold water as well as warm water in the kneading of his dough to make his loaves of bread, for preventing their crumbling too much. To do which, after he had mixed his yeast with warm water, and had a little kneaded his dough, he now and then poured a dish of cold water over it, and proceeded to knead his dough till he had worked it enough. This, he said, would keep the bread from crumbling too much. And it is this same method that this woman always followed, when she kneaded her dough, and made bread for her numerous family.

The Damage of letting Bread lie too long in an Oven.—IT is a rule among our country housewives, that if loaves of bread stand longer than three hours in a well heated oven, they will fall and be lumpy, like as a toast toasted beyond its due time will be too hard.

Of making Bean and Pea Bread.—THE bean flower makes a rank hearty bread, even the rankest in taste of all others made in *England*, and which cannot be made into loaves so well as other bread, because it will crack and be brittle, therefore it is commonly made into cakes in some parts of the North; its meal is of a yellowish colour, and so is its bread. Pea bread is much sweeter; yet in some parts of the North they grind beans and make bread of them, and sometimes they mix bean flower with barley meal for bread.

Of making Bread with Oats and Tills.—TILLS is a grain that will grow well on poor chalky and gravelly soils, and is about one third part lesser than common pease. Tills being ground into flour, and mixed with fine oatmeal, make a coarse hearty bread; but tills of themselves make a bad bread, and thetches worse.

What occasions bread to be ropy and musty, &c.—WELLS and ponds, that lie in the reach and influence of the sea and salt-water rivers, have their waters generally of a brackish nature and taste, insomuch, that without great care is taken in managing the dough, the bread will soon become ropy. So if bread is made from dough that is over water'd, it will be apt to rope and soon grow mouldy; the same if bread is kept in a damp cellar too long. I had once a lazy maid servant that would not knead her dough enough, and then the bread crumbled, and would not keep sweet long; but another, that kneaded her dough well, and work'd it stiff into loaves, made as good bread as the other did bad. In short, if bread is kept in too moist a place too long, it will rope, or hoar, or mould. And if it is kept in a very dry place too long, it will eat hard, and be apt to crumble. A place between both extremes is best.

What the Laplanders *and* Norwegians *eat for bread*, &c.—IN the month of April 1748, a *Sweedish* gentleman, Professor of Natural History in the University of *Obo* in *Finland*, and one of the Royal Society of *Stockholm*, was at *Gaddesden*, above a fortnight together, to see my ways of husbandry, and among other things he told me, that the *Laplanders*, who are under the *Sweedish* government, are never troubled with the scurvy; because their bread is dried fish, and other diet accordingly; which causes their bodies to be so lightsome, that a *Laplander* will walk over their white mossy land a long way in a day without tiring, will lay his leg on his shoulders, and that a *Laplander* of eighty years of age, would tire the youngest, stoutest *Englishman* in walking. He also informed me, that in some parts of *Norway*, the inhabitants dry and grind the inner bark of the fir-tree, for making bread of its powder or meal. In *Sweden* many also dry and grind the buck-bean and marsh-trefoil-root after they have got out its bitterness by scalding water, and then make it into bread.

The Management of a Bushel of Barley-Meal by a Labourer's Wife.—THIS woman having four children, her husband, that is a day-labourer at threshing, hedging, &c. bought a bushel of barley of me on the 27th of *October*, 1746, to grind into meal, and by sifting it she got a peck and half of the finest part of it, which she baked into bread; and for the next baking, she sifted the remaining Meal, as she did the first, through her hair brewing sieve, and got out a peck and half more, which being somewhat coarser than the first, she mixed a pottle of wheat meal with it, and made it into bread; and after this she had a peck of coarse branny stuff left, that helped to make good wash for her hog. This she did to make the penny go the farther, although wheat was then but four shillings per bushel, and barley eighteen-pence. And to make her barley bread in the best manner, she mixed milk and water, or made use of all skim milk in the kneading of her barley dough, because the milk, she says, holds it better together than all water, makes the bread whiter and eat sweeter. Barley meal, she says, requires the same quantity of salt, but rather more yeast than wheat-meal does. And as to the degree of heat the water or milk should be in, the same will serve for barley meal as for wheat-meal; lukewarm in summer, and hotter in winter. But there is this nicety, she says, to be observed in making bread of all barley meal; the dough of it must not be kneaded stiff, for if is, and put into the oven stiff, the loaf will crack, and be so hard, as hardly to be cut. The knowing housewives therefore work this barley-dough till it is tender and soft, and then make it into loaves, which when baked about three hours, will come out in good order.—The use of barley-meal in making bread was very much in practice amongst the poor people in *Hertfordshire* and elsewhere, in the great frost of 1740, which began about *Christmas-Day*, and held near a quarter of a year, which so cut off the wheat in the field, that the last year's wheat sold for seven or eight shillings a bushel, which necessitated many to make use of barley-meal, not only for bread, but in several other shapes, as I shall give an account of in the following manner, *viz.*

Bread said to be made in Fingal *in* Ireland.—It is reported that they here grind wheat, rye, and pease, to make their bread of, or beans instead of pease, saying, barley-bread slips through them too soon.

N.B. *In my next and second book, I shall give my readers an account, how to make a loaf of bread with barley-meal and another ingredient, that has deceived persons who thought themselves good*

*judges of bread, and made them think it really wheaten bread, tho'
there was no wheaten flower amongst it, and yet it eats better than
a loaf made with all wheaten coarse flower. It is a very valuable
receipt, that has escaped the notice of all authors.*

Of the several Uses of Barley-Meal, and Fat, in making Pye-Crust, Pancakes, Puddings, &c.

*A VERY cheap Way to save Butter or Fat in making Pye-Crust,
with a Mixture of Barley and Wheat Meal.*—THE flower or
meal of barley and wheat made use of in equal quantities,
makes good pye-crust, thus;—Warm skim milk, and mix a
little yeast with it, just enough to enliven it, then work this
into the two meals, for making it into a standing paste for any
sort of pye, and it will keep the crust a little hollow and from
burning, make it appear whitish, and eat short and sweet,
somewhat like a common wig, to the saving of butter or fat;
but if sugar was added to the paste, it would then eat like a
wig. And although crust is made in this cheap manner, some
think it better than if made with all wheat meal, because this
would eat dryer and harder. This cheap way has escaped the
knowledge of all authors before me.

Mary Weeden, *a poor Woman, her Way to make Fat go the
farthest in making Paste of Barley-Meal for Pyes or Pasties.*—THE
flower or meal of barley always requires a little fat to be mixed
with it, because it is too harsh and short of itself with only
water, to make crust for apple or other pyes or pasties. A poor
woman that uses to make apple or other pyes with barley-
meal, for her family, refuses to melt her fat over the fire in
water as the usual way is, but mixes her hogslard or butter with
the meal, by putting bits of it in several parts of the whole;
then she pours her hot water over the same, which melts and
disperses the lard or butter throughout the barley flower, by
the time it is thoroughly kneaded together; but observe, that
this woman's way is not to be practised when the fat is in a

hard body, as dripping-fat and suet commonly is; for in this case such hard fat must be melted in water over a fire, till both are boiling hot. And though I have mentioned this poor woman's method of mixing soft fat cold, in bits with the barley-meal, it is out of the common practice; and she only does it because she thinks this way prevents the waste of her fat better than if she melted it in water over a fire. And in thus preparing her barley-meal paste, for apple or other pyes or pasties, her allowance is, a quarter of a pound of lard, or other soft fat, to half a peck of barley-meal.

The cheapest Way of all others to save the Expence of Fat in making of Pye or Pasty Crust for a Poor Man's Family.—THIS is a most save-all way, and what some poor people are glad to make use of to hitch out the penny, when they cannot afford to buy fat; then it is that they boil skim milk, and while it is boiling hot, they mix wheat flower with it, by stirring in a spoonful at a time, till it is brought into a stiffish consistence, and cool enough to work into dough or paste, chiefly for making a crust for turnover, or flap-apple, or meat patties; and if the flower is good, and the management accordingly, it will make a short, white, and sweet sort, even as good as if only a very little fat was melted in water and mixed with flower.

A Barley-Meal boiled Pudding, as made by the Country Housewife of a poor Family.—SHE stirs the meal with water, a little salt, and a little yeast, and when well mixed, she puts it into a pudding-bag and boils it; when enough, she cuts it into thin slices in a platter, and directly puts between the slices, hogslard sprinkled with a little salt, or melted dripping without salt, and it will eat puffy and palatable, and give a dinner to a poor family, without any thing else. But where milk can be afforded instead of water, it will make the barley-meal pudding so much the better.

A Barley-Meal baked Pudding as made by the Country Housewife, a Farmer's Wife.—THIS pudding is made with such cheap, wholesome, and palatable ingredients, that it may justly be called a right country housewife's pudding, as being composed with those things that stand the yeoman or farmer in but little, because they are commonly ready provided in the house, and of his own produce. Our housewife, in doing this, stirs her barley-meal with water, a little pepper, salt, and apples, cut small; these being well mixed, she puts it into a pudding-pan, with a piece of pickled pork in the middle of it, and when baked, it will prove an agreeable nourishing dinner to her family.

Barley-Meal palatable Pancakes; how to make them for a Yeoman's, a Farmer's, or poor Man's family.—CUT apples very small, and stir them into the barley-meal with some milk and salt, and a little powder'd ginger, for the ginger hollows the pancakes, gives them a good relish, and warms the stomach. Then fry this mixture into pancakes with pot-fat, lard, or dripping-fat, and without any sauce they will eat hollow and palatable. By all these ways of using barley-meal, a poor man is not obliged to lay out his money in wheaten flower, or wheaten bread, and yet by these good managements his family may enjoy a hot bellyful of wholesome food, prevent his having a score to pay off on a *Saturday* night, and give him a shilling in his pocket, which for want of such frugal housewifery he would be obliged to lay out; for according to the old proverb, *A penny saved is a penny got.*

The several Ways of preparing Barley-Meal, for subsisting a poor Man's Family in the hard Frost of 1740.—IN this frost a peck of fine barley-meal was sold at our country shops for one shilling, because wheat-meal was as dear again. This necessitated some poor men's wives to make it go as far as possible, and to this end one of them made no bread of it, but only mixed water with some of the barley-meal, and kneaded it into paste or dough for making cakes with the same; this being done, she broiled these cakes on a gridiron, and they served her family instead of bread.—At other times she made her barley-meal into hasty-pudding, and now and then made it into a boiled pudding, saying, that her family had rather eat barley-meal under these preparations, than the coarse wheaten bread of the shops. And this woman told me, that her husband grew fat chiefly by this barley-meal food (for her husband is one of my day-labourers) and further, that most of the poor men's families in her neighbourhood made use of barley-meal for the greatest part of their subsistence.

Barley-Meal Bread with Turneps, Rye, &c.— IN the great frost of 1740, some of our poor boiled turnips to a mash, and put them and their liquor into a bushel of barley-meal, and then made it into dough, and made one loaf more than if there had been no turnips used; but the bread eat sweetish and disagreeable.—Barley-meal and rye-flower make good bread, because the rye is moist, and the barley dry and short.—Half a peck of rye-flower and a peck of wheat-meal makes good bread; or half one and half the other.—In the great frost of 1709, barley-meal was sold for 8*s. per* bushel.

Pancakes and Fritters made with Wheat-Flower, their several Ways of Preparation, and their Uses in Farmers, Yeomens, or Gentlemens Families, in Harvest, and at other Times of the Year.

How commodiously Pancakes answer the Farmers, the Yeomens, and Gentlemens Interest.

PAncakes are one of the cheapest and more serviceable dishes of a farmer's family in particular; because all the ingredients of the common ones are of his own produce, are ready at hand upon all occasions, saves firing, are soon cook'd, are conveniently portable, and supply both meat and bread; insomuch that in harvest, and at other times, they become a pleasant part of a family subsistence, to the saving of much expence and trouble in a year, by causing the less consumption of fleshmeat, &c. This piece of frugal œconomy likewise affects the yeoman's and gentleman's family; for altho' the master and mistress of these can afford to eat better than the plain sort of pancakes, yet their servants may be often supplied with them as a changeable, light, and pleasant diet, for either breakfast, dinner, or supper. And that a proper sort may be made for both masters and servants uses, I shall be the more particular in giving various receipts for the same as followeth, *viz.*

The Hertfordshire *plain cheap Pancakes for Farmers Families,* &c.—ARE made with wheaten flower, milk, eggs, and powder'd ginger. To a pottle of wheat-flower they put two quarts of new milk, four eggs, and some powdered ginger; these they stir together into a batter consistence, and fry them in hogslard; when one side of the pancake is fried enough, our housewife, or her maid-servant, turns it in a clever manner, by giving it only a toss with the frying-pan, and when this is dexterously done, it is the best way of turning them. Thus she goes on frying pancake after pancake, and as she lays them one upon another, in a platter or dish, she sprinkles some coarse sugar for their sauce; but takes what care she can that the family eats them hot, for the hotter they eat them, the less danger there is of rising in their stomachs, if the lard should be rankish. But whether they eat them cold or hot, if the ingredients are fresh and good, they are agreeable victuals; and though I mention sprinkling of sugar over the pancakes after they are fry'd, as sauce to them, yet some think it the better way to mix sugar in the batter, for mixing it the more regular to the taste.

How a Woman made three Pancakes that dined herself and three Men.—THIS housewifely woman, that lives in our neighbourhood, made her batter for her pancakes thus: In the first place, she pared, cored, and chop'd her apples very small, then prepared her batter with wheat-meal, four eggs, milk, and powder'd ginger; these being all mixed, she put some of the batter into a large frying-pan, with a good quantity of hogslard, and though she laid her batter in thinnish, the pancake came out thick, because all the several ingredients contributed to it. And when she had fry'd three of these pancakes, herself and three men eat them without any sauce, saying, They had a dinner to their satisfaction.

How Small-Beer or Ale Pancakes are made.—THESE are sometimes made, not only by the poorer sort of people, but also by farmers and yeomens wives, when milk cannot easily be had; for although most farmers and yeomen keep cows, they are not always in milk, as being in calf, or that they go, what we in *Hertfordshire* call, guess or dry: In this case milk may be supplied by the use of small-beer, or better with ale; but whenever either of these are wanted, it should be of the mildest newest sort, and free from the bitter taste of hops. Then mix this liquor with wheat-flower, a few beaten eggs, sugar, and ginger, and fry it into pancakes with lard or other fat. I must own, that a pancake made with malt liquor is not so palatable as one made with milk; but where the bellyful is mostly consulted, it will do well enough. And here I take the opportunity to observe, that all authors whatsoever, in their writings on country housewifery, have in no little degree been wanting to answer one main end of their title-page. For as I take it, the chief art of good housewifery lies in bringing much into a little compass; or for explaining this better, to make a little cost answer the end of a great expence; which to do, I shall make it my endeavour in the greater part of this work to shew in the cheapest, plainest, and most practical manner. And that the more curious and abler persons may have their choice, I shall add how the richer and more palatable sorts of things may be made to their satisfaction.

How Water Pancakes are made by poor People.—THIS pancake is made by many poor, day-labouring mens wives, who when they cannot afford to make better, make this; by stirring wheat flower with water instead of milk, for if they can get milk, they generally think it put to a better use when they make milk porridge of it for their family. The flower and water being stirred into a batter consistence, with a sprinkling of salt and powder'd ginger, they fry the pancakes in lard, or other fat, and without any sugar they and their family make a good meal of them.

How Pancakes are made for rich People.—RICH pancakes are made by some to eat as the finishing part of a dinner; to make such, they melt three quarters of a pound of butter with a pint or more of cream; when this is done, stir into it as much flower as will make a common batter for thickness; fry with butter or lard, and turn each pancake on the back of a pewter plate; strew fine sugar over them, and they'll be rich pancakes indeed: But for a farther choice of rich pancakes, I shall add the receipts of several authors.—One author by an old receipt directs, that to make good pancakes, three eggs should be beat till they are very thin; this done, beat them up again with an addition of water, powder'd cloves, mace, cinnamon, nutmeg, and a little salt, next thicken them with fine flower, and fry them with lard or sweet butter into a thin substance till they are brown, then strew some white sugar over them, and they are ready for eating. Upon which this ancient author remarks and says, there be some, who in pancakes mix new milk or cream; this, says he, makes them tough, cloying, and not crisp, nor so pleasant and savoury as clear water makes them.—Another author says, make use of eight eggs to a pottle of flower, powder'd ginger, cinnamon, nutmeg, mace, and some salt: Make, says he, these into thin batter with milk, and beat the whole well together with half a pint of sack; then put the pan on the fire with a little butter or other fat, and when hot, rub it with a cloth; the pan being thus cleaned, put in a sufficient quantity of fat to melt, and your batter on that, very thinly spread, which in frying must be supplied with little bits of butter, lard, or suet; toss the pancake to turn it, and fry it crisp and brown.—Says another author, for making pancakes in the thinnest manner, mix eight eggs with a quart of cream, six spoonfuls of flower, six of sack, one of rose-water, a pound of butter, and two grated nutmegs; the butter must be melted with the cream, and the whole mixed together into a batter. Observe also to butter the fryingpan for the first pancake, but not afterwards, and spread the batter as thin as possible each time you fry. This pancake, says he, being so very thin, needs no turning, for if one side of it is brown, it is enough, and this quantity of batter will make above thirty pancakes; and as they are fry'd, strew fine sugar over each pancake and lay one upon another for eating; or (says he further) if you think fit, you may beat up the eggs with a pint or a quart of water instead of cream, which when mixed with the other ingredients, will make good thin pancakes; but you must take care you do not burn them in frying. Also, that if you make this sort of batter early in a morning, to stand till dinner time, it will make the better pancakes.

Apple Pancakes for Gentry.—FOR this, after you have pared your apples, cut them in round slices, first taking out the core part; these fry in fresh butter; next beat up twelve or sixteen eggs in milk, or better in a quart of cream, which mix with ginger and nutmeg powder'd each two drams, powder'd sugar six ounces; then pour this batter on the fry'd apples, and fry altogether: Sprinkle with sugar, and they'll be good eating. Others mince the apples, and then mix them with batter.

A quick and plain Way to make Apple Fritters.—In *Hertfordshire*, to make these, we cut large apples in thin slices, and only dip them in batter, and fry them in lard or dripping.

A quick and plain Way to make pickled Pork Pancakes.— To do this, we make no more to do in *Hertfordshire*, than to cut thin slices of pickled pork, and dipping them all over in batter, we put them among batter in the fryingpan, and fry them in large pancakes.

The Dugdale Flower Pancake.—THIS is a wheaten pancake, because it is made with wheat-flower, tho' with one of the coarsest of *English* wheat. Yet it is well known to many yeomen and farmers, who sow this Dugdale or Rivet-Wheat, that if the flower of it is sifted fine, it makes the best of pancakes, because its flower or meal is of a sweet short nature.

To make fine Pancakes fry'd without Butter or Lard, according to an old but good Receipt.—TAKE a pint of cream and six eggs, beat them very well together, put in a quarter of a pound of sugar, and one nutmeg, and as much flower as will thicken it like ordinary pancake batter. Your pan must be heated reasonably hot, and wiped with a clear cloth. This done, put in your batter as thick or thin as you please.

To make Rice Pancakes.—THE same author says, boil a pound of rice in three quarts of water till it is very tender, then let it stand covered in a pot a while, and it will become a sort of jelly; next scald a quart of milk and put it scalding hot to the rice jelly, when this is done, mix 20 eggs, well beaten, with three quarters of a pound of butter first melted over a fire, and stir all these together with salt, and as much flower as will hold them frying in butter. This mixture is best done over night.

The Hertfordshire *Bacon Pancake, or what some call Bacon-Fraise, for Plowmen and others.*—CUT the best part of bacon into thin pieces, about two inches square, then with milk, flower, and eggs make a batter; when the eggs are well beaten, mix all of them together, and then put into your fryingpan hogslard or good dripping, which when thoroughly hot, lay in your bacon batter according to discretion, and as the pancake fries, cast some of the fat on it;—when it is enough on one side, turn it. This pancake needs no spice nor sugar, and serves well to fill our plowmens and others bellies instead of intire flesh.

The Hertfordshire *Apple Fritter.*—BEAT the yolks of four eggs and the whites of two well together, which mix with a pint of milk, seven spoonfuls of flower, a quartern of brandy, some grated nutmeg, ginger, and salt; next slice some apples very thin, dip each of them in your batter, and fry them in lard over a quick fire. Or you may mince the apples.

The Hertfordshire *plain Fritter.*—To make these, our housewife makes use of six eggs well beaten, and mix'd with two quarts of milk, a quart of flower, and good store of powder'd ginger, because ginger makes the fritters hollow and hot. She also mixes some coarse sugar with her batter, by which there needs little or no sugar afterwards to eat them with. Batter fries hollower in fritters than in pancakes; but then it employs more time and fat in dressing them.

To make a better Sort of Fritter.—Mix cream and flower with six yolks of eggs and two whites, six spoonfuls of sack, cinnamon, nutmeg and ginger powder'd, and a little salt. Beat these an hour together into a batter, and put your quantity of it into lard at discretion for frying it in fritters.—Some to make richer fritters still, grate *Naples* biskets in cream, and mixing this with some white wine, eggs, sugar, and spices, form a batter for frying it in lard.—Others beat eight yolks with four whites of eggs and a pint of cream, then stir in some powdered spices, two spoonfuls of ale-yeast, and a little salt with some wheat-flower; and set it all, so mixed, within the reach of the fire, to rise and swell; when it does, add four or five spoonfuls of sack, and beat all once or twice again. Thus the batter is made; into which put thin slices of apples, and lade what quantity of it you think fit into boiling lard, for frying it into fritters.—Others first make a *hasty-pudding*, and when coolish, beat it in a mortar with eggs, salt, and sugar, till it becomes a batter, and so dropt into lard and fry'd.

Potatoe Fritters.—Mix *potatoe* pulp with milk, shred suet, currants, salt, and Jamaica spice, and fry it in fritters.—Or you may mix minced apples with the pulp of potatoes or parsnips, and milk, Jamaica pepper, and a little sack for fritters, and eat them with the sauce of lemon juice and butter.

Of making Puddings with Wheat-Flower, in Harvest, and at other Times in the Year.

THE Hertfordshire *Way of making Plumb-Pudding in Harvest Time.*—Pudding is so necessary a part of an *Englishman's* food, that it and beef are accounted the victuals they most love. Pudding is so natural to our harvest-men, that without it they think they cannot make an agreeable dinner. Therefore in *Hertfordshire* our rule is, to make plumb-pudding during wheat harvest, which generally lasts a fortnight; and plain-pudding during the rest of the time. Now to make a plumb-pudding of the better sort for six harvest-mens dinners, our housewife makes use of a pottle of flower, a quart of skim or new milk, three eggs, half or three quarters of a pound of raisins, and half a pound of chopt suet. This being stirred and well mixed together, with a little salt, is to be tied up in a linen cloth or bag; but not too tight, that it may have room to swell. Boil it three or (better) four hours; and if they cannot dine on this with good boiled beef, or with pork, or with bacon and roots, or herbs, they deserve to want a dinner.

A second Receit to make a cheaper Plumb-Pudding is this.— WITH a pottle of flower mix some plumbs, suet, skim milk, coarse sugar, and a little salt, and boil all in a pudding. The sugar will supply the eggs, for eggs in harvest time are not so plenty as in the former part of summer, because the hens now generally begin their moulting. But to make richer puddings at other times, do as follows.

A Pudding to bake or boil.—MIX a quart of new milk with half a pound of currants, and half a pound of raisins, a pound of chop'd suet, five eggs, some nutmeg and salt: These stir with flower till it is of a thick pudding consistence, and either bake or boil it.

A second Pudding to bake or boil.—Is to shred a pound of raisins and a pound of suet together; to this put a few spoonfuls of flower, and five or six eggs beaten up with some sugar, salt, cloves, and mace in powder: Bake this, or boil it four or five hours.

A Pudding in haste.—THIS I was informed of by a woman in our neighbourhood, who having formerly been in service at *London*, was ordered by her mistress to make a pudding in haste. Upon this she asked where she should get milk, as thinking to make a hasty-pudding; but she was answered, there was no occasion for milk, and bid to fetch half a pound of rice and a quarter of a pound of currants, which when picked and washed was bound up in a cloth mixed, and just boiled; for it is enough if boiled a few wallops.

Hasty-pudding, by Mr. Houghton—HE says, to make a substantial hasty-pudding, take a quart of milk, the grated crums of a penny loaf, and boil them together; then sift over it half a pound of flower, first dried before the fire, with a little salt; stir also into it some butter, and a quarter of a pound of currants.

The common Farmers Hasty-pudding.—FOR this, they make use of new or skim milk, or milk and water. A pint of flower will require two quarts of milk. Boil the milk first, then take a pint of cold milk, and mix a little hot milk with it till it is blood warm; then mix the rest of the boiled milk and the flower'd milk together off the fire, and when so mixed, stir the whole over the fire, while it boils a quarter of an hour; then take it off, and add butter, or sugar, or both.

A poor Woman's Pudding for her Family.—TWO women, that lived in a house near me, made each of them a pudding. One put two eggs among other things into hers; the other made her pudding without any eggs, using only hot water wherein some bacon and turnips had been boiled, with a little salt and flower; and yet the latter proved to be the best pudding, as it was full of little holes, light, and better than the former; so great a difference there is in good housewifery and management!

A rich baked Pudding.—TAKE a penny loaf and slice it into a quart of cream with a little rose-water, then break it small; next, take three ounces of almonds blanched, and beaten small with a little sugar, put in seven eggs beaten, some marrow, and two pippins sliced thin; mingle these all together, and bake the pudding.

A boiled Plain-pudding.—TAKE a pint of new milk, or better so much cream, and mix five beaten eggs with it, three spoonfuls of wheat flower, sugar, salt, and nutmeg, a little of each; tie this mixture up in a cloth first butter'd, and put it into a pot of water as it boils, and in about half an hour's time it will be enough. The sauce, melted butter alone, or mixt with sugar.

Rabisha's *baked Hasty-pudding.*—SET on three pints of cream, the crumb of two penny French loaves sliced and minced, put to this a grated nutmeg, a few cloves, mace, cinnamon, and ginger beaten; add thereto half a handful of flower, mingle it together, and stir it into your milk; when it boils, throw in a piece of butter; then having four or five eggs beaten, with the whites of half cast away, put them also into your pudding, with a handful of sugar, and a little rose-water; stir them together again, till they begin to boil and thicken, then pour it into the dish it is to be eaten out of, set it on a heap of coals, make a fire-shovel red hot, and hold it close over your pudding till it is brown on the top, then scrape loaf-sugar over it, and send it up.

Rabisha's *baked Rice-pudding.*—TAKE three pints of milk, and a handful of rice beaten to powder; boil it, and keep it stirring till it is thick, which will be in a quarter of an hour, with a piece of butter and cinnamon, and mace in it, then put it into an earthen-pan and let it be cold; next add to it two handfuls of currants, some sugar, a little salt, and six eggs, leaving out three of their whites; beat the whole together, and after you have butter'd the bottom of your dish, lay your pudding into it, and garnish the brims of it with a paste; when baked, scrape on some sugar, and 'tis done.—Or, boil rice till it is full tender, and mix eggs, a little salt and nutmeg with it; this lay on a thin paste in a dish with bits of butter, and bake.

A plainer Way to make a baked Rice-pudding.—BOIL half a pound of powder'd rice in three pints of milk well, then take it off, and when almost cold beat up six eggs, and add these with half a pound of chopt suet or butter and a grated nutmeg, and bake it half an hour.—Or if you think fit you may put some fine puff-paste at the bottom of the dish.

A Buckinghamshire *Farmer's Way to victual his Family with Pudding,* &c.—THIS farmer rented a farm of eight score pounds a year, consisting of arable and meadow ground, kept eight horses, twelve cows, two taskers, two plowmen, a shepherd, and horse-keeper, besides several day-labourers; and as his family were but eight in number (for the farmer was a widower) his maid servant made every day one or two boiled puddings, which, with a piece of bacon, was the chiefest of their food all the year; for I do not remember I ever saw them dine on any thing else, except now and then a calf's pluck that the farmer bought at *Leighton* market in *Bedfordshire.* Now you must know, that as eggs and butter helped to pay his rent, he would seldom allow an egg to be put into the pudding, but obliged the maid to make it of a quart of skim milk and about a pottle of wheat flower, a little salt, and powder of ginger; which she stirred into the consistence of a hasty-pudding, and commonly boiled it in two bags, which she first flower'd to prevent their sticking; when they were boiled enough, they cut the pudding in slices, and poured melted butter on it or sugar'd milk.

This Author's Servant-Maid's Way to make a Boiled-pudding.—IT is also my way to have a plain pudding made most days in the year; and for doing it, my servant-maid mixes a pint of new milk with a quart of flower, one egg, a little salt, and powder of ginger. This, when she has flower'd her pudding-bag, she puts into it, and boils it an hour and a half, or two hours, against my plowman and boy come from plow; and when it is taken up, she for sauce mixes some sugar and milk together. And I assure my reader, that with such a pudding and a piece of pickled pork boiled, my family makes a dinner to their satisfaction; for where they eat one pound of bacon, they eat more than fifty of pickled pork, for reasons I shall hereafter assign.—Or to make a boiled pudding better than this, you may mix grated bread and minced suet together in equal quantities; upon which pour scalded milk, and let all lie under a cover about twenty minutes, then add a spoonful of sugar, ginger, nutmeg, and a little flower, and boil it in a pudding-bag an hour and a half, or two hours.

Bread-pudding.—TAKE the crumb of the whitest bread, and cut it in thin slices, to the quantity of about half a pound, or grate it; then boil a pint of milk, and put it boiling hot on the bread, grate half a nutmeg into it, and when cold add three beaten eggs and a little sugar; stir all well together, with a handful of fine flower to hold it together, and boil it half or three quarters of an hour; for sauce melt butter, or mix butter and sugar together.

Apple-pudding, the Hertfordshire *Way.*—THIS sort of pudding I have frequently made in my family, because in some years I have great quantities of apples, which more than ordinary pleases my people. To make it, my servant-maid boils a pint of milk with a quarter of a pound of lard or dripping, then mixes it with as much flower as will make it into a dough or paste, rolls it, and when the paste is cool and stiff enough, she puts on it sliced or minced apples, which she incloses in the paste; then puts it into a cloth, ties it up, and boils it two hours and a half at least; our sauce is melted butter with sugar, or sugar and milk.—But to make a richer apple-pudding, you may scald your apples and pulp them through a cullender; then mix them with cream, bisket, and eggs, a little nutmeg and sugar, which bake in a dish, with a sheet of puff-paste.

Potatoe-pudding.—THIS is a most serviceable and most wholesome root, because it is of a nourishing satiating nature, and admits of being eaten in several shapes; as with bacon, pickled pork, salt beef, mutton, salt fish; in pyes, in puddings, with butter, or with milk, &c. &c. And as they are easily propagated, no farmer, labourer, yeoman, nor gentleman, should be without them, as they value their pockets; for potatoes with good management may be kept all the year, so that where there is ground enough to plant them on, there need be no want of this profitable vegetable to save expence, and this by many ways of using them. Here indeed I shall only shew their service in a pudding; but more by and bye. Boil, peel, and mash the potatoes; this done, mix two pounds of the pulp with half a pound of butter, four eggs, pepper, salt, and ginger, and when they are all beaten together into the consistence of a pudding, it may be either boiled or baked; when enough, eat it with melted butter.—Or, you may mix with potatoe-pulp, scraped carrot, sugar, butter, nutmeg, salt and eggs, which put in a dish with paste round it, and bake it half an hour in a quick oven.—Or, if you have a mind to make a potatoe-pudding richer, mix minced apples with potatoe-pulp, cream, fine sugar, powder'd cinnamon and cloves, and being beaten all together into a pudding consistence, put it in paste and bake it in a dish.—Or, buttered eggs may be mixed with potatoe-pulp and other ingredients for a baked pudding.—Or, thin little slices of pickled pork or bacon may be baked with potatoe-pulp for a pudding, with some other ingredients as abovesaid.—Or, a potatoe-pudding may be made with their pulp, whole oatmeal, currants, salt and pepper, and butter, baked in a dish or earthen-pan; for sauce, melted butter or cream, with slices of lemon, &c.

To make a Black-cherry-pudding.—BEAT an egg, and put it into a pint of milk; then mix about a quart of flower, and a pound of black Kerroon cherries, with the milk and egg; stir them together till it is of a pappy consistence, for being put into a pudding-bag, first wetted or flower'd, and boil it about an hour or an hour and a half; for sauce melt butter and sugar, or milk and sugar: If you have not Kerroon cherries, any other sort, if ripe and sweet, may do.—This pudding we commonly have made at times during the cherry season, and proves a pleasant eating to my family.—Which puts me in mind of what one of our country wenches said to her *London* mistress: Madam, says she, pray let us have a black-cherry-pudding for dinner. A black-cherry-pudding! I never heard of such a thing in my life! that must be physick. No, Madam, says the girl, we have it often in the country, and it is a very good pudding indeed.

A Flower-pudding for a Farmer's Family to boil.—A pottle of flower will make two good bag-puddings, or they may be tied up in a cloth; and to make them they commonly take skim milk, which is near as good as new milk for stirring of puddings; to this pottle of flower three eggs are sufficient to beat and mix with the rest; when they are boiled enough, instead of melted butter, some farmers wives melt hogs-lard and lade it over the pudding for sauce, with a little salt strewed over it; or, instead of lard, they melt some sweet pot-fat-dripping. This sort of fat is preferred by some to butter, as being cheaper, heartier, and more ready at hand, when butter cannot be had.

A Flower-pudding to bake.—BOIL a pint or a quart of milk, and thicken it with flower; if you make use of a quart of milk, there should be half a pound of butter, four ounces of sugar, eight eggs, a little salt, and a grated nutmeg mixed; this put into a butter'd dish, may be baked in an hour's time.

Of Apple-Pyes, and Apple-Pasties, for Harvest and other Times.

APPLE pyes and pasties are a main part of a prudent, frugal farmer's family-food, because the meal and apples that make them are commonly the produce of his land, and are ready at all times to be made use of in pyes or pasties, for giving his family an agreeable palatable repast; a covered or turn-over pasty for the field, and the round pye for the house; the first being of a make and size that better suits the hand and pocket than the round pye, and therefore are more commonly made in farmers families; for one, or a piece of one, being carried in the plowman's and plowboy's pocket, sustains their hunger till they come home to dinner, and oftentimes pleases them beyond some sort of more costly eatables; nor is it less wholesome than pleasant, for that the ingredients of the apple-pye are rather antidotes against, than promoters of the scurvy. In short, it is the apple pye and pasty, and apples made use of in some other shapes (particularly the famous Parsnip apple) that I take to be some of the cheapest and most agreeable food a farmer's family can make use of; but for displaying their value in a more elegant manner, I hope the following poem will not be unacceptable to my reader.

Of APPLE-PYES: *A poem, by Mr.* WELSTED.

O F all the delicates which *Britons* try,
To please the palate, or delight the eye;
Of all the several kinds of sumptuous fare,
There's none that can with apple-pye compare,
For costly flavour, or substantial paste,
For outward beauty, or for inward taste.
   WHEN first this infant dish in fashion came,
Th' ingredients were but coarse, and rude the frame;
As yet, unpolish'd in the modern arts,
Our fathers eat brown bread instead of tarts:
Pyes were but indigested lumps of dough,
'Till time and just expence improv'd them so.
   KING *Coll* (as ancient annals tell)
Renown'd for fiddling and for eating well,

Pippins in homely cakes with honey stew'd,
Just as he bak'd (the proverb says) he brew'd.
THEIR greater art succeeding princes shew'd,
And model'd paste into a nearer mode;
Invention now grew lively, palate nice,
And sugar pointed out the way to spice.
BUT here for ages unimprov'd we stood,
And apple-pyes were still but homely food;
When god-like *Edgar*, of the *Saxon* line,
Polite of taste, and studious to refine,
In the dessert perfuming quinces cast,
And perfected with cream the rich repast:
Hence we proceed the outward parts to trim,
with crinkumcranks adorn the polish'd rim,
And each fresh pye the pleas'd spectator greets
With virgin fancies and with new conceits.
DEAR *Nelly*, learn with care the pastry art,
And mind the easy precepts I impart;
Draw out your dough elaborately thin,
And cease not to fatigue your rolling-pin:
Of eggs and butter, see you mix enough;
For then the paste will swell into a puff,
Which will in crumbling sound your praise report,
And eat, as housewives speak, exceeding short:
Rang'd in thick order let your quincies lie;
They give a charming relish to the pye:
If you are wise, you'll not brown sugar slight,
The browner (if I form my judgment right)
A tincture of a bright vermil' will shed
And stain the pippin, like the quince, with red.
WHEN this is done, there will be wanting still
The just reserve of cloves, and candy'd peel;
Nor can I blame you, if a drop you take
Of orange water, for perfuming sake;
But here the nicety of art is such,

There must not be too little, nor too much;
If with discretion you these costs employ,
They quicken appetite, if not they cloy.
    NEXT in your mind this maxim firmly root,
Never o'er-charge your pye with costly fruit:
Oft let your bodkin thro' the lid be sent,
To give the kind imprison'd treasure vent;
Lest the fermenting liquors, mounting high
Within their brittle bounds, disdain to lie;
Insensibly by constant fretting waste,
And over-run the tenement of paste.
    TO chuse your baker, think and think again,
You'll scarce one honest baker find in ten:
Adust and bruis'd, I've often seen a pye
In rich disguise and costly ruin lie;
While the rent crust beheld its form o'erthrown, ⎫
Th' exhausted apples griev'd their moisture flown, ⎬
And syrup from their sides run trickling down. ⎭
    O BE not, be not tempted, lovely *Nell,*
While the hot piping odours strongly swell,
While the delicious fume creates a gust,
To lick th' o'erflowing juice, or bite the crust:
You'll rather stay (if my advice may rule)
Until the hot is temper'd by the cool;
Oh! first infuse the luscious store of cream,
And change the purple to a silver stream;
That smooth balsamick viand first produce,
To give a softness to the tarter juice.

    A Character of the famous Parsnip Apple, and its Uses.—FROM
whence this apple is so called, I cannot tell; but this I know, that
it is the very best of apples for pyes, pasties, and puddings in
harvest time, and for eating (baked or raw) single as they are;
they are always the first apples that are ripe with us, for they
commonly begin to drop from the tree about the middle of

August, some of them weighing four ounces apiece; and I think I can affirm it for truth, that I have had above twenty bushels in one season off one tree only; part of which I made use of for present spending, part for cyder, and the rest I hoarded, for these will keep till near *Christmas*. These apples are also of the greater value, for their agreeable quality of eating well in an apple pye or pasty without sugar; for when they are ripe, pared, and cored, my servant-maid bakes considerable numbers of two-corner'd pasties without any sugar, because they need no other sweetening than what a little water with their own juice affords; and yet in this manner of making them, our men commonly prefer eating such pasties alone, before bread and cheese: Hence it is that we say the Parsnip apple saves cheese. And for supper (in harvest time especially) these apples make almost a constant part of it, by being coddled or baked, till they are so tender, as to be easily mixed in messes of bread and milk. In short, the Parsnip apple is endowed with such excellent qualities, that they may truly be accounted a pleasant repast, from the lord's to the peasant's table, in the shape of pyes, pasties, apple-puddings, apple-dumplings, or baked, or coddled singly. This apple tree is not to be had in any of the nurseries near *London*, as I have been informed, when I was amongst them, by some of their own nursery men; for it is only in growth at *Gaddesden*, and at some miles round it. But as I keep only three sorts of nurseries always by me, one for the black large Kerroon cherry-trees, one for the Parsnip apple-trees, and one for the Bell-orange pear-trees, I am ready to furnish any gentleman with any of these sorts for one shilling each tree at my house: And I further add, that as these apples, either eaten raw, or better under some preparations, serve in some degree for meat and drink, no gentleman, farmer, yeoman, or labourer, ought to be without one or more of these trees, where they have ground convenient for planting them.— Next I shall likewise give an account of the excellent quality of the Bell-orange pear, as follows, *viz.*

The Character of the famous Bell-orange Pear.—THE tree of this pear I am owner of, and is so large a one, that it has borne above twenty bushels at once of pretty sizeable pears, which are always ripe in harvest; it is of an orange colour, grows in the shape of a bell, therefore is called the *Bell-orange pear.* And as it is thus early ripe, it gives our harvest-men a pleasure to eat them raw for they have a delicate taste, but are most of all agreeable in pyes or pasties, because these pears in these shapes taste somewhat like sweetmeats; and to say no more than they deserve, a pye may be made of them fit for the table of a potentate. I have made perry of these pears directly from the tree, and found it good liquor, if drank in a little time, for it will not keep a great while; and it has such a delicate smell, that if a person hold his nose over the bunghole, the scent is just like that of an orange. My maid bakes them loose in an earthen glazed pot, for being eaten with milk or with milk and bread. I have been in several of the nurseries about *London,* and inquired for the like fruit, but they own they have it not; nor do I know of any other tree of this sort in all our country, nor in all my several years travels: And the way I came by this was, by purchasing the farm I now live in, and hold in my own hands, which has enabled me to raise a nursery of these very sort of pear-trees, so that I am ready to furnish any gentleman at the price of one shilling each, and send them to any part of *England, Wales, Scotland, Ireland,* or to any of our plantations abroad. And I further say, and aver it from the truth of experience, that the juice of the black Kerroon cherry (which may be conserved till this pear or Parsnip-apple is ripe) mixed with that of the Parsnip-apple, or with the juice of this Orange-pear; will, with a little assistance, make a tawny colour'd wine, little inferior in my opinion to some foreign wine.

The Character of the famous black Kerroon Cherry.—THIS famous serviceable cherry is accounted the best of the black sort in *England,* for its firmness, delicious juice, and smallness of kernel: I believe I have above fifty of these sort of improved cherry-trees growing in my plow and meadow fields, that seldom miss of producing great quantities of cherries, that we make use of in puddings and in two-corner pasties; but we reckon they eat better in the pasty than in a pye, because in cutting one of these through its middle, the liquor may be kept in to the last of its eating: Likewise, when this excellent black Kerroon cherry is eaten in a little time after gathering, the eater enjoys a most wholesome pleasant sort, that will bear a long carriage, and therefore are good market cherries.

The Farmer's Wife's plain Way of making or raising Paste for Apple or Meat Pyes, Custards, or Pasties.—Her allowance is half or a whole pound of lard, or dripping-fat, or pork-fat, or any meat-fat is it is tried up, to half a peck of flower; which she boils in water, and as soon as it boils, she mixes it with the flower, and works it into as stiff a paste as possible; and when it is well kneaded, she wraps it up in a linen cloth, to keep warm for using it in a requisite heat; for such pye-crust should be raised while the paste is warm, because it cools in making, and stiffens the better: With this, apple-pyes, meat-pyes, custards, and several other pasties are made both cheap and palatable, for farmers uses.—Or, if you will make the crust somewhat better, melt three pounds of fresh butter in boiling water, as soon as it boils take it off the fire, and mix all with a peck of flower, and work it into a paste, for apple-pye, meat-pye, or any other that requires a standing crust.—Or take it this way, melt two pounds of butter in a saucepan with water, when it is melted skim off the butter, and with some of the water work it in the flower to a stiff paste; the flower should be half a peck; if not used quickly, wrap it in a cloth, and let it lay before the fire.

A Puff-paste.—TAKE one pound of fresh butter, and one pound of flower; mix two ounces of the butter and two eggs with the flower, and make it into paste with cold water; then work the other part of the pound of butter into a stiff paste, and with a rolling-pin roll it thin; when so done, put bits of butter here and there in most parts of it, roll it again, then double it up, and make each end meet, and roll it again, till all the butter is thoroughly well incorporated. But to make this receit the plainer to my reader, observe what *Rabisha* says.— Take a pottle of flower and the whites of six eggs, make it into a paste with cold water, let it not be very stiff; when it is well wrought, roll it forth foursquare like a sheet of paper as thick as your finger; then take three pounds of butter, and beat it well with a rolling-pin, then lay it on in slices all over your paste about as thick as your finger, and strew a little flower over it; then roll up your sheet of paste like a collar with the butter within, squeeze and roll it at both ends broad and long-ways; then clap up the ends, and make them meet in the middle one over another, and fasten it down again with your rolling-pin, rolling it forth every way as thin as at first; then flower your board well underneath, and spread it over with butter, roll it up, and work it as before; thus do three or four times, till your three pounds of butter is made use of. In the *Summer* make this paste in the morning with the stiffest butter you can get, and lay it in a cold place till you make use of it. In *Winter* you must beat your butter well, otherwise it will be harder than your paste, and break holes through it.—Or, mix two pounds of flower with half a pound of butter, and the whites of three or four eggs well beaten with cold water, and work into a paste; then roll it thin, and by degrees roll in one pound of butter more; roll it again and again, adding flower each time for five or six times, till this quantity or more butter is well worked into the paste, for making a puff-paste for nice small pyes or tarts.— Or, to make a good crust, you may use cold milk instead of cold water, with an addition of as much brandy as an egg-shell will hold, and fine sugar, with two pounds of butter, and three pounds of flower for pyes, tarts, &c. Thus having given my reader an account of making poor pastes and rich pastes, I proceed now to the making of apple-pyes, pasties, &c.

How a Farmer disgraced himself by having Apple-pasties made at a dear Rate, and how he might have had them made cheaper and better.—THIS farmer lives about three miles from *Gaddesden*, in a farm of about two hundred pounds a year rent; and being in low circumstances, endeavoured to save the penny in several managements of his kitchen; amongst the rest, he had his apple-pasties made with wheat-meal in the following manner: His apples he caused to be chop'd small with their cores and stalks (as they were gathered from the tree) in a tray or wooden bowl unpared; this being done, he had his paste made with water, and chopt suet, or fat, in the usual way, which he bought at a dear rate, having no hogslard or other fat of his own; and in this paste he wrapt up his chopt apples in form of pasties, and baked them to his disgrace, for he could hardly get a good servant to live with him, and those that did, grumbled much, and worked the worser for it. Now had this farmer caused his crust to be made with a mixture of half wheat and half barley meal, and not have pared his apples, but quartered them, and threw away the stalks and cores, and made use of skim milk and yeast, instead of water and fat, as I have before observed, he had pleased his servants better, and come cheaper and more creditably off; for the skim milk and yeast would have made the crust puffy and white, and eat well without sugar, if the apples were of the right sort, and in right order.

How another Farmer has his Apple Pyes and Pasties made something better than the last Farmer.—A farmer near me has his apple-pasties made, by first paring the apples and taking away the stalks and tops of them, but chops the apples with all their cores very small, for by being so small chopt, they fill the apple-crust or coffin in every part of it, better than if they were quartered, and the cores thereby less perceived in eating.

How a third Farmer has his Apple Pyes or Pasties made.—THIS farmer has his apples quartered, as thinking the fewer of them goes to fill a pye or pasty, and because the apples will bake redder than when chopt small.

This Author's Way of having his Apple Pyes or Pasties made.—ONCE every week or ten days, from *August* to all the time that my hoarded apples last, my servant-maid bakes apple pyes or pastries with her bread, but does not pare her apples, only cores them, takes away their stalks, and cuts them in small bits with a knife; if the apples are not full ripe at using, or if they are of the sharp-tasted kind, as the *Holland* pippin, or the green *French* pippin, and such like, she then puts a little sugar amongst them; but when she makes use of the Parsnip apple, or the Gold-Rennet, or when she mixes the sweet apples with a few sharp apples, she puts no sugar amongst them.—By what has been said, may appear the great conveniency of having the Parsnip apple-tree, and the Gold-Rennet-tree (which are constant bearers) together with the sweet-apple-tree growing on a farm; for by having these apple-trees at command, much sugar may be saved, and yet good apple pyes and pasties may be made of them: It is my good fortune to have many apple-trees of various kinds growing in rows in my plowed fields and meadows, besides those in my orchard, and wood of my own planting, which in some plentiful years return me large quantities of apples for making cyder, and for kitchen uses. And here I am also to observe, that I have several trees of the sweet apple the best sort of which are of a pretty large size, and will keep to *Lady-day* or longer; which I find of great service in making apple pyes and pasties alone for servants, without any other sort of apples or sweets. But if you are for finer sorts, scald apples till tender; when you have so done, skin them, and beat them to a pulp; then beat some eggs, and mix the whole with grated bread, sugar, ginger and nutmeg, and some melted butter; butter your dish, and bake it in a moderate heated oven.—Or, pare pippins, quarter them, and near cover them with water; put two pounds of sugar to about a pottle measure of pippins, and boil these all together on a gentle fire close covered, with some beaten dill-seed, cinnamon, orange-peel, and rose-water; when cold, make it into pasties or tarts with a rich paste.

Of Victualling Harvest-men in Hertfordshire.

IN this county we hire harvest-men long before harvest, by way of security, that we may not be at a loss for them when we most want them; and give each man thirty or six and thirty shillings for his month's service, besides victualling and lodging them in the house all that time, for then they are ready early and late to do our work. Now in victualling these men there are variety of ways practised by country housewives; and she that can do it cheapest, and most satisfactory, is the best house-wife. To this purpose, I, and many other farmers, single out some of our older ewes, that are what we call broken-mouth'd sheep (that is to say, such who by age have lost most of their teeth before) and timely put them into good grass, for their coming out fat time enough to kill in harvest. Or instead of ewes, others kill a fat barrow-hog of twenty or thirty stone weight (one or more) the offald of which we eat fresh, and the rest we salt down, as is my way every harvest. Others that occupy very large farms, and employ eight, twelve, or more harvest-men, have an old cow, or a small *Welch* runt fatted against this time. And if a farmer cannot dispense with the whole himself, he lets a neighbour or two have the rest; and when his neighbours kill the like, they furnish the same to him. In any of these cases we have the less meat to buy of the butcher, however, some beef we commonly take of him every week during the harvest, and suet with each lot or parcel, for making harvest-puddings; which is so necessary a part of our victuals, that the men think they cannot make a good dinner without either a plain or plumb one; and it is this last sort that most of our farmers have during wheat harvest, and the former sort afterwards. These with several other preparations of food, with strong beer and ale, are what we victual our month or harvest men with. And if we cannot get our harvest in by that time, by reason of rainy weather, we keep them longer, some even six weeks or two months, till our ricks and cocks of corn are all compleated and thatched. In short, it is our notion in *Hertfordshire*, that that gentleman, yeoman, or farmer, manages best, who victuals his harvest-men with beef, bacon, or pickled pork, beans, pease, puddings, pyes, pasties, cheese, milk, with other culinary preparations, and with well brew'd strong and small beer and ale; for such a one ranks the best chance of hiring the best hands, that will go on briskly with their work, and do a good deal of it in a day. Not that I write this as a general rule, for I know a certain farmer, that lives within three miles of me, who although he employs six month-men, besides his own servants, has bought but six stone of beef in a harvest; because he supplied this meat with the flesh of fatted old sheep and swine, &c. I also am sensible, that much further north, bacon, pork, and pudding are almost the whole feed of their harvest-men, as believing a bellyful is sufficient, and that the less variety of meats causes the men to eat the less, which may perhaps in these parts answer the end of preventing their buying beef, &c. But as such œconomy will not be agreeable to southern men, our housewife's art lies in furnishing variety of eatables, and yet to do it in the most frugal manner. And that it may be so done not only in harvest-time, but also at all other times throughout the year, is the main design of my writing this treatise *of the Country Housewife.*

To preserve Beef or Mutton Suet sound and sweet all the Harvest Season and longer.—THIS I take to be a very material article and piece of good housewifery, as beef or mutton suet is extraordinarily necessary to be kept in readiness, throughout the harvest time, for mixing it, to make plumb and plain puddings, &c. and it is on this account that we southern farmers have always a parcel of beef suet weighed with every lot or parcel of beef we buy of the butcher, who by custom should allow a pound to every stone of eight pound. But for the best and most suet, some buy the surloin, that is weighed with the leg; or if we will pay a penny a pound extraordinary, we may have all the suet of a surloin alone. Now as such a quantity of suet cannot be made use of presently, it highly concerns a right country housewife to preserve it sound in the sweetest manner; which that she may effectually do, let her chop the suet as small as she can, and then sprinkle it with pepper and salt at discretion: This done, it must be potted down as close and as hard as she can well do it, and it will keep good not only the whole harvest, but near a year together. Whereas if such chopt suet was not well seasoned with pepper and salt, and laid loose or hollowish, it would surely stink in a little time. Observe also, that suet so potted should have a close covering over it, and be kept in some dry part of a house, for if it stands in too moist a place it will be apt to mould and hoar.

The good Housewifery of a Farmer's Wife to furnish herself with a due Quantity of Suet against Harvest-Time.—IN view of wanting suet in harvest-time, this woman took care before-hand to provide for it; therefore as often as she bought beef or a loin of mutton, she chopt the fat and potted it down, with pepper and salt as aforesaid; knowing that in harvest-time, enough of good suet is difficult to be had, and because beef, mutton, and suet, sell cheaper before than in harvest; which the more encouraged her in time to provide this most necessary ingredient, which she kept thus managed in an earthen glazed pot, with only a wooden loose cover over it, placed in a dry part of the house.

The best Way of salting Beef, to preserve it sweet and sound in Harvest, and at all other Times of the Year.—BEEF in harvest-time is mostly eaten fresh, as best agreeing with the farmers and workmens interest; for by boiling a piece fresh with bacon or pickled pork, the one pleasantly relishes the other. And if the beef or mutton is lean, the fat bacon or pork helps it the better out; this is much observed by our country housewives, because it frequently falls to the farmer's lot, to have lean pieces amongst the meat he buys. And when there is so much bought in at once as requires salting, some will directly salt it down in a pot or tub. Others, who manage much better, will first sprinkle some salt over it, to extract and draw out the bloody juice (that it may take salt the freer, keep sweeter, safer, and longer, in the hot season of the year) and when it has lain a few hours under such a sprinkling of salt, will then salt it down for good. Or, take it this way, which is still a more sure way of proceeding: After the beef has been sprinkled with salt, and lain to drain out its bloody juice six or seven hours, wipe every piece dry, and rub them all over well with dry hot salt. This done, pack them close in a pot or tub one upon another.

The Benefits of getting Roots, Herbs and other culinary Vegetables against Harvest-Time.—IN our Chiltern country of *Hertfordshire*, several of our prudent housewives foresee the great conveniency of having broad beans, pease, carrots, turnips, potatoes, cabbages, onions, parsley, and other kitchen ware, ready for use against a want of them in harvest-time; for that some of these not only prove a sauce, but also help meat to go the further. And here I think it necessary to inform our country housewife, that she ought to have a bed of grass-onions ready all the summer time for her pot uses, even 'till *Allholland-Tide*. Now what I mean by grass-onions, are *Welch* onions; whose green large flaggy stalks will endure cutting many times in a year, and will last ten or twenty or more years, provided the bed is dressed once in three years with soot, ashes, or malt-dust, and not suffer'd to run to seed. This I yearly prove to my great conveniency, as being thus furnish'd with early and late onion-stalks, when roots and stalks of others are not easily had; and for having these onions, its seed may be had at any of the *London* seed-shops, by asking for a penny-worth or two of *Welch* onion seed: But I have further to inform my reader, that this is the seed which produces the forward sort of young onions, which are drawn by *May-Day* to be eat with sallads; therefore this *Welch* onion seed may be sown for an early drawing of them, as well as for a durable crop to cut in flags. And as for broad beans, they serve, in some measure, as a second sort of meat as well as sauce, and are so necessary to a family in harvest-time, that that gentleman, yeoman, or farmer, who does not provide a sufficient crop of them against such an occasion, is very much wanting to his own interest; for it is this most cheap and serviceable vegetable which allays thirst, and so relishes fat bacon, or salt pork, that the men often eat it with a good stomach, to the saving of much expence in the consumption of beef and other meat; it is easy of carriage to the field, will keep hot some time, and prove a very wholesome nourishing eatable. Pease also are valuable, as a change of satiating diet, and are cooling and pleasant to the taste. In the harvest of 1748, as well as in former harvests, I fed my harvest men almost every other day with bacon and beans, or pickled pork and beans. Carrots, turnips, cabbage, and potatoes, are also good kitchen provision to be eaten with salt or fresh meat. Onions, sallary, leeks, parsley, thyme, and savory, are also necessary in harvest-time, because with these our country housewife cooks up her lean orts of beef, her pieces of bacon or pork, her offald cold turnips, carrots, cabbage, or potatoes. And if the meat is a little tainted, yet by her skillful management in the use of some of these roots and herbs, she may recover such meat, by causing it to be hashed or minced according to the art of good housewifery.

Of the Nature and Uses of Pork in Harvest and at other Times of the Year.

SWINES flesh, says an eminent physician, nourishes very plentifully, and yields firm nourishment; therefore is most profitable to those that are in their flourishing age, sound and strong, who are exercised with much labour. Now, as such, I would here introduce it, and for its being a most pleasant serviceable meat, especially for the diet of harvest-men now and then, because a porker, newly killed, admits of many ways of dressing it, is cheaper done, is less cloying, and keeps (salted) sweet and sound longer than any other meat whatsoever: Witness the approbation it meets with in the county of *Kent*, where pickled pork is in such general esteem, that they make very little bacon there, because a dish of pickled pork, with apple dumplins, *&c.* is there deemed an agreeable repast, from the peer to the peasant. And as thus, it stands the most ready and cheapest of flesh victuals to tradesmen and farmers in particular; for here the common plowman thinks himself not rightly provided, if he cannot carry a piece of pickled pork and apple-dumplin into the field, to bite on till he comes home to dinner; as ours in *Hertfordshire* take a piece of bread and cheese with them; for pickled pork is more profitable to a family than bacon, because there is no reason to commit waste in eating it, as too often is seen in the case of the latter, when its burnt thick rind or skin, and the rusty inside of the fleshy part, tempt many to throw them away. Bacon is likewise very apt to have its gammon-part damaged by the breed of very minute insects of the vermicular kind, that are first generated in it, and when a little aged become winged, for it is then that they skip or fly about, and from hence it is that they are called the hopper-fly, that will, if not prevented, eat into and spoil the whole gammon; and how to prevent it without making a present consumption of the bacon, is above the art of most people, as I shall in my second part *of the Country Housewife* further observe. Whereas these damages are intirely avoided in pickling of pork, as well as the disagreeable rankness of taste that bacon is very subject to have in it, if kept aged.

Of killing a Barrow-Hog for a pickled Porker in Harvest Time.—THIS is a late practice in *Hertfordshire*, but takes more and more every year, because the fresh meat of a porker lessens the farmer's expence in beef, &c. For this sort of meat being of his own feeding, not only stands him in less charge than beef, but when it is managed by a good housewife, will go further than any other sort of flesh in a family. And why the killing of a porker in harvest has not been long practised is, because most people imagine that the weather at this season of the year is too hot for making the flesh take salt kindly, so as to keep sweet afterwards. But the contrary of this erroneous opinion, I and many others every year prove, by an artful and careful management; for we, in the first place, take care to keep a porker from meat two days and two nights before we kill him, because if a porker was killed with a bellyful of meat, the flesh of it would not keep so long sweet and sound, as one killed when its belly is empty of food. This is so well observed by butchers, that they not only follow this rule in killing a porker, but do it also in killing all other beasts, whenever their conveniency allows it. So when a porker is killed in the summer time, it should be done in the evening, that the flesh may be the sooner cold, by the approaching night; and when the hair is scalded off, and the guts taken out, my way is to hang the carcase up in the cellar, or other cool place, where the great blue blow-fly cannot come. This I did by one I scalded in *August* 1746, about the third day after I had began harvest, that weighed five and twenty stone, as I did another in *August* 1748, and is what I generally practise every year, as one of the best pieces of husbandry belonging to a farmer's house for lessening the total of a butcher's bill.

Of cutting out the Carcase of a Porker for pickling.—THE next morning we cut out the carcase into many pieces. First the butcher cuts off the head and cleaves the porker asunder, then takes out the spare-ribs, or chine, or both; if a chine is saved, the spare-ribs will be the less. Next he chops off the four hocks, then cuts out the two blade-bones, and two butt or buttock pieces, and last of all the short or broiling ribs. The rest, being all flesh is pickled; and for this, the butcher cuts it out into square pieces according to the bigness of the family.

Observations on killing several Sorts of Sow-Hogs for pickled Pork.—A YOUNG sow, that has had but one litter of pigs, and is gone near half her time with pig again; if such a one is fatted and killed then, her flesh will eat almost, if not quite, as well as the flesh of a spay'd sow, if pickled for pork. The next observation is, that I killed, on the thirteenth day of *May,* 1745, a sow that had had two litters of pigs; her last litter was pig'd on the 11th of *March* and on the 4th of *April* I sold off her pigs. On the 30th of *April* she took boar, and thirteen days after I killed her, being near the middle of three weeks after her brimming time was over; and she eat exceeding sweet and fine, as being fatted with barley-meal after a particular method; for though she was fattening but a little while, yet by being kept well before, she was thought to weigh thirty-five stone, tho' fattened for pickled pork. It is also become a late practice to kill an old sow for pickled pork, notwithstanding she be seven years old, or more, but then as her skin by such an age is got thick and tough, she is better pickled with her skin first taken off. This has been done to my knowledge for harvest and other uses, to a good purpose; for as such an old sow is fatted on a sudden from a very lean condition, with barley-meal or other sweet food, the flesh eats tender and luscious, like that of a young barrow-hog. And as to her skin or hide, a profit may be made of it, by selling it to the tanner, for that with tanned hog-skins many saddles are covered, and sold for a better price.

How a Farmer in Hertfordshire *singed the Hair off his Hogs, to make pickled Pork of them.*—THIS farmer rented about a hundred year in *Great-Gaddesden* parish, and was of opinion, that singing or burning off the hair of hog made the flesh harder and firmer, and better for pickling, as pork. Accordingly, after the hog's hair was burnt off with straw, he rubbed the skin with a brickbat dipt in hot water, till he got it white and clean. But I cannot say I am of his opinion.

Of pickling Pork in Harvest and at other Times of the Year.—
WHEN the carcase of a porker is cut out, and the bony pieces
separated from the fleshy ones, we lay the fleshy pieces on a
clean brick cellar-floor, in harvest-time, or any other summer
weather; but if a porker is killed in winter, we lay them on a
table or bench, somewhat in a sloping posture, close by one
another, out of a cellar. The pork so laid, we sprinkle common
salt over all of it, and let it remain in this condition a day, or
a day and night, to drain out its bloody gravey or juice; for if
this is not first carefully done, the pork will stink, notwithstanding it is well fatted. Then to a porker that weighs five and
twenty stone (which is the bigness I commonly kill mine at)
we make use of a peck and a pottle of common salt, well mixed
with two ounces of salt-petre, finely beaten. These two salts
being well incorporated, our housewife salts every piece of
pork with it all over; and as she salts them, she lays or packs
them very close in a glazed earthen pot or powdering tub (but
we account the first best) and between every layer of pork
sprinkles some coarse sugar, till a pound of it is thus made use
of. When all is potted, she lays over it a wooden cover.

The Practice of an old Hertfordshire *Housewife in the
pickling of Pork.*—THIS old *Hertfordshire* housewife, who lived
many years at *Market-street*, and boarded persons who were
under the care of the late —— *Copping*, Esq; for the cure of
cancers, *&c.* often said, that sugar helps to preserve pickled
pork, and therefore should be always used with salt, to make
the pork eat sweet, short, and well colour'd; but first of all her
practice was to rub over every piece of pork as thin as possible
with powder'd salt-petre, and then to rub the mixture of salt
and sugar over them; for that the salt-petre hardens the flesh,
and the sugar softens it, and greatly lessens the fiery sharp taste
of it. One pound and a half of sugar, she says, is enough to mix
with a peck of common salt, and four ounces of salt-petre is
enough for a porker that weighs five and thirty stone: She also
says, that a board or cloth, or both, should be laid, and kept

always over the pot or pickling tub, to keep out the air, for that if the air gets much to it, it will never recover its first fine taste, do what you can: She likewise strictly observes to take out every piece of pickled pork with a fork as she wants it, for that if the fingers touch it, they are apt to taint and spoil the pork.

The Practice of a second Hertfordshire *Housewife, in the pickling of her Pork.*—THIS woman's way is to mix common salt, bay-salt, and salt-petre, beat very fine with sugar in a bowl; then with this mixture she rubs over every piece of her pork, and thus salts it all down in a pot or tub, saying, that this is a better way than to strew sugar between the layers of pork.

The Practice of a third Hertfordshire *Housewife, in the pickling of her Pork.*—TO a porker, weighing twenty stone, she made use of a quarter of a pound of salt-petre mixt in powder with common salt to the quantity of a peck, and after the pieces of pork were sprinkled with salt, to extract the bloody part that remained in them, she rubbed them well all over with the salt mixture; and if, after the pork had been potted down about a week, the briny dissolution of the salt did not appear to her liking, she drained off what was liquid, and boiled and scum'd it, and in the boiling added more salt and water, which when cold, she poured on her pickled pork. But there are some that in such a case will take out every piece of the pork, and salt it over again with common salt, and then pour over it this refined brine, as thinking all such preparation but little enough to preserve pork a year together sweet and sound, especially if the hog is killed in harvest, or at any time in the summer, because they are sensible it is the heat of the weather that chiefly endangers pickled pork to eat rank, wherefore if the fresh pieces of pork, as I said, are laid on a cellar-brick-floor, or in some other cool place, to draw out the heat that remains in the flesh, it will be in no danger of eating rank or being otherwise damaged: A trouble that ought not to be grudged, since one night's time is sufficient for this, if the cellar is of a very cool sort.

How a young Maid-Servant spoiled the Flesh of a Porker for want of knowing how to pickle it.—THIS happened to my certain knowledge, for I was an eye-witness of it, by seeing the spoiled pork when it lay abroad on the dunghill, occasioned merely by the ignorance of a young maid-servant, who having no mistress to look over her, pretended herself capable of pickling a porker. But it happened otherwise, for after the pork had been a little time in the pickling pot, it began to smell rank, and as it continued longer, it became worse; insomuch, that she was obliged to throw most of a fine fat porker to the dunghill, for that none of the farmer's servants would eat it. Now this damage was occasioned by her not first sprinkling the pieces of pork with salt the night before they were pickled, for the bloody juice to drain out of them; for had she so done, and the pork lain thus but twelve hours before it was pickled down, this loss had been prevented.

A famous Receit for pickling of Pork.—Is this: Put as much salt into water, as will cause an egg to swim; boil and scum it well; when cold, put it into a pickling pot or tub, or earthen jar, and put your pieces of pork into it; here they are to remain a whole week, for the bloody gravey to be extracted; then take out all the brine, and boil and scum it again, with an addition of salt and water, if you find it necessary; when cold, put in the pork to stand a week longer, do the same a third time a week after, then stop it up close for keeping: In this manner, pork may be made to keep sweet and sound a long time; and by this method you may preserve your offald-pieces for a great while, as hocks, tongues, chines, spare-ribs, butt-pieces, &c. And if you approve of the pork being of a reddish colour, boil an ounce, two, or three, of salt-petre in the brine, and it will not only bring it under this colour, but secure your meat the better from tainting.—*A second receit is,* When the pork is cut from the bones, rub every piece well with salt-petre; this done, take one part bay-salt, and two parts common salt, and with this rub every piece thoroughly well; then strew common salt

(104)

over all the bottom of the pickling pot or tub, and lay in and cover every piece of pork with salt; pack them as close as you can, and fill the hollow places with salt; likewise when you perceive that the top salt melts down, strew over more salt, and you need not fear the pork keeping sound a good while.—*A third receit.* Some make use of half petre-salt, and half salt-petre, to mix with common salt, as having a notion, that petre-salt mix'd makes the flesh red and soft, when salt-petre alone makes it red and hard: However, they allow, that all these three mixed with sugar, shortens the flesh, gives it a pleasant relish, and makes it eat somewhat like ham, and keeps it from sliming. And for the better preventing any corruption breeding among the pork, some will, after it has lain a month salted down, take out every piece, and lay them in a fresh pot; and as they are laid in, will sprinkle a little salt over every one of them; and after the old pickle is boiled, and scum'd, when cold, will pour it over the pork; for though pork is potted with only salt, yet it will all turn to brine in less than a fortnight: Now all this cost, care, and pains in pickling pork, is no more than what is necessary, since (according to the opinion of some) it does not come to its full perfection of goodness under one year's time.

How a Hertfordshire *Housewife damaged best pickled Pork.*—IN pickling her pork, by mistake she put too much salt-petre amongst it, and thereby gave it such a disagreeable rank taste that it could hardly be eaten, especially when it was hot, for when the pork was eaten cold it did not taste so bad; therefore this housewife said, that two ounces of salt-petre was full enough to mix with common salt, for salting a porker of twenty stone weight; and although this woman tried, by washing some pieces of the pickled pork with hot water, to take off the ill taste, yet it proved past her skill, for that the flesh retained its disagreeable twang to the last.

Why Pork, that is to be pickled, should be first sprinkled with Salt, to soak and draw out its bloody Part.—THE reason is, because there are veins in the flesh, that contain some blood in them, which, if not first extracted and discharged by the salt, will corrupt and taint the pure flesh. On this very account, some are so careful, that they will not pickle down their pork till it has lain under a sprinkling of salt a night and a day; others refuse to let it lie more than six or eight hours, as believing, that if it lies longer, the gravey part will be also drawn out: However, this is certain, that if the bloody water is not first got out, it will mix with the brine, and corrupt and spoil all the pork.

A new and safer Way to pickle a Porker in Summer-Time.—THIS is in case you have not the conveniency of a close cold cellar; then kill your porker in the evening, and as soon as his guts and appurtenances are taken out, sift some black pepper through a fine sieve, and strew it all over the inside of the carcase; then hang it up till morning, when you are to lay the two sides of it in a strong pickle for five or six hours; for in this time the brine will extract and draw the bloody juices and jelly out of the flesh; this being done, cut the whole into convenient pieces, and salt and pickle it as before. By this means the flesh is delivered from the damage of its great enemy the blow-fly, that are very apt to get to it through the small holes and crannies; but if they do, they cannot meddle with the inside of the porker, because the pepper dust defends it. And as the pork is pickled, the pepper taste will be entirely overcome and lost by the greater power of the salt.—Or kill a porker in the summer evening, and hang him in a cellar with a wet cloth round it, if there be danger of the fly, for cutting it out next evening.

A particular Way of salting down a Porker for pickled Pork.—I will here suppose the porker to be scalded, (which is what I always do) for then the flesh will take salt better than when it is singed, because the fire locks up the pores of the skin, when scalding opens them; after the porker has been killed about fifteen hours in cool weather, cut it out, and sprinkle some common salt over the pieces, as before directed: This done, if the porker weighs thirty stone, take a peck and a half of salt, a quarter of a pound of salt-petre powder'd, a quart of petre-salt, and a pound and a half of coarse sugar; put these ingredients well mixed into an iron-pan, and heat them very hot, and with it salt every piece of pork thoroughly well, and pack the pieces very close in an earthen glazed vessel; then put a round board over the mouth of a round pot, and a weight on that, and a thick cloth tied fast over all: The weight presses down the pork into the brine, and the cloth keeps out the air; for it is the air that corrupts and breeds a nasty film on the top of the pickled pork. *N.B.* In salting down a porker to pickle, there must be salt enough made use of to raise a brine, as the *Kentish* housewives do, or else the porker will be in danger of corrupting.

A Country Woman's Way to manage a Porker that is too small, for pickling a long Time.—Of a por[k]er about eight or ten stone weight, that is to be eaten quickly, she has the spare-ribs cut likewise, then salts the pieces but very little, even only to a sprinkling, for drawing out the bloody juices; twelve hours, she says, will do this in calm weather, four and twenty in frosty; then she salts them for good: Of such a small porker she makes two haslets, one with only the heart, lights, and sticking-piece, stuck on a great skewer, with sage mix'd with salt, and baked as it lies over an earthen pan in the oven.— Another haslet may be made with the short bony pieces spitted, roasted, and eaten with apple-sauce and mustard.

The Kentish *and* Suffolk *Ways of pickling Pork.*—THE pickling of pork, I believe I may say it for truth, was first practised to the greatest perfection in the county of *Kent*, as is well known to me, that have lived in three several parts of this famous country; since which the *Suffolk* farmer has fell into such an approbation of it, that he refuses to make bacon, for giving the preference to pickled pork: Here their general way is to kill porkers at two several times of the year; the first sort are those smaller porkers that have run in the stubble, and got some flesh on their backs, which comes in for a first and present supply of meat, after their old pickled pork is expended; and as small porkers are to become a family subsistence for about three months, they salt the pieces accordingly, without salting them so much as to create a deep brine; and as the weather at this time of the year comes in colder and colder, such salting will prove sufficient to keep the flesh sweet till *Christmas* following, when they begin to kill their large hogs, to pickle for the ensuing part of the year. And when at this time they kill their large pickling hogs, after they are scalded, and the fleshy pieces have been sprinkled with salt, for drawing out the bloody gravey, they cut almost all the lean from off the fat, and leave the pieces as fat as they well can to be pickled down; and for putting the lean part so cut off to the best use, they think it so done, when they make sausages of it; then when they salt down the pieces of pork, a man is there on purpose to press down every one as tight as he can possibly; and this he does to prevent the[i]r swim[m]ing in the brine, for if they swim, they will rust and spoil: The pork being thus salted and pressed down in a pickling tub (for here they refuse the earthen glazed pot) they have a wooden cover in a hoop, that shuts or covers the tub so close, that it prevents the air getting to the pork. And when they want to take out a piece, they do it with a fork as it lies on the top, for they never meddle with an under piece, to the displacing of an upper one; and to prevent the necessity of using such a tub of pickled pork too soon, some of their best housewives keep a stock of old pickled pork by them; for, as they manage it, it will keep years together sound and good; and therefore they bestow a second security on it, by boiling a very strong brine about *Lady-Day*, which when cold, they put over the pickled pork, and then begin to make use of it. And so opinionated are these *Suffolk* housewives of their pickling pork in the best manner of all others, that they say, it will eat almost like marrow when it is rightly boiled; and thus their pickled pork becomes the chief, and almost the only meat the *Suffolk* farmer's-family feeds on: Accordingly, it is said, that when one of these farmers rents two hundred a year, by this, and other frugal managements, his butcher's bill amounts but to a trifle in a twelvemonth's time.

To bake the Ears, Feet, the Nose-part, Mugget, or gristly lean Parts of a Hock of Pork.—THESE, or any part of them, may be made a good family pleasant dish, thus:—Lay them in a glazed earthen pot, and strew over them some salt, pepper, onions, one or more bay leaves; over these pour water till it is above them, bake it two or three hours, and keep it as it comes out of the oven till wanted, then cut and fry it in slices; the sauce is a little of the pickle, flower, and butter melted with some mustard.

To roast Pork in a Collar.—THERE is a pretty way of doing this with a breast, or any other part of the hog that will admit of rolling into a collar: The flesh must be taken from the bones, and rubbed over with salt, thyme, sage, nutmeg, cloves and mace, all in powder, then roll and tie it up, and run the spit through it long ways. Or you may season such a collar of pork with only thyme, parsley and sage; roll it in a hard collar in a cloth, tie it at both ends, boil it, and when cold, keep it in a soucing drink.

Rabisha's *Way to souce a Pig in Collars.*—CHINE your pig (says he) in two parts, take out all the bones, and lay it to soak in water all night; next day scrape off all the filth from the skin or back part, and wipe it very dry; then strew some pepper over it, with a little powder'd mace, ginger, and a bay leaf or two; roll it in two collars, and let your water boil before you put it in, keep it scumming till it is half boiled; when boiled enough, keep it in a soucing drink.—Or take it this way: When you have cut off the head of the pig, slit the body in two, taken out its bones, and washed the flesh in several waters, you should then scrape the skinny part, and wipe it dry; this done, season it with a mixture of salt, thyme, and parsley; roll it hard with filletting, and boil it in two quarts of water with the bones; which put into about a quart of vinegar, a handful of salt, sweet herbs, and spice, and a bay leaf or two, and when boiled tender, keep it in this pickle or soucing drink.—Or what I think is a better way still: Boil the two collars only in water, till they are very tender, and when so boiled, take only a little of this water, and add to it a little white-wine (and isinglass if you please) some salt, vinegar, mace, and two or three bay leaves; this boil by itself a very little while, when cold put in the two collars, and keep them in it as a soucing drink or pickle; if this pickle is made strong, it is said to preserve such collars sweet half a year together, but the head must be eaten presently. These several ways were printed by old authors, and inserted by several new ones, in their late collections.

Rabisha's *Way to bake a Pig.*—SCALD it (says he) and slit it in the midst, flay it and take out the bones, season it with pepper and salt, cloves, mace, and nutmeg, chop sweet herbs fine, with the yolks of two or three new laid eggs, and parboiled currants; then lay one half of your pig into your pye, and herbs on it, then put in the other half with more herbs aloft on that, and a good piece of sweet butter aloft upon all: It is a good dish (says he) both hot and cold.—But the farmer's wife, when she bakes a pig, makes no more to do, than to lay a pig (after it is scalded, to get the hairs off, and gutted) in an earthen pan, with a paper over it to keep it from being scorched; and for sauce, she employs the brains, gravey and currants.—But *John Murrell* gives his printed receit thus: To bake a pig, says he, cut it in quarters, season them with pepper, salt, and ginger, lay them in pye crust, and strew over them shred parsley and savory, minced hard yolks of eggs, blades of mace, currants, sugar, and sweet butter: In two hours time it will be baked, then mix some vinegar and sugar, and pour it by way of a layer over the pye with scraped sugar.—Again *Rabisha* says, to improve a pig pye, bone the flesh, and season it with nutmeg, pepper, salt, and chopt sage; then slice thinly a boil'd neat's tongue or two, and lay the slices on some pig, then more pig, and then more tongue, and so on: The pig is to be laid in quarters, and over all put a few slices of bacon, cloves, butter, and a bay leaf or two; make the paste white and good, and after it is out of the oven, put in some sweet butter.

To roast a Pig.—*Murrell* says, to make a pudding to put in its belly, take grated bread, half a pound of minced suet, a handful of currants and cloves, mace, nutmeg, and ginger in powder, with salt and sugar, two eggs, rose-water, and some cream; sew the pudding up in the pig's belly, and roast it; when almost roasted, squeeze the juice of lemon over it with grated bread; the sauce is vinegar, butter, and sugar, and minced hard yolk of egg with it.—But I think the plainer way better than this, which is to mix salt with chopt sage and parsley, and sew it in the pig's belly; put paper round it, to keep it from scorching, and roast it; the sauce, butter, brains, gravey, vinegar, sugar, and currants.

The Farmers Way of dressing a Porker's Head, Feet, and Ears.—WE make no more to do, than to boil them tender, and eat them with mustard; and if any of them are left cold, we fry them in lard with some onions, and eat with mustard.—Or else, mince the flesh of them, and lade butter over it for eating.—But to eat the feet and ears in a nicer manner; when they are boiled, chop them small, and mix butter with gravey, shalot, mustard, and slices of lemon; then stew all together.

To fry collar'd Pork.—BEAT up some yolks of eggs with grated nutmeg, then cut slices of your collar, and dip them in it; then fry them, and eat with mustard and sugar. Or you may broil a chine, or other proper piece of pork, and sauce it thus; cut turnips in bits, boil them in broth and milk, then toss them up with butter and vinegar, and pour it over the broiled pork.

Pork-Balls to fry.—THESE are pretty ready victuals, made with the fat of bacon and the lean of fresh pork mashed together in a mortar or otherwise, with powder'd spices and shred sage, crums of bread and flower, fry'd in little balls, or in little square pieces, in a pan of lard.

A Yorkshire Cook-Maid's Way to pickle Pork.—SHE rubs the pieces over night with only brown sugar, and lays them sloping on a table or bench to drain, next day she rubs on them salt-petre powder, mixed with common salt and some loaf sugar, then pots it up; no way, she says, exceeds this.

How to bake or roast a Hog's Haslet in the cheapest Manner the Hertfordshire *Way.*—A hog's haslet is to be composed of the sticking-piece, the lights, the heart, and sometimes the milt; these being well washed, and cleansed from their blood, are cut into pieces about the bigness of one's hand; then we get ready beaten pepper, salt, shred sage and onion: This being done, we run a stick, or very large skewer, through every one of the pieces of meat; but before we put them on the skewer, we roll every piece in the seasoning, and when skewer'd, strew over them the shred sage and onion; next we fasten the kell or caul of the hog round the haslet, for preventing its scorching, and causing it to come moist out of the oven with gravey and fat in the earthen-pan it lay over; if the caul is from a small hog, it is but little enough to lay over and cover the haslet, but if from a large hog, half the skinny part may be sufficient, and the thick fat part cut in bits, for being melted and try'd up with the fat of the belly-piece; both which, being a sort that will not keep sweet so long as lard, may be made use of to fry pancakes, *&c.* This is the most profitable way of all others to dress a hog's haslet, because it is thus made palatable and wholesome without waste, for by thus baking it, the haslet of a large hog has yielded a pound or more of fat, which, as soon as the haslet is out of the oven, is scum'd off, and put into a glazed earthen pot, to be kept for frying meat with, *&c.* And as the gravey liquor is left behind in the pan, it serves for palatable sopping, and in the whole, gives a family a delightful nourishing dish.—But if the haslet is to be roasted, the very same preparation will do, only instead of running a skewer through the pieces of meat, they must be spitted; but as roasting a haslet is more troublesome and costly than baking it, where a person has an opportunity, the last way is to be preferred.—A second way to roast a haslet, though more costly than the first, is, to cut the heart in thin and the liver in thicker pieces, about the bigness of a hand, with the fat crow, sweetbread, and sticking-piece only. This done, besmear the pieces with beaten eggs, and then rub them over with a mixture made of grated bread, shred sage, pepper, salt, and marjoram, and as you spit the pieces so prepared, put a few thin bits of fat bacon amongst them, and wrap the caul over all. When roasted, eat it with vinegar, mustard and melted butter for sauce.

The Hertfordshire *cheap Way of making Family Mince-Pyes with a Hog's-haslet.*—FOR this we make use only of the lights, the sticking-piece, and heart; and if they are of an old hog, they must be first boiled an hour, or till they are tender. This being done, they must be first chopt or minced very small, and mixed with plumbs, currants, coarse sugar, and Jamaica spice at discretion, then put it into a pan-paste, or into raised paste, or into pasties, for baking.

The Hertfordshire *Way to make Mince-Pyes for a large Family, with a Haslet, &c. is this.*—AGAINST the time that a hog is to be killed, many of the *Hertfordshire* women provide a calf's chauldron; and when these guts are cleaned, they likewise clean the hog's guts, and boil them together till they are tender. Next they chop and mince both very small, and likewise boil and mince the haslet, and other odd bits of meat from a porker or bacon hog. And when plumbs or currants, or both, with some *Jamaica* spice, is mixed with such minced meat, there may be several pyes made, to be eaten hot or cold, which may be baked in earthen or tin pans, or as pasties in turnover crust. This is much in practice in and about the town of *Tring* in *Hertfordshire*, partly because there is much veal brought to this market (that lies thirty miles from *London*) from the adjacent country, which is famous for producing the whitest sort in *England.*

The Hertfordshire *Housewife's Way to make Pork Pyes, or turn-over Pork-pasties in Harvest-time.*—As it is one of the best pieces of husbandry, on the victualling account, to kill a porker at the beginning of harvest; so it is a good piece of housewifery to make the best use of the offald-pieces of the same. To do which, our housewife takes the two kidneys, the two butt-pieces, the mouse-pieces, that grew at the end of the blade-bones, the two blade-bones, and other odd pieces, and chops them into bits, about the bigness of a pidgeon's egg; then peppers and salts them pretty high, for at this time of year this is more than ordinarily necessary to be done, because these pyes or pasties are to be kept some days for being eaten cold: This done, make a regular mixture of the fat and lean pieces; if there be not fat pieces enough, the pye will eat dry, and if there be too much fat, it will be apt to make the harvest-men sick. Now with these fleshy and bony bits of meat, several large pyes may be made, and baked, either in raised paste, in earthen pans, or in pewter dishes, or in the shape of turn-over two-corner'd pasties, and thus they become a most necessary and convenient food at this time of the year, for farmers families in particular, because the cold pyes or pasties are a portable, wholesome, and satiating victuals for breakfast or dinner; but in cold weather, the blade-bones of a porker are generally broiled, and not chopt in bits to bake in pyes. *N. B.* Thus it is our *Hertfordshire* way to make pyes of the short bony pieces, and boil the coarse fleshy pieces first; so that our housewife salts down or pickles only the fine fat pieces clear of all bone, as being the only way to eat all the flesh of a porker in sweet order; for if the bony pieces are salted and pickled down, it's a great chance if they do not stink. And it is by these housewifely good managements that we dare to kill porkers, even of thirty stone weight, in the hottest weather of summer, with an assurance of keeping the meat from tainting, provided we have a good cellar.—A second receit is, To cut the lean part of a porker, with some of its fat part, and mix and beat them together. This done, season them with nutmeg, mace, pepper, and salt; and between every piece of this beaten meat, lay a small thin cut of hard fat, as that of the chine or such like. When all is put into the pye-crust, put bits of butter on the top of it, with some claret, just as the pye is put into the oven.—A third receit is, that in case you roast or boil a joint of pork, and it prove to be under boiled or roasted, it may be recovered, by making it into a pye with the following ingredients, *viz.* take as much of potatoes as there is pork, pare them, and cut the potatoes and pork into small bits; season it with salt and pepper, and lay it in a pye-crust, putting pieces of butter at bottom and on the top of it; then as it is going to be put into the oven, pour in some water, and bake it moderately.—An excellent way is to skin the pork, and cutting it into flat pieces, a hand's breadth, rub them over with salt, pepper, and grated nutmeg; lay these in a pan of paste, with minced apples, sugar, and white wine, over which lay bits of butter, then close up, and bake the pye.

The Hertfordshire *(or this Author's) Way of baking pickled Pork.*—THIS is much practised in my own family, and many other families in *Hertfordshire*, as a valuable piece of good housewifery; because no meat comes so cheap to the farmer as pickled pork, rightly managed, for preventing a butcher's bill, and is performed in two different manners; one is, by baking a piece of pickled pork in an earthen pan or dish, with a pudding by its side. The other is to lay a piece of it singly a little hollowish on a pan, with apples or potatoes under it. But in either case, the piece of fat pickled pork should be soaked and shifted in fresh water several times, for a day or two before it is made use of, to lessen the sharpness of the salt. This dish, if the pork is cut or hack'd in the skin, baked and eaten with apple-sauce or potatoes, will prove so much like roasted pork, as hardly to be distinguished from it. And thus by only changing the form of dressing pickled pork, a family eats it with a good appetite. Whereas if it is dressed always one way, it is apt to cloy, and cause a grumbling for having too often the same food dressed in the same manner. This and many other receits plainly prove, that no one can be duly qualified to write a book on Country Housewifery, unless he lives in the country, and carries on the farming business, for then he has an opportunity of writing from experience. And if he is informed of (what is called) a serviceable receit, he is then in a way of being capacitated to judge whether he is imposed on or not.

To make a Pork-pye to be eaten cold.—CUT the meat from off a loin of pork into thin pieces, and the same of veal, both which must be beaten flat with a cleaver. Then mix salt, pepper, minced sage and thyme, with some yolks of eggs, and put it amongst the meat. Next lay your pieces of pork in the crust of a pye, and on them lay pieces of veal, and so on, one after another, till your coffin has its due quantity, and bake it. When cold, fill it with melted butter.

A Leg of Pork to boil.—BOIL a powder'd leg of pork; boil also a handful of sage, and mince it very small. This done, put it into a little strong broth with butter and pepper. This must be mixed with some boiled turnips, and some more melted butter, and lay the same over or upon the leg of pork for being eaten with it.—A second way to boil a leg of pork is, first to stuff it with parsley and sage, and boil it with cabbage; when the cabbage is enough, chop it small and mix it with melted butter.

A Leg of Pork broiled, according to Rabisha's *Receit.*—HE says, take part of the fillet, skin it, and cut it into thin collops, then hack them thinner with your knife. Then take sage and a little thyme minced exceeding small, with a little powder'd pepper and salt, and strew it over them; then put them on the gridiron, and when broiled on one side, strew the same on the other side. This done, mix mustard, vinegar and sugar, with melted butter.

How to roast Pork-Steaks.—CUT and hack the steaks, then mince suet with sage, spinage, pepper, salt, and nutmeg, which strew over the stakes, and roll them up. Spit and roast them, and eat them with sauce made of mustard, butter, and sugar.

To broil Pork Steaks.—THE best steaks for this purpose are those cut off a loin of pork; after they are beat thin with the broad part of a cleaver, and strewed over with a mixture of salt and sage minced very small, broil them on a gridiron. When enough done, put over them mustard and vinegar mixed with a little sugar.—A second way is, to make a mixture of sage, parsley, and thyme, chopt very small, with pepper and crums of bread; rub this over the steaks, and broil them; then sauce them with melted butter, vinegar, shalot, gravey, and mustard.

The Hertfordshire *Way of roasting Joints of Pork.*— SOME roast, or bake, or boil the butt or gammon part of a porker; if the butt piece is roasted, some stuff it with suet chops very small, eggs, grated bread, shred sage, salt, onions, and pepper. The same they do by the chine, which also is very good stuffed and roasted. But then these two sorts should not be too much salted. The hind and fore loins are likewise excellent meat when roasted, and sauced with a mixture of lemon-peel, mustard, butter, and sugar. When they are roasted about a quarter of an hour, cut the skin or hack it about an inch broad. Others take this way to roast a joint of pork supposing it to be a breast, they will take out the bones in the manner they do the breast-part of venison; and when it has been rubbed over with salt, they will strew over it minced sage and thyme, beaten cloves, mace, and nutmeg. When these are well rubbed in, they will roll it with the skin outward, then tie it about with a string, and put it on a spit long-ways for roasting, and give gravey or apple-sauce to eat with it.

To salt a Piece of fresh Pork at once for boiling it directly.— TAKE six ounces of common salt, and mix it with a quarter of an ounce of salt-petre finely beaten to powder, which rub over all parts of a piece of pork, whether it be a small leg or other joint, for the piece should not be large for this quantity of salt. Then flower a linen-cloth pretty much, and tie up the meat close in it, which when boiled will be as salt as if it had been salted some days before. If you think fit, you may leave out the salt-petre; but then you must make use of more of the common salt.

A second Way to salt a Piece of fresh Pork for boiling.— THIS is chiefly done, when time will not permit for salting it regularly; therefore when haste requires it, the water must boil before it is put in, then rub your piece of pork very well with common salt, and boil it, and while it is boiling, you must put salt into the pot by degrees, little by little, till the water or pot liquor is well salted. Cover all close, and the heat will drive the salt through the meat, if the piece is not too big.

To salt fresh Pork on the Spit.—TO do this, boil salt in water to a strong brine. When the pork is heated on the spit, baste it with this hot brine by degrees, and in a very little time it will be salted enough, as you may know by the dry whitish salt scum or scurf that appears on the meat; for by the heat of the fire, the salt is made to enter the fresh pork forthwith; and then you may baste it in the usual manner.

The Hertfordshire *Farmers Wives Way of dressing the Liver and the Crow of a Porker.*—THE liver, the crow, and the sweet-bread, is the first meat we dress of a hog, for this sort is fit for frying as soon as it is cut out; our farmers wives therefore make no more to do in dressing this, than to cut the liver, the crow, and the sweet-bread, in pieces about two or three inches square, and fry them in the same fat the crow yields; and if they prove too thick she cuts them thinner. When fry'd enough, it is eaten with mustard for an agreeable dinner to a whole family.—A second way to fry liver and crow is, to cut the liver into short thick pieces, because being short and thick they will fry the tenderer, but the sweet-bread and crow rather long ways, about the same bigness; then soak the pieces of liver first in scalding water, and while this is doing, make a composition with eggs, water, flower, salt, shred sage, pepper, and grated bread; in which dip all the pieces of meat, and fry them in lard or butter, over a quick fire. For sauce, melt butter, and mix it with sugar and mustard.

The Service that souced Pork is of to Farmers and other Families.—THE soucing of a hog's head, feet, ears, hocks, guts, &c. is of such importance to a farmer's family, that many set no little value on this great conveniency; because such souced meat is not only the cheapest sort, but is ready at a minute's wanting it, to become a pleasant, wholesome, hearty meal; either eaten cold from the soucing-drink, or being cut into pieces and fry'd. For these reasons it is, that most of the good housewives of farmers who live about forty miles from *London*, and so on northward, commonly prepare and keep souced pork by them (at times) from about *Michaelmas* 'till *Lady-Day*; for that at this season of the year the weather is generally cold enough to agree with soucing-drink for preserving pork in sweetness a month or more together.

A Country Housewife's Way to make her Soucing-drink, to preserve Pork sweet.—THIS woman's way was, as she lived near a town, to go to a neighbouring public house, and ask the favour (when she had not the opportunity at home) to have the liberty of putting some water over their grains, after the strong beer was brewed off; for you must know, that most of these publicans have not a full vent for as much small beer as they could brew after their strong, and therefore rather than pay excise for small beer they are not sure to sell, which they leave the grains in a hearty condition, and consequently seldom refuse to give a neighbour leave to run some water through them. Now it is this water or wort, that thus runs through the grains, which is the proper liquor to make soucing-drink of, because it is perfectly new, and free from the fermentation of yeast, for if yeast were put into it, it would be improper for a soucing-drink, as yeast in boiling would rise, and then the fermentation would not only induce staleness, but would give the pork a disagreeable twang. When this is done, she puts a handful of salt or more into about two gallons of this malt-liquor, and boils it; and, when it is cold, it is a soucing-drink, fit for preserving pork sweet in. Or you may boil some bran in it. Or in water you may boil some bran and salt for a soucing-drink; but then the bran must be drained off through a cullender or better through a hair-sieve. But for a further account of making souce-drink, see what *William Rabisha* says of it.

Rabisha's *Way to make Soucing-drink.*—TAKE, says he, beer brew'd on purpose, then boil a pan of water, throw therein a peck of wheaten bran, and let it boil. Strain it through a hair-sieve, and throw in two handfuls of salt, so mix it with your beer aforesaid, and souce your pork therein. You may also take half a peck of fine flower of oatmeal, mix it with some liquor, and run it through a hair-sieve, and it will cause your souce to be white. Milk and whey is used in this case; but your milk will not keep so long: you may put both in boiling thereof, it will cause it to boil white. Keep your souce close cover'd; and when it begins to sour, you may renew it at your pleasure, with adding fresh liquor.

To souce a Hog's Head, Feet, Chitterlins, and Hocks, &c.— BOIL them till they are so tender that a straw may be run through them, and when cold, put them into the cold soucing-drink; but take care to scum off the fat that in boiling will swim on the top of the liquor, and reserve it to join a greater quantity, to be try'd up or refined for after uses; as for frying of pancakes, or for making crust for pyes, *&c.*

Harvest-Men fed in various Manners.—IN wheat harvest time, which commonly lasts about a fortnight, our men set out for the field by four of the clock in the morning, and return home about eight at night. In *Lent* grain harvest time later in a morning, and sooner at night, as the days are shorter. In either, the men generally eat five times a day: At their first setting out, they eat a little bread and cheese or apple-pye, with a draught of small beer, or half a pint of strong each man, in part of his quart for one day: At eight o'clock some send, for breakfast, boiled milk crumbled with bread; others, milk-porridge with bread; others, posset with bread, and bread and cheese besides, or instead of bread and cheese, apple-pasty; others send into the field, for breakfast, hashed or minced meat left the day before; others send it cold (as left) but hashing or mincing is best, because if it is a little tainted, it is thus taken off by a mixture of shred onions and parsley, or with butter and vinegar, which relishes it, and makes it well suffice for a breakfast, and now they drink only small beer. At dinner time, which should be always at one o'clock, the victuals should be in the field; for it was the saying of a notable housewife, that as the men expected it at that hour, if it was not brought accordingly, they would lag in their work, and lose time in expecting it. Broad beans and bacon or pork one day, and beef with carrots, or turnips, or cabbage, or cucumbers, or potatoes, another day, is, with plumb-pudding in wheat-harvest-time, and plain-pudding in *Lent* harvest, good dinner victuals. But this method of victualling harvest-men is not a general rule; for I know a farmer that rents above a hundred a year in *Hertfordshire*, and employs half a score hands in harvest time, who kept his men almost a week together on only fat bacon and pudding, and when at other times his wife dressed beef for dinner, she seldom boiled it enough, on purpose to prevent the mens eating too much. Now the flesh of a new killed porker, or that of a fatted old ewe or weather sheep, or of an old fatted cow, comes in a right time for saving the expence of buying meat at market; the dressing of which to the greatest advantage, I have, and shall further give an account of by and bye. At four o'clock in the afternoon, is what we call cheesing-time, that is to say, a time when the men sit on the ground for half an hour to eat bread and cheese with some apple-pasty, and drink some strong beer; then to work again, and hold it till near eight of the clock at night, when all leave off and come home to supper, where is prepared for them, messes of new milk crum'd with bread, or posset sugar'd and crum'd with bread, or fat bacon or pickled pork boiled hot with broad beans; but although fat bacon at night is in common use with some farmers, with roots or with beans, yet others refuse to make this supper victuals, because it is apt to make men sick. No matter, say some, we must give them that which cloys their stomachs soonest. But my way is this: I allow them most nights a supper on hot milk crum'd well with bread, apple-pasty, and bread and cheese if they will eat it.—Others sometimes give harvest-men wigs sop'd in ale for supper, or a seed loaf or cake cut in pieces, done after the same manner.—A yeoman, owner of a farm worth a hundred a year, of more than three parts arable land, who therefore employs about ten harvest-men, feeds them with fresh and salt meat, which is chiefly that of his own providing, by fatting old ewes or weather sheep in summer, for killing in harvest; but whether they be ewes or weathers, they are commonly those that have lost some of their teeth by age; and what of this meat the family does not eat while it is fresh, they make into pyes or pasties, so highly seasoned with pepper and salt, that they will keep sweet and sound a week or two, provided the fly is kept off; but, besides his killing such an old sheep now and then in harvest, he kills one or two porkers, which his family eats fresh as long as it lasts so, and salts the rest: These, with a lot of beef now and then from the butcher's shop, supplies his harvest people all the harvest-time with fresh meat, and for his salt meat he has all the year pickled pork, or bacon, or both by him, which proves a good friend to his pocket.—A small farmer, that employed about four harvest-men, generally boiled oatmeal in skim milk for the mens breakfast, well crum'd with bread, and as soon as they had eaten this, they had pancakes to eat hot after it.—A great farmer had a mess of hot milk got ready for his harvest-men to eat as soon as they arose, and about eight o'clock sent them minced meat, bread and cheese, and pasty.—By this method each man is allowed a quart of strong beer or ale in a day, and is fed five several times, to support him under his early and late hard work in reaping, mowing, loading and unloading of corn, grass, hoeing of turnips, &c. and other slavery; in any of which cases, a brisk foreman (whom in harvest-time we call lord) is a valuable servant; for that on his diligent, careful, nimble performance, depends in a great measure the more work of the rest that follow him, because his pace is a rule to all the company: And it is for these, and other reasons, that such a foreman (who is generally the head plowman) is better worth ten pounds a year wages, than some of the more ignorant, slow, and careless sort are half ten pounds; for such a right workman, with us, is up first in harvest-time, blows his horn to awake and get ready the rest, leads them to their work, and has two paces upon occasion, an ordinary and extraordinary one.—Some also of our *Aylsbury-Vale* housewives feed their harvest-men with rice-milk, and at other times with furmity.

The valuable Uses of Cheese to Yeomen and Farmers Families in Harvest-time.—THIS family article, I think, deserves a paragraph in my book, because cheese is an indispensable necessary food in all yeomens and farmers families throughout the year, but most of all in harvest-time; for so great a stress is then laid on this eatable, that every day while the harvest lasts, the men about four of the clock in the afternoon (as I have before observed) sit down in the field for about half an hour, which they call *cheesing-time*, by reason that in this space of time they eat a piece of bread and cheese, and commonly drink a pint of strong beer or ale each man, in part of a quart which we allow them a day; and this they punctually observe to do, especially in wheat harvest, because at this time they are obliged to work in harvest the hardest and longest, and therefore more than ordinarily covet this sort of refreshment, as well to ease their backs from their stooping reaping labour, as to refresh their bodies by thus eating and drinking. And as to the management of this cheese diet, I have to observe, that some of our farmers think it no lost time to ride to *Baldock-Fair*, which lies about five miles from *Gaddesden*, and is held on the 24th day of *February*, there to buy *Leicester* or *Warwickshire* cheese for harvest and other times, because we imagine we buy it here much cheaper than at any country shops. But to save the cheese-penny in another shape, some yeomen and farmers are so frugal as to keep the thick strong *Cheshire* cheese, as well as thin cheese in their houses for using the *Cheshire* at supper, and the thin at other times: Wherefore as cheese is eat at almost every meal in harvest-time, it concerns a yeoman or farmer to keep by them or buy old, and not new cheese; for though new cheese, perhaps, may be bought for a half-penny or more a pound less than old, yet some sort of it will go away near as soon again as old.

To make Harvest Posset, the Hertfordshire *Way.*—THIS is very commonly done for supper, and but seldom for breakfast; because, for the latter, we send into the field either broth made from yesterday's meat crum'd with bread, or milk-porridge with bread; but for supper, we often give the harvest-men a posset crum'd with bread, made in this plain manner: The maid-servant boils new milk, and when it is so done, she puts about a pint of it into each man's wooden dish, and immediately adds a quarter of a pint of stale strong beer, some coarse sugar and crumbled bread, which turns the milk into a posset, and gives the men a palatable supper; but if our country housewife has a mind to make a better posset she may:—Take a quart of new milk, and mix it with a pint of ale, the yolks of eight eggs, and the whites of four, which when beaten must be put in the milk and ale; then add some sugar and nutmeg, and stir it all the while it is on the fire till it is thick (but it must not boil) and it's done for eating; but if you will have the posset richer, use cream instead of milk. Or to make a sack-posset:—Take a quart of milk or cream, boil it with sugar, mace, and nutmeg; then take half a pint of sack, and half a pint of ale, and boil these well together with sugar; then put your milk or cream to your sack and ale in a bason, cover it with a hot dish, and set it two or three hours by a fire before you eat it. Or you may bake a sack-posset thus:—Beat eight eggs, and strain them into a quart of milk or cream, season them with nutmeg and sugar, then put to them a pint of sack, stir them together and put them into a bason, and set it in the oven no hotter than for a custard; let it stand two hours.—Or, grate three penny Naples-biskets, and boil them with nutmeg and sugar in a quart of milk or cream; then warm a pint of sack and put it into a bason, and on that pour your boiled cream by a high fall, when after a little time standing it may be eaten. But for an ordinary sack-posset—Sir *Kenelm Digby* says, boil a pint of milk, and as soon as it boils take it off, and let it cool a little, for by so doing, says he, the curd will be the tenderer; then pour it into a pot, wherein are two spoonfuls of sack and four of ale, sugar it, and let it stand by a fire-side till you eat it.

To make Wigs for Harvest-men the Hertfordshire *Way.*— OUR way is to make use of no butter, because we cannot well spare it from market; and therefore we use only a little cream put among new milk, which serves instead of butter; neither do we use any eggs, because this is rather too costly, wherefore we mix only the warm milk with some flower, ale, yeast, carraway-seed, sugar and salt, and knead it into a paste or dough, which, after it has stood to ferment and rise, we make into wigs, without colouring them with yolks of eggs, as the usual way is; neither do we put them into tin pins, but set them on a peal, and lay them to bake at the oven's mouth (as we do our common dough cakes) for about half an hour; and this we generally do about six o'clock in the evening, that they may be hot against the men come home to supper from reaping, when we toss one of these large wigs to each man for his dipping it in a bowl of ale, which serves for an agreeable cooling supper with cheese or other things. Thus, as we think

THE COUNTRY HOUSEWIFE'S FAMILY COMPANION

these sort of plain wigs are a cheap and pleasant food to our workmen, our frugal housewives generally make some of them twice a week, sometimes alone, and sometimes they bake them when they bake bread; so that the farmhouse is seldom without some of these wigs, or seed or plumb cake all harvest; for the making of which I shall give directions by and bye, after I have shewed our housewives to make richer wigs, if they think fit.—Take half a peck of flower, and mix it with an egg-shell full of carraway seeds, and half a pound of sugar; then melt twelve ounces of butter in a pint of warm milk, and with three parts of a pint of ale-yeast knead all together into a paste, and after it has lain to ferment and swell, make it into wigs and bake them.—Or, take three quarters of a pound of butter, and mix it with a pottle of fine flower, and half a pound of sugar, nutmeg, mace, and grated ginger, four beaten eggs and half a pint of ale yeast, with a little Canary, if you please: These mix with a little warm milk, and knead the whole into a light dough, to stand about half an hour before a fire to ferment and swell; then just before they go into the oven, wash the wigs over with beaten yolks of eggs; if the oven is quick in fire, they will be baked in half an hour on tin plates.

A common Country Baker's Way of making Wigs.—THIS baker lived about a day's journey from *London*, in the *Dunstable* road, where he made wigs as well as loaves of bread for sale: Now it was this baker's method to use milk-porridge as one of his chief ingredients in the making of wigs (saying, he thought it help'd to make them whiter, hollower, sweeter, and more substantial, than when milk only is employed for this purpose) with flower, ale-yeast, some sugar, and carraway-seeds; but you must know that the milk-porridge he thus made use of, was from the finest of oatmeal, as it came from *Braetch-Mill* at *Luton* in *Bedfordshire*, where it was ground almost as fine as flower.

To make a Hertfordshire *Seed-cake for Harvest-men.*— THIS cake is made much after the same manner as wigs are made, by stirring flower, yeast, milk mix'd with some cream, sugar, and carraway-seeds, which, after being kneaded and fermented, is baked in a round, deep, earthen or tin pan, on a hearth, or at the oven's mouth, and serves for beaver victuals upon a change; that is to say, it is sent into the field about four of the clock in the afternoon with some cheese, for the harvest-men to eat this cake dry with, or to dip it in ale; and sometimes it serves for supper victuals, as also for entertaining a neighbour or stranger with a cup of ale; so that a good housewifely farmer's wife is seldom without this cake or wig, or plumb-cake, especially in harvest-time, and thinks this seed-cake good enough for these purposes without eggs or butter, though some of the abler sort add hogs-lard or butter for making it better. In either form it is a very agreeable repast, when every harvest-man is allowed a wooden dish of ale to sop a piece of this in as a cooling beaver or supper, after hard labour in hot weather. Others of our country housewives make use of a tin hoop, and laying doubled brown paper at the bottom of it well flower'd they put the paste into it, and when it is out of the oven they unscrew a pin, and the hoop parts free of the cake. But, for a choice of better sort of seed-cakes, take the following accounts how to make them.

To make a good Seed-cake.—WORK two pounds and a half of fine flower, with a pound and half of fresh butter, seven eggs, a tea-cup full of cream, and three spoonfuls of ale-yeast, into a paste, which set by a fire-side to ferment and rise; then work in a quarter of a pound of carraway comfits; an hour or thereabouts bakes it in a butter'd tin hoop. Or—Mix three grated nutmegs with some beaten mace, and put it to half a peck of flower; then take two pounds of fresh butter, and melt it with two quarts of hot cream, and when cooled, mix it with a pint of yeast, and a pound and half of carraway-seeds, and some chopt orange or lemon peel; knead the whole into a thin paste just before it goes into the oven, and bake it in less than an hour's time: Some add a little sack.

A Hertfordshire *Spice-loaf for Harvest.* —THIS loaf is made with wheat-flower in the shape of a common loaf, and for a large family in the bigness of half a peck one: It must have more yeast work'd into the flower than is allowed for a houshold-bread loaf, because it must be hollowish and spungy, somewhat of the wig kind; then melt butter, and knead it into dough with sugar and carraway seeds, and bake it not quite so long as bread is. This seed loaf, like seed cake, is to be eaten dry, or in slices dip'd and sop'd in ale for beaver or supper, or with cheese or spread butter.

A Hertfordshire *Plumb-cake for Harvest.*—THIS cake is made with a quart of flower, a quartern of currants, or half a pound of *Smyrna* raisins (for we reckon that currants go as far again as these plumbs in a pudding or cake) a quartern of sugar, four spoonfuls of yeast, some warm milk made better by the addition of a little cream, grated nutmeg, and some carraway-seeds; mix and knead these into a paste, and after it has lain to rise and ferment, make it into a cake and bake it at the oven's mouth, when bread is baked: Such a cake some farmers wives bake twice a week, to have one of them constantly by them during the harvest; not only to give the harvest-men now and then a slice, but is also a sort of entertainment for a neighbouring visiter, as being a ready bit with cheese and a mug of ale, without butter, because, as I said, this must go to market; about half an hour bakes it. But how to make richer plumb cake, the following receit will shew.

To make a good Currant or Plumb Cake.—YOU may with half a peck of flower mix one pound of melted butter, two pounds and a half of currants, a little salt, some powder'd cinnamon, cloves, and nutmeg, half a pound of white sugar, rose-water and ale-yeast; work the whole well till it swells in working, and bake it in a tin hoop; if you will you may add sack. Or—Mix four pounds of flower with twelve eggs, a quarter of a pint of cream, a pound and half of butter, and two powder'd nutmegs; mix the butter cold, and do not wash but rub the currants dry; to these add two pounds of loaf-sugar, half a gill of sack, and some rose-water; knead it well, and bake it half an hour.—Or rub half a pound of butter into half a peck of flower; this done, boi[l] half a pound of butter with cream, let it be luke-warm then mix with it powder'd mace, nutmegs, and hal[f] a pound of fine sugar: The whole being mingled together, put to it half a pint of ale-yeast, four or five eggs, or half a pint of sack, and one pound of currants; this being kneaded, let it lie by a fire-side till it rises, and bake it in a tin hoop. But if any one wants to make a richer plumb-cake than any of these, he may—Mix six pounds of currants with seven pounds of flower, powder'd cloves, mace, and cinnamon, candied lemon-peel, a quart of ale-yeast, whites of eggs, and a pound of butter melted in a quart of cream, with two pounds of sugar.

The Benefits of saving the Fat of boiled, roasted, or baked Meats.

THIS I take to be one of the best pieces of housewifery belonging to a farmer's, yeoman's, or gentleman's family; because it is in a large family attended with considerable profit, when bacon or pickled pork, salt beef, or any sort of fresh meat is boiled, roasted or baked, and the fat is in quantity enough to be scum'd off and saved: Wherefore she that does not this, but suffers such fat with the pot-liquor to be given to hogs or dogs, is a sorry housewife indeed; and yet as great a fault as this is, there are too many guilty of it.—Or, if they give themselves the trouble of scumming and saving it once, some of the worser sort are apt to neglect it twice; but a good housewife will be sure to let little or none of such fat be spoiled, because a mixture of such fats will, if not used at home, sell to the tallow-chandler for two-pence half-penny or three-pence a pound: But when the fat of roasted or baked meats is saved and try'd up, that is to say, when it is boil'd, scum'd, and after it is settled cold in a glazed earthen pot, and the jelly dross taken from the pure hard fat, it will then keep several months sound and sweet, fit to make good pye-crust, fry pancakes, and be otherwise very serviceable in the kitchen. And the clearer the fat is poured off from its watry dreggy parts, the longer it keeps sound; and for its better coming out of such a glazed pot, it should be just rinced with water as the fat goes into it: Others, when the fat is cold, pour half a pint or more of cold water on its top, for that by this the fat will the easier come loosely out, and if shifted now and then with fresh water, it will be preserved sweet some time. The fats from only boiled bacon or pickled pork are soft fats of the worser sort, yet may serve, when try'd up to fry pancakes, or make ordinary pye-crust for farmers servants and poor mens families; but these are improved when try'd up with the fat of salt beef, or fresh roasted, baked, or boiled meats; however, at worst, these fats will serve for greasing cart-wheels, preserving white-leather harness, and making candles for country villages, &c.

Of saving the best Fat of a Porker or Bacon Hog.

HOW we try or dry up the pure fat Part of a Porker or Bacon Hog, which we call Lard or Seam.—IN a day or two after the hog is killed, we generally try or dry up the fat of it, and begin with tearing off the skinny part of the flair, and cutting off the coarse ends of it, for then there will remain nothing but the pure lardy fat part. This we cut into bits a little bigger than dice, and put them into a metal pot, to heat over a gentle fire to melt by degrees; and as it melts we take it off the fire, and thus we serve it several times, to drain away the fat through a pewter or earthen cullender, by keeping back the gross part with a brass or other ladle; and when the remaining fat becomes somewhat dryish, we put the whole into a cullender, to squeeze out the liquid part, and thus renew the melting and squeezing several times, till no more fat can be forced out. A good housewife commonly lets a sprig (two or three) of rosemary be amongst the fat in melting, for giving the lard an agreeable flavour.

How we try or dry up the offald fat Part of a Porker or Bacon Pig.—WHAT I call the offald part of a hog is, first, the kell or caul; secondly, the ends of the flair; thirdly, the fat of the guts. If the caul be that of a porker, it is but small enough to put over and cover the haslet, that is to be roasted or baked, for preventing the lean meat being scorched or dried too much, and for keeping the herbs in their place: But if it is that of a bacon hog, the caul is generally large enough to use part of it for this purpose, and part to melt or dry up for keeping fat. Or if none of it is employed this way, the whole is cut into little bits and melted down. Secondly, as the ends of the flair consist of a coarse bloody fat, we generally cut them off from the better fat, and melt them with the caul fat. And, thirdly, we do the same with the thickest end of the belly-piece of a large porker, or bacon hog; with this difference, that as this fat is of a kernelly and harder nature than the other two sorts, we cut it smaller. This done, we melt these last three fats in a pot or kettle, over a gentle fire, and as it melts we squeeze and press it out thro' a cullender by degrees, till nothing is left but the dry dreggy part, which we call crinklings, that are commonly eaten by our plowmen and other servants, with only a little salt strew'd over them. Now these three offald sorts of fat, so melted together, we keep in a glazed earthen pot, by itself, for present occasions, to fry pancakes, make pye-crust, and using it on some other culinary accounts, because this sort of fat will not keep so long sweet, nor is it so white and palatable as the more pure flair fat part is; but as to the gut fat, we generally melt it by itself, and save it for greasing our waggon and cart wheels, for if this was melted with better fat, it would taint it, because it retains the strong scent of the dungy guts.

How to preserve Hogslard or Seam fresh.—As I said, we seldom do any thing else, for preserving our lard sweet, than to boil it with a little rosemary, and squeeze out the pure from the gross part: But there is an old receit, that says, to preserve lard sweet and fresh for some time, it should be boiled up with a little old verjuice, till all the verjuice is wasted in boiling; then put it into a glazed earthen pot, or into a hog's bladder, and keep it in a dry place, and it will remain untainted from mustiness, or any other ill scent, some years; for if lard is kept in a damp cellar it will grow rank, and if too much in the sun, the same: Therefore keep it in a dry room. Others, instead of rosemary, boil a few bay leaves among the lard, to give it an agreeable flavour. A pint of verjuice is but enough to boil with six pounds of lard, till it is wasted, according to the opinion of some, but I think a lesser quantity of that liquor may serve. Most of the hogslard that is sold in *London*, is sent out of the country in hogs bladders, because it is the lightest, safest, and cheapest carriage, else it would be sent in glazed earthen pots.

Of making Sausages.

*H*OW *to prepare Guts or Skins for filling them to make Sausages.*—Sausages are generally made with sheeps guts, and to prepare them right is the chiefest part of the business: Many authors have wrote on making sausages, but not one of them has told his readers how to prepare skins for them; which deficiency I here undertake to supply, by giving a plain account of it, as it is now in practice.—Take the fresh guts of a sheep, and cut them into fathom or six foot long pieces; one parcel of guts will cut into six or eight such pieces; stroke the dung out, and put them into water just to wet them, then turn them inside-out, by the help of a stick, wash them, and scrape a piece at a time as it lies on a table, with the back of a knife drawn along the inside skin thus turned outwards, and it will come off in two or three times scraping, and without breaking the gut, if it be rightly done; and in the same manner, the outward skin with scraping will come off at the end of the gut; then there will only remain the middle skin, that will appear about the bigness of a wheat straw. And when all the pieces of the guts are thus scraped, cleaned, and prepared, put them into water made just lukewarm, for if it is too hot, they are all spoiled. Now in this lukewarm water the guts must be washed clean; then put them into a glazed earthen pot, with salt enough strewed over them, and they will keep sweet as long as you please. And that the skins may appear truly fine and clear, put one end to your mouth and blow it, and then you may easily perceive whether the gut is entirely free of all outward skin or fur; for if it is nor, it must be presently taken off.

How to prepare Pork Meat for making it into Sausages.— THE next thing is to prepare the meat for filling the skins with it: For this purpose, a fine hind loin of pork is the best part of a hog, though some make use of a fore loin, but the former exceeds; yet there is a profit to be made sometimes of a fore loin, which cannot be done with the hind loin, and that is, when sausages are made in a town where gentry live, they sometimes bespeak and buy the bones of a fore loin to broil, and then there is the more meat left on them, because for these they generally give an extraordinary price, as the sweetest meat lies next to the bones, and eat somewhat like that of a spare-rib; otherwise the flesh is cut quite off from the bones, as clean as can be well done. The meat, thus taken off the bones, must be cut into little bits, and chopt as small as possible, till a whole bit cannot be found in it bigger than a pea free of its skin, for the skin must be first taken off the loin; and while it is chopping, four or five spoonfuls of water must be now and then mix'd among the meat, for this will cause it to chop the better, increase its gravey, make the sausages eat the more pleasant, and if they are to be sold, will add to their weight. A secret never yet imparted by any author whatsoever, in the exact method this is done; and is of such importance, as occasioned a person to give out selling sausages, merely for want of knowing this piece of good management.

How a Person set up to sell Sausages in a Market Town in Bedfordshire, *and broke for want of knowing how to make them in a right Manner.*—ONE, that was a thorough master of this business in this town, made great quantities of sausages, which he not only sold in the market town he lived in, but carry'd many to other places for publick sale; and as he sold these, with pyes, and tarts, and other pastry ware, he got money apace, and lived in such a manner, as tempted one of his neighbours to endeavour the same. Accordingly this person began to make sausages, but not knowing how to mix water with the meat in chopping, soon gave over his new employ, because his sausages eat dryer, harsher, and were not near so good as the old Sandard's were. There are indeed many receits how to make sausages: One in particular says—The fillet part of a young hog chopt very small, and mixt in the proportion of half a pound of fat to two pounds of lean, season'd with pepper, salt, and nutmeg, and grated bread added to it, will make sausages, if the meat is stuffed into the guts, with salt and water; but no mention is made of what sort of guts, nor how they are to be prepared, nor how to mix the water with the meat in chopping, and therefore is an imperfect one, for meat cannot be chopt full small without watering it in chopping, and if it be beat much to supply watering, the meat will be dryer and eat worse.

How to make compleat Sausages for Sale, or for a private Family.—THE meat being prepared as before mentioned, as it lies on the chopping block, we grate white bread as small as possible, and sprinkle over it; which, when mixed, hollows the meat, makes it go the further, weighs more, and makes the sausages eat the pleasanter, half a pound of such grated bread is enough for one loin of pork; then beat black pepper and *Jamaica* pepper, as much of the one as the other, and mix them with salt, which sprinkle over the meat and bread, and mix them well with the chopping knife: Then chop green sage very small, and mix this likewise with the meat, though some dry it and rub its powder in, but in this manner the sage is apt to lose some of its virtue; therefore sage is kept dry in its leaves in winter, and chopt as the green sage is, by which means the sage will make an agreeable green spotted appearance through the gut when filled. The mass of meat being thus all got ready, take an instrument, which we call a tin fill-bowl, made hollow and in the shape of a syringe, only wider at top and narrower at bottom, about four inches in length, an inch and half wide at top, and three quarters of an inch wide at bottom. This being filled with the chopt meat, and the little end put into the gut, the meat is forced into it by a finger pushing it down; and when a pound of it is thrust thus into a fathom-long piece of gut, and made all alike round, at every six inches in length a link is twisted off, and a sausage compleated.—Thus, sausages may be made in a good and cheap manner for a gentleman's, yeoman's, and farmer's family, clear of that extraordinary expence that some receits may lead people into; as when white-wine, eggs, oisters, and other chargeable ingredients are made use of: Therefore, those receits that direct the making of sausages in a plain, palatable, and wholesome way, must be the best for a private family's use, as this which directs—To chop a leg of pork very small, and mix it with a sufficient quantity of hog's hard fat, some *Jamaica* pepper, black pepper, salt, marjoram, and sage, all cut and minced small, which being put into sheeps or hogs guts, makes sausages.

To make Sausages as good as those from Bologna, *according to the receit in* The Way to get Wealth.—TAKE, says this author, the fillets of young porkers, three parts lean, and one fat, to the weight of five and twenty pounds; season it well in the small shredding, and beat it in a mortar with pepper and salt, a little grated nutmeg, and a pint of white-wine mixt with a pint of hog's blood; then stir and beat it all together, till it is very small;

add a few sweet herbs, chopt small and bruised, as pennyroyal, sweet marjoram, and winter savory; then with a whalebone bow open the mouths of the guts you are to fill with this meat, and thrust it leisurely down with a clean napkin, lest, forcing it with your hands, you break the gut. Make divisions of what length you think convenient, tying them with fine thread, and dry them in the air two or three days if it be clear and the wind brisk, then hang them in rows at a little distance one from the other in your smoak loft, and when they are well dried, rub off the dust they have contracted with a clean cloth; anoint them over with sweet oil, and cover them with a dry earthen vessel, and, either roasted or boiled, they will equal those so much boasted of from this city in *Italy.*—Or make use of the gammon part of a bacon hog, which shred small with a like quantity of lard and sweet herbs as above; work it with red-wine and the yolks of eggs, till it becomes a paste fit to be put into skins, so that the sausages ought to be as thick as a child's wrist; then hang them up in a chimney, and when sufficiently dried, they are ready to be eaten with vinegar and oil.—But to make these *Bologna* sausages keep long, mix as much fat as lean of a porker, and then add to it cloves, pepper, mace, salt, parsley, and sage, all shred small into a paste and fill the biggest guts of a sheep, or instead thereof the guts of an ox; then hang the sausages in a dry place not too near the fire, and they will keep a twelve-month round; their usual size is a foot long, and should be boiled just before eating.—Or *Bologna* sausages may be made with the lean of beef, whereof the buttock part is best, and is chopt with some bacon fat, and some beef suet, with pepper, cloves, mace, and a little salt-petre and bay-salt, into a paste consistence, it will be fit to fill large skins with; some add the powder of a few dried bay leaves: then dry them in or near a chimney.

To make Sausages without Skins.—Take the leg of a young porker, and cut all the lean free of skin and strings; then take two pound of beef suet, and shred it small; this done, chop sage and onion, and mix them with pepper, salt, and nutmeg;

all which ingredients must be cut and minced small, and when minced small enough, add the yolks of two or three eggs, and make the compost into a paste: Now this paste may be kept sweet a fortnight, and when used, it must be cut into the shape of sausages and fry'd.—Or take the receit with this variation; make use of a leg of pork of a small size, two pounds of suet from an ox, two handfuls of sage, the crumb of a two-penny loaf grated, salt and pepper to your taste, and chop all pretty small together; but, in the first place, be sure to cut out all skin and gristles, and when all is well mixed together knead them into a paste pretty stiff with the yolks of two or three eggs, and roll it (when you are ready to use it) into the shape of sausages, and fry them.

How to preserve naked Sausages.—To make sausages for keeping them sweet and sound some time, mix the meat pretty high with pepper, salt and herbs, as before directed, then press it down in a glazed earthen pot very close, and they will keep, if season'd enough, almost half a winter good. And when such potted down meat is to be used, take some of it out, roll it in flower in the shape of sausages, and fry them, or broil them: This is the most in practice amongst farmers for their family uses.

How to preserve Sausages in Links.—If sausages in links are to be kept some time, they may be so done by laying them in a glazed pot, and when they are all placed in it, then pour on them salt water. This method is observed in particular by those who make and sell sausages for their livelihood, because if they cannot sell them quickly, they preserve them this way; whereby the sausages may not lose any thing of their weight.—Another receit says, make use of double the weight of fat to the lean of pork, and mix with four pounds weight of this meat a nutmeg in powder, and as much cloves and mace as the nutmeg, with pepper and salt; then chop a handful of sage, a small parcel of thyme, and mix the whole with a handful of grated bread, all mixed very small, and put into skins. Thus far the receits are pretty well; but here is no mention made how to chop the meat with water, how to prepare the skins, nor how to fill them, &c. &c.

To make Sausages by an old Receit.—It says, take the largest chine of pork, and first with your knife cut the lean thereof into slices, and spread it over the bottom of a dish; then take the fat of the chine, and cut it in the very same manner, and spread it upon the lean; then cut more lean, and spread it upon the fat; and thus lay one lean upon another fat, till your quantity of pork is shred, observing to begin and end with the lean; then with a sharp knife cut it through and through divers ways, and mix it all well together; then take store of sage, and shred it exceeding small, and mix it with the flesh; then give it a good seasoning of pepper and salt, take the guts made as long as possible, and not cut in pieces as for puddings, first blow them well to make the meat slip, and fill them; which done, take thread, and with it divide them into several links as you please, then hang them up in the corner of some chimney clean swept, where they may take the air of the fire, and let them dry there at least four days before any be eaten; and when they are served up, let them be either fry'd or broiled on a gridiron, or else roasted about a capon.

Rabisha's *Receit to make Sausages of Pork, or with the Flesh of a Fowl or Rabbit.*—Take pork, but not as much fat as lean, mince them exceeding small together; then take part of the flair of pork in bits about the bigness of the top of a finger, season it with minced sage, good store of pepper and salt, some cloves and mace; then take small sheeps guts and cleanse them, so fill them with your funnel, always putting some of the pieces of flair between the minced; you may sprinkle a little wine on the top of your sausage meat, and it will fill the better. I have made (says he) rich sausages of capons and rabbits flesh, and could shew a receit for it; but allow, that no flesh eats so savoury in a sausage as pork, by reason sage and pepper are not so suitable to the other two sorts. Tie up the sausages in links, and keep them for use.

Of making Black and White Hogs Puddings.

HOW to prepare Skins for filling them to make Black Hogs Puddings.—To prepare these in a pure sweet housewifely manner, the guts of a barrow hog should be extraordinarily well cleansed; for which purpose, one person should hold open a gut, while another by a funnel pours water into it, for driving and washing out all the dung, and is what must be nicely done, till the gut is clean emptied, and discharged of all the filth; then we turn it inside-out, and wash it thoroughly two or three times; at last we scour all the guts well with salt, and put them into a tub of cold water, where they are to lie twelve hours, and then this first water is to be thrown away, and fresh put in its room, and so on every twelve hours, for three or four days together; or better, if it be so done a whole week.

How to prepare Meat for filling Skins with it to make Black Hogs Puddings.—As soon as the hog is stuck by the butcher, the blood should be catched in a glazed earthen pot, some salt first put into it, and stirred about all the while with a wooden paddle. When you have thus got the blood, the salt will preserve it sweet without clotting a week together in winter; then get ready a composition of meat for filling your prepared hogs guts with it. And to do it, boil whole oatmeal, or what we call grouts, in water only, a wallop or two, and immediately take it off the fire, for emptying both oatmeal and water into an earthen glazed pot or pan, wherein some salt is first put; here let it lie all night to harden; next morning mix as much blood with the oatmeal as will colour it, and add to it some crumbled bread, pennyroyal, and onion cut small, with some chopt bits of hogs hard fat. These being all well mixed together, begin to fill a gut a yard long, with the same tin fill-bowl instrument that you did the sausages with, and when it is about three parts filled, and squeezed all of a thickness, tie each gut so filled at each end with thrum-thread; and while water is boiling, put these puddings into it, and boil them till they become dark colour'd and tender, which will be in about an hour's time; then take them out of the water, and while they are hot, twist them into links, ready to be dressed, by either broiling or frying them.—Thus black hogs puddings may be made in the very best housewifely manner for cheapness, and yet good enough for a farmer's family, or for sale: Not but that there are several other ways to make black hogs puddings, according to different receits. One whereof says—Grind oatmeal a little, and add to every quart of it the inside of a half-penny loaf grated, both which ingredients are to lie soaking in milk twelve hours, and after that twelve hours more in warm'd hog's blood; then mix chopt fat with pennyroyal and winter savory, and stir the whole together with sprinkled salt. The meat thus made, it says, guts are to be filled with it, and when tied up in lengths, they must be boiled and hung up near a chimney to dry.— Another says, boil a haslet in about five gallons of water till tender, then drain out the liquor, and while it is boiling, put in a peck of whole oatmeal, which is to boil but fifteen minutes: Then let the grouts and water stand cover'd in a pot about six hours, and with half the oatmeal mix thyme, pennyroyal, parsley, cloves, mace, and salt, all minced small with a quart of hogs blood and some hogs fat of the flair cut into dice bits; which put into the guts, till every gut is three parts of it filled, and then put the puddings into boiling water to boil thirty minutes, pricking them now and then to prevent their bursting; when boiled, lay them on clean straw, and with the rest of the oatmeal make white hogs puddings.—Another says, beat a quart of cream, and as much sheeps blood, with ten eggs; this done, stir into it grated bread and oatmeal finely beaten, each a like quantity; then with powdered cloves, mace, nutmeg, marjoram, lemon, thyme, pennyroyal and salt, make a mixture, and when all is mixed, fill the guts, and boil them directly.—Another says, boil the liver of a hog till it is enough, and bruise it in a mortar with half the quantity of hogs fat cut small; mix these with hog's, goose, or sheep's blood, salt, pennyroyal, butter'd yolks of eggs, some spice, and some oatmeal grouts just cut in the mill, after being first soaked twenty hours in water: When all these are brought into a requisite consistence, put it into the guts, tie them up, and boil them in a kettle of water with hay at bottom; when swell'd enough, dry them on hay.

How to prepare Skins for making White Hogs Puddings.— As the eating variety of viands enlarges the appetite, our country housewife may make white hogs puddings as well as black ones; and indeed, it is the more necessary so to do, where persons have an aversion to the eating of blood, as many have. Good wholesome white hogs puddings may be eaten with pleasure, with a very little trouble of cooking them, for on a gridiron they are presently broiled: But to make these good as well as cheap, is the art of the housewife; and that she may do all this, I here present her with a receit that has been in practice many years with a frugal manager, as follows, *viz.*—Take hogs guts, and after the dung is washed out of them, scour them well with salt, then turn them once a day, and shift and wash them twice a day in spring water for a week together, to soak out all the tincture of the dung, and make them white. It is true, that many stand not on this nicety, but scour, wash, and fill the guts in a day or two after they are begun with; however, by the way, this is a sort of sluttish proceeding, for if the gut is not made thoroughly white and sweet, the meat cannot be agreeable.

How to prepare the Meat for filling Skins to make White Hogs Puddings.—THIS receit as well as my first for making black hogs puddings are genuine sorts, calculated for the use of a country family, or for common sale, because they are composed of cheap, sweet, and palatable ingredients; for which purpose, let our country housewife provide herself with a pottle of grouts or whole oatmeal, half a pound of white sugar, half a pound of currants, the crumb of a two-penny white loaf, and three quarters of a pound of hogs fat chopt;

the oatmeal must be boiled over night, in as little water as will just suffice, and this only for a quarter of an hour, and by morning it will be in right order, neither too hard nor too soft. Next morning therefore mix all the ingredients with cold new milk, and some *Jamaica* spice in powder, into a pudding consistence, and put it into the prepared hogs guts, after the same manner as was done for sausages of sheeps guts; and observe, that for these white puddings we make use of only the smallest guts, for if they were of the larger sort, they would take up too much of the meat. The guts being thus filled, boil them in yard-long pieces, about three quarters of an hour at most, for these must not be boiled so long as black puddings; and as they boil, they must be reared up with a fork to the top of the water now and then, and pricked with a fine fork to prevent their bursting. This done, take them out of the kettle with a stick, and lay them on wheat straw first put at the bottom of a basket; then with thrum-thread, and while the puddings are full hot, tie them up in links, two, three, or four in a bunch, and place them singly on a table. Thus the process of this receit is finished under a plain preparation, free of those costly compositions with which several receits to make white hogs puddings are stuffed, as may appear by the following accounts of them, *viz.*—Mix some of the finest white crumb of bread with a little flower, mace, and nutmeg, steep these in milk to become a pappy consistence: This done, add four ounces of currants, and as much almonds, marrow, and sugar, which beat and thoroughly mix together for filling hogs guts with it; they must be boiled, and the puddings afterwards kept in a dry place till used.—Another receit directs to make use of twelve or more eggs, and half the whites, which are to be beat up, and when a quart of cream boils, stir in the eggs on a gentle fire; to this must be added, when the cream is cooled, a pound of grated bread and nutmegs, two pounds of chopt suet, and half a pound of sweet almonds minced and beat fine with orange or rose water, salt and sugar, with which fill the guts and boil them, and prick them as they boil to keep them from breaking.

How to make white Hogs Puddings by an ancient Receit.— STEEP grouts in milk twelve hours, then boil a pint of cream, and put these grouts into it, and let them soak here twelve hours more; then put to this the yolks of eggs, a little pepper, cloves, mace, saffron, currants, sugar, salt, and some swines suet, or for want of this, beef suet; all these being prepared according to art, fill the guts with this mixture, and boil the puddings on a gentle fire, and as they swell, prick them with a great pin, or a small awl, to keep them from bursting; and when you are to serve them on a table, first boil them a little, then take them out, and toast them brown before a fire, and so serve them, trimming the edge of the dish either with salt or sugar.—But here is no mention made how the hogs guts are to be prepared, which is a strange deficiency, and seems as if the authors were persons ignorant of the matter, for neither ancient nor modern receits shew this first and most necessary article.

How to make Gut Puddings with Hog's Liver, by an ancient Author.—TAKE, says this author, the liver of a fat hog and parboil it, then shred it small, and afterwards beat it in a mortar till it is very fine; then mix it with cream, and put to it six yolks of eggs and two whites, and the grated crumb of a half-penny loaf, with good store of currants, dates, cloves, mace, sugar, saffron, and salt, and the best swines suet or beef suet; but beef suet is the more wholesome, and less loathing; then after it has stood a while fill the guts with it, and boil them as before shewed: And when you are to serve them to the table, first boil them a little, and lay them on a gridiron to broil gently, but do not scorch them, nor in any wise break their skins, which is to be prevented by often turning and tossing them on the gridiron, and keeping a slow fire.

To make Gut Puddings with Hog's Liver, by one new and two old Receits.—TAKE a pound of beef suet, and mince it with the crumb of a two-penny white loaf small enough to pass through a cullender; then boil a pound of hog's liver, which grate and sift very fine. This done, boil a quart of cream with some mace, and grate a nutmeg into it; mix all this with six eggs, currants, a little salt, and rose-water, into a pudding consistence, and fill hogs guts with it.—This receit seems to me to be the last ancient one reformed, as being somewhat better put together in a truer proportion of ingredients. But to shew the maker of a hog's liver pudding in a more particular manner, I shall add the two following old receits, *viz.*—Boil a hog's liver very dry, when cold grate it, and take as much grated manchet as liver; sift them through a cullender, and season it with cloves, mace, cinnamon, and as much nutmeg as of all the other; half a pound of sugar, and a pound and half of currants, half a pint of rose-water, two pounds of beef suet minced small, eight eggs, put away the whites of four; temper your bread and liver with these eggs, rose-water, and as much sweet cream as will make it something stiff; then cut the small guts of a hog about a foot long, fill them about three quarters full of the aforesaid stuff; tie both ends together, and boil them in a kettle of fair water, with a pewter dish under them with the bottom upwards, and it will keep your puddings from breaking; when the water boils, put in your puddings, let them boil softly a quarter of an hour, and take them up; and so you may keep them in a dry place a week or more: when you spend them, you must broil them.—The other receit runs thus, *viz.* Boil a hog's liver well, let it be thoroughly cold, then grate it like bread; then take grated bread, new milk, the fat of a hog minced fine, and put it to the bread and the liver, the more the better, divide it into two parts, take store of herbs that are well dried, mince them fine, put the herbs into one part, with nutmeg, mace, pepper, anniseed, rose-water, cream and eggs; wash the skins, and then fill them up, and let them boil enough: To the other part, put barberries, sliced dates, currants, new milk and eggs, and work them as the other.

To make Hogs Guts Puddings with Hogs Humbles.—AFTER the hogs humbles are tender boiled, take some of the lights, with the heart, and all the flesh about them, picking them from all the sinewy skins; then chop the meat as small as you can, and put to it a little of the liver very finely searsed, some grated nutmeg, four or five yolks of eggs, a pint of good cream; two or three spoonfuls of sack, sugar, cloves, mace, nutmeg, cinnamon, carraway seeds, a little rose-water, good store of hog's fat, and some salt; roll it in rolls two hours before you go to fill them in the guts, and lay the guts to steep in rose-water till you fill them.

Of Chitterlins, their Make and Use.

*H*OW *to make Chitterlins.*—THESE, if made as they should be, are pleasant and hearty victuals; and that they may be such, take the guts of a barrow hog, a year, or a year and half old, especially of one well fatted with barley meal, oatmeal, or pease; for these guts will eat sweeter, than if the beast is fed with beans or a ranker food. In the first place, after the guts are cleansed from their dung, they must be turned inside out, and well scower'd with salt; then put them into cold spring water, and for three days together they must be shifted into fresh water twice a day, and turned and scoured with salt several times, till they are got thoroughly clean and sweet. This done, the smaller guts are generally platted or woven together, and tied in a knot at their ends, in order to keep in their fat, while they are boiling. Then, on a clear fire, boil both small and great guts four hours for making them rightly tender, though some boil them only two or three; but this is too short a time for causing such tough meat to eat soft and palatable; and if you put some milk into the water they are boiled in, it will add to their whiteness and sweetness of taste: But some, after the guts are clear'd of their dung, and at their first scouring with salt, will with the salt rub them with sage: Others boil sage in their water to take off their hogoo, for the preparation of chitterlins will prove the cleanliness or sluttishness of a housewife, as much as any meat whatsoever will.

To make a Chitterlin Pye.—This may be made a delicious family pye, if the chitterlins be duly prepared according to the foregoing receit; then chop and mince them with some offald meat of the hog; this done, put it into a paste laid on the bottom of a pan; and on the meat put some minced apples, currants, plumbs, powder'd coriander and carraway seeds, *Jamaica* spice, and nutmegs grated; then lay your cover of paste over all, and bake it. Others make use of no offald meat, but make the pye with only chitterlins and the other ingredients, and with the maw or mugget of the hog, which mugget being first skinned and boiled with the chitterlins, and chopt and made into a pye with them, will become a hearty and pleasant food for either a farmer's, a yeoman's, or a gentleman's family. It is true, that in harvest time, our servant maid is rather too busy to employ so much of her time, as chitterlins require for cleaning them; besides which, the very hot weather, that generally happens at this time of the year, is another discouragement; but at other times, when the weather is cooler, it is ill housewifery to throw away the guts of a sizeable porker or bacon hog.

To boil, broil, or fry Chitterlins.—Is another preparation, and the most common way of dressing them of all others; after they have been scoured with salt, and boiled the several hours before mentioned, they are presently cook'd and made ready for a breakfast, dinner, or supper, by boiling them on a gridiron, or frying them till they are brown; but boiling them is most in use with some farmers wives, and when they are so done, they will not eat right, unless boiled exceeding tender, and eaten with mustard.

Of Bacon in general.

THE necessary Uses of Bacon.—BACON is a serviceable, palatable, profitable, and clean meat, for a ready use in a country house: Ready I say, because it requires not to be kept in a cellar, or at any distance from a kitchen or chamber, but may be had at all times of the year for being cut to broil, fry, boil, or bake; and if it is not in the house, it is ready at the next chandler's shop. For bacon is so universally traded in, that it may be had at almost any part of the kingdom; and so serviceable to both rich and poor, that it saves much expence in firing, time, and trouble, is a very palatable viand, and the more so, as it agrees with fowls, veal, pancakes, beans, *&c.* And it is so profitable, that like pickled pork, it saves much in a numerous family, by preventing the large total of a butcher's bill; for bacon in many farmers houses is the stay of the family. Where there is bread and bacon enough, there is no want; for these satiate the keenest appetite in a little time, will bear living on the longest of any meat, with a little change of another sort. In the northern parts of *England*, thousands of families eat little other meat than bacon; and indeed, in the southern parts, more than ever live on bacon, or pickled pork, or on both, since trade has lessened, and the number of families increased. One of the biggest and ablest farmers in our part of *Hertfordshire* fed his harvest-men most part of the harvest time with bacon. Near *Rickmansworth* in *Hertfordshire*, a farmer that kept five horses, and rented a hundred a year, gave his servants hardly any other meat all the year than hogs flesh and old mutton. A *Hertfordshire* yeoman, that occupies his own estate of about a hundred and fifty pounds a year, kills five large bacon hogs, and five large porkers in a year, and now and then an old toothless ewe fatted, which they would for the most part make into pasties; and by the agreeable sweetness of the hogslard, the pyes proved so short and pleasant, that his people generally eat them greedily; for this yeoman, like many others, was afraid of a butcher's large bill.

The Hertfordshire *Way of curing Bacon for a private Family.*—THIS is the best way of all others; for where the bacon is rightly cured, the fat will look clear, and eat hard and sweet, and I may assuredly add, that it will keep longer sound than any other sort of bacon whatso[e]ver. For bacon, we seldom kill a hog under a year old, but many older, till some weigh fifty or sixty stone, for we cannot have too fat nor too large a flitch. And that it may be the safer and better cured, our season for killing is, from *Allhollantide* to *Lady-day*, when the weather is generally cool enough for this purpose. In *Hertfordshire* we generally singe or burn the hair off our bacon, and when it is so done, we hang up the hog, and let it remain hanging all night; next morning we cut out the whole chine, two spare-ribs, two but-pieces, two blade bones, and two short ribs, for we leave no more bone in the flitches than we can help. Then we rub the two flitches of a thirty, or forty, or fifty, or sixty stone hog, with a sprinkling of salt on the fleshy sides, and let them lie singly on boards a day, or a day and a night, for causing the bloody juice to drain out of them; which when discharged, we employ two ounces of salt-petre finely powder'd to the flitches of a thirty stone hog, and so in proportion to a larger one: Then we presently make use of a peck of common salt, a small part of which we rub the skinny sides with, the rest on the fleshy sides, and lay the skinny side of one flitch on the fleshy side of the other, and so let them remain ten days before we salt them again; and then we lay on half a peck of more salt, and put the bottom flitch on the top one, to lie together ten days or more: At the end of which time, we hang them up in our wide country chimney corners to dry for a week or two, or three; if the chimney is a very wide one, and a slow fire is left, they may hang the longer, but if it be a narrow one, the less time; in either case, if the flitches are heated too much, they will rust and spoil. Hence it is, that when we kill a thirty or forty stone hog in *March* or *April*, we let the flitches hang but three or four days in the chimney corner, and then lay them upon a rack, that is fixed over the kitchen, to dry leisurely; for at this time of year the air alone is almost sufficient to dry them. By this method our country bacon is salted and dry'd very white and sweet, free of that nasty, unwholesome, unpleasant smoak twang, which the ignorant regard not, when the knowing refuse it.

Bacon made in several Parts of the West Country.—In a certain part of this country, after the flitches have been a little salted, and laid on a little descent for the bloody juice to drain off, the next day they mix some salt-petre with as much sal prunella, and rub it on both sides of the flitches. Next day after they mix some bay salt among their common salt, and salt the flitches well, and while they lie salted one upon another for two or three days, they shift their posture, and so on for two or three weeks, at the end of which they hang them upright over an oven, and in six weeks time they will be very sweetly and whitely cured.—In another part, they kill a hog in the evening, cut him out next morning, and throw the flitches into a strong brine to lie a few hours; they then take them out, and rub on two large flitches four ounces of powder'd salt-petre, then immediately salt them well with all natural salt, and let them lie so three weeks, shifting them once or twice in that time, before they hang them up in their chimneys to dry. But some let their flitches lie ten hours in brine, then salt them, and let them lie a month salted; when they take and smoak them a day and a night, or more, as the weather is more or less open.—In another part, as in *Wiltshire*, they kill hogs for bacon almost all the year, and send great quantities of it to *London*. In summer they kill in the evening, and strew some fine powder'd pepper over the inside of the carcase very lightly, for preventing the flies damage; next morning they cut it out, and lay it in brine six hours, to discharge the bloody part of the flesh; then with a mixture of some powder'd salt-petre and common salt they salt the flitches soundly and lay them one upon another, and shift every second day, laying the bottom flitch uppermost, and salting them more at three different times in a fortnight; at the end of which time, they strew over every flitch some bean flower, to give the bacon a fine brown or golden colour, keep it the better from rusting, and for forwarding its drying; then they hang the flitches over one another, in a very great chimney or smoak-room, to dry leisurely a week or two. And thus their great hogs, that weigh some above sixty stone, at eight pounds to the stone, are ready to be cut for bacon in a month or six weeks time. But even these are not such quick ways to prepare bacon for a market as is practised in another part, where their wash-fatting of hogs, their salting and quick drying, give the bacon a sweetish taste, and an artificial hardness and colour, in order to take the eye of the buyer; but in the pot, in the pan, and on the gridiron, it shews its loose nature, by its ready and easy parting with much of its fat, to the loss of the owner.

What I was told by a London *Seller of Bacon.*—THIS person in conversation, little mistrusting who he told the story to, was free in telling me, that some in very open weather begin to kill their hogs about three o'clock in the morning, and cut them out at seven or eight o'clock at night; then directly throw the flitches into a very strong pickle for five, six, or seven days; then smoak them twelve or four and twenty hours, and away to market with them. Otherwise, when they take them out of the pickle, they salt the flitches for four and twenty hours, then shift and salt them again for as long a time; next they hang them in their smoak-room for a little while, and send them to market. These ways, he said, are sometimes practised when there is a quick sale for bacon; but what must we call this? It hardly deserves the name of bacon, rather the name of pork-bacon, and is a most profitable sort for the seller; for it will weigh to his satisfaction, and may eat sweet and good for present spending, particularly in pease and beans season, but in course must grow rank if kept long, because, as one said, the fat of such bacon is so little cured, that it is rather tallow than true bacon. Therefore, when such bacon cannot be vended at *London*, much of it is sent to country markets, for selling it to poor people at low prices, to prevent its spoiling to intire loss. But this is not the case of all the *London*-made bacon, for I am very sensible, that there are vast numbers of their wash-fed flitches of bacon laid in salt for two or three months together in their cellars, piled up one upon another, and shifted at times for preparing and curing them in their smoak-rooms, and undoubtedly may be good bacon. As to their smoak room, it is a profitable contrivance, because they have plenty of smoak at a cheap rate, by their burning of saw-dust, old spokes of wheels, *&c.* without any excessive heat of fire: And thus they dry several large flitches at a time as leisurely or as quick as they please; and thereby the bacon may be impregnated with smoak to such a degree, as will make it want the less salt, give the outside of it a golden colour, and help the better to cure it for keeping some time; but then they cannot dry the bacon so white, as we do in our large country chimneys, nor cure it so fine as we can; nor do they preserve it in so sweet and delicate a manner, as is done in the country.

The Practice of curing Bacon in some Country Towns.— WHEN a hog is cut out, they throw it into brine for three hours, and then salt it for two or more months, and just before they hang them up in their smoak-room they wash their flitches in fair water, because the salt that remains without-side of them would else help to rust the bacon. And although the flitches are yellowish, when they come out of the smoak-room, yet if they are hung up in a large chimney corner, the fire will add a whiteness to them.

A Farmer's Wife's true Country Way of preserving Bacon in a white Colour.—THIS is a matter of importance, because it is not only a cure to bacon, by salting it for a month and drying it well, but likewise to preserve it white, sweet, and sound, for a considerable time after: Which to do effectually, our country housewife, after drying the flitches leisurely for three weeks or a month in a chimney corner, by a wood fire, free of smoak, in a moderate degree of heat, takes care, as soon as the bread is drawn out of the oven, to put some wheat straw into it, for divesting it of all humidity and thoroughly drying it; this done, she lays some of it at the bottom of a chest kept in her chamber under the bed, and on that the skinny side of a flitch of bacon; then she puts another layer of dried straw on this, and a second flitch upon that: And if she has several flitches of bacon to preserve, she thus lays one flitch upon another with straw between them, and never shifts the straw, but cuts the bacon as she wants it for her private family. And I do avouch it for truth, that of all the bacon I ever eat in my travels, I never met with any that out-did this sort for pala-tableness, firmness, cleanness, and whiteness of flesh; and am not a little surprised to find, that no author I have hitherto read has taken the least notice of this most excellent way of preserving bacon. And what consequence this way of drying and preserving bacon is of, I shall shew by what follows, viz.

How a Gentleman living in the north-west Part of England *would not suffer his Bacon Hogs to singed, on Purpose to avoid the ill Qualities of the Smoak.*—THIS curious gentleman, owner of a large landed estate, was a person who made it the greatest pleasure of his life, to improve and enjoy one of his farms, of about 50 *l.* a year, which he kept in his own hands. This gentleman, having a due knowledge of the ill effects of smoak, would not suffer those hogs he killed for bacon to be singed, but scalded them as we in *Hertfordshire* do our porkers, not only for avoiding the nasty unsavoury tang that smoak impregnates the rind or skin and flesh of a hog with, but also for avoiding the unwholesome qualities that attend all singed, smoaked bacon, when eaten with fowls, veal, or other viands; for that he thought such smoaked bacon gives these meats a disagreeable relish, and makes them become somewhat offensive to both palate and stomach. And since such smoaky bacon is as unwholesome as unsavoury, it ought to be the more refused; and the fine white dried bacon, free of that pernicious smoaky quality, preferred to it. For smoak, by naturalists, is defined to be a stupifying keen fume or vapour, full of dark sulphurous excrements, void of all real virtues, and very pernicious to health; for that it proceeds from those poisonous juices that the fire and air send forth. Fire, says one of these virtuosi, divides and separates the forms and properties of nature, and manifests both vices and virtues of things, which so long as they remained in one body intire, nothing of this pernicious quality has been seen or known. Smoak therefore, says he, is an excrement that all people endeavour to avoid, as being the most prejudicial to the fine volatile spirits, and therefore most offensive to the eyes; for they are the gates of the whole body, where the natural spirits have their ingress, egress, and regress, and for this cause, smoak first offends the eyes, and so does any other stupifying fume or vapour, either internally or externally. Therefore when any eat ill prepared food, or drink the like drink, and when the heat of the stomach and concoctive faculty separate such foods and drinks, they do as naturally send up into the head gross excrementous vapours, very offensive to nature, and especially to the eyes; for smoak contains in it two poisonous qualities that are of a bitter and astringent nature.

How the same Gentleman scalds his Hogs.—FOR these reasons, this gentleman scalds his bacon hogs thus; when the hot water is ready, in that degree of heat as will scald the hair, he puts into a pail-full of it two or three handfuls of oatmeal-dust, which is what remains after the oatmeal is made. This water, so dusted, he puts over the dead hog, as it lies upon a bench or form, and as the dust is well mixed with it, it will lodge at the bottom of the hair, and cause the water to have the greater effect in making it come regularly and easily off, better than the common way of doing it only with hot water.

In this work the butcher uses an iron instrument, somewhat like a horse's curry-comb, that has two edges, but no teeth. This scrapes off the loosen'd hair, and then a knife follows which cleans the skin and compleats the work; and when one side of the hog is thus done, they lay a little straw at bottom, and turn the lower side uppermost, to be scraped and cleaned as the other was. This same way is made use of in some parts of the north for both baconers and porkers, with good reason, for it makes the bacon look white, and take salt better than if singed. Thus prepared, it will not damage soup or broth, as they are dried free of any burnt tang, and therefore fitter to be boiled with fowls, veal, beans, &c. This is much the better way than to scald the hair off (as we do in *Hertfordshire*) by putting the dead hog into a tub or cistern of scalding water, which is a sort of parboiling, and undoubtedly renders any bacon or pork so served, subject to keep the less time sound; for the hulls or dust of the oatmeal serves, in this case, instead of resin.

Fatting Hogs for Bacon or Pork in London.—A LONDON distiller told me, that although he did not keep any hogs, yet he knew one that kept eight hundred by him at once, at some time of the year, for fattening them to sell for baconers or porkers: When porkers sold well, he fatted his hogs accordingly; if baconers sold well, he fatted them accordingly; and said, there was no sweeter pork or bacon than these hogs make, which are fatted with only hot wash and grains, being as sweet as those fatted in the country with barley-meal, but then (as he said) their bacon will not keep so long sound as the country-fed bacon will, nor will it retain its fat in boiling like that. And no wonder it is so, if it is true, as I have been informed, that some feeders of hogs with distillers hot wash and grains have killed their hogs and made them into bacon in a fortnight's time, by first laying the flitches in a very strong brine three days, seven in salt, and three in a smoak-room, at the end of which time they were carry'd to market for sale; so that in about a fortnight such bacon is compleatly made and sold. And although salt-petre makes part of their brine, and some of it is mixt with common salt afterwards, to salt down their flitches, by which they stiffen their bacon fat, and give it a reddish cast, yet such fat will boil more out than that from bacon made from the feed of pease or beans, &c.

The Care and Art made use of by a Country Housewife in curing her Flitches of Bacon.—As soon as her hog was cut out, she strewed some salt over the fleshy sides of the flitches over night, to extract and drain out the bloody juice of them; next morning she laid one of the flitches on a table, and opened a place in the shoulder part with a knife, in which she forced in some salt, for here is the most dangerous place of breeding taint; when this was done, she did the like by the other flitch, and then laid a peck of salt over both the flitches, which weighed near thirty stone; this done, she laid one flitch upon the other, the skinny side on the fleshy side, and the tail of the upper one to the head-part of the under one; at the week's end she shifted the undermost by laying it uppermost, and where she perceived a barish place, she strewed some more salt over it; this she did twice in two weeks more, and when the flitches had thus lain three weeks in all, she hung them up to dry near her wide chimney, by a wood fire that burnt leisurely.

N. B. Next to the bone in a flitch of bacon is the greatest danger of taint, and therefore she applied more salt-petre than ordinary, as well as common salt, to this part.

Why a Sow is better to make Bacon of than pickled Pork.— THIS as well as hundreds of other useful matters, in country housewifery, were never exposed in print. A sow by being made bacon of, her flesh will eat shorter than if it was pickled for pork, because both the salting and drying causes it. Besides which, the belly-piece of a fatted bacon hog is almost all fat, and is the toughest part of the carcase; which when melted, near half of it will become a coarse lard, good enough for present spending, to fry pancakes, and make ordinary pye-crust, &c. But when the flesh of a sow is pickled for pork, this tough fat belly-piece is pickled with the rest of the carcase. And although it be an old sow that is to be made bacon of, she will, by being baconed, eat very tender, as having got new young flesh in fatting. Such a sort of case as this has caused a dispute between a man and his wife: Says the woman, I will have the skin of my old sow (for she was seven years old) taken off, and pickle her flesh for pork. No, said the husband, she will make better bacon. And it proved so, for I heard the woman say, that nothing eat tenderer or sweeter.—But observe, that whether a sow be killed for pickled pork or for bacon, it concerns every owner of such sow, that she be not killed in brimming-time; for if she is, her flesh, whether pickled as pork, or dry'd for bacon, will assuredly eat rank and very unsavoury; which evil to prevent, we either have such a sow spayed before fatting, or boar her, and kill her fatted about the end of eight weeks, which is about the expiration of half her time: Or if she is fatted without boaring, we kill her at ten days end, after her brimming is over, because there is an interval of 21 days between each brimming or boaring time. This is what I duly observe myself, in fatting of a sow, by managing her according to one of these three ways, for I have practised all of them, and have therefore further to say, That as spaying of a sow is a somewhat hazardous operation, it is not so much in use of late as formerly, because many have died by it, either by the unskilfulness of the operator, or by the mismanagement of such a sow afterwards.—These material articles are certainly so necessary to be known and observed, that if I had not wrote them, my book must have been so much the more imperfect.

A black Hog of the foreign Breed was killed with so thick a Skin, that it was thought it would be worth more to sell to the Saddler than to eat as Rind to Bacon.—A FARMER, that kept the wild sort of breed of hogs, fatted one that weighed 35 stone, for bacon, which had so thick a skin, as was thought by his neighbours would have sold for more money than to eat it, as rind to bacon, because such a thick skin would have tann'd into a good substance, very fit for the saddlers use, who give the most money for hogskins of any tradesmen. Therefore such a very thick skin (especially if it be of a very old hog) is better sold to the saddler, and the flesh pickled for pork.

How a Quaker living at Eaton *in* Bedfordshire *used to prepare his Bacon for drying and keeping.*—It was the practice of this man, for his own family's use, to wash his flitches of bacon very clean, just before he hung them up to dry; and when he was asked, Why he differ'd, in this action, from all his neighbours? he said, He could not find what good a crust of salt did his bacon, after it had lain a month under it, for that in this time the flesh had had all the virtue it could have of the salt; and said, that by so doing he could eat his bacon with less waste of salt than others did, and much cleaner.

How a Country Bacon-monger left off smoaking his Bacon, to dry it without Smoak.—THIS was done in *Buckinghamshire*, where a publican bacon-monger, every year, is said to kill 100 hogs for making bacon of them. It was this person that made an attempt, in imitation of the *London* bacon-man, to dry his bacon in a smoak-room, by burning sawdust in the same. Now, whether he managed the drying art as they do, I cannot say; but this I know, that he was soon out of love with his new way of hastily drying bacon altogether in a smoak-room, and did afterwards without smoaking them at all; for as soon as the flitches had lain their due time in salt, he laid them upon a rack near the cieling, in the kitchen, within the reach of some heat from the fire: Where after they had gradually dried, he took them away, and laid others in their room; and thus he proceeded to cure all his bacon, giving it a most white colour, free of all smoak, and likewise free of all rust, that might be occasioned from too much heat of the fire. For this is a true maxim in the drying of bacon, that so far as the heat of the fire enters the flitch, so far the rust will breed in it. Not but that there are two extreams in drying bacon. Some hang up their flitches in the side of a chimney, to be dried and cured by the sooty smoak, for two or three weeks, so that when they are taken down, they appear black. This way, indeed, may help to keep the bacon from tainting a long time; but its unwholesome nature and unpleasant taste want no rehearsing. So likewise is the under-drying of bacon another extream, for then the fat will be like tallow, and taint in a little time.

How another Country Bacon-monger cured his Bacon so as to make it look very white, eat sweet, and keep sound a long Time.—THIS bacon-monger, I am here writing of, is a tradesman besides, for you must know, that in many country towns and villages there are shopkeepers and others, who kill many hogs in a year, for selling bacon wholesale and retail, as grocers, chandlers, publicans, butchers, *&c.* most of whom make use of abundance of pickle for steeping their flitches in, to prepare them for salting and drying, and have likewise their smoak-houses built on purpose for the drying of their bacon, in the same manner as many *London* bacon-men have. But this country bacon-man makes use of no pickle nor smoak-house: His way is fairly to salt the flitches with a little powder'd salt-petre, mixed with common salt, and once a week, for three or four weeks, he rubs a little more salt on each flitch, and shifts them; then he hangs them in his chimney-corner, where no smoak comes at them, nor too much heat from the fire, when dried enough, he carries them up into a chamber, and lays the first flitch on wheat-straw, and when he has put some straw on that, he lays another flitch over it, then straw, then flitch, and so proceeds, till he has laid ten or fifteen flitches in one heap. And thus many more may be laid in one chamber, cover'd over with wheat-straw. A way that keeps bacon in the sweeter and soundest condition of all others; for here is no excess of heat, cold, or moisture to annoy it. Therefore it was that this man sold his bacon, when others could not theirs, who do not cure it so well as he does.—But there are some who think it a good way to preserve their flitches of bacon sweet and sound, by laying them in a heap of malt, and it may answer the end, if the malt is fully dried, and of the brown sort, free of any smoak-tang; otherwise it is apt to damp it, and give it an ill relish.—I also know a farmer's wife that never lets her bacon hang in the chimney above three days, and then puts it on a rack near the outside of the chimney to dry; for her notion is, that if it hangs above three days here, it wastes.

The different Qualities of Pork and Bacon.—It was in *March*, 1745, that I had the honour to be in conversation with a worthy and curious Member of Parliament, whose seat lies about 100 miles eastward from *London*, who told me, he had sent to a friend of his in *London* a present of pickled pork, which for its good relish, and for retaining its fat in boiling, made him declare, he had a very ill opinion afterwards of the common pickled pork sold in *London*, because it had not so good a relish, nor would it retain its fat in boiling like this country gentleman's pork; which leads me to observe, that there are several sorts of pork and bacon, whose good and bad properties are chiefly owing to the food the swine eat: Some are fed (near the north seas especially) with fish; in other parts, with tallowchandlers graves; some with horse-flesh; some with whey and skim milk; others with wash and grains; some with the offald and blood of beasts; others with bran and pollard; some fatted on clover, turnips, potatoes, parsnips, and carrots; others with horsebeans; some on oatmeal, and some on beech-mast and acorns; some on barley, or French-wheat, or on pease, *&c.* Now to avoid prolixity, in writing of all these in particular, I shall only touch on a few of them. The feed of whey and skim milk, wash and grains, bran and pollard, potatoes, parsnips, carrots, turnips, clover, the offald of beasts, oatmeal, and barley-meal, *&c.* are all sweet food, but create a loose flesh in comparison of the more firm feed of corn; and of all corn food, there is none that comes up to the pease. And therefore many of the knowing ones (with a great deal of reason) will buy our pease-fed bacon, in refusal of all other bacon; as being sensible that this particular sort of corn-fed bacon has not only a very close flesh, but likewise a very sweet one. And of this sort is all the bacon I make; a quantity (little or more) of which I am ready to supply any person with, or with pickled pork, upon a proper order.

How to prepare Flitches of Bacon for drying, so as so prevent their rusting, and for securing their Gammon Parts from the Breed of the Hopper-fly.—THIS is a matter of no little consequence to families, because where they consume little or much of this most necessary, ready, pleasant, wholesome, cheap food, they would willingly have it preserved from these two pernicious accidents, which (for want of knowing how to prevent it) happens to thousands of flitches of bacon, and renders them of little value. As to rustiness, I take it to be the first beginning of the bacon's decay, and consequently is the first worst part of it, which is so disagreeable to all stomachs, that if much is eaten of it, it surely causes sickness for a little while. Rustiness is occasioned two several ways; one is, by letting too much heat come at the bacon, as I have before observed; the other, by keeping it too long before using. Now to prevent the first, the old country practice is, that when the flitches have lain long enough in salt, and are ready to be hung up in or near the chimney to dry, they spread over the fleshy side of each flitch a good quantity of long bran, which they pat down with their hand, for making the salt lie the closer to the meat, and to keep it from falling off when it is got dry. Many are of opinion, that by such branning the flitches, it helps to keep them from rusting: But I say, that whether bran is put to them or not, bacon will rust, if the fire is made so hot near it as to melt a little of the outside fat; but, I think, I know a better way than to make use of bran, and that is, when the flitches have lain long enough in salt to be hung up for drying, we sift over their fleshy side some fine wood ashes (made from beech or ash) pretty thick, which having a penetrating salt in them, it enters a little way into the flesh, and sticks some time to it, helps to keep off rust, and discharges the breed of the hopper-fly, that in ill-cured bacon, especially, is very apt in time to breed, increase much, and eat the gammon part of it, for here they first begin, and are succeeded by maggots. This application of ashes is of late become a practice in *Hertfordshire*.

An Account of a Lord's Butcher who salted and managed his Flitches of Bacon in so wrong a Manner, that great Part of them were spoiled.—THIS case I know to be true, because it was acted not far from *Gaddesden*, where a lord had so large a family, that he kept a butcher all the year on purpose for killing his oxen, sheep, calves, swine, *&c.* It was here they fed their swine extremely fat for bacon. And although this butcher was an elderly man, yet he committed a very gross mistake in the management of his salted flitches of bacon; for as the thick back-part of them lay higher than the thinner belly-part, the salt in melting run down to the thin part, and left the thicker part bare of it. Thus they lay some weeks without disturbance, for the butcher thought he had well secured them with a sufficient quantity of salt; but so it was, that when he came to displace them in order for drying, he found all their fat back-part stunk to that degree, as made them be boiled only for getting out their grease, to grease cart-wheels with. And to this use only was it put, notwith-standing the lord kept a pack of hounds, that would have greedily eaten all this damaged bacon; but then it would have done them a great prejudice. For if hounds were to be fed with salted meats, it would certainly lessen their scent. However, as the thin part of the flitches had the greater share of salt, they proved to be as good bacon as need to be used. And there were large quantities of it.

The Nature of Salt-petre, Bay-salt, Petre-salt, and Sal Prunella.—SALT-PETRE is a bitterish salt, and of a sulpherous nature, for it is the main ingredient used in the making of gunpowder; yet it is of a coolish nature, very penetrating, and resists all putrefaction; therefore of excellent service in the preservation of hog-flesh, especially in hot weather, because the powder of salt-petre presently enters into pork or bacon, and greatly prevents their tainting.—Bay-salt likewise is good in a mixture with common salt, provided too much is not thus made use of, for if it is in excess, it will give the flesh a disagreeable taste. Some say, petre-salt is only bay-salt dusted; but this I am not certain of. However, I heard a gentleman's cook say, that petre-salt makes pickled pork or bacon red and soft, when salt-petre makes them red and hard. Either or both of these, when mixed with coarse sugar, preserves pork or bacon in an admirable manner, and gives them such a pleasant relish, as makes them eat much like *Westphalia* ham. But sal prunella exceeds all, if applied in a right quantity, being a more purified salt, and therefore is sold at a greater price.

A Butcher's Notion of Salt-petre.—THIS butcher kills many hogs for bacon in a year, and says, he never dares to use above a quarter of a pound of salt-petre to the greatest hog; for he says, you may lay on as much salt-petre as will make bacon stink, or at least taste nauseously rank.

Why a Vale Housewife refuses to make use of any Salt-petre in the curing of her Pork or Bacon.—THIS housewife is wife to a man that lives on his own estate at *Eaton* in *Bedfordshire*, who is seldom without half a dozen hogs in his yard, which he feeds for his own family's use; now it is a constant notion of this woman, that salt-petre does more harm than good to pork or bacon, she therefore refuses it, as believing it to be of so penetrating a nature, that it eats out the gravey and goodness of the meat, makes it unpleasantly dry, and gives it an unsavoury twang. For, as she says, if bacon is rightly salted and dry'd, there is no danger of its tainting; and as to the redness of the colour, and hardness of the flesh, which she allows salt-petre may be the cause of, she thinks common salt may fully supply both these qualities, if enough of it is made use of, and the bacon passes through a leisure drying, and is rightly preserved afterwards.

To make a Pickle for pickling Flitches of Bacon, in order to prepare them for being Smoak-dry'd.—THIS is the practice of many of the great bacon-mongers both in town and country; and is indeed a very safe way to secure flitches of bacon from the blow-fly, and from taint; because such a liquid is sure to affect all their outsides at once, and as it is composed of very potent strong ingredients, their insides too in a little time. On this account it is, that several of these bacon traders venture to kill their hogs for baconers even in warm weather, by depending on the security of this penetrating liquor. But besides all this, bacon thus prepared weighs much heavier than that prepared by only salting the flitches three or four weeks, and gradually drying them as long by a country wood fire. As pickling therefore is most to their interest by increasing the weight, and saving much salt, time, and trouble; one sort of it may be made thus.—Mix half a peck of white common salt with half a peck of bay salt, two pounds of brown sugar, two ounces of sal prunella, and two pounds of salt-petre.—These boil in such a quantity of spring water as when cold will pickle two flitches at a time, to lie a fortnight in the same. Then take them out and smoak them over a saw-dust fire, or by that made with old wood.

To cure Hams by an unboiled Pickle.—TAKE six pounds of coarse sugar, a peck of bay salt, a quarter of a pound of finely powder'd salt-petre, and half an ounce of allum; put them into spring water, so that the quantity of the brine may come up to the standard of bearing an egg; when the liquor is at this proof, lay in your hams to lie in it three or more weeks; then take them out of the pickle, dry them with a cloth, and rub them over with common salt; then it is that they are fit to be dried.

To cure Hams by a boiled Pickle.—YOU may pickle two or three hams in the following pickle at a time; take two pounds of coarse sugar, two ounces of sal prunella, half a peck of common salt, four pounds of bay salt, one ounce of allum, and five ounces of salt-petre; they must be all in a powder'd condition. then infuse them in six gallons of spring water, in which boil all of them briskly for only fifteen minutes; scum it well, and when the liquor is perfectly cold, put in your hams to lie in it three weeks at least; at the end of which time take them out, rub them dry with cloths, and work in some dry salt all over them with your hand, and then they are fit to dry and keep for your leisure uses.

To make English *Hams like those of* Westphalia *in Shape and Taste.*—THE following receit has been collected from one author to another, and as it is somewhat curious and serviceable, I shall also transcribe it in the same words.—Take the legs of a porker, and lay them in cloths, to press and dry out the remaining blood and moisture as much as may be, laying planks on them, and on them great weights, which will bring them into form. Some have boxes purposely shaped for them, with screws or weights to press down their lids; when they are thus ordered, salt them well with bay-salt finely beaten, and lay them in troughs or wicker panniers one upon another, close pressed down, and covered with sweet herbs, as hyssop, winter-savory, thyme, pennyroyal, *&c.* which will infuse into them a pleasant flavour; let them continue thus a fortnight, then rub them well over with petre-salt, and let them lie three or four days till it soaks out, it being of a wonderful penetrating nature; then take them out, and hang them in a dry close smoak-loft, and make a moderate fire under them, if possible of juniper wood, but so that it may last long, and let them hang to sweat and dry well; then hang them up in a dry place that is somewhat airy three or four days, to purge them of the ill scent the smoak has put into them, and then hang them up for good in a dry place, that is somewhat airy, against you have occasion to use them; which when you have, wrap them up in sweet hay, put them into a kettle of water when it begins to boil, and keep them well cover'd till they are boiled enough, and they will cut of a curious red colour, and eat short and savoury, so that few can discover them from the right *Westphalia* hams.—There are several other ways of curing legs of pork to make hams of them, too tedious to insert here, and therefore I shall only touch on a little more of this subject.—Salt-petre hardens and colours flesh, and on this account it is a very proper ingredient to rub into a leg of pork, for making it into a ham; and as the bloody juice should be extracted before it is salted for good, some have rubbed fine powder'd salt-petre, with some coarse-sugar, all over the leg once a day for three days, before they salt it well with common salt, and when it is so done, it may lie a month or two in the same, turning it now and then with your pocket fork; then it may be hung up in paper to dry for use.—Others mix sal prunella with salt-petre, and rub a ham with them, to keep in a strong boiled pickle twelve days; then re-boil the pickle, and re-salt the ham as before, and after it has lain a fortnight in it, it is to be bran'd and dried; and as to the boiling of such a ham, it is best done as aforesaid with hay. But for boiling oak saw-dust with a ham, to give it the deeper red colour, it ought to be inquired into, how wholesome or unwholesome it is.—Others rub a leg of pork with coarse sugar two days together, and taking a mixture of sal prunella and common salt rub it well in it, and let it lie in the same till taken out to dry.—Others, as in *Yorkshire*, where land, workmens labour, and hogmeat, are extraordinary cheap, and their water carriage of goods to *London* as convenient, send great numbers of hams every year out of that large county to the opulent city of *London*, so that there are now few cheesemongers shops there, but what sell these hams for about five-pence a pound: But this art is not only practised in *Yorkshire*, for there are many gentlewomen that delight in this piece of good housewifery, as well as tradesmens and farmers wives who may make hams as before-mentioned, or thus—Take the leg or ham of a barrow hog, about a year, a year and a half, or two years old, when they are at their full growth, and salt it a little for extracting the bloody juice, which it will do in about ten or twelve hours time, as it lies in a glazed pot: This done, wipe it dry, and bruise half a pint of bay-salt, and mix it with one pound of coarse sugar, four ounces of powder'd salt-petre, and a quart of common salt: These being well incorporated, put them in a saucepan or an iron dripping-pan over a fire, where the composition must be well stirred till hot; and while it is so, you must rub it soundly over every part of your ham; then let it lie two or three weeks under this salt mixture, turning it several times, and it will be ready for being dried in a chimney or smoak-stove, by burning saw-dust or otherwise.—Or order your hams partly after the method they practise in the city of *Wells*, in *Somersetshire*—Let your ham be thoroughly cold, then beat it on both sides well with a rolling pin, for making the flesh tender, readier to take salt, and eat the shorter; when you have so done, powder three quarters of an ounce of salt-petre with a quarter of an ounce of sal prunella, which mix and rub all over the ham, lying thus four and twenty hours: Then beat one ounce of sal prunella more very fine, and mix it with a pint of bruised bay-salt, two quarts of common salt, and one pound of coarse sugar; which heat in an iron pan over a fire, till it is hot, but not so hot as to melt, and rub it over the ham at your turning it every day for three weeks: At the end of which time hang up the ham to dry, and when dried, wrap brown paper about it to keep off flies, and preserve it in a dry part of the kitchen.—Or take this shorter way—Hold your ham near a fire-side, and rub half a pound or more of coarse sugar over it; this done, let it lie so a day and a night; next, you are to rub it all over with four ounces of powder'd salt-petre, and four ounces of petre-salt, mixt with three pints of common salt: Thus salted, let the ham lie in an earthen pan or wooden bowl or tray, three weeks, turning it now and then, and rubbing a little common salt over it, at the end of which time wipe it well, and dry it in your chimney by a wood fire.

The Power of Brine and the frugal Management of it, in the Cure and Preservation of Bacon, Hams, Tongues, &c.—IN many of the *London* cellars, where they keep great numbers of flitches of bacon in heaps under salt for two or three months together, ready for drying and selling them at a beneficial time, they have a reservoir to catch and retain the brine that descends into it by a dissolution of the salt; which brine they boil and scum till it is perfectly clear, and make it serve (with more salt) for a pickle to preserve other bacon, pork, or beef in; and if they want to make it very strong, they add sugar and common salt, or salt-petre, *&c.* to their liking. Thus flitches of bacon, hams, spare-ribs, tongues, clods of beef, legs of pork, or other pieces of a hog or bullock, may be pickled, by lying in the pickle of either of the foregoing receits; hams four or five weeks, the clods of beef three weeks or a month, tongues twelve or fourteen days, and thinner meat accordingly: These brines, if made to the proof of swimming an egg, will last good three months, and if they are found to decay, or are bloody-foul, it is only boiling them up again with some addition of common salt, which when scummed, and discharged of all flesh, will be clear and new for another trial. And it is from such pickle, that hams, tongues, or other pieces of meat may be taken to dry in a chimney or stove, or a smoak closet or room, over or near the burning of charcoal, sawdust, or old spokes of wheels, or other dead wood that has lost its sap. An innkeeper of *Leighton* in *Bedfordshire*, that had some-what a greater trade than his neighbours, and kept plow'd ground in his hands besides, always kept his beef and pork in one large powdering tub in brine; and for preserving his brine and meat sweet and untainted, his maid-servant all the summer long was obliged to boil up her pickle once every fortnight or three weeks, in order to scum and purify it, till it was as clear as rock-water; when cold, she return'd it into the tub, and having new salted her old, or salted her new fresh meat, it was laid in this clarify'd pickle. And thus he went on all the year, shifting his brine often in summer, and seldom in winter, but never intirely discharged his powdering tub of brine, except once a year, and then it was for using it to keep his wheat-seed in at sowing-time. But his tongues he kept in a pickling pot by themselves, and shifted the brine now and then that they laid in, by boiling and scumming it, and new salting them. But Mr. *Houghton* is more particular in his fourth volume (page 257.) *of Brine* ; for there he says, that in the strongest unboiled brine he could make, he potted two porkers in *February*, and in *July* he thought it exceeded all the bacon he ever eat with beans.—That in such brine, that he kept two years without boiling, he sunk a brisket of beef for eight days, in *February*, and then took it out, dried it in a temperate open place for six weeks, and it eat very well with boiled sallad.—That about the same time he sunk another piece of beef for twenty days, and afterwards hung it up in an open place for the whole summer, and at *Michaelmas* it was very good.—That he sunk a leg of mutton in brine all night, then hung it up in a string in defiance of the season and flies for ten days, and after dressing it, found it excellent; and so fresh as to eat salt with it.—The use of making such a strong unboiled brine that will answer this end, I will shew by an example of preserving a leg of pork in it, so that it may be made to eat like true *Westphalia* ham. It is certainly true, that the leg of the wild foreign black breed of hogs is the best to make a ham of, because their flesh is naturally shorter and sweeter than the *English* breed. After the leg has been cut out ham-fashion, let it be a day or two before it is meddled with, then beat only the fleshy side of it with a rolling-pin, rub the leg all over with one ounce of powder'd salt-petre, and let it lie thus eight and forty hours; next mix two handfuls of common salt, with one ounce of sal prunella finely beaten, one handful of bay-salt, and one pound of coarse sugar. These, as I said before, must be warmed in a pan till they are near melting, and then when they are so warm, must be soundly rubbed with more common salt all over the ham, in an earthen glazed pot; when the ingredients are all dissolved into a brine, turn the leg or ham twice a day with a pocket fork for three weeks together, then take and dry it as bacon is dried.—This is a very strong brine, and may serve as an excellent pickle for bacon, pork, beef, &c. &c.—The use of coarse sugar in salting or pickling of bacon, pork, beef, mutton, &c. may perhaps be wonder'd at, particularly if mixed in a pye with salt and pepper, &c. but it has been often found to add a tender shortness to the meat, and give it a delicate relish besides. Thus when sugar is used in the cure of bacon or pickled pork, it is said to be as effectual in the curing of them as salt. And it is well known, that salt causes all meat it is applied to for keeping, to be hard and dry; whereas sugar makes the flesh eat tender, short, and sweet. Thus as sugar has a great spirit in it, it is thought that it will, with half the quantity of common salt that is usually made use of, preserve flesh a year together sound and good.— But to be further particular in making a right pickle or brine for keeping bacon, or hams, or tongues, or other meat in— Boil in five gallons of water (whereof the spring sort is best) a quarter of a pound of salt-petre, one pound of petre-salt, four pounds of bay-salt, two ounces of sal prunella, and eight pounds of brown sugar; boil all fifteen minutes, scum it well, and when cold put in your meat, to keep five or six weeks, more or less.

Rabisha's *Method to bake a Gammon of Bacon.*—HE says, first boil the gammon tenderly, then take off its skin, &c. season it with pepper and a little minced sage, stick the upper side with lemon-peel, and then put it into a good butter'd crust, or in an earthen pan, or pewter dish, cover'd over with a pasty crust; but before you put on the cover, lay on it some pieces of butter, and when it is out of the oven, pour melted butter over it.—Or boil an onion or two in claret with minced sage, and a few sweet herbs, thicken'd with butter.—This is good, eaten hot or cold.

To roast a Ham.—THIS is to be done by first boiling it tender, and then stripping off its skin; when on the spit, besmear it with the yolks of eggs, crums of bread, and shred lemon-peel, and make this serve for basting it several times as it roasts.—A gammon, either boiled, baked, or roasted, may be made an exquisite dainty dish with pigeons, or chickens, &c. or eaten with brocoli, cabbage, or collyflower.

The ill Qualities of Bean-fed Bacon, and that from Swine fatted on Distillers Wash, Butchers Offald, &c.—Bean-fed pork and bacon is somewhat like horseflesh in comparison of pease-fed pork and bacon, because the beans make the hog's flesh of an ill colour, and coarse withall, give it a thick rind or skin that will crack and part in boiling, eat rank, and is accounted by the knowing ones to be a groat worse in a stone than a pease-fed hog.—So swine fatted on distillers wash, as thousands in a year are at *London* on that and butchers offald, &c. I say, that the pork and bacon of these are of a flabby nature, and will (notwithstanding the hardness that salt-petre gives it) lose much of their fat in boiling. In *September* and *October* 1748, great numbers of wash-fed hogs (I was informed) were driven from place to place in *Hertfordshire*, to sell ready fatted for pork or bacon, because, as it was said, *London* was glutted with their bacon. Therefore it concerns all gentlemen, tradesmen, and others, in cities and towns, particularly in the opulent city of *London*, who buy all the bacon and pork they use, to prefer sweet, wholesome, good pease-fed country pork and bacon, as fed in *Hertfordshire* and other Chiltern countries.

To roast a Gammon of Bacon.—FRESH it by soaking it in warm water, then tear off the skin, and let it lie with only a quart or three pints of raisin wine, mountain wine, or sack, in a glazed or pewter dish, one day; then spit it, and roast it with paper before it, baste it most part of the time with the same sack, &c. and at last strew over it minced parsley mix'd with crums of bread.

To boil a Gammon of Bacon.—SOAK it in cold water for three days, scrape and rub it with a brush, boil it with sage, rosemary, thyme, marjoram, and fennel, with some bay leaves; this done, tear off the skin, and stick it with cloves; to be eaten hot or cold.

Of the Feeding of Boars, and making Brawn of them.

THE Case of a Gentleman, who had a Boar almost spoiled by the wrong Management of a Servant.—THE boar I am writing of had been kept by a worthy nobleman indeed, who for his hospitality, and generous entertaining his neighbours, is in very great esteem in the country about him. The boar was almost three years old, when he was put up to fat for brawn against *Christmas* 1745, and although he was for this purpose feeding near twelve months, was yet in a lean condition at killing-time. The reason of which was, the gentleman's servant had no more wit than to put the boar up in a stye, that was contiguous to several others, where sows and barrow hogs were kept; so that there was only a bare partition of boards between one and the other. This made the boar fret to that degree, that his meat did but little more than keep him alive. However, when the time of year was come for killing him, the nobleman sent for our *Gaddesden* butcher, because he understood this art better than all others in the country about him. When he view'd the boar, he told the lord, he was not fit to kill for brawn, as being too lean for the purpose; but this did not satisfy him, for he insisted upon his being killed for brawn. On this the butcher, who lived seven miles from him, said, if he would but send the boar to his house, where he had good conveniencies, he would do his best to make brawn of him; accordingly a stout man was appointed to drive the boar, but when he was out of the stye, he ran about the nobleman's park which way he pleased, so that they were obliged to have him into the stye again, where they halter'd and bound him, and carried him in a cart to the butcher's house, who in two days time killed him.

How the Boar before mentioned was dressed by the Butcher for making Brawn of him.—AFTER the boar was stuck and dead, the butcher poured scalding water over its carcase, and then directly rubbed in a quantity of powder'd resin, and upon that more scalded water, to make the hair rough and matt, for the better being pulled off; in the same manner as he does the least pig. For a porker, the water must not be boiling hot, because if it was so, it would set the hair, rather than help to make it part easily from the flesh; but a boar-skin will admit of scalding water. Now to make the best of such a lean boar, the butcher cut off all the fat and all the lean from off the bones of a neck of pork, and stuft this meat in between the lean and shield of the brawn, for that the fat of a neck of pork is harder than any other part of the hog, and therefore fittest for this purpose. This done, he with sufficient help made rollers of the brawn, by twisting up the flesh as tight as they could with a cord, and when they had well girted it, they immediately bound the roller about with tape: Thus they did by every roller of brawn, and then hung the rollers by strings on cross sticks placed over a copper of water, and boiled them; and when the rollers, that before hung down lengthways, turned broadways in boiling, they were taken out and bound tighter, and thus boiled on for about nine hours in all, which is enough for the flesh of a young boar, because there ought to be three hours difference in the boiling of a young boar and an old one; for if a young boar's flesh was to be boiled twelve hours, as an old boar's should, the fat would be apt to boil out too much. Yet this happens more or less, as the feed of the hog is; for if he was fed with hard hog pease or beans, the flesh will not lose its fat, like that fed with flashy meat. However, as this boar was fed with such hard meat, and the fat and lean of a neck of pork was added to it, it made this young lean boar's flesh look marbled-fat. And thus it eat moist, sweet, and very tender.

The Case of another Gentleman, who in buying and feeding a Boar for Brawn, lost most of it.—THIS gentleman lives in

Hertfordshire, about twelve miles distant from the other, who, in the year 1746, bought a boar, about seven years old, that was extreamly poor, for making brawn of him; when it was brought home, his servant put him up to fat on good pease; but in about six weeks time the boar fell off his stomach, and would not eat. Upon this he was advised to alter his meat, and feed him with barley-meal, and then the beast recovered his stomach, and fed till he was killed, three weeks after, nine weeks in all. This gave the old boar a quick but flashy fat, insomuch that it boiled almost all away; for as such an aged boar requires at least twelve hours boiling, to get the shield tender and soft, near all his fat was boiled out, and lay at the top of the water, to the quantity of almost a pail-full, which was good for little else than to grease cart-wheels with. This occasioned the butcher, who killed the boar, and managed the brawn to the last, to new bind the collars of brawn several times in their boiling (for altho' he did with much help bind up the stubborn shield of such an old boar, yet he could not prevent the loss of the fat:) And to know when the collars wanted new binding, they were tied by a string to a stick, that lay cross a deep copper (for a shallow one is improper for this work, because they must not touch its bottom) and the collars of brawn, that before hung pendent longways, now turned broadways: Then it was that they were new bound with broad tape, and boiled again, and this was done several times, till, at last, a roll or collar, which at first was as big as a child's body, by such waste of fat became no bigger than a man's arm is thick, insomuch that there was hardly any fat left in it; nor would this brawn have been fit to be brought to a table, had not the butcher interlaced the lean of it with some fat bits of a porker.

Observations on the Case of this Gentleman, who had bad Brawn instead of good Brawn; and how Brawn is to be managed to have it good.—THIS misfortune happened, as I said, thus, The gentleman bought a boar for making his *Christmas* brawn, that was very poor, and also very old, and by feeding him a very short time on barley-meal, his fat became so very loose and flabby, that it melted out in boiling; not but that he was obliged so to do, because as the boar was a very old one, and very poor withall, his stomach could not digest the hard, dry, grey hog-pease he at first was fed with, for he at last dung'd them whole, and then went off his stomach, and must have been worse than he was, had he not been fed with the soft meat of barley-meal. Now an old boar by some is preferred to a young one for making brawn of, and they assign you this reason for it, saying, that the shield (the best part of the brawn) of an old boar is thicker than that of a young one. Others with more reason prefer a boar of three or four years old, as the fittest to make good brawn of, because he will feed and fat the kindest on hard grey pease, which will give him a hard fat, a mellow lean, and a good shield; when such a boar is thus fed fat, if the butcher does not make a delicate brawn of him, it is his fault. And to do it, he first soaks the flesh of the boar ten or twelve days in cold water, every day shifting it, and duly observing at every shifting to scrape and thin the shield, for by this cleanly management the fresh water not only extracts and washes out some rankness of the boar's flesh, but also adds to it an agreeable whiteness. When this is done, the next thing is to bind and boil the collars of brawn; to bind them requires the help of two men at least, for they must be bound extreamly hard with white tape of a penny a yard, of which there must be employed many; as this gentleman's boar took up above an hundred. To boil them, there must be a copper of water provided, wherein must be put a peck of the finest whitest oatmeal, with some milk, bay-leaves, and rosemary, for increasing a whiteness in the brawn, and giving it a savoury pleasant tang: Here it should boil as gently as possible ten or twelve hours, till a straw can be run through the brawn; but I am informed, that some, instead of tying up the collars with tape only, put them besides into a trunk or mould of tin, made so, that as the brawn shrinks in boiling, a collar is taken out of the copper, and directly screwed tighter; by which means the fingers are prevented scalding, and much time and trouble saved, that otherwise must be expended in drawing the collar tighter with tape and hands.

Rabisha's *Method of collaring and sousing Brawn.*—YOUR brawn being scalded and boned, of each side you may make three handsome collars; the neck-collar, the shield-collar, and the side or flank-collar. If your brawn be very fat, you may also make the gammon-collar behind, otherwise boil and souce it. This being water'd two days, shifted three or four times a day, and kept scraped, wash it out, squeeze out the blood, and dry it with cloths. When it is very dry, sprinkle on salt; so begin at the belly, and wind it up into collars; but in case you can stow more flesh in the flank, or in the collar, you may cut it out of other places where there is too much, or from the gammon. This being bound up, as you would bind a trunk, with all the strength that can be obtained, put it into your furnace or copper, and when it boils scum it; but you must be careful it is kept full of liquor, and continually scummed for the space of six hours; then try with a wheat-straw if it be very tender, and cool your boiler by taking away the fire, and filling it constantly with cold water, so shall your brawn be white; but if it stands or settles in its liquor, it will be black: Then take up your brawn, and set it up on end on a board. Your souce-drink ought to be beer brewed on purpose, but if it be of the house-beer, then boil a pan of water, throw therein a peck of wheaten bran and let it boil, strain it through a hair sieve, and throw in two handfuls of salt, so mix it with your beer aforesaid, and souce your brawn therein. You may take half a peck of white flower of oatmeal, mix it with some liquor, and run it through a hair sieve, and it will cause your souce to be white: Milk and whey are used in this case; but your milk will not keep so long: You may put both in the boiling thereof, it will cause it to boil white: Keep your souced brawn close covered, and when it begins to be sour, you may renew it at your pleasure, by adding fresh liquor.

What Mr. Bradley *says of feeding, making, and soucing of Brawn, in his* Country Housewife, *page 186.*—IT is to be observed, that what is used for brawn, is the flitches only, without the legs, and they must have the bones taken out, and then sprinkled with salt, and laid in a tray or some other thing to drain off the blood; when this is done, salt it a little, and roll it up as hard as possible, so that the length of the collar of brawn be as much as one side of the boar will bear, and to be (when it is rolled up) about nine or ten inches diameter. When you have rolled up your collar as close as you can, tie it with linen tape as tight as possible, and then prepare a cauldron with a large quantity of water to boil it. In this boil your brawn till it is tender enough for a straw to pass into it, and then let it cool, and when it is quite cold, put it in the following pickle: Put to every gallon of water a handful or two of salt, and as much wheat bran, boil them well together, then strain the liquor as clear as you can from the bran, and let it stand till it is quite cold, at which time put your brawn into it; but this pickle must be renewed every three weeks. Some put half small-beer and half water, but then the small-beer should be brewed with pale malt; but I think (says he) the first pickle is the best. *Note*, the same boar's head, being well cleaned, may be boiled and pickled like the brawn, and is much esteemed.—In another place, page 110, he says, A boar ought to be put up at *Midsummer* to be fed for brawn against *Christmas*, when it sells best, even for one shilling per pound; and it should be an old boar, because the older he is, the more horny will the brawn be. We must provide for this use a frank, as the farmers call it, which must be built very strong to keep the boar in, and somewhat longer than the boar, but in such a manner, that the boar must not have room to turn round. The back of this frank must have a sliding board to open and shut at pleasure, for the conveniency of taking away the dung, which should be done every day; when all this is very secure, and made as directed, put up your boar, and take care that he is so placed, as never to see or even hear any hogs; for if he does, he will pine away, and lose more good flesh in one day, than he gets in a fortnight, he must then be fed with as many pease as he will eat, and as much skim milk as is necessary for him. This method must be used with him, till he declines his meat or will eat very little of it, and then the pease must be left off, and he must be fed with paste made of barley-meal, made into balls as big as large hens eggs, and still the skim milk continued, till you find him decline that likewise, at which time he will be fit to kill for brawn. These directions to make brawn, by Mr. *Bradley* and *Rabisha*, are all pretty well to the purpose; but to make brawn by the following printed receit, in a Housewife's Book, is very insipid indeed; it begins thus— *To make brawn*—When it is cut up, says the author, and boned, let it lie two days and nights in water, shifting it each day into fresh water; when you come to roll it up, dip it in warm water, and salt it well; then roll it up, and boil the least roll six hours, and the biggest nine.—Another printed one, more insipid than the last, says thus, *To keep brawn*, Take some bran, put it in a kettle of water over the fire, and two or three handfuls of salt; boil this up, strain it thro' a sieve, and when it is cold, you must put your brawn in it.

To bake Brawn by an old Receit—WHICH says, take two buttocks, and hang them up two or three days, then take them down and dip them in hot water, pluck off the skin, and dry them very well with a clean cloth. When you have so done, take lard (that is to say, the flair of a hog) cut it in pieces as big as your little finger, and season it very well with pepper, cloves, mace, nutmeg, and salt; put each of them into an earthen pot; then add a pint of claret wine, and a pound of mutton suet, and so close it with paste. Let the oven be well heated, and so bake them. You must give time for their baking, according to the bigness of the haunches and the thickness of the pots; they commonly allot seven hours for the baking of them. Let them stand three days, then take off the cover, and pour away all their liquor; then have clarify'd butter, and fill up both the pots to keep it for use. It will thus keep very well two or three months.—Or you may pickle a boar's head, by either scalding off the hair of it, or burning it off with wheat-straw. If by the latter way, rub off the stubbed ends of the bristles with a brick-bat and knife; then open the head by its under side, and take out all the offald bones, brains, and tongue; but not cut the skull-skin in two. Next lay it in salt two or three days, at the end of which make several holes in the flesh, and stuff them with salt; then tie up the head in a linen cloth, and put it into a kettle of water with sweet-herbs, bay-leaves, onion, rosemary, and spices, and (if you will) a bottle of claret; boil it eight or ten hours, till it is very tender.— This is to be eaten cold like brawn, by laying the whole head on a table, and cutting it out at pleasure. And by the same way any hog's head may be prepared and eaten.—Or you may prepare and keep a hog's or boar's head in this manner: Scald or burn off the hair or bristles of it, as before directed, very clean, then take out the brains, and boil the head so tender, that all the bones may easily be taken out, then take the flesh from the skin, and mince it while it is hot; season it with spice, and squeeze it very tight down in a glazed earthen pot for keeping; or you may keep it in a pickle made of the water it was boiled in, with salt, and a very little pepper. This is to be cut out in slices at pleasure, and eaten with vinegar or mustard is excellent.

To roast the Flesh of a Boar.—Sɪʀ *Kenelm Digby* says, that at *Frankfort* in *Germany* they roast a wild boar; but first, they lay the flesh to soak six, eight, or ten days in good vinegar, wherein are salt and juniper-berries bruised (if you will, says he, you may add bruised garlick or what other haut-goust you please) the vinegar coming up half way to the flesh, and turn it twice a day; then if you will you may lard it; when roasted it will be very mellow and tender. They do the like with a leg or other parts of fresh pork.

Rabisha's *Way to bake Brawn to be eaten cold.*—TAKE (says he) your raw lean brawn, that is not useful to collar, and as much fat bacon, mince them small together, and beat them in a mortar; beat a good handful of sage with them; season them with some pepper, salt, and beaten ginger; pour in a little vinegar, and break in a couple of eggs; you may make a cold butter paste in a sheet form, and lay this your prepared meat on it; put in butter, and a few bay-leaves on the top, and so close up your pasty for baking.

Sir Kenelm Digby's *Way to bake Collars of Brawn.*—IT must, says he, be a very hot oven, and therefore be eight hours heating with wood; if the brawn is young, eight hours in the oven will do; if old, ten or eleven. Put but two collars into an earthen pot, with twelve pepper-corns, four cloves, a great onion quarter'd, and two bay-leaves; fill the pot not quite full of water when you set in, but fill it full when in the oven. The cloths on the collars must not be pulled off, till they have been three or four days out of the oven. To keep the collars afterwards in a soucing drink—Boil salt in table-beer, when cold put to it two or three quarts of skin milk to colour it, and change the liquor once in three weeks. Such pickled brawn cut in thin slices, and eaten with a mixture of pepper, salt, vinegar, oil, and mustard, is by some esteemed good eating.

The Management of Sows and their Pigs.

WHY the Inspection and Care of a Sow and Pigs belongs to the Country Housewife.—As there is one or more sows generally kept in a farm yard, I think it may be said the inspection and care of her belongs to our country housewife when she has pig'd; because the pigs, if they are not her perquisites, yet as she makes wash from her kitchen, skim milk from her dairy, and grains from her brewings, she has here an opportunity for, putting them to a profitable use, by feeding her sow with them, and fatting her pigs with the greater expedition; for on this account, no meat comes up to wet meat, as it produces the most milk. Therefore all wash made of pot liquor, skim milk, or whey, or from brewing, when mixt with barley-meal, or bran, or grains, is a proper food for a sow that suckles pigs.

The Management of a Farmer who lived at Eaton *in* Bedfordshire, *whereby he generally had sucking Pigs all the Year.*— THIS farmer kept twenty cows and a bull, and also three breeding sows, which brought him so many pigs, that he seldom was without some all the year, for as he had much milk and grain besides, he was furnished with the very best of food, for maintaining his sows in the greatest heart, and in the most milk. Accordingly he gave them full quantities of skim milk and no whey, because he thought whey was not good enough for milch sows, and would let them go abroad, during the summer season, to graze in his meadows next his house; and when they came home, he would give them two or three dishes of horse-beans every day (for in this Vale of *Aylesbury* there are but very few pease sown) to keep them in heart for sustaining the suckling perhaps of ten, twelve, or more pigs each sow. Nor can any make whiter, sweeter, or fatter pigs than dairymen-farmers; because they certainly have the greatest conveniences for doing it, as I shall shew in my next account of it.

How a Woman made near four Pounds a Year, by the Pigs of only one Sow.—A FARMER'S wife, that kept five cows, had the sole management of the sow and pigs, and took such care, that when she went out, and but daubed her legs, she obliged her maid to wash and clean them, lest her tail might dirty the milk and give the pigs a distaste of it; she also saw that the maid duly litter'd the sow and pigs with clean wheat-straw twice a day; and for increasing and preserving her milk, she always kept a sack of pollard by her, in readiness for mixing a handful or two in some skim milk every time she fed the sow, for she preferred the pollard to barley-meal and all other soft meats: (As to barley-meal, it is a notion many are possessed of, that it is too hot a food for a milch sow, and thereby tends to the drying up of her milk, yet allow, that kernel is necessary to be given to a sow besides milk and pollard) For as a sow with many pigs will grow lean and faint, if not sustained with good meat, she, as most people living in vales do, thinks that horse-beans are the most strengthening food of all grain; and therefore two or three dishes of them are given every day to a suckling sow, which hold about a pint each. Thus this farmer's wife went on feeding her sow in the best manner, causing the pigs to have white flesh, white skin, and white hair; so that at three weeks old, or thereabouts, she commonly sold them for three shillings, or three shillings and six-pence, each pig, to the *London* higler, at *Dunstable* market, or at *Hempstead* market; but if they did not answer their character, the pigs were either returned to her, or else she must take a very low price; for these higlers are such connoisseurs, that when they (according to their custom) hold up a pig by its hind leg, and perceive any thing of a reddish colour between them, they are displeased, and the owner must come off with the less money: So when a sucking pig is kept a month or more before it is sold, it then by age acquires a reddish skin, that lessens its value, for the higler well knows, that aged pigs will eat rank and displease his customers; but when a sucking pig is three weeks and a half old, it is then of a right age: And if a sow-pig is thus aged, and white fatted in the sweetest manner, it is (if rightly dressed) a dish for a king. Now there is no loss in keeping a suckling sow up in the greatest heart, for if she don't pay keeping fat, she won't pay keeping lean; and if she is thoroughly well kept, she will certainly take boar, on the turning of her milk, (which will be presently after the pigs are sold off) and breed again. By this method, this woman had generally five litters of pigs in two years from one sow, that she sold fatted for near seven pounds; for if a sow is kept on a full allowance of meat, there need little time be lost in her breeding, because the general part of these creatures are so prone to take boar on full keeping, that some sows will take him before the pigs are sold off. But when it so happens, it is an observation made by hog-dealers, that the sucking pigs of such a sow are the worse for it, by reason it damages her milk.

The Method that a prudent Person took to manage a Sow before and after Pigging, and to cause his Pigs to have white sweet Flesh.—THIS person, more careful than hundreds of some others, always observed to let his suckling sow feed every time from her pigs, lest the pigs were made the worse, by letting the sow feed in the same stye where they lay. To this end, whenever he fed his suckling sow, he always let her out of the stye from her pigs into another adjoining stye, for if she was fed out of a trough that stood in the same stye, the pigs would be apt to lick the wash or other soft meat that is slobber'd about it, lose part of their appetite, and acquire a coarse reddish flesh. This method is duly practised by a near neighbour of mine, who I am persuaded makes as much money of his pigs as any man in our country, and is what every good husband and housewife ought to practise, where conveniency allows it; for which purpose, I have two styes ready to feed and keep my sows from their pigs at pleasure, and find no little benefit by it. Hence I am to observe, that it is not only to write of fatting a hog, and making his flesh into pickled pork or bacon, but you may see here, that there are several important matters besides, that are absolutely necessary to be wrote of in a book intituled *The Country Housewife*, relating to these serviceable animals, although never taken notice of by any author before, which occasions me therefore to be the more particular on this subject. But I must further observe to my reader, that it is mine as well as the person's practice I write of, never to let a stye be litter'd with much straw, when a sow is going to pig because if it is, the pigs are apt to be smother'd; and when she has pig'd (if she pigs in the day-time) carefully to attend the taking away her glean, though some are careless of it. And when she has pig'd her litter, and is gone out of the stye the first time, we scatter a handful of wheat-straw over the pigs, and when she returns to them, we take the straw off, that she may the better see and suckle them. Then we take the opportunity of scattering a little more straw on the sow; and so on, increasing the straw by degrees, and giving the pigs and sow a small matter of it at a time twice a day: Thus we think such management tends much to nourish the pigs, keep them clean and white, and force on them a quick growth.

The Case of a Gentleman, who lost several of his sucking Pigs, by Means of his Sow eating sourish Apples.—THIS worthy gentleman, whose delightful seat I was at in 1746, lying in the county of *Kent*, for delivering to him some of my fine profitable Ladyfinger natural grass-seed, Tyne grass-seed, and Honeysuckle grass-seed, for sowing them, to convert his plow'd ground at once into a natural sward, for making a little park or paddock of it, to keep a few deer in, *&c.* was pleased to tell me he had a sow that, while she suckled her pigs, eat some stampings of apples that were a little sourish, which had such an influence on her milk, as to alter it so much for the worse, that it killed several of her pigs.—Which leads me to observe to my reader, by way of advertisement, that I sell these most excellent grass seeds, that may give an opportunity to convert plow'd ground into grass ground at once, without loss of time; by sowing these seeds amongst barley or oats, under such a peculiar management, by my information, as will assuredly keep the seeds and the infant crop of grass from the damage of insects and weather, and produce a plentiful crop of such grass, presently after the grain is carried off, and continue such for ever, if husbanded accordingly. Thus a person may come by the very best of grass ground, free of those nasty prejudicial seeds of weeds, that accompany hay-seeds taken promiscuously out of hay-lofts; and thereby the cows which feed on this grass will yield milk, butter, and cheese, that excells, I believe I may say, most or all other sorts, fats a beast presently, and gives them the sweetest of flesh. And thus this gentleman inclosed about forty acres of land with pailing (park-like) chiefly because it prevents the approach of huntsmen too near his seat by day, and poachers by night; a new sort of management, and which, very probably, may give a gentleman more pleasure, than if he occupied a thousand acres of field land.

Sow bursted.—A FARMER living near *Ivinghoe*, in the Vale of *Aylesbury*, having a sow kept up that fed on beans for fatting, gave her such a large quantity of whey at once, as swelled the beans in her maw to that degree as bursted her; for if a fatting hog is neglected giving water to, and comes to drink greedily on sweet whey, it alone will endanger its life, but much more when it is drank in great drought on a belly-full of dry horse-beans. Therefore where great dairies are carried on, persons ought to be more than ordinary careful on this account, lest they meet with the same loss this farmer did, whom I was well acquainted with; but I suppose it to be the fault of his servant, for he himself was a man of good judgment in the farming business.

Sow killed by Accident.—IN the harvest-time of 1747, a woman living at *Edlesborough* in *Bucks* kept two sows, one was to pig the same day she died, which was occasioned by the sow's getting her head through a hedge or pale, where, by straining to draw her body after her, it so squeezed her belly, as to kill her and her pigs: The other was killed in the following manner.

A Sow killed by a wrong Medicine.—THE same woman having lost one sow, the other pig'd well; but they had given her something that had alter'd her milk so, that the pigs all scour'd: This made her get advice, how to cure her pigs; and to do it, she boiled twelve dozen of corks in milk, and gave it to the sow, which bound both the sow and pigs to that degree, as killed them all. Thus the poor woman lost her two sows, and their litters of pigs, almost at a time.

An Account of a Hog-doctor's Procedure to cure Swine that ailed nothing.—A THRESHER being at work in a barn, as he came out of it, he happened to put his foot on hog's-dung; the stink of which so offended our nice workman, that in a passion he struck a hog on the head with his flail, and made it reel. Now as a hog is one of the most sulky creatures upon earth, if a little out of order, it went to a straw-rick just by, and there lay, till next day; when the farmer finding it, he sent for a hog-doctor from *Redbourne* in *Hertfordshire*, who, on viewing the hog, said it had the murrain, and would infect the six others it went with (for the man that struck it, would not own it) upon this he was employ'd, and had half a crown a drink for all of them.

A Sow poison'd by drinking Broth.—A WOMAN having a sow, she committed a mistake in boiling a poisonous herb for a healthy one, for giving the broth to her sow, it poisoned and killed her: The case was this, she wanted some herbs to boil with her meat, and as it is usual with country-women to gather them in the fields in the spring time of the year, this woman gather'd what they call *Jack in the Hedge*, which she took for the white-ash herb, a herb which grows amongst grass; but it proved to be the first, that stinks like onions, and yet by some is accounted a wholesome herb. But whether she made the broth too strong of it, or it happened by some other unknown means, the loss of the sow was imputed to this herb.

A Hog soon choaks.—THEREFORE what is given it by a horn must be done with a jirk, for if its head is held up too long in giving it a drink, it will be apt to choak.

A Sow killed by eating Brandy Cherries.—A SOW has died by eating too many cherries that were steep'd in brandy.

Several Hogs cured, that were jogg'd under their Throats by eating Acorns.—A FARMER, in our parish of *Little Gaddesden*, having several of his hogs, in a plentiful year of acorns, jogg'd under their throat by eating them, made no more to do, than to heat an iron red-hot, about the thickness of one's little finger, and run it through the corrupted knob or bunch, which brought on a suppuration, that run out a putrified matter, and cured the hogs. This way he took without bleeding them by cutting off a piece of each hog's tail, for then the hog is apt to bleed to death, especially in hot weather.—This year (1747) the acorns dropt the greenest that was known in the memory of man.

Hogs died with rotten Livers.—A PETTY farmer had eight small hogs or rather pigs that were kept so poor and stunted, that if they fell in a cart-rut they could hardly get up, and thus were forced to eat the little grass they could find on a common, and in eating it were forced to eat much dirt, which rotted their livers, and killed them.

Some Hogs killed by eating Acorns, and others cured.— IN the great acorn year of 1747, several hogs died after they had done masting, because they had acorns given then uncured.—A woman near me had one that seemed mad by its running about and screaming, insomuch that it was thought bewitched; at last, they gave it flower of brimstone in milk out of a horn, but not curing it, the next day they gave it some soot mixt in piss out of a horn, which effectually unbound it, and made it dung a prodigious quantity, so that it recovered and became a valuable hog.

How to prevent Hogs being bound too much by eating Acorns. —OUR way is to give our hogs a feed of boiled turnips mixt with bran, every morning fasting, before they go into the fields and woods to feed on acorns.

To keep Hogs in Health that feed on Beans or Pease for fatting.—THESE are apt to bind hogs much; if they are bound too much, it takes away their appetite, therefore I commonly put some pollard or bran into the water I give them to drink, for taking off its rawness.

Sucking Pigs killed by giving the Sow Hops amongst Grains.—
THIS was true matter of fact, as it happened to a neighbour of
mine, who ignorant of the ill effects of hops, gave the grains
and hops together to his suckling sow, as they came out of a
copper, from being boiled to make a small beer which we call
Kettle-gallop; that is to say, we put the ground malt and hops
into water and boil them together, then strain out the liquor,
and work it with yeast for small beer; the grains of which, with
the hops, were given to the sow, and caused the death of five
pigs out of ten, and two of the rest pined to that degree that
they were near dying. Now I cannot account for this damage
otherwise, than that I think the hops being of a toughish
nature, the sow could not digest them without much
difficulty, or that their acid quality turned and curdled her
milk so as to spoil the pigs. But to avoid this evil, I have in my
treatise on brewing malt liquors, (intituled *The* London *and*
Country Brewer, sold by Mr. *Astley*, bookseller, at the *Rose* in
Pater-noster-row, London) shewed a way how to make
kettle-gallop small beer, and yet to feed a sow safely on the
grains, free of the damage of all hops.

A Sow, just ready to pig, was poisoned by drinking yeasty
Wash.—THIS was my own case. On the 26th of *August* 1746,
I had a sow just ready to pig, when my silly maid-servant gave
her a pail-full of wash, made up with the yeasty grounds of
barrels, in the evening; and next morning she was found dead,
prodigiously swelled, with much froth, that she had
discharged at her mouth.—Now why the yeasty grounds of
barrels poisoned the sow, in my humble opinion was, because
yeast is of an acid nature; and as the grounds lay some time
in the barrel after the beer was drawn out of it, it acquired such
an increase of its acidity, as to gripe, poison, and swell the sow;
for whether yeast is stale or new, it has a poisonous swelling
quality in it, witness the experiment I published (in my said
brewing treatise) of a dog purposely kept hungry for eating a
yeasted toast, which in a very little time swelled and killed

him. And why it has not the same effect on the human body by bread is, because there is but little used in making it, and that being mixed with much water and flower, the fire of the oven renders it entirely harmless: Therefore let this be a warning to all that read it, never to suffer any yeasty grounds of barrels to be mixed with any meat that is given to hogs, lest it kill them as it did my sow.

Hogs damaged by eating Hens Dung.—This happened in my neighbourhood thus: A farmer bought two pigs for fourteen shillings of a hog-dealer, to keep and fatten; but was forced to sell them again for the same money, after keeping them long enough to be worth near as much more, and this because they took to eating the dung of a parcel of hens, as it fell from under them, while they roosted upon an elm-tree that stood near the farm-yard.

How a Sow brought a Litter of four and twenty Pigs, and how she was managed to bring them up, till they were sold for five Shillings a Piece.—My next neighbour, who keeps a breed of hogs between the *Berkshire* and *Leicestershire* sort, had a sow of an ordinary size, that on the third day of *August*, 1747, brought him four and twenty pigs all alive at one litter, but all of them died except three, in a very little time; yet I know a brewer that lives at *Albury* near *Gaddesden*, who had the like number of pigs at a litter from one sow, and preserved them all alive, till he fatted and sold them for five shillings a piece; but to do this, he was obliged to keep the pigs in two styes, and the sows as well as possible. *N. B.* I knew a sow of the black foreign breed kill seven pigs ought of nine, because the farmer was so silly to confine her contrary to her nature in a stye.

How cheaply a Woman kept a breeding Sow.—A woman that has an orchard containing about one acre of ground in my neighbourhood says, she gave no more than a single half peck of pollard in a day, at twice, mixt in wash, to her large sow, which with what grass she eat besides in her orchard, during

the summer season, maintained her well till she pig'd.—
Others give only a little wash at night, after the sow's grazing
all day in clover.

A Sow that eat Chickens.—THERE are sows that will eat
chickens, and none are more prone to this mischief, than those
of the wild foreign breed, or those between that breed and the
English breed. A neighbouring farmer had one that would run
after them, and thus devoured his chickens and young ducks:
The same has been my own case; the best cure for which I
think is, to fat and kill such a sow, and buy in a more gentle
sort, and that I think is either the *Berkshire* or *Leicestershire*
breed, for most of these are truly gentle.

To dry away a Sow's Milk.—IN summer time, when sows
that suckle pigs are fed in clover, or other green vegetables, or
when they are kept altogether on wet meat, this is very
necessary to be done, to prevent that destructive disease, the
garget in her bag or udder, which if neglected may prove fatal
to her; tho' if a sow, when her pigs are sold off, is fed with
horse-beans, or other dry meat, we then seldom do any thing
to her; but when it is necessary, you need only to rub in some
brandy over her bag, and it will dry away her milk at once
using. But as farmers have seldom brandy by them, the tarring
of a sow's bag will do as well.

To wean Pigs.—AT a month old, pigs may be weaned, but
if older, it will be rather better; and to wean them to make
the best hogs, it should be done in the month of *May*, for then
the summer hot weather is before them, when good wash and
grains is then almost as good as whey in winter; and to wean
them in the cheapest manner we commonly let them go
abroad with the sow in clover or other grass, and at their
return home, in the evening, we feed the pigs apart from the
sow, by giving them skim milk, whey, or good wash, with
some barley-meal, pollard, or bran amongst it, and some dry
beans or pease upon the ground or barley, oats, or thetches.
Others, who have no corn, give them only pollard or barley-

meal, mixt with wash or water; but a little kernel best keeps them from being stunted; for if a pig is once stunted in its growth, it requires some time and extraordinary cost to recover it. Thus if pigs are well fed with wash and grains, &c. and corn, besides their sucking the sow, the sow's milk will soon decline, and in time she will beat them off, and wean them from her. This way of weaning pigs by degrees, by letting them go with the sow in the day-time, and feeding them besides by themselves, is, in my humble opinion, the best way of all others to make good hogs.

When a Sow should be killed for Pork or Bacon, in Pig or not in Pig.—IT is a common opinion that a sow may be safely killed for pickled pork or for bacon, when she has gone eight weeks with pig, or half her time, for a sow goes sixteen in all, and pigs in the seventeenth. Others are of opinion, that she may be safely and profitably killed at nine weeks end, because the pigs do not begin to hair till that age; but when they are so old as to hair, they feed on the sow's flair, which lessens her flesh, and alters it for the worse.—I killed a yelt or young sow on the 17th day of *November*, 1747, that weighed near thirty stone, with nine pigs in her belly, when she was gone nine weeks and three days, and she proved good pickled pork, for the pigs had hardly begun to hair. I might have made bacon of her; but it sometimes happens, that when a sow has taken boar, and we put her up to fatten, that she stands not to her boaring; in this case, we either drive her to boar again, or else venture to fatten her without her taking boar at all. Now, when it so happens, we observe as well as we can to kill her in the mid-time between her boaring, which is about ten or eleven days after she has shewn signs of it; for we reckon a sow goes to boar at every three weeks end till she stands to it, that is to say, till she proves with pig. Now to know which is the best use to put such a fatted sow to, I shall here give my opinion, and that is, for making bacon of her; because common salt mixt with salt-petre, sugar, &c. with good drying, makes the flesh of a sow eat shorter and better, than when it is pickled. For in the making of bacon, the belly, thick-skin'd, fat, tough part, is quite sever'd from the flitch, and mostly put to the use of making an offald lard for kitchen frying uses, &c. whereas, if the sow is made pickled pork of, this coarse, fat belly-piece is pickled with the rest of the meat. And although she may be an old one when killed; yet being fatted with a sweet pea, or barley-meal, or pollard, her flesh will eat sweet, and if rightly bacon'd will eat short and pleasant.

Of Cheap, Approved, and Experienced

MEDICINES *and* REMEDIES

FOR

Divers DISEASES incident to Human Bodies.

THE first medicine I here present the public with is, according to the gentleman's character of it, the greatest one in the world (and which I rather believe, as it comes from a disinterested, worthy person, owner of a considerable landed estate, and one who, by his great learning, travels, and experience, has found out and made many excellent discoveries in medicine, agriculture, mechanics, *&c.*) and from his recommendation of it, it has been try'd at and about *Gaddesden* in several cases of diseases in the human body, and done great service; particularly to my near neighbour Mr. *Richard Hanowell*, who, having been afflicted with the King's-evil a long time, in and about his head, so as to have several running sores or ulcers next his cheek and throat, was at the expence of about five pounds, for bottles of liquor to cure the same, from a famous *London* practitioner in physic and curer of evils, which, as Mr. *Hanowell* declared to me, made him worse instead of better; then by my advice he drank the quicksilver-water, which he made from time to time by my lending him a pound of quicksilver that I bought for my own use (for I take half a pint of the same water every morning fasting, which frees me from all cholicks, *&c*) which has had such salubrious effects on Mr. *Hanowell*, that on the 25th *October*, 1748, he shewed me the places where his ulcers for years together run, so sound, that he pinched the parts as a proof their soundness, and they seemed to me to be as well as any other part of his face. And what is singularly honourable in this generous gentleman, he, without any obligation to me (though I am under much to him) has been pleased to correspond with me, I believe, to the exchanging of near thirty letters; not only on the subject of quicksilver, but likewise upon many secrets of great importance for the good of his country; which, with many others from different gentlemen, I intend (as I have leave for so doing) to publish, if I can meet with tolerable encouragement.

The best Cure in the whole World for the *Pox*, *King's-Evil*, *Leprosy, Itch, Gout, Rheumatism, Scurvy*, &c. &c. according to the following Letter, by the Use of Quicksilver-Water.

To Mr. *William Ellis*, a Farmer, at *Little-Gaddesden*, near *Hempstead*, in *Hertfordshire*.

London, Nov. 12, 1745.

S I R,

I AM very sorry to find your friend afflicted with the gout once or twice a year; however, I cannot but think it very happy for him, that he has already met with a medicine (though not a very agreeable one to take) that acts so quickly, and restores him to walking so effectually. I know a friend of mine that used to take one spoonful at a time of spirits of hartshorn, in the midst of great fits of the gout, which by repeating every night, and sweating much by it, soon carried off the fit, and enabled him to mount his horse, and as he was old and gross, the horse brought him, by degrees, to his feet. Now I look upon sal volatile to act in the very same manner without any material difference, and every body knows the gum guaiacum to be a most noted specific in the rheumatism, and very laudably so in the gout too, so that I would have you regard your medicine very much. However, as the mercury-water has such grand effects in rheumatick cases, and can do him no harm, in or between the fits, by way of diet-drink, I will venture to say, if it does not actually free a temperate person of a youngish gout, yet it will certainly reduce the frequency of his fits; and by the same laws, much abate the rigour of them; and I would willingly have you try, tho' I cannot really warrant this opinion from practice, or trial, though there is great reason to be certain of the good effects intended, as I could evince at large; assureing you at the same time of the innocence and salubriousness of this water. You may depend on it to cure your neice's eyes, if she drinks half a pint night and morning, and about a pint with her dinner; two or three times a day bathing her eyes with a warm spoonful of it, provided her complaint is really scorbutick. And I doubt not but it would much allay, if not cure a confirm'd evil. I would advise the issue to be continued. The doctor's application is good [he means Sir *Hans Sloan's* eye-salve] but will not remove the cause, *viz.* a scurvy in the habit, which if it be her case, his medicine may repell it from the eyes, and throw it (if there was not an issue) upon the lungs, so as to induce a consumption, or perhaps vitiate the blood, so as to bring on fevers, *&c.* She can but try this agreeable kind of drink, for as many months as she pleases. Therefore a pound of quicksilver, which costs but about four shillings and sixpence, or five shillings, I think will serve many years, boiled or rather simmer'd in any quantity of water, in an iron pot, or a glazed earthen pot, for no other metal will do, for the space of five or six hours or more. The water should never be drank freezing cold, but set a little before the fire. By what I find lately, it is a water that will not corrupt in bottles for a long time, if ever: For it destroys all kind of animalcula, and resists and destroys all manner of acidity and fermentation in the water it is boiled in, which shews it to be the highest alcali in the world, and certainly the most minute and divisible and I am persuaded, all the particles of the effluvia that mix with the water are perfectly and minutely globular, and fitted by such form and smoothness to enter and pass in the circulation thro' the imperceptible vascular system, or it could not effect what it does. Let a mangy horse or any other beast drink constantly of it, and bathe the scrophulous parts with it by a spunge, they will soon fall off, and the blood be purified, which I desire you will try the first opportunity. I cured some time ago a pointer of my own of an universal mange, so bad, that he had scarcely a hair left on his body, and that too within four weeks, by the last mentioned method. I observed the itching much allayed in seven days. In seven or eight more, the scabs began to dry and shell off, and clean new hair appeared growing underneath, and in less than five weeks he was entirely sweet, clean, and new cloathed, which my groom, and the chymist I bought the seven ounces of mercury of, to boil, can testify.—The way I came by this secret was from a surgeon, who shewed me his nephew, a *London* apprentice, whom he had cured of the pox by this water alone, after having been twice salivated, and had not strength enough to go thro' a third course. He said he met with the secret in a *German* old manuscript of a practitioner, but had always despised it till this lucky opportunity offer'd. *I am, Sir,*

Your sincere Friend and Servant.

P. S. These and other reasons make me expect it will cure the pox in the gentlest and most merciful manner. Pray give it to any poor body that has the itch, without telling them what it is. After this you are at liberty to publish it, at any time, or indeed as soon as you please.

A second Account of the great Virtues of Quick-silver-Water in the Cure of the *Pox, Scurvy, Mange, Scald-Head, Rheumatism, Worms,* &c.

London, Nov. 30, 1745.

S I R,

ONE pound of quicksilver will infuse and communicate its effluvial virtues to five hundred or one thousand boilings of fresh water, and yet suffer little or no diminution in its weight; if it is boiled in the water 10 or 11 hours, it will turn the water of an ash-colour, which is only owing to a stronger impregnation of its dusky and most minute effluvia, and this is perhaps the best cure in the world for an inveterate scurvy, mange, or scald-head, obliging the patient to drink constantly of it with his victuals, and in a morning fasting, half a pint, and the same going to bed; washing the scabious head, body and joints, with the said water once or twice a day, and avoiding all other drink, except a chance glass or two of wine. Avoid all salt meats during the cure. You will be surprised how the stubborn symptoms will yield, subside, and vanish, sometimes in a few weeks, generally in a few months, restoreing the patient in rest, health, strength and complection, in a most surprising manner, without uneasy or torturing physic; for this medicine acts as an alterative, and may justly be said to be the noblest bathe in the world. I speak this from the field of experience, and think you deserving the knowledge thereof, myself by mere chance having come by this excellent secret. I also find it will destroy worms and botts in man or beast; and I have very great reason to believe, it will by a continuance and perseverance very safely and easily cure the pox and rheumatism; it is certain it pervades all the capillaries, even to the pores of perspiration; and is a most irresistable alterative, allaying and mollifying all the corrosive matter in the animal system, or it could not effect the truths I have mentioned above, and been an eye witness of under my own direction, tho' I do not profess physic.

I am, sir,
Your faithful humble Servant.

S I R,

I have to subjoin, that if you add to the mercury-water regimen, the giving the patient every night going to bed the bigness only of a small pea of the crude mercury, swallowed down in half a glass of water, it will much facilitate the cure in scorbutic or rheumatic cases. The common itch, as it is presently catched, falls before these two, generally, in three weeks time: Worms in a few days. But it will require a longer time to eradicate old scrophulous complaints, scald-heads, and stubborn rheumatisms, which seem to be universal rather than local. And I can assure you it is excellent in the stone and gravel; also for bilious cholicks, occasioned by pungent hot humours in the intestines; because I find it allays and qualifies their pungency, by its alcalous quality (or something else that we cannot account for) as chalk, &c. mollifies vinegar or sour beer. And the water should be continued even after cure (by way of bath or spaw drinking) for some months. Not but the water itself has been found to effect a certain cure in obstinate cases; but it is as certain, that the least quantity of the gross quicksilver (and the less the better) taken every night, till the symptoms vanish, does much expedite the cure. Yet this water alone has also absolutely eradicated the pox without the least ruffle to the constitution. And it will kill the bugs in beds and furniture, provided they be washed with it, or well sprinkled by means of a brush, as bookbinders spot their leaves.

An Account of a most cheap and famous Cure made on the face and eyes of Mrs. Knight, *of* Betloe-ground, *in* Buckinghamshire, *by the use of Cows Milk. And also how a Person's wounded Thigh was cured by a most easy Remedy.*

THIS woman now living (in the year 1748) wife to the late Mr. *Knight,* an eminent grazier, living within a few miles of *Ivinghoe* and of *Aylesbury* in *Buckinghamshire,* whose character for hospitality and honesty will remain a lasting example to others, was grievously afflicted with an inflammation in her face and eyes, to such a degree as obliged her to be under the hands of that noted surgeon, the late Mr.

Roland of *Aylesbury*, during almost the space of one year, till the expence amounted to about thirty pounds, but without a cure. Now it happened, that in this interim of time, Mr. *Edward Thorne*, a butcher, of great dealing, living at *Little Gaddesden* in *Hertfordshire*, and who killed all or most of the Duke of *Bridg[e]water*'s beasts for his numerous family, had a violent scorbutick humour broke out in his thigh, that so lamed him, as to necessitate his having recourse to a profess'd surgeon, but notwithstanding his application Mr. *Thorn* was still in a very painful sad condition; insomuch that the late good *Scroop* Duke of *Bridg[e]water*, who was a nobleman remarkably easy of access, and ready (unless a case was falsely represented to him, as I have known done) to assist a neighbour in distress, seeing this man (his butcher) in a very decrepit condition, ask'd him what was the matter? He told his Grace how lame he was by a wound in his thigh, and that he was hardly any thing the better for what his surgeon had done to him. Upon this, the Duke offer'd to give him his letter for carrying it to *London*, and to wait on that celebrated surgeon the late Mr. *Bouchier*, for his advice; for you must know, that this person was so skilful as to be encouraged (as I am informed) by a large yearly salary from the government, for giving his advice *gratis* to his Majesty King *George* the Second's subjects; and abundance of service he did to great numbers of people, amongst whom was this Mr. *Thorne*, who when he had presented him with the Duke's letter, and seen his wound, asked him who was his surgeon? He told him. Says Mr. *Bouchier*, Go tell him he is a blockhead, for proceeding thus in a wrong manner, and bid him get a black-lead pipe thrust into the wound, there to remain for the pus to evacuate through it, and as the wound heals, it will push out the pipe by degrees, which must from time to time have its end clip'd off with a pair of scissars, lest the shirt catch it and tear it out, for no salve will affect this sort of wound. When Mr. *Thorne* had received this sort of direction, he thanked him and retired;

but just as he had got out of the parlour, a woman with a child in her arms, and bolsters on its inflamed face and eyes, entered the same, for asking Mr. *Bouchier's* advice; which raising a desire in Mr. *Thorne* to hear what he would say on this case, he stood at the parlour-door, and heard him ask her, Who had been her surgeon? She told him such a one. I thought, said he, he had had more wit, than to go on so. Woman (says he) go and wash the child's eyes morning and evening with warm milk directly taken from the cow, and it will cure it; but do not take off the bandage all at once; leave it off by degrees. Mr. *Thorne*, hearing this, came away; and when at home, soon went to Mr. *Knight*, with whom he usually grazed and fatted his horned cattle; and there related to Mrs. *Knight* this child's case, and the surgeon Mr. *Bouchier's* advice, which made such an impression on her mind, that she directly applied the same remedy to her inflamed face and eyes, and in a little time got a perfect cure of both.—The like happened to two of my neighbours about *March*, 1747. One was in prodigious pain and almost blind with an inflammation in her face and eyes, insomuch that she was not capable to make her straw hats, for that was her profession, but every now and then was obliged to lie down on her bed, or sit up by the fire-side. Upon this I told her husband the virtue of cow's milk, and advised him to have it applied to his wife's eyes, accordingly, the woman morning and night duly bathed her face and eyes with the warm milk, and soon recovered her sight, which induced her to acquaint her sister, that was much in the same condition, with her success; and as she made use of the same means she had the like cure. This most excellent medicine of warm milk (tho' seemingly a mean one) I recommend to cure all inflammations of the face and eyes, whether they be blood-shotten, or otherwise damaged by hot scorbutick humours.—*N. B.* The black-lead pipe was at first four inches in length, with a hole in the middle of it, a little bigger than that of a common tobacco-pipe, and of its shape, which by the help of a bandage kept in the wound, till it descended by leisure degrees, and was diminished by frequently clipping of it, till the cure was perfected.—I have also to add, that upon a more particular inquiry into the distemper that affected the above-mentioned woman's eyes, she told me herself, that before the application of the cow's milk she had a hot water, that now and then discharged so fast through her nostrils, that it would sometimes run, and was of so sharp and hot a nature as to raise little blisters on that part of her face it fell on from her eyes; so that they were inflamed to a degree of forcing her to keep her head in darkness a great part of the day, because she was not able to behold the light, nor the fire, which render'd the poor woman incapable of providing for her family as she used to do, by platting of wheat straws, and sewing them into hats; but by the balsamic cooling milk alone she was in a little time restored to good sight, and capable of following her business.

How a young Man had the sore Piles, by tippling too much October *Butt stale Beer, and how cured.*

THIS young man lives at *Market-street*, in *Bedfordshire*, four miles from *Little-Gaddesden*, and who so accustomed himself to drink strong, stale butt-beer, that he became sadly tormented with the piles. Upon which he applied to the late famous surgeon, *John Copping*, Esq; in *Market-street*, who directed him to take half an ounce of flower of brimstone every morning, in milk, till it cured him; and cure him it did, as he declared to me. And no wonder, since, as the learned Dr. *Quincy* observes, "The flower is certainly balsamic and cleansing, and good against all diseases of the breast, and several other parts of the human body, used either inwardly or outwardly."—Others say, sitting over the smoak of frankincense and pomegranate shells will cure them.

A Gentleman Traveller's Character of the Flower of Brimstone.

THIS gentleman said, He had been a traveller almost all over *Europe*, and that it was his real opinion, That no body need take physic, if they took half an ounce of flower of brimstone in milk every morning, as he did, and drank sage-tea after it.

Dr. —— his Method of taking Flower of Brimstone for his pimpled Neck.

THIS gentleman, a famous doctor of divinity, well known in *Surrey* and *London*, took as much flower of brimstone every morning, throughout the year (except in frosty weather) as would mix in a spoonful of milk, and would drink a large tea-cup of milk after it, for dispersing and curing of pimples, that were apt to come out in his neck. And Dr. *Quincy* says, "That it is the plenty, in a great measure, that lessens its esteem.["]

An excellent experienced REMEDY for the *Gravel*.

Notwithstanding this is a Chronical, and a Disease that has proved fatal to Thousands, its direful Effects are easily prevented, if the following Directions are timely applied, and duly observed.

SWeeten water-gruel with honey, and eat a mess of it without bread every morning fasting. And if a person is much afflicted with the gravel, let him eat the same mess oftner. This receit was communicated to a gentleman, my neighbour, by a physician at *London*, who telling another of it, they said, Of all the things they had made use of for this purpose, none did them so much good as this. For as the gruel and honey are both of an open slippery nature, they consequently make the parts slippery, and bring away the gravel easily. But yet this remedy may be made much more effectual, if their cheap, common, small drink is composed according to the following receit, and drank indeed of small malt-beer.—To twenty-two gallons of water put nine pounds of treacle, which mix and boil one hour briskly, and so a lesser quantity, if thought fit, in the same proportion, with hops, or better without them, and work it with yeast till it is fit to barrel up.—By these two liquors, that are of an opening cleansing nature, the cause of breeding gravel will be much prevented, and if bred, will be easily discharged.

A Diet Drink.—Eight ounces of sena, 4 of carraway seeds, 4 ounces of sweet-fennel seeds, 4 ounces of anniseeds, 4 ounces of sassafras, four ounces of sarsaparilla, 4 ounces of hartshorn shavings, 2 ounces of ivory shavings, 6 ounces of stick-liquorice, 1 ounce of rhubarb, liverwort, brooklime, water-cresses, water-dock-root, wild fetches, clivers, dandelion-roots, parsley-roots, elder-buds, nettle-tops, scurvy-grass, one dozen of Seville oranges. The seeds to be bruised, and the liquorice to be sliced, the rhubarb to be grated, and put into the vessel last. The sena to be infused in a pitcher of the beer. The scurvy-grass and wild-fetches to be bruised and put into a flannel bag in the vessel at last, and the oranges to be squeezed and put into the vessel rind and all. All the other things to be boiled well together and strained off. Two or three handfuls of each of the herbs and roots.—This diet-drink was made by Mrs. *Sibley*, a yeoman's wife, at *Water-End*, in *Hertfordshire*, and sold by her at 18 *d.* per quart, chiefly in the spring season, for curing and preventing the scurvy, rheumatism, and other distempers; being infused in a firkin quantity of middling beer.

London, June 1, 1749

S I R ,

HERE follow the receits which I promised on *Friday* last, having now found the memorandum, which I had (as I surmised) put up very carefully together, and then overlook'd. The first my wife presents you with, being what she practised when she lived with her aunt in *Wales*, who kept fourteen cows, *&c.* and generally killed two large hogs every year.

The Welch *Way of preparing Hogs Guts for Puddings.*—FIRST take some of the fat off, and cut the guts in proper lengths (longer or shorter, as you chuse) letting water run through them till the dung is clean out of them, then with clean hands turn them by the help of a round stick, and wash them clean with water; put them into a pail or pan, with two or three handfuls of salt among them; get a whisp of clean straw, and work them well about with that in your hand, till they froth; then wash them well, and repeat the salt and agitation; then wash them again, and put more salt, and two or three handfuls of crabs mash'd to pieces; lastly, scour them well with your hands, taking care not to break them; then wash them very clean, and put them into water with a handful or two of salt, and let them lie till next day; repeat fresh water and salt to them two or three days, and, when you are about to fill them, wash them out with fair water only.—*N. B.* When they are thoroughly clean, they will lie on the back of your hand without slipping off.—Hogs or sheeps maws, when intended for puddings, should, after their contents are emptied and washed, be first well scraped and scalded, and then served as aforesaid.

Welch *Black-puddings.*—WHEN you kill your beast, receive the blood in a clean earthen pan, with a handful of salt in it, stirring it continually as it flows from your hand, till you find a large coagulum, or lump, stick to your hand, which throw away; then drain the blood into a clean pan, and let it stand till you use it as follows: Pour scalding hot milk upon some whole oatmeal-grouts, let it stand all night, then mix near one half milk with your blood, adding thereto some of the hog's fat or leaf, a little winter-savory, thyme and pennyroyal, all chopt very fine, and season'd with a little salt and black-pepper. Mix all these very well of a due consistence, that the composition be not too thick nor too thin, and fill your guts; but be sure to leave room enough for them to swell in boiling, and then tie them up in the form of a figure of eight circular. Lay them but one upon another in a wide kettle of water, just ready to boil. Let them boil, very gently lest they burst, about six or seven minutes; then take them out, and lay them upon clean wheat-straw on a sieve before the fire; turn them, and they will be soon dry; then repeat the boiling, dry them as before, and they are done. Keep them upon fresh dry straw in a sieve for use. Let them have air enough, and they will keep a fortnight or three weeks, wiping them now and then.

Welch *white Hogs-puddings*—ARE made by pouring warm milk upon whole grouts, letting them soak 12 hours or more; then add some of the best hogs fat cut very fine, and season them with salt, pepper, nutmeg, a little honey to your palate, and a few currants well wash'd and pick'd. With this mixture fill your larger guts, but not too full, and boil them about as long again, as the smaller black sort, and in the same manner.

Welch *Way of making Puddings with Hogs or Sheeps Maws.*—IN *Wales* they do not throw away the hogs or sheeps maws, but after they are cleansed as above, they fill them with the following composition, *viz.* Blood prepared as aforesaid, and about half as much milk, stir in a proper quantity of oatmeal, to which add a good quantity of suet, shred very small; some of the herbs to be winter-savory, thyme, marjoram, parnel, and lambs-tongue, some cives or young onions, and the white part of leeks cut small, with pepper and salt; observing that none of the ingredients are over predominant when filled, and leaving a little space to swell; skewer them up and tie them, throw them into boiling water, and boil them very gently near half an hour. These eat very well, if cut in slices, and fry'd with a little butter.

Sussex *Pudding.*—There are two ways of making this famous pudding, a flat way and a round way. On the 13th of *June*, 1749, baiting at the *Cat-Inn* at *East-Grinstead*, I saw the cook-maid seemingly put a flat cake of dough on a wooden paddle, about the bigness and shape of a round trencher, into the boiling water of a pot that had meat in it for dinner, which, by a long handle to it, she held in the water till it boiled hardish; then she drew away the wooden paddle or skimmer, and left the pudding-cake to sink and boil longer. Now this pudding, she told me, was made with flower, milk, eggs, and a little butter kneaded together, and when boiled enough, it was taken out, slit in two, and butter put into it. Thus she made this *Sussex* pudding, that was to be eaten with meat instead of bread.—The other way is, to make a round pudding of the same ingredients, which (I suppose) is to be tied up in a cloth, and in the middle of this pudding they put a piece of butter, and so inclose it with the dough that the butter cannot boil out. When boiled enough, they find the butter run to oil, and so well soaked into the pudding, that they eat it with meat instead of bread, or without meat as a delicious pudding.

How to boil salt Meat to the greatest Advantage.—As the ignorance of some may lead them to commit a gross mistake in boiling of salted beef, bacon, or any other salt meat, I thought it not foreign to my present undertaking to inform them, that if salted meat is put at first into boiling water, it will surely keep in the salt, and further harden the flesh, so as to make it eat very disagreeably. Now to prevent this, it is only putting the salted meat at first into the water cold, and then as the meat gradually heats with the water, the salt will boil out, a sufficient scum arise, and the flesh will hereby be made to eat fresher, tenderer, and much more agreeable, than if it was at first put into boiling water.

To pickle Sprats.—ONE of our country housewives pickles sprats in the following manner: The sprats, she says, must be washed and laid in a glazed pot, and between every layer salt must be spread, and so on till the pot be full; thus they should lie three days, then taken out, and put into the same or another glazed pot, filled up with a mixture of vinegar and water, which must be put into an oven, as soon as the bread is drawn. Thus, she says, sprats may be kept, for eating like anchovies, some time; but, I think, sprats will not retain an anchovy colour and taste so well this way, as if a few bay leaves were first put into the pot, and then between every layer of sprats, a mixture of bay-salt and salt-petre; and this is better in an anchovy-tub than in a glazed pot, because the tub may be turned bottom upwards every now and then, for by this method the sprats will be cured without baking, and in about two months time fit to eat raw like an anchovy.

To pickle fresh Herrings.—OUR country housewife says, its only washing them, and putting them into a barrel or glazed pot in layers or rows, with some salt between every layer. But I am sure it would be better done, if their heads were cut off, and then between every layer or row of herrings, a mixture put of bay-salt and salt-petre, till a glazed earthen pan is full, and baked in a very gentle heat of an oven.—In *Kent* they have a custom to give pickled sprats in their public houses to their customers (drinkers); and in *London* some do the same by pickled herrings, or rather baked ones, which by their reddish colour and agreeable taste please much.—But if you would be at a greater expence, after they are scaled, gutted and washed, you are to lay the herrings in a heap, and strew a little salt over them (as they do at *Dover*, for preparing them to dry over smoak in their herring hang-room, for making red-herrings of them, as I have seen done) to drain two or three hours their bloody part out. Then rub each herring dry between a cloth, and have ready a mixture of pepper, salt, cloves and ginger, a little shred onion and lemon-peel, for with this you are to sprinkle every layer of herrings, till the pan is full; and after you have put a pint and half of red wine over thirty herrings, and tied paper over the pot, bake them with bread.

The case of Mr. Glanville, *of* Edgware, *in the County of* Middlesex, *who was very near poisoned by eating Muscles.* THIS person being a great lover of this shell-fish, after he had eat a boiled parcel of them, began to be sick, and his sickness increased upon him to that degree, that he swelled so much, as not to be able to see out of his eyes. Upon this there were several medicines given him, but none of them did him any service, till at last, when he could hardly speak, he was heard to call for oil; they gave him some, till it made him vomit up the muscles, and at the same time anointed his body all over with oil, which had so quick an effect on him, that he was presently cured, and became a sound man. Now it was not the muscles (though at first thought so) that poison'd Mr. *Glanville*: No, it was a very little crab insect, that lodged in the open part of the muscle's body, and yet lies so hid, as not to be perceived by the eyes of the careless ignorant eater, for this crab insect is hardly bigger than a thetch or small pea; it has a round body (crab-like) and a broad tail, with its legs shaped like lobsters claws, as plainly appeared to me by the sight of one kept in spirits of wine, and so preserved by Mr. *Glanville*, to shew that which once had very near killed him.—To remark on this case, I have to add, that there are few muscles (as I am credibly informed) without one of these crabs in its body. And although it is common for people to take out what is called the beards before they eat them, yet most are ignorant of this poisonous insect. And if such an ingenious person as Mr. *Glanville* is, who seems to me to be possess'd of brighter parts than any other tradesman I ever conversed with, was through ignorance insnared to eat this dangerous crab, how much more easily will a more vulgar person eat a muscle without any suspicion of such a fatal quality harbouring in it, hence I am also led to observe the great carelessness and supine neglect of our *English* virtuosi, who study much the refined sublime parts of natural philosophy, and yet neglect numerous matters, to my knowledge, which ought to be made known to people, who for want of timely instruction may innocently eat poisonous things, and be killed by them.

A Woman poison'd by eating a roasted Duck.—Mrs. *Bell*, a *Cornish* woman, and wife of Mr. *James Bell*, that now keeps the fine *Green-Man-Inn* at *Gaddesden*, tells me that one Madam *Beazely* at *Falmouth*, about the year 1738, bought a duck in the market that was well fleshed. This she roasted, and when she had eaten her bellyful of it, she began to sicken and swell; upon which three doctors were sent for, but notwith-standing all the medicines they gave her, she continued swelling, and died in less than half an hour's time. Now, I suppose, the duck had swallowed a young toad, and that those who draw'd the duck might have broke the poisonous part of the toad in drawing; and not being wash'd before roasting, the poison might have had this fatal effect, for Mrs. *Bell* says, it was the doctor's opinion she was poisoned in this manner.

How a Hertfordshire *Woman, her Family, and a Hog, were poisoned by eating an Herb.*—In the hard frosty spring of 1740, a poor woman that lived at *Studham*, two miles distant from *Gaddesden*, gathered a herb that grew in a hedge, called Jack-jump-about, for boiling it with a piece of meat. It was like mint, and as hardly any other boiling herb was then to be got, she made use of this. One child died by it, and another had like to have had the same fate, and the mother narrowly escaped, but the hog that eat the pot-liquor was killed by it.

How two Buckinghamshire *Girls were poisoned by eating Henbane-root.*—At *Pitstone*, about three miles from *Gaddesden*, liveth a widow woman that holds a farm in her hands, who had three girls that one day took a fancy to dig up some henbane-roots that grew in and about the farm yard, and scraping one it appeared to them like a little white carrot; one of the girls refused to eat any of it, but the other two did, who in the night-time were taken so bad, that the mother thought them bewitch'd; at last, the healthy girl confess'd the matter, and discover'd how her two sisters had eat henbane-root, which made their mother send to *Leighton* for a doctor, who by proper medicines made shift to cure them; but he said, that if they had eaten and drank after it, he could not have cured them.

How a Man accustomed himself to cure his Tooth-ach with Henbane-seed.—THIS man named *Richards*, lying at *Rinxsell* near *Gaddesden*, when troubled with the tooth-ach would first put some tobacco into the bowl of a pipe, and some henbane-seed on that, then tobacco, then henbane-seed, till his pipe was full. This he smoaked, and declared it had such virtue as to make worms come out of his teeth, to the cure of the tooth-ach, for that time; for this man never smoaked, but when troubled with the tooth-ach, and then it was in this manner: And no wonder it thus effects a cure, since it is of a stupifying nature like tobacco. It grows in yards and dry ditches, and has pods that hold much small seed.

A School-boy poisoned by Vitriol.—A BOY that went to school at —— put a bit of vitriol into his mouth about the bigness of a nut, and suffered it to dissolve into his stomach; the consequence whereof was, that his chaps and belly swell'd, and he was poison'd to that degree as endanger'd his life; wherefore many schoolmasters will not suffer their scholars to lick a pen, because vitriol is a chief ingredient in the making of ink.

A Cow poisoned by eating Laurel-Leaves.—AT *Bovingdon*, five miles from *Gaddesden*, a gentleman had his laurel-hedge cut, and his cow having free access to it, eat what she would, but quickly swell'd and died.

A Man poison'd by eating a Toad.—IN the *London-Evening-Post* news-paper, dated *March* 26, 1741, there was inserted the following account, from *Salisbury*: Last night was buried at *Hinton*, near *Bradford*, in *Wiltshire*, one *James Silcock*, who being very much accustomed to eat horse-flesh and dog-flesh, and other disagreeable things, did undertake to eat a frog and a mole; after he had eat the mole, the person that undertook to provide the frog, by mistake brought a toad, which he having eaten, and swallowed a plenty of liquor, immediately died.

Several Persons poisoned by Poison laid for Rats.—DUBLIN, 26 *Novemb.* 1748, we hear from *Carlow*, of a very melancholy accident which happened there last week; one Mr. *Buttler* having mixed up poison with some oatmeal for the rats, a maid-servant, who was not acquainted with it, made use of it for breakfast; by which means two men, two maid-scrvants, and a child, were poisoned; one of the women died that night, and the other is despaired of, but the men and child will recover.

Rabbits poisoned by Hemlock.—THIS herb grows in meadows of the wetter sort, and other places; it has killed many tame rabbits by ignorant gatherers of it giving it them instead of dog-parsley, though it is easily known by its smell, for this has a stinking scent next to assafœtida, but in make very much like dog-parsley, that is excellent rabbit meat, for it will not pot a tame rabbit. Dr. *Quincy* says, at page 195, that this plant grows so much like common parsley, that it is difficult to distinguish it when young, therefore in all probability they have sometimes been gathered and sold together; for, says he, there have been many instances of persons, and sometimes whole families being suddenly taken ill, so as to occasion suspicion of poison, when they had reason to suspect it in the parsley, by having eat stuffed beef as is common, or some other food where that had been used. It first affects persons with giddiness and dimness of sight, and afterwards operates violently by vomit and stool; fat broths and oily liquids are the antidotes.

Of Poultry and their Eggs.

POULTRY and their eggs come more immediately under the care and management of our country housewife, than any other outward part of the farmer's business; and accordingly many farmers think it their interest to let their wives have all the profit of their eggs and poultry, for raising money to buy what we call common or trivial necessaries in the house, as sugar, plumbs, spices, salt, oatmeal, &c. &c. which piece of encouragement engages our housewife and her maid-servants to take special care of feeding her poultry in due time, setting her hens early, and making capons at a proper age.

The best Feed for Dunghill Fowls, to make them lay early Eggs, and many of them —Is horsebeans and hempseed. Of the first, a particular woman had such an opinion, that she preferred it to all others, and the rather as horsebeans in some wet summers grow in prodigious plenty, and are sold very cheap, sometimes for less than two shillings a bushel; hempseed indeed is dearer. As this last is furnished with much hot oil, as the horsebean is with a very hot quality, they both cause hens to lay in winter, when no other common seed can so well; but if hens were confined always in a room, it hinders very much their laying. The game hen lays most eggs, but they are commonly the least sort.

Sorts of Hens.—THE *Hertfordshire* dunghill fowls and their eggs have been in great esteem a long time, and at this time their eggs have the greater reputation of all others, insomuch that the very cryers of eggs about *London* streets take particular care to make the word *Hertfordshire* be well known; for our country is a Chiltern one, abounding with many hills, dry soils, gravelly rivers, plenty of most sorts of grain, and allow'd by professors of physick to be the healthiest air in *England*, all which undoubtedly contributes to the breeding of the best of eggs and soundest of dunghill fowls; a proof of which is very demonstrable, by the game cocks bred in *Hertfordshire*, that beat for the most part those bred in other counties. But I can't say our dunghill fowls exceed all others, for there are excellent sorts of the *Poland*, the *Hamburgh*, and the *Darking* dunghill fowls; the character of the last of which is hereafter inserted.

Of Hens sitting, and of Chickens and young Ducks.—THE game hen sits oftner than the dunghill hen, and will fight the hawk better in defence of her chickens: But as their legs are commonly as black as their feathers, few farmers keep them, because their blackish chickens will not sell like the white-leg'd dunghill sort. When a hen sits on her own eggs, she commonly hatches in three weeks, but when she sits on duck eggs, a month. If she has sat a week on duck eggs, and by accident the eggs are broke, or the hen too much disturbed, so that if she is set again on other duck eggs, she will not sit out her time; in such a case, if she is set again on the hen eggs, she will, because on these she sits a shorter time than on the duck eggs. A hen that sits beyond her time of three weeks seldom brings all her eggs to perfection, which is chiefly owing to her being set in a cold place, or going too far for her meat when off; but that is the best hen that hatches a day or two before the usual time. It is a fault to set a pullet with too many eggs. One was set with eighteen eggs, which she sat on well till the first chicken chirp'd, and then she was affrighted, ran away, and forsook the rest, so that our housewife could preserve but three, and for bringing them up she was forced to use more than ordinary care.—To have early chickens, an industrious housewife living at *Gaddesden* had a brood of chickens a fortnight old this 25th of *February* 1747-8; she set her hen in a chimney corner that had no fire near it, but on the back of the same chimney there was a daily one kept, which struck such a sufficient heat to the corner, as enabled the hen to sit close in this cold season, and hatch twelve chickens, which our housewife kept in this place, giving them offald wheat, that was screened at the mill from good wheat, and now and then some wetted pollard; with these the chickens went on well, and for eating up what the chickens and their hen left, our housewife let in a laying hen now and then, so that here was no waste made.

Dunghill Fowls, their Nature, by Mortimer.—THE oldest are best sitters, and the youngest best layers, but good for neither if kept too fat. To breed right chickens is, from two to five years old; the best month is *February*, and so any time between that and *Michaelmas* [here Mr. *Mortimer* is wrong, for when a hen begins to moult, she ought not to be set, because her chickens then seldom live.] A hen sits (says he) twenty days; geese, ducks, and turkeys, thirty; let them have always meat by them while they sit, that they may not straggle from their eggs and chill them. One cock will serve ten hens. If fowls are fed with buck-wheat, they will lay more eggs than ordinary, and the same with hempseed; the buck-wheat whole, or ground and made into paste, which is the best way: It is a grain that will fatten hogs or fowls speedily, but they are commonly fatten'd with barley-meal made into a paste with milk; but wheat-flower is better.—*Mortimer*, vol. I.

To fatten Hens, Pullets, Chickens, Capons, or Turkeys.— THEIR coops must be kept very clean, for all ill smells and nastiness is prejudicial to the fattening of fowls, as contributing towards giving their flesh a bad tang, and an unwholsome quality; to this purpose, they should have also two troughs, that one may be scalded and dried, while the other is in use, and both meat and water, or other liquor, should be kept from each other free of any mixture. As to their meat, there may be several sorts made; one by boiling barley till it is tender in water, another parcel of it in skim milk, another in strong ale; when so boiled, a little coarse sugar may be mixed with it. Or make a paste with barley-meal, and water or skim milk. And as to their drink, let them have strong ale or skim milk, or water wherein a little brickdust is mixed; for if they have not something to scower their maws or crops, they will not thrive to expectation, therefore if brickdust is not put into their drink, either a little of that, or fine sand, should be mixed with their meat now and then, to get them an appetite, and make them digest their food the quicker; the ale will intoxicate them, and cause them to sleep much and fatten the sooner, but the milk tends most to the whitening of their flesh. Now it wants no demonstration by argument, to prove that variety of meats forward the expeditious fattening of any animal; in this case, therefore, give any of these fowls these several sorts of foods alternately; so will they be creating them an appetite while they are fattening, to the making of them exceeding fat in a little time.

An ancient Author's Way to fatten Chickens.—BOIL (says he) bread in milk, as though they were to eat it, but make it thick of the bread, which slice into it in thin slices, not so thick as if it were to make a pudding; but so that when the bread is eaten out, there may some liquid milk remain for the chickens to drink; or that at first you may take up some liquid milk in a spoon, if you industriously avoid the bread; sweeten very well the pottage with good kitchen sugar of four-pence per pound, so put it into the trough before them; put therein but little at a time (two or three spoonfuls) that you may not clog them, and feed them five times a day, between their awaking in the morning and their roosting at night. Give them no other drink, the milk that remaineth after they have eaten the bread is sufficient, neither give them gravel or aught else; keep their coops very clean, as also their troughs, cleansing them well every morning. To half a dozen very little chickens, little bigger than blackbirds, an ordinary porringer full every day may serve, and in eight days they will be prodigiously fat. One penny loaf, and less than two quarts of milk, and about half a pound of sugar, will serve little ones the whole time; bigger chickens will require more, and two or three days longer time; when any of them are at their height of fat, you must eat them, for if they live longer, they will fall back and grow lean; be sure to make their pottage very sweet.—Or you may pound rice in a mortar till it is very small, and the smaller the better, for then it may be made into a paste with scalded milk and coarse sugar, which if given to chickens by a little at a time, so that they are not gorged, will fatten them in a very little time; let them have ale or good small beer to drink, and give their meat warm.—But there is a receit that directs the fattening of chickens with rice without pounding or grinding it, only to boil rice in milk till it be very tender and pulpy, as when you make milk-pottage; it must be thick, that a spoon may stand an end in it; sweeten this very well with ordinary sugar, and put it into their troughs where they feed, that they may be always eating of it; it must be made fresh every day; their drink must be only milk in another little trough by their meat-trough; let a candle (fitly disposed) stand by them all night for seeing their meat, for they will eat all night long. You put the chickens up as soon as they can feed of themselves, which will be within a day or two after they are hatched, and in twelve days or a fortnight they will be prodigiously fat; but after they are come to their height, they presently fall back, so that they must be eaten. Their pen or coop must be contrived so, that the hen (who must be with them to sit over them) may not go at liberty to eat their meat, but be kept to her own diet in a part of their coop that she cannot get out of; but the chickens must have liberty to go from her to other parts of the coop, where they may eat their own meat, and come in again to the hen to be warm'd by her at their pleasure. You must be careful to keep their coop very clean.—Or you may scald oatmeal in milk, and feed the chickens with it the first week, and rice and sugar the second week; in a fortnight they will be prodigiously fat; a little gravel will now be necessary sometimes to cleanse their maws and give them an appetite.

Sir Kenelm Digby's *Receit to make a luscious Food to fatten Chickens in the sweetest and quickest Manner.*—STONE (says he) a pound of raisins of the sun, and beat them in a mortar to pulp, pour a quart of milk upon them, and let them soak so all night; next morning put to them as many crums of grated stale bread, which beaten together will bring them to a soft paste; work all well together, and lay it in the trough before the chickens (which must be about six in a pen, and keep it very clean) and let a candle be by them all night. The delight of this meat will make them eat continually, and they will be so fat (when they are but of the bigness of blackbirds) that they will not be able to stand, but sit down upon their bellies to eat.

Gaddesden *Farmers Way to feed Chickens.*—NOTWITH-STANDING we live on a high hill, and on a red clayey soil, yet some of our farmers venture their early bred chickens abroad, and let them take their chance in going with the hen abroad from the first, even in *February* or *March*, though the weather is frost or snow; but then we take care to give them a hearty food, for enabling them to withstand the cold; and that is whole oatmeal and barley mixt together, which will so hearten them, that they will not kill themselves with chirping and pain, as those chickens are apt to do, that are fed with sloppy meat, such as wetted pollard, *&c.* And if the chickens should fall sick, we give each one sow-bug or wood-louse, and it often recovers it; but a hen as well as a chicken is killed by musty corn. The chicken is cured by the bug, or both the hen and chicken are sometimes cured by rue.—Butter and scouring-sand must be given a little in large pills or pellets.—For the same reason, put rue into the water the chickens drink, which will keep them in health, and from the cramp.

To make Capons.—THIS operation belongs to the country housewife. I know a yeoman living near *Hempstead* in *Hert-fordshire*, whose estate is but about fifty pounds a year, that makes (as it is credibly reported) fifteen pounds a year by the sale of capons; his wife and daughter cut the young dunghill cocks, but I don't suppose they were all bred on his farm, for some for this purpose make it their business after harvest-time to go to markets for buying up chickens, and between *Michaelmas* and *Allhollantide* caponize the cocks, when they have got large enough to have stones of such a bigness that they may be pulled out, for if they are too little, it can't be done; and to know when a cock is fit for it, he should be pretty well grown, have a good comb, and be well fleshed, for these signs shew they are bigger than those of leaner fowls. To cut them, the cock must lie on its back, and held fast, while with a very sharp knife she cuts him only skin-deep about an inch in length, between the rump and the end of the breast-bone, where the flesh is thinnest; next she makes use of a large needle to raise the flesh, for her safer cutting through it to avoid the guts, and making a cut here big enough to put her finger in, which she thrusts under the guts, and with it rakes or tears out the stone that lies nearest to it. This done, she performs the very same operation on the other side of the cock's body, and there takes out the other stone; then she stitches up the wounds, and lets the fowl go about as at other times, till the capon is fatted in a coop, which is commonly done from *Christmas* to *Candlemas*, and after. Now if the stones are but big enough, as they lie to the back, they may be safely taken out with a greased fore-finger, without much danger of killing the creature, but when they are too small there is danger. This way of caponizing a cock, I have had done at my house for my information, by a woman deemed to be one of our best capon cutters, else it would have been a difficult matter for me to give a description of it; for they that never saw such an operation, and venture at it, must expect to kill one or more, before he or she gets master of the science. And indeed it is for want of this knowledge that the art of caponizing fowls is not so much practised as formerly; but as I have given a pretty good account I hope of it, I am of opinion the art will be revived, and capons sold in greater plenty than ever.

The Character of the famous Darking *Dunghill Fowls.*

Kings-Head-Inn *at* Darking, Jan. 24*th*, 1747-8.

S I R,

I AM very glad to oblige you with the best account I can give of our fowls; they are large, and in general white-leg'd; they that are most curious of their breed chuse a cock all white, and the hen of a speckled mixture of feathers, but white leg'd, that making a stronger breed than both being white: They are all round us very careful of their feed, cramming them with fine ground down corn made in rolls and dipped in milk; they are received by all people as the finest of poultry that any place affords. *I am, Sir,*
    Your most humble Servant,
        BENJ. BARNSLEY.

Of the T U R K E Y

THIS is the largest tame land-fowl we have in *England*, and by many is preferred to others, if they are well fatted. There are two sorts of this species, the common *Suffolk* or *Norfolk* turkey, and the *Blue Virginia* sort: The first are bred in vast numbers in those two counties, from whence *London* is chiefly supplied with these excellent fowls, as appears by the many large droves of them, frequently seen on the roads thither. A turkey, sold at *Artleborough* near *Norwich* for fourteen-pence, at *Stratford* near *Bow* in *Essex* was sold for twenty-pence, so cheap are they in *Norfolk*; for here they have many dry sandy grounds, that produce abundance of turnips, barley, *&c.* which tend much to the growth of turkey poults. The other blue sort are of the flying kind, and will settle and roost on trees, yet may be kept as tame fowls, but they must have one wing cut, if they are to be hinder'd from flying, which is practised by some, and by others not, because some gentlemen delight in their flying behaviour; and where many of these sort are kept in parks, or other large inclosed grounds, a boy may attend them, and by the frequent use of a whistle, to call and invite them to a feed of corn now and then at a particular place, it will be a great means of naturalizing these turkeys to the part, and keep them from straggling too far from home; as it is practised in a nobleman's park, to my knowledge. One cock is enough to seven hens.

Of breeding Turkeys.—As they are of a more tender nature than most other tame fowls, they are somewhat difficult to rear, especially in a cold country, or on a wettish cold soil; in a warmer one, they may, if kept well, be made to tread twice a year; but few do this, but are contented with one brood only. They are commonly set with thirteen or fifteen eggs. The turkeys are very apt to lay their eggs in hedges, where they live near them, and sit abroad: But of this, our right sort of country housewives are aware, and take care to set them in a barn, hovel, or other large cover'd place; for to stint them of room, is prejudicial to this bulky body'd fowl in their hatching and bringing up their young. When the young turkeys are strong enough to be admitted abroad, they are liable to be hurt by several accidents, by hawks, pole-cats, nettles, &c. before they attain an age of security. A nettle will sting them to death, by making their head to swell, till they pine and die; therefore many good country housewives, to prevent this, where they have nettles grow near their houses, will before-hand pull them up.

To feed young Turkeys.—To a quart of pollard, put a hard egg, and as many leaves of wormwood as will make all green, both cut very small, and mixed with as much boiling milk as will make all into a soft paste; after young turkeys have been fed with bread and milk one or two days, feed them with this paste for a week, it will keep them alive. And if you will feed them with scalded bran for a month afterwards, they will shift for themselves bravely, when otherwise they often die very young. But there are several other sorts of food that some give young turkeys, till they are big enough to range for a living abroad, as fennel, curds, &c. But in dry sandy grounds, they are certainly brought up in the cheapest manner, because in this loose earth they easily find and pick up seeds of weeds and corn, worms and other insects; and as they in particular love to stock their craws with particles of sand, here they have it in plenty. Some spring seasons of weather are attended with so much cold and wet as destroys many broods of young turkeys, notwithstanding all the care that has been made use of.

Of fattening old Turkeys.—A TURKEY is not to be fatted like a dunghill fowl; if we fat them by crams, we mix barley-meal with pollard and water, with which we make pellets or crams, and put as many down the turkey's throat as it can well take in, every morning, for three weeks or a month, and turn him loose all the rest of the day. This we commonly begin to do before *Christmas*, that the turkeys may be fatted for a market or a friend. Barley-meal crams dipt in milk make their flesh appear the whiter.

A further Account of the Breeding and Feeding of Turkeys.— THESE fowls are bred by some farmers as the most profitable sort; others reject them for their troublesome breeding up, and being too great devourers of corn. One author observes, that when they have a large range of liberty they will feed on herbs, and seeds of herbs, without trouble or charge, except in breeding and fattening time, and then they require very careful attendance, as they are a tender chilly fowl; that where they have a wood or grove near a house, the hen turkey will seek her nest abroad, conceal it from the cock, and bring up her brood with more success than the more tame; that they seldom fatten before winter be well spent, when they forget their lust; that the cold weather gets them a stomach, and the long nights afford them much rest; and observes, that the whitish or light colour'd turkeys are much better meat than the blacker sort, but withal, that they are more tender in their nursing up; when young turkeys are hatched, to give them a pepper-corn, one corn with a little milk to each turkey poult, as being a great preservative against the cramp, which these fowls more than ordinarily are subject to suffer by; that an egg boiled till hard, and chopt small with wormwood or cloves, is a good first food for warming their bodies and creating an appetite, and so is cheese-curds and wormwood. They should be kept from rain while they are very young, in shelter till a warm day, and then they may be brought out in the middle of it for an hour or two, under a coop, at about a week old; and so on, longer and longer, till they can shift for themselves without the hen. It is reported, that a turkey may be improved in bulk and goodness of flesh by castration; and I think, that if the eggs of the bustard were search'd for in *April*, and set under turkeys, they might be brought up as tame as dunghill fowls. But of this most noble fowl the bustard, more is designed to be wrote, when I publish my *Treasure of new Discoveries in the Improvements of Instrumental Husbandry, &c.* In short, as the turkey for its large body and delicate flesh is kept by many farmers and gentlemen, and that the chief art of breeding them lies in their right managing of the poults, I have further to add, that if they are timely fed with a proper food, and kept under cover for the first four or five weeks from rain, slugs, or snails, that are apt to scour and kill them, and a turf of grass every day given them, there needs little care in their attendance afterwards. And if they are bred near oak or beech trees, their mast in a plentiful year will fatten them without any other meat, as is often seen by those turkeys bred on *Gaddesden-Hill*, and fed amongst our many beech trees, that are of the largest sort in *England*.

Of DUCKS.

THE Profit of keeping Ducks.—THE duck is not fit to be kept where there is but little water in ponds or ditches, for if there is but little, they mud and spoil it for kitchen uses, and for watering of cattle; but they are certainly very profitable where there are good conveniencies for keeping them, because they run up in growth very fast for an early market, eat up the weeds on waters, devour spawn and young frogs, caterpillars, slugs, and snails, *&c.* return downy feathers, live cheap, and when fatted under confinement, with a pure meat, they are dainty food for the nicest palates; where there is a river or a springy moor, they will get three parts of their living abroad.

Of the several Sorts of Ducks kept in England.—THE common white duck is preferred by some, by others the crook-bill duck, some again keep the largest of all ducks, the *Muscovy* sort; but the gentry of late have fell into such a good opinion of the *Normandy* sort, that they are highly esteemed for their full body and delicate flesh; they are very great devourers of grain, insomuch that if they were wholly to be maintained on it, it must cost a person many times more than ducks are sold for at the poulterer's shop. A good parcel of ducks will do great service in a turnip or rape field, where they are seized by the black caterpillar, and so will a turkey or a goose, for all these fowls are very greedy of such insects, and accordingly have proved a cure, when no other applications could.

Of breeding Ducks.—ONE drake will serve for near twenty ducks. In the hardest weather, one quart of barley will be sufficient to feed ten or twelve ducks one day; however, the better they are fed the more eggs they'll lay, and so fed they'll lay abundance at intervals of time, beginning after moulting time about *Allhollantide* or about *Christmas*. Those who have no duck eggs of their own seek out to buy some, for having them in readiness to set the first broody dunghill hen, that they may have the earliest ducklings to market, for when they are very early sold, they may fetch eighteen pence apiece, in *February*; but then such an early brood must be kept in a house, unless the weather is very mild indeed; and for their first meat, it should be a very hearty sort, made with bread and milk, and pollard mixt together; so that in breeding ducks, the dunghill hen, which commonly sits first, and keeps house better than ducks, becomes very serviceable, and thus there is the greater opportunity to enjoy a brood of ducks both by the hen and the duck's sitting, and of bringing up the more young ones. On this account many farmers sell their duck eggs to a good advantage. Our Vale farmers wives duly observe to dip the bills or beaks of the ducklings as soon as they are hatch'd in milk, and where they make cheese to give them curd.

Of *G E E S E.*

S ORTS *of Geese.*—THERE are several sorts of *English* tame geese, some smaller bodied than others, but the largest and finest sort that I ever saw was at Sir *Jeremy Sambrook's*, at his seat near *Northaw* Common; but that truly honourable and very worthy gentleman, Sir *John Rawdon*, shewed me, at his seat near *Brentwood, Essex* (when I carried to him fourteen young tame pheasants) a breed between the *English* and *Portugal* sort, which he prefer'd for their good qualities.

Geese sitting and hatching.—THIS business comes in particular under the country housewife's inspection, and for managing it to profit, she should feed her geese well betimes, even from *Christmas*, that they may lay early eggs, and enough of them for setting her geese in *February* or *March* at farthest, and therefore some oats ought to be given them or other corn, or wetted bran or pollard, besides what food they get abroad; coleworts raw or scalded, or turneps boiled and bran mix'd, or raw carrots chopt small, or guts and garbage will very much contribute to their laying and sitting betimes, that their goslings or green geese may come to an early market for fetching the best price; feed them in the out-house they are to lay and sit in, for naturalizing them to the place; provide them wheat or other straw, and make them a nest with it as far off the company of other geese as conveniently can be, and as a goose sits about a month let her have water and gravel constantly by her, and meat in due time; set her on her own eggs, for it is thought by some that her knowledge extends as far as this, to approve of, and sit better on her own than those of other geese. And that if a dunghill large hen is broody first, it is profitable to set her with five or six goose eggs; but this is very seldom done, because a goose well fed will lay and sit early enough, and cover thirteen or fifteen eggs. The goose having hatch'd, if the weather is severely cold or wet, she and her brood should be kept in till the goslings get older and heartier, by giving them at first bread, bran, pollard, yetted barley, or other corn scalded in milk, with chopt clivers, lettice, cole-worts, or turnips boiled to a mash, with bran or pollard mixt with them, or minced raw carrots amongst it, till after a week or more that they can eat buck-wheat, barley, oats, or other raw corn, and shift for themselves. Likewise be sure to put fennel in all their water. Thus the goslings may be prevented having the cramp or other illness, which, for want of a careful and right management at first, sometimes kills them; and for their greater security, let them go and be kept out a little at a time, till they are able to endure the weather, and preserve them from eating musty corn, from the kite, from the pole-cat, and *Baltick* rat, from hemlock, henbane, and other poisonous herbs by land, and from the pike or large jacks in water, for that all these are enemies to young ducks and goslings.

The Loss and Profit of keeping Geese.—THEY are not fit to be kept where there is a scarcity of water, but only where there is much pond water, or near a river, or on a common. Here geese may pay better than any other tame fowl; because they are great devourers (hog like) of meat, and bite grass rather closer to the ground than a sheep, and therefore their keeping is disallowed of on many commons; but where they have plenty of water, grass, and weeds, they'll live and thrive with very little expence all the year, except in feeding time for laying eggs, in sitting time, and in bringing up their young. Then it is that some geese-owners buy oats or other meat, as those do who live on *Box-Moor* near *Hempstead*, to whom I have sold oats for this purpose; but for the rest of the year, the old geese are very little expensive. A goose, it is said, may live forty or fifty years, as has been proved; and although she is very old when she comes fat out of the stubbles, yet her body being furnished on a sudden with new flesh, she may eat to satisfaction: Which leads me to observe, that notwithstanding it is the custom of many farmers in *Hertfordshire* and elsewhere, to fatten geese chiefly in stubbles, yet it is the custom of many others to sell them lean, as may every year be seen by the great droves of such geese travelling towards *London*, from *Flag-hundred* near *Yarmouth*, in *Norfolk*. In one drove there were fourteen hundred sold at *Stratford* in *Essex*, for twenty-pence a piece, to fatten for the *London* poulterers. If geese are fatted in stubbles, when they are brought home every night, they should have some pollard or bran mixt with skim milk, broth, or water, or corn soaked and given them in water; but in a morning they should eat nothing before they are drove to the field, because they'll search for their meat with the greater diligence. Again, in case geese are to be fatted altogether in a house, that house is best for this purpose that has the least light, and is farthest off the noise of other geese. There are several sorts of meat to fatten them with, as *French* wheat just broke at the mill and given in water, or the flower of it made into a pap or paste is a great fattener; so is ground malt mixt with pollard and given them in water, or barley-meal wetted into a thin paste; but let the meat be what it will, they must always have a pan of water by them, wherein is some gravel or sand; and if with any of these meats, some coleworts, lettice, or clivers are given besides, it will increase their appetite, and cause them to fatten apace, in a fortnight or three weeks time; for goslings especially are such extream lovers of lettice and coleworts, that they'll almost fatten upon them alone, and so they will on carrots cut small, or on turneps boiled to a mash and mixt with pollard, which is the cheapest meat they can be fatted with. A goose is easier brought up than a turkey, for a turkey, when as big as a pigeon, may bc stung to death by a nettle.

Eighteen Goslings killed and carried away in one Night's Time by a Polecat.—A Man who lives on *Box-Moor*, near *Hempstead*, had eighteen goslings carried away in one night; and believing they were carried away by a polecat, diligently searched amongst the hedges to find his hole, but finding none, they proceeded to search about a bay of hay in a barn, and perceiving a hole, they cut down into it, and there found a polecat lying in the midst of it, with most of the dead goslings, for which they had only the satisfaction of killing him.

Of SWANS.

*T*HE *Pleasure and Profit of keeping Swans.*—SWANS are stately beautiful birds, and are said to be a very proud, but chaste fowl; and are so sensible of affronts, that I have often seen a cock swan scare both women and children in wing-running after them. They are chiefly kept by gentlemen, who regard them more for fancy than profit; not but they will pay indifferently well, if kept under a right management in large ponds or in a river. Nor will they leave the place if pinion'd, but keep strictly to it, even if it be only a pond of no great compass, as has been seen in *Ashridge-Park*, for some years, in the time of *Scroop* the late Duke of *Bridgewater*; but if they go unpinion'd, they are apt to take flights, tho' they seldom entirely forsake their first habitation. They are a very hardy bird, and are not devourers of fish to any great damage, for they never dive deep, hardly ever farther than their necks will reach, so that they can only take a few of the smallest fish. And as to the expence of their maintainance, what they get in and about the water, and the grass that grows on the land contiguous to the pond or river, with a few oats now and then, will suffice, except in a hard frost, when they are deprived of the benefit of water; then, indeed, they must have a greater allowance of oats. The young swans, called cignets, if fatted, are a dainty dish, and eat excellently well in a pye, provided they have not exceeded two years of age. Their long neck, broad feet, and broad bill, are necessary; their neck to reach, and their broad mouth to take up much slime at once, in order to take up worms and other insects from the bottom of ponds; the upper part of their bill is pierced, in order to discharge the water.

Of Breeding Swans.—SWANS make their nest with flags or rushes, which they build on the water, amongst flags, to a very great bulk; here they generally lay their eggs, in *March*, to the number of four, five, or six, and then sit on them for seven or eight weeks before they hatch; in which time, as their nest is always pretty near the shoar, they must have oats given them. When they have hatch'd, the young swans have nothing given them besides what the old swan provides, which are flies, worms, or other insects, weeds and grass, carrying them now and then on her back, and so will the cock swan, and provide his share for them; but after three weeks age, the cignets will eat oats, which are placed in a trough fix'd in the water about two foot from the land, to which both old and young have always free access; and now it is that the cock swan is most furious at spectators, as being very jealous of his mate, and fond of her brood. Where there is not good room in a pond for their large nest, or conveniency to make one with flags or rushes, grass, straw, and such like stuff must be laid near the edge of the water, on the land, and the swan will, if not much disturbed, lay her eggs in a nest she builds there.

How to fatten Swans.—TO fatten these large water fowls, they must not be totally deprived of water, and therefore for accommodating them in the most natural manner, stakes must be drove into the ground round a place in the water, by the shore-side, and on part of the contiguous land; so that one half must be land and the other half water, that is to be thus inclosed for about half a pole square, that the swans may have liberty allowed them enough to be on either. Here the cignets, or old swans that are to be fatted, must be confined to feed on oats, and nothing else, and if well supplied with them, they will fatten in three weeks or a month at farthest. Swans are of a dunnish colour for the first year; but before the second is over, they will be perfectly white. Then the cock may be partly known from the hen, by the larger comb, neck, and legs. About *Michaelmas* time they should be pinion'd, and for doing it safely a person should have some fore-hand knowledge of it, and not venture at random, lest he kill them by being an ignorant operator, as one I know did, who was thus the death of four young swans out of six; therefore observe the following method.

Pinioning a Swan.—MR. *Bradley*, in his *Farmer's Monthly Director*, page 132. (sold by Mr. *Brown*, at the *Black-Swan*, without *Temple-Bar*, *London*) says, That the feathers must be pick'd clean round the first joint of one wing, then take a strong pack-thread, and knit hard enough round the place, a little below the joint, to stop the bleeding, when the pinion is cut off with a very sharp knife. For doing this, the month of September is a good time.

Of E G G S.

HOW to preserve Eggs sound.—DR. *Godfrey* in his book says, That eggs have been laid under a running water, and after two years lying in the same have been found perfectly sound for eating, and breeding of chickens. He also further says, that if eggs are covered with a proper varnish they will hold sound a year, as has been proved by putting them under a hen that produced chickens; for by these means the air is kept from entering their shells, and so are preserved from rottenness.

A second Way to preserve Eggs sound.—THIS is done by the art of packing them in a wicker-basket, hamper, or cask, for if you place their large ends downwards, they will keep sound two or three months. The reason for this is, when you place them the reverse way, the air has a greater contact with the wind-bladder in the large end of the egg, so as to waste and exhaust it much the sooner thro' the pores of the shell, for as this wind-bladder (which supports and helps to keep the yolk from sinking and running amongst the white) becomes more or less damaged, so will the egg be in proportion.

A third Way.—WHEN you pack eggs for carriage or keeping some time, always set their broad ends downwards, and between every layer of them put straw, and keep them out of the power of cold air, that it may not freeze them; therefore reserve the hamper, basket, or cask, in a warm room in winter, and in summer in a cellar. The broad ends of the eggs, which are porous, have a thick skin, which the egg feeds upon while it lies in this posture; but when the eggs lie long ways, there is little else but skin, and when that is fed on, and eat up by the rest of the egg, the egg begins to rot. It is also observable, that the chick's bill lies next the bottom, and here through the little holes it fetches its breath. Now if these little holes lie uppermost, the air has the more power to enter and spoil the egg.

A fourth Way.—A farmer's wife, to save her eggs in a cheap time against a dear one, used to put them on wire or other sieves, or on other bottoms, and by laying them thus, she turned the eggs once every week, from *August* till towards *Christmas*, in imitation of the common higlers way, who, when they meet with a disappointment of sale, turn their pack'd-up eggs in a hamper bottom upwards, and by so doing once a week, they will keep sound four or five weeks.

Rotten Eggs sold knowingly.—IT is too often practised by some farmers wives, to save their eggs from harvest-time to sell near *Christmas*, and though many be rotten, yet they will sell them as sound ones if they can, though they know them to be rotten. Therefore,

To know rotten Eggs.—WHEN they are rotten, on holding them against a fire, candle, or the sun, they appear of a dirty or blackish colour.

Hertfordshire *Eggs.*—WE generally are so careful of sending clean eggs to *London*, that when we find any of them sully'd, we put them for a minute in warm water, and rub them with scouring sand; then lay them on a cloth, and they presently dry.

The D A I R Y.

*T*HE *Benefits of making use of a brass Skimming-dish.*—IN my way home from *Sussex*, on the 15th day of *June*, 1749, I rode along with a grazier, that lives near *Towcester* in *Northamptonshire*, who informed me he had lost sixty horned beasts by the reigning murrain distemper; nine of which number died this last spring. He says, he received eighty pounds from the King for forty of them; that he now keeps forty cows for carrying on a butter dairy, and sells his butter all the year, at a *London* market, for seven-pence a pound in winter, and six-pence in summer. He says, there is sold at some shops a brass skimmer for milk, about the bigness of a common wooden skimming-dish; this, he says, takes the cream away right, because it lets the milk through its little holes, and retains the cream. But he says it must be done exceeding quick, by putting the cream into a porringer or pan, which is to be held by the other hand, lest the cream pass also through the holes. This, says he, is an improvement; for by discharging the milk from the cream, the butter will keep sweet the longer, be better tasted and firmer, milk being weaker than cream. Thus the purest cream may be gathered for making the very best of butter, far exceeding the old common way of blowing off the cream in the skimming-dish with the mouth, which does it less cleanly, and less free of the milk. But, say some, the more milk the more butter; true, but then that butter is so much the worse, as there is milk mixt with the cream. This also proves the setting of milk over embers for scalding it, and thereby raising a clouted cream, to be much more profitable than to wait the taking cream off cold milk, because the clouted cream is easily taken neat and intirely off the milk, without a mixture of it, at once.

The Nature of what the Dairymen call Second-butter, by which may be discovered how ignorant Persons are imposed on that buy Butter.—THIS great dairyman says, That to make the first and best butter, his wife skims every 12 hours in summer, and forbears to do the same but a little longer in winter, and thus skims twice for making this prime, best butter: And for making a second butter, she likewise generally skims the same milk twice at every 12 hours end. By this method, he says, his wife gets cream enough to make a dozen pounds of this second butter, after 12 or 13 dozen pounds are made of the first butter from the same milk. Now this second or back butter is worth but very little more than half the value of the first prime butter: Yet our *London* butter-woman-seller sells it all alike, for one and the same price, either to ignorant buyers, or to those who are more knowing, who, by being in her books, dare not dispute the badness of this butter. And that for informing this butter-seller, he tells me, that leaves, or some other mark is laid to this second butter, for preventing a mistake, lest unwarily she sells the worst butter for the best to her best customers.— If he skims so often in summer, he must have a very cold dairy-cellar indeed, for these several skimmings are not in common practice.

Whey Butter.—HE tells me they can skim their whey but once at 12 hours end. This whey-cream, he says, makes worse butter than the skim-milk second or back butter, for it will not keep, and presently eats rankish. I must confess that the square, leaden, milk-coolers in a cellar will very much contribute to the keeping of milk sweet a long time, which he tells me that he uses altogether, else I cannot understand how he can skim so often, and yet get such sweet butter as to hold good in summer time to *London*, after it has been drawn in a waggon about fifty miles.

How in the Management of a Vale Great Dairy they get their Fewel, and keep their Cows from having the red Water, or pissing of Blood.—IN *Buckingham*, *Bedford*, and *Northampton* shires there are many great cheese and butter dairies carry'd on, without so much as an acre of plow'd ground, who have only a dwelling-house and one or two calf-houses belonging to them. In such a grasing farm they perhaps keep forty, fifty, or sixty cows, and always milk them abroad summer and winter, and if snows fall deep, they fodder, and sit on a stool in the snow to milk. And when a calf falls, it is housed, and the cow kept in a night or two, but they quickly sell off the calf for employing the milk to make butter or cheese. Here many have few or no hedges, but part their grounds by rails, banks, or ditches, which constrains them to get cow-dung, and cut (if there be any) scrubbed black-thorn or gorze, for two reasons, one is for fewel against winter, the other is to prevent their cows cropping the young shoots of these vegetables; for if they are let to grow any thing long, they are apt to cause cows to piss bloody water. Fewel being thus scarce, they go with a cart or wheel-barrow, and take up cow-dung soft or hard, and continue doing this at times all the summer, for getting good store of it against a long winter, and for relieving the ground from a cover of it; for if cow-dung is let alone, it will grow hard, and kill the grass underneath it; for this dung, though very soft at first, will harden to that degree, as not to be washed away by rains for a year or more. Now the value of this cow-dung does not end here, for after it is burnt, by way of kitchen-fewel, the ashes of it are excellent to dress their grasing grounds, and therefore the poor people sell them to the grasing farmers for a crown a cart-load.—If your cow should piss bloody water; you may give the following medicine:

To stop bloody Water piss'd by a Cow.—TAKE pennygrass, scabious, and camomile, a little of each, a few cloves bruised, or some cinnamon; boil these in a quart of old verjuice; give a pint of this warm to a cow fasting out of a horn; if it does not answer at first, renew it three or four mornings.—But for four other receits to cure this malady, see my *Modern Husbandman*, sold by Mr. *Thomas Osborne*, in *Gray's-Inn, London*.

The good and bad Properties of Cows.—A BOOK entitled *The Country Housewife*, without an account in it of the advantages that cows may yield, and how such advantages may be acquired, would, in my opinion, render me a preposterous author, and be a tacit declaration I was never owner of a cow; or if I was, that I knew not how to write of her qualities, which is perfectly necessary in the work I have here undertaken; for cows are certainly the most useful beasts belonging to a country-house, because at gentlemen's country-houses and at farms, their produce of milk, cream, butter, cheese, and the management of them, generally belongs to and comes under the woman's province; wherefore their qualities ought to be enumerated. Yet so necessary as this is, many of them have slipt the notice of most authors; therefore as I am an owner of cows, and find them pay me well, by their enabling me to make butter or cheese, or for suckling calves for the butcher, especially in the summer vacation time, while my crops of corn, grass, fruit, and wood are growing, I have to say that that cow is a very valuable one that gives 4 gallons of milk in one day, in her prosperity; though I have heard of a cow, thought to be worth ten pounds, that gave five gallons a day, in the months of *May* or *June*, on a full bite of grass, and continued giving milk till near her calving (but I say, it is a good cow that gives three gallons a day) while some others go dry two or three months: She was a healthful one, hardy, gentle, and easy

(233)

milked. Such a cow as this deserves to have her breed increased; for where one cow merits this character, there are twenty that do not. I have one cow, and she is of the *Holderness* breed, that would give milk almost to her calving; but this no prudent farmer will suffer, because it would surely damage himself and her; for it is well known to us cow-keepers, that although it is a common braggadocio saying with some sellers of cows, that she'll give milk till she calves, yet I am sure, if this is allowed, it will not only reduce the cow's flesh and make her lean, but cause her to bring a very small calf. However, I knew a farmer at *Eaton* in *Bedfordshire*, that was perswaded, by the ignorant sort, a cow would not be the worse if she milked within a week or fortnight of her time, and he took their advice; the cons[e]quence of which was, it sunk the cow's flesh, caused her to bring a very small calf, and made her give a very little parcel of milk for some time after: Whereas had the same cow been dried a month or better before her calving, she might very probably have kept herself in good flesh, brought forth a large calf almost half fat, and have given a large quantity of milk besides. This is now so well known among judicious experienced dairy farmers, that there are few or none but what observe to dry their cows a month, before calving, if they don't dry of themselves; as many do, for there are some sort of cows, especially the red sort, that give the most milk for a time, and then they'll dry of themselves within two or three months of their calving. And it is this sort therefore that bring the larger and fattest calves, and give the greatest quantity of milk, till they thus dry of themselves: For the same reasons, when a cow is wanting of this quality by nature, the drying of her in due time should be forced; a case contrary to the notion of a late famous author, who, in his *General Treatise on Husbandry*, has these words—"Nor can I find any reason, why the black cattle, which are thus constantly in milk should not bring a well-grown calf; for seeing how moderately they dispense their milk at each meal, we may reasonable infer, that they give only what nature allots them to spare from their nourishment, and rather seems to be a necessary discharge of juices than any inconvenience, either to the cow, or the calf she is pregnant with. For in such a case, the calf will naturally draw to itself from the mother what juices are necessary for its support, and if it required more than the cow could conveniently furnish, the cow must then necessarily languish, and as surely lose her milk, so that while we find milk in a cow, we cannot reasonably suppose, that either the cow or calf want nourishment." Thus far this author.—Next, I have further to observe, that to have a right sort of cow, either of the red or black sort, she should be thin-skin'd, taper-headed, slender-neck'd, low-leg'd, well-shoulder'd, smallish teats, with a round thin-leather'd bag, in refusal of those cows that are furnish'd with parts of a different make and shape.

How to milk an unlucky Cow and prevent her Mischief.—As insignificant an article as this at first may seem to appear, I am sure there are thousands that stand in need of its information. In *Cheshire* and many other places the milk-maid wears a black hat, partly because she is obliged to push and hold her head hard against the cow's flank, to discourage her from kicking the pail of milk down, for such pressure somewhat diverts the motion, because as the maid pushes her head hard against the cow, the cow naturally leans her body hard against the maid's head, by which she can feel the cow's intent to strike, and so take away her pail in time; yet I call this only discouraging, for it will not always prevent it, for some cows will kick to that degree, that they must have their legs fetter'd, by tying them above the hind middle joints. Others again are so unlucky, that to prevent the damage of their kicking, they must be milked through a hurdle. Of this sort are many of the *Holderness* breed, that have large bodies, short horns, taper-headed and necked, thin-skin'd, and give a great deal of milk, but are very apt to kick, break through hedges, and leap over gates and stiles. And when they are so very mischievous, as some of them are with both head and heels, they are better parted from than kept; if kept, the milk that is got from them must be by only milking a single teat or dug at a time into a pint wooden or earthen dish or bowl, and that in such danger, as makes it perhaps not worth while to keep her. But this is not all the mischief that belongs to an unlucky cow, for many of these kickers are very apt and prone to buck other cows, spoil their bag (as I have known an instance of) and sometimes the calf in the cow's belly; for which last reasons, all cows should have wooden tips fastened to the end of their horns, to prevent the great danger that weak and underline cows are liable to suffer by those we call master cows; for woeful experience has given us many deplorable cases of mischief done by cows horns to men, women, children, and beasts. Therefore I have always every one of my cows horns thus served, whether they be of the unlucky or the gentle sort; for although a cow may be gentle at other times, yet when she has a calf by her, there is danger in feeding, milking, and suckling her. The next thing I have to advance is, that if the maid milk cross-teated, that is to say, if she milks a backward dug of the further side with the forward dug of the hither side, it is thought the cow is not so prone to kick, as if milked by the next two side dugs, but that she'll give her milk down the freer for it. And indeed, this cross-milking is both easier for the cow and the milker. Again, it is the necessitous case of many farmers to feed their cows at a considerable distance from the house, in summer-time especially, which travel brings a beast under great heat and pain, with their full bags of milk; therefore cross-teat-milking is here a beneficial service, because it discharges the milk from both sides the bag in equal quantities, and thereby cools, eases, and refreshes the cow at once. It is likewise to be observed as a material point in milking of cows, and which is the custom of some dairies, that after all the cows are milked, the milker begins again to milk, or what we call drip that cow which was first begun with, and so on, dripping every one of the rest.

One intent of which is to prevent milk being left in the bag; for some of the idle sort of milkers are frequently guilty of this, and then it greatly damages the beast, and prejudices its owner, by lessening the after quantities of milk, and drying the cow the sooner. A second intention is, that by thus dripping or milking a cow over again, that cow which held up some of her milk the first time, may give it all down at the second milking. A third intention is, that by this dripping of cows, there will be got what we call stroakings, which being little inferior to cream may be added to it and increase its quantity. But for performing this with judgment, it is hardly worth while to do it, where there are but few cows kept, and where there are many there should be more hands than ordinary to dispatch the dripping, else the cows may be obliged to stay too long from feeding, and their bags or udders replenished with new milk, to the lessening of the next meal. Again I have to observe, that a slow milker damages a cow, by lessening her milk; when one that milks briskly, and is used to milk her, preserves her milk in good order. And for her longer continuance in plenty of milk, that cow that calves in *April* or *May* stands the best chance for it, because the first spring of grass meets her; and although some of the small *Welsh* cows will live on a shorter bite of grass, and are hardier than the larger sort, yet their carcases are of the less value to fatten. Therefore where there is meat enough for a large beast, I am of opinion, they'll pay more than a smaller one, because when they go guest and have done milking, and are fatted for the butcher, their price will be large accordingly, as I have proved, by fattening my own cows abroad and at home.

The kicking Cow.—THERE are many cows brought under very ill behaviour, by means of a young ignorant milker, who, because the cow don't just please her, rashly strikes or scolds at her, when a gentle behaviour would incite the same in a beast, witness what some cows are brought to by the like. I have seen more than one cow led by a string in the hand of a boy or girl, for the better confining the cow to feed on common field ground between corn lands; and it may be depended on as a true maxim, that if a cow can't be broke of her ill tricks by fair means, it can never be done by foul.

How to hinder a Cow from holding up her Milk.—FOR this there have been several devices made use of: As first to twist a rope hard about the cow's body while she is milking: Secondly, to fling cold water over the loins, and then directly to milk her: But this should be done for several days: Or if the cow is to be suckled, milk her first, and let the calf draw away the rest, for a cow will (or is forced to) give it a calf, when she will not to a milker.—Or to make her less regard holding up her milk, let her have hay or other meat before her while she is milking.

The Life of a Cow saved by the Care of a Servant-Maid.— IT was the maid-servant of a very small farmer, who kept but one cow in all (but of so kind a breed as to give milk enough to supply his house, and some to sell besides.) And thus this cow became part of the poor man's bread. Now it happened that as the farmer had but little ground, and that under crops of grain, he was necessitated to turn this his cow into the high-ways, to pick up and get a living as well as she could, without any mistrust of her doing ill by eating what she could find; but so it was, that in being thus sharp set to get a living she was obliged to eat nettles, and by custom she came to love and eat them so greedily, that at last she hoved and swell'd with them, as if she had eaten clover-grass. This being perceived by the maid-servant (for no body was at home but her) she in all haste drove the cow towards the farrier's shop, which was about half a mile off, and in driving her she dropt down by the way, and became such a sight as brought the neighbours about her; some of whom advised the maid to send in all haste for some gin and pepper. And by giving her a penny-worth of pepper in half a pint of gin, the cow immediately discharged abundance of wind (which was the cause of the malady) and perfectly recover'd on the eleventh day of *June*, when the nettles were in their greatest rankness of sap; but for an antidote against such destructive accidents, our country housewife should endeavour to have the following remedy given to each cow at its first turning into clover, rapes, turneps, or into any other dangerous feeding.

Of Antidotes for preventing the hoving or swelling of Cows while they Feed on Clover, Rapes, Turneps, &c.—CLOVER, rapes, and turnep-tops, are accounted the three worst sorts of vegetables for causing cows to hove, swell, and die: Therefore it is of great importance to endeavour a security against their fatal effects, and how to do it deserves the notice of all such whose beasts are liable to these accidents. In some vales indeed, where they sow no clover, rapes, or turneps, they are in no danger of this fatal malady: But in chiltern countries where they are, none ought to be without the knowledge of the following ingredients: When a cow first goes into clover, rapes, or turneps, *&c.* let one man hold her by the horn, while another takes hold of her tongue, and thrust down her throat an egg-shell full of tar, then let her go.—Or you may cut off the head, tail, and fins of a red-herring, and dip it in tar for giving it as before.—Or you may give the cow a belly full of good hay just before she goes into clover, and if she is kept in every night on hay, and turned out every morning, it will be a greater security.—A tar and hay preparation is what I generally every year observe to make use of, when I put my cows to feed on any of these hoving vegetables, lest I suffer as an old farmer did, who being necessitated to turn his cow to grass, put them into a field of clover on the 31st of *March*, 1740, and lost the best of them, for she quickly swelled, hoved, and died after being turned into it; and yet this old farmer is justly accounted an acute one as any is in our parts for his management in the old way of farming, but as to any new way he is averse to it, because he can't give credit to what his forefathers never knew nor practised: But this he might have known, that clover, though short at its first bite, is full of sap (as this was) and therefore very windy, and the more apt to swell a beast, as I have found by many trials.

How a Cow's Life was saved that was hoved in Clover, when internal Remedies failed, shewn by a Case of my Neighbour's Cow.—A Cow that was hoved and swelled in feeding on clover-grass fell down and must have died, had not an accidental stander-by stabbed her with his pointed pocket-knife; for he had learned that such a method was the lest thing that could be done to a hove cow past any other remedy, and that it was safe stabbing her in the paunch clear of her kidneys, as it proved by this fact; for as soon as he had stabbed her, out came dung and wind in a very violent manner. Upon which they directly tarred the wound, and cover'd it with a plaister of common pitch, to the entire curing of her.

The best Remedy perhaps that ever was found out for curing Cows of the Murrain; or a famous Cure made on a Butcher's Cow, that was seized with the Murrain Distemper at Little-Gaddesden.—On the 28th of *November* 1746, Mr. *Edward Thorne*, a butcher at *Little-Gaddesden*, bought two fat cows to kill (for about this time they were very cheap, because many beasts were sold in apprehension that the fatal malady would seize and kill them, which at this time raged in *Buckingham-shire, Bedfordshire*, and in some other adjacent counties) but finding them in calf, he resolved to keep them for milch cows, and they went on very well till the 5th of *December* following, when one of them fell amiss, seized with the murrain or plague, which made her grate her teeth, run at the eyes, hang down her head, scour, and would not eat: Upon this the butcher first blooded her, then clapt four rowels in her, one in each buttock, the others on each side her neck, made with horse-hair and tow twisted together, with horse turpentine. Then he made a drink with half a pint of gin, a pint of ale, about an egg-shell full of fine wood soot, one ounce of the flower of mustard-seed, and two eggs mash'd with their shells. This drink he gave her out of a horn, and at every two hours end some thin malt mash out of a horn, with a very thin malt mash standing before her, that she might drink of the liquor of it, for he gave her no water, and it answered the intent; for in about eight and forty hours time, this drink and one more knit her, by altering her scouring, and caused her to dung thickish, and in two days time more she kick'd up her heels and was perfectly well: And what was very surprising, the other cow that was kept in the same yard all the while was not infected, for the butcher was afraid to take the well one away, lest he should give offence to his neighbours by endangering their cows.—To account for this success, the butcher is of opinion, that the mustard and the other hot ingredients threw out the distemper, by sweating the beast, and told me he came by this receit accidentally as he bought cattle of a *Leicestershire* grazier, who declared to him, that this same medicine had saved of one man's cow's twenty out of two and twenty that were seized with the murrain distemper. The parts where the rowels are fixt will swell much, but on their running the swelling will sink and draw the fever out of the cow's head.— And it is my humble opinion, that there was never a better remedy ever found out than this, for the cure of the murrain, because here are several operations performed on the cow's body at once, both inwardly and outwardly, which gives her two chances for her life; if the rowels run, we say there is no great danger of the cow's doing otherwise than well.

How to prevent the Murrain Distemper spreading amongst Cows.—THE following has been used with great success in several places where the distemper among the horned cattle has raged very violently, and comes recommended by a very able physician.—Take tar and flower of brimstone, of each half a pound, oil of turpentine four ounces, assafœtida two drams: Mix these well together, and with a painter's brush do the nose and muzzle of the cow night and morning.

Of Thefts and Robberies, with Precautions to prevent them.

ACCOUNTS of this nature may perhaps be of more consequence to gentlemen, yeomen, farmers, and others, than all I have wrote before: For if a gentleman or farmer runs out and gets into a ruinous condition for want of knowledge, inspection, and careful management of his affairs both at home and abroad, he may thus be deprived of the means to live happy. And I am well assured that many gentlemen, yeomen, farmers, and others, have run out their income, merely by their servants carelessness and pilfering, and too often by the thefts of ill neighbours: Wherefore I have thought it necessary to publish the following accounts of thievery, for examples, that others may learn to avoid falling into the like misfortunes.

How two Threshers stole much Corn from their Master.—A MAN living near me, coming into the possession of a little farm of twenty pounds a year ready sowed with grain to his hand, after harvest employed two threshers to thresh out his corn, believing they would not wrong him, as he paid them well for their work, but it otherwise happened; for as the owner followed the farrier's business at four miles distance from the farm, these threshers lived at discretion, and therefore, being very great rogues, took the advantage of their master's absence, and carried several bushels of his wheat to the mill to grind for flower, besides what they conveyed away for raising ready money; for the farrier believed they stole in all forty or fifty bushels of wheat, and several of pease, and for furnishing themselves with meat they stole mutton; upon which one was taken up, and sent to *Hertford* gaol in *January* 1748-9, where he died, before the assizes, of the gaol distemper; the other confessed he stole only two bushels of the wheat, but for want of other evidence, and for the sake of his large family, that must have fell on the parish if he had been hanged or transported, he was not prosecuted. Now this farrier was brought up from his cradle in the country, was near fifty years of age, and accounted as sharp a man in his way as most is, yet proved a mere *ignoramus* in the management of a farm.

How a villainous Servant of a Farmer, by a false Key he got, had free Access for a long Time to his Master's strong Beer Cellar.—THIS fellow was servant to Mr. *Linny*, a famous farmer at *Beckwood*, tenant to that late generous worthy gentleman Sir *Thomas Seabright*, Member of Parliament for *Hertfordshire*, where, after he had been some time, he got possession of the key of his master's strong beer cellar, long enough to take its impression in clay, and have it match'd at an ironmonger's in *Dunstable*; and being (as he thought) thus compleatly furnished, he put the original key in the way of being found by his dame. After this he took his opportunity of trying his new key, which was a little twisted, and every way like the old true one, except its being too short in the hollow: However, to cure this, he made use of a gimlet, and bored so long till he made it do, and then he had free access when he thought fit to fill his belly with any of the liquors he found in the cellar; for this tenant kept a good house; and thus this villain went on till he went into another farmer's service near his former master, yet was not deprived of having a belly-full of Mr. *Linny's* strong beer once a week, for when a new servant came into his place, he quickly got acquainted with him, telling him how he had gone on, and that if he would every *Sunday* give him liberty, he would give him his key. This was agreed to, and both of them every *Sunday* got into the cellar, and there drank at their pleasure for almost another year, till at last the master and mistress miss'd so much of their liquors, that they mistrusted a bite; upon which the mistress lock'd herself into the cellar, and by waiting catch'd the present servant, who confess'd the other, and who for fear of prosecution left the country for some time, till he heard his master would pardon him, if he would come and make an ingenious discovery of the whole matter, which he did in the manner I have related it.—Persons ought to take particular care of this piece of villainy, for it is too commonly practised: I knew two fellows in our parish that did the same, and reigned in their roguery a considerable time, by which and other misfortunes their master sold his estate of forty pounds a year, and became poor.

How a Taylor undertook a Farm who knew nothing of it, and how he was robbed.—THIS man lives about four miles from *Gaddesden*, and wanting hay I sold him some the 8th of *April*, 1749, when he told me, That having marry'd a wife, and got a house and land, he was desirous to take a little farm near him: This he did, and kept, I think, four horses; but being ignorant in many branches of the farming business, among other discourse he said to a friend of his, He could not tell when a labourer had done his day's work. Oh, says his friend, they will soon make you know that, and something else. And so they did, for one he catch'd stealing his bacon, by cutting a piece off as it hung up in the kitchen. Another stole this or that thing, which he detected them in; however, by being thus bit to his loss, he took courage, look'd out sharp, and now makes a tolerable good farmer.

A Gentleman of a considerable Estate run out by his Servants holding a Correspondence with bad Neighbours.—THIS gentleman coming to an estate of above a thousand a year, at a young age, left his servants to manage his domestick affairs; who managed so, that he run out considerably, though in a single life; till at last his eyes were opened, and he perceived how the loss happen'd, which was by his servants holding a correspondence with vile neighbours, for in order to please them, they pilfer'd from their master those things which brought him under great losses; but on discovering their villainy, he forbid any of his family so much as to talk with a neighbour. If they did, he or she was to be directly turn'd away. And his prohibition (as he lived in a lone house at some distance from others) had so good an effect, that he recover'd his losses, and is now a very rich gentleman, living, northward, about a hundred miles from *London*.

How a Yeoman's Maid-Servant pilfered her Master's Flower, Bacon, Cheese, &c. and exchanged them for Gin.—A YEOMAN in *Hertfordshire*, whose landed estate is about sixty pounds a year, kept a maid-servant that so loved gin, as to carry now and then some of her master's bacon, flower, or cheese, to an adjacent shop where they sold gin, where she would drink till somewhat intoxicated; and as her mistress was an indolent sort of woman, she perceived not the maid's wickedness, for a long time, for when she got a little tipsey, she told her mistress she was seized with a pain in her stomach, was pity'd, and thus frequently obtained leave to go to bed sooner than ordinary; till at last her wickedness appeared palpable, and she was discharged, leaving a score of five shillings at the gin-shop unpaid.—I could record many more such villainies, but my room will not allow it.

The Character of that great Oeconomist Scroop Egerton, *late Duke of* Bridgewater.—THIS nobleman was certainly possess'd of many fine qualities, particularly that of temperance in eating and drinking, and in many other branches of living. He was (I believe) never known to be intoxicated with liquor, for he and his Duchess seldom or ever exceeded a pint or a quart bottle of wine at dinner. His breakfast was a mess of water gruel, and as he always rose betimes, while in the country, when he had eaten it he would ride or walk out till ten, and then come home to a tea-breakfast with his Duchess and daughters. His supper was tarts, hasty pudding, pancake, or other light food, in refusal of flesh; but he generally eat as hearty a dinner as any man, having extraordinary plenty of all manner of dainty provisions, and two men cooks to dress them. His exercise was walking amongst his many workmen, with whom he was so delighted, that he seemed never better pleased, than when he was giving them orders and seeing them work in the best planted park in *England*, in his many inclosed fields, woods and garden. And so extremely fond was this gentleman of a country life, that he would every now and then take a trip, even in winter, down to his seat at *Ashridge* from *London*; and notwithstanding the fatigue of his journey, I have seen him, the same day, walk through a great shower of rain to a considerable distance in his great coat, to view a new-made pond or other novelty. His number of cart, race, and other horses was one hundred and fifty at least; his red and fallow deer, above one thousand; his menial servants of all sorts, about sixty; and his day labourers, thirty: And although he kept a large pack of the finest fleetest hounds in the country, yet he would latterly seldom go with them; but on the contrary has been heard to say, he wish'd in his youth he had minded them less, and the improvement of his estate more. However, he pretty well redeemed his lost time, for he planted much, and seldom felled a tree, unless at a very great age indeed. His houshold and other parts of his œconomy were attended with a very close inspection, particularly that of his servants accompts; his housekeeping was exercised in plenty, yet with frugality; and there was always enough of every thing that was good; his corn-fields furnished his house with bread, malt, oatmeal, *&c.* and he sold much grain besides, at *Hempstead* market; his cows supplied milk, cream, and butter, but his cheese he bought: He was such an admirer of the Lady-finger natural grass, that grew in his meadows, that he would now and then recommend its excellent virtues to others; his oxen, sheep, lambs, and calves he generally fatted in his own grounds, and commonly killed an ox every week or fortnight, besides smaller meat, giving large quantities of it every week to the adjacent poor people, to the making of their families hearts glad. His *London* house he also, in winter, supplied now and then with mutton, lamb, veal, venison, bacon, pork, pigs, fowls, eggs, and flower; likewise with fruit and other garden-ware, strong beer, wood, charcoal, pond and river fish, to the furnishing his table with wholesome pleasant viands, and to the saving of much expence; for which purpose the Duke had a waggon or cart every week loaded, almost throughout the winter, with these provisions. His servants had one of the mildest masters upon earth, seldom, if ever, being in a passion with any of them, nor did he ever turn any of them off, without a very capital offence indeed; and when superannuated, they were sure of a comfortable subsistence during the remainder of their life. He delivered some of his low meadows from inundations of water, by causing *Great-Gaddesden* river to run round instead of passing through it, as formerly. He seldom denied a neighbour a favour, an instance of which is my own case, by his giving me leave to remove a barn of three bay from off his copyhold land, to my freehold land. He made many fine purchaces of landed estates, and yet left behind him ('tis said) a prodigious quantity of ready money, besides a most bulky yearly income. He died in *January* 1744-5, at his *London* house, greatly lamented by his relations, friends, servants, and particularly by the poor, after complaining (the day before his death) he was not well at his stomach; however, he seemed pretty well next morning, and eat his breakfast as usual; but in the afternoon lay on the bed, to take a nap, having a cord given him in his hand to ring when he waked; but lying longer than ordinary, without hearing of him, his Duchess, with another person or two, went to his bedside and found him dead, with the bell-string in his hand, and without the least ruffling of the bedcloaths; so that it is thought he went away in his sleep: However, he was directly blooded in the jugular vein, which bled pretty well; yet he was thought by the doctors to have died about an hour before, at the age of about sixty-two. He was a constant churchman, a loving husband to his excellent Duchess, a most affectionate father, and a true friend to all he profess'd himself so.

Country Family's Profitable Director:

According to the Present Practice of the Country Gentleman's, *the* Yeoman's, *the* Farmer's, *the* Labourer's *Wives, and Others, of the Counties of* Hertford, Bucks, *and other Parts of* England.

PART II.

Of WHEAT.

HE Uses of Wheat.—This king of grain is, according to Mr. *Mortimer's* notion of it, the most general grain used in *England* for bread, although it is not unfit for most of the uses the other grains are fit for; as for beer, a proportion of which being added to the malt, helps much the keeping of it: If a little wheat-bran is boiled in our ordinary beer, it will cause it to mantle or flower in the cup, when it is poured out; which sheweth what a rich spirit wheat is endowed with, that so much remains in the bran. If wheat be malted, and a small quantity be added to other malt, it will add much strength to your beer; but it is something more fulsome, being reputed to be the principal ingredient in the making of mum. Starch is also made of musty unwholesome wheat, and of the bran thereof, than which there are few things whiter.

How much Fewel may be saved by the Make of a particular Oven.—MR. *Mortimer* says, it may not be improper for the baking of bread to insert an oven, which a friend of mine (says he) has made, at the further end of which he has made a vent for the smoak, which, if he had carried upright, would have obliged him to have been at the charge of a particular funnel for it; besides, he could not have well come at it, to stop it up when the oven was hot, and therefore he brought it with a pipe over the top of the oven, by which means he can stop both the mouth and vent together. He tells me, That the air drawing through the oven, his wood kindles presently, and that any green wood will burn in it. He says, It takes up but one third part of the wood, that another sort of oven takes up to heat it; also that brick ovens heat much sooner and better than those made with stone.

Of a Sort of wheaten Bread made in a Gentleman's Family in Derbyshire.—THIS worthy gentleman, although possess'd of a plentiful estate of one thousand a year, yet both he and all his family, throughout the twelve months, eat their bread made from wheat flower, as it came from the mill, with all the bran in it, except now and then, when he himself eat fine manchet bread spread with butter for his tea breakfast. And it was the practice of his servant that made it, to let it stand in the oven all night, which they believed added to its sweetness; for as his servant told me (whom I sent out of *Hertfordshire* to be his plowman, where he always eat wheaten bread free of the bran) he thought it the best bread he ever eat; and there are many other good families eat the same wheaten bread, made of the flower as it comes from the mill. Though this sort may at first seem a little rough and harsh to a stranger, yet by custom it will prove pleasant, wholesome and strengthening. And why they let their loaves stand so long in the oven was, I suppose, because they were peck loaves, which require more and longer heat than smaller bread.

How in a certain Part of Suffolk *their Farmers make three Sorts of Bread out of Wheat-meal, as it comes ground from the Mill.*—HERE many of their farmers live in the most plenty, by the help of that excellent and very cheap manure called cragg, which is composed of sea sand, shells, loam, *&c.* and is dug out of that ground, formerly thought to be overflowed with salt water, with which, and their other industrious husbandry, they are enabled thus to live. Now one chief part of their profitable management is in their making the most of the wheat-meal, of which they make three sorts of bread: One sort for manchet to eat with tea, a second for the master's and mistress's table, and a third for the servants; and this they do by help of a boulting hutch, or what some call a gigg, that sifts and dresses three sorts of flower at a time out of it, by a lawn cloth, and two sorts of hair cloths; by which they get a very fine flower for making roles, cakes, or as I said manchet, pyes, and other sorts of kitchen rarities; then a table-bread for masters and mistresses, and a third to make a coarse brown bread for servants; for here they use all or most of the bran in their bread. And it is remarkable, that most of the people of this country look with a fresher colour than those in any other county in *England*; but whether this is oweing to the branny part of their bread, that scours their stomachs and guts, and delivers them from that scorbutick acid fur which the finer softer bread has not power to do; or whether it is owing to their particular breed or climate, I cannot say: But this I am sure of, That a certain Duchess had this sort of coarse branny bread made with wheat-flower, just as it came from the mill, for her own eating, in order to scour her stomach, and create her the better appetite; and I must needs say, it is well known to me, that few persons enjoy a better state of health than she does at this day.

Barley-Bread.—MAKE use of half barley and half wheat-flower, and for this purpose some millers grind both together, as they did in the hard frost of 1740. It makes good bread, but better pye-crust, for thus it eats crisp and pleasant; and because the barley-flower shortens the wheat-flower, they put some new milk into the warm water it is kneaded with, which makes it whiter, sweeter, and stiffer. But old skim or fleet milk should not be used in this case, lest it sours it too soon. Also observe that this dough must be kneaded with more yeast than all wheat-flower, and worked and squeezed more.

The Hertfordshire *Barley-Bread made to eat like Wheaten-Bread.*—THIS is a very serviceable secret, and thought to be of such importance by a common baker, that on his imparting it to his good friend and neighbour Mrs. ——— he enjoined her not to divulge it. However, as he is since dead, and the widow is since become my next neighbour from a distant part of *Hertfordshire*, and lives on her means, independent of following any business; she, for the good of the world, thought fit to discover the secret to me, by telling me, that she believed the invention was first put in practice, in this county, about forty years ago, when wheat in some parts was sold for ten shillings a bushel, by reason of the hard frosty, long, snowy winter, that then happened, which occasioned this common baker, as well as many private families, to bake barley-bread that was highly improved by the following method, Take a pottle of fine oatmeal, and lay it in water to steep all night; next morning it will appear (if too much water is not put to the oatmeal) like hasty-pudding: This break into several parts of a peck and half of barley-meal, to which add warm water and yeast, and knead it into dough, as all wheat-meal is commonly done. Then mould it into loaves and bake them. Thus a barley loaf may be made hollow, white and sweet, so as to be hardly known from coarse wheaten bread. For as barley-meal alone naturally makes a heavy, hard, coarse, harsh loaf of bread, the oatmeal being of a more hollow sweet nature and white colour, adds these fine qualities to the barley-meal, and thus produces a much more wholesome and pleasant loaf of bread, than all entire barley-meal can; and where a person has the conveniency of making use of skim milk instead of water, it will make the bread better still.

To make good Servants Bread.—THE greater the quantity of flower, the more profit it is to make bread of it, as the same is in using much malt at a time in brewing. Take two, three, or four bushels of coarse wheat-meal, and mix it with the like quantity of barley-meal, to make one batch of bread, and so in proportion for a greater or lesser quantity. And supposing they are made finer than they are ground, by sifting their meals, take one bushel of it, and put a piece of leavened dough into the same at nine a clock at night, which cover with the same meal. If this is done in winter, the water must be made very hot, even as hot as can be endured with the hand; but if in summer, only bloodwarm, and so according as the weather is hot or cold; then early next morning leaven the rest of your meal, and knead the whole together, till by working it well it is brought into a right stiffness; for it is observable, that the softer and lighter the dough is, the less time it will keep. Now to make this bread go the farther, knead the dough stiff and close, for the lighter the bread, the more will be eaten of it; and when the dough is thus kneaded close, make two or three deep holes in it with your fist, and let it remain some time under a warm cover of cloths till the holes are swell'd up, for then the dough is in right order; and this will happen sooner or later, as the weather is warmer or colder. By this time I will suppose your oven to be in a forwardness of heating, by one that tends and looks after the fire, while you are cutting and moulding the dough into the form of half peck or peck loaves, that as they are made should be lain on a linen cloth, or on a board well flower'd, at a little distance from each other, to prevent their touching and sticking. Next examine your oven's heat. If on rubbing a stick the sparks of it fly briskly about, it is enough; then sweep it clean, and rub the bottom of the oven with a broom first, and presently after with a wet mop, or what the bakers call a maukin; then if it is over-hot, shut up the oven's mouth, lest it scorch the bread too much, and make it harsh; after this set in your loaves as fast as you can, placing the larger at the further end and round the sides, and the rest in the middle. It also should be observed, that in heating an oven, the dead coals or ashes of wood, furze, fern, straw, or other fewel, should be taken now and then out with the peel and thrown away, because these rather check than increase the heat. Care likewise should be used to burn the fewel in all places alike, by firing it sometimes on one side and sometimes on the other; which done, stop the mouth of the oven close. If it is an iron-plated door, wet rags are sufficient, and so they will be to a wooden stopper if it shuts very close, else we lay wet rags first and dirt over them. Three hours time is enough to bake a batch of half-peck loaves; if peck loaves, four or five hours must be allowed, and when this time is expired, draw your bread; and if you find one or more loaves not baked enough, put them in again, stop up, and let them remain longer, but not too long, lest it give the bread a brown colour and an ill taste. Observe likewise to act the good housewife in keeping stale bread by you, while new is baking, for when new bread as I said is eaten, it goes away sooner than older, and if some loaves are not baked so much as others, eat them first.

To make French *Bread.*—TAKE a peck of the finest wheat flower, and ferment it with half a pint of good new ale-yeast, and half a handful of salt first dissolved in warm water, with three quarts of milk; then about an hour after add three pecks more of flower, and knead it well, but not too much; let it rise in a tray or kiver, and mould it into loaves of what size you please, which set into the oven, and draw about an hour after.

A second Way to make French *Bread.*—TAKE a peck of the finest wheat flower, with some leaven, yeast, and hot water, which let rise in a bowl or kiver. If it is in winter cover it warm;

in the mean time this is rising, work three pecks more of fine flower with very hot water or milk, four ounces of salt, and a pound of fresh butter; and after this has stood two hours to rise, mix it with the first dough, and knead all together into one mass, which let stand a proper time to rise. Then give it a thorough working and kneading again on a dresser or table, and when the loaves are ready to be put into the oven, you may brush their tops over with yolks of eggs beaten up with water.

A third Way to make French *Bread.*—MIX half a pint of new ale-yeast with a peck of flower, and the whites and yolks of six eggs beat up thinly, a little salt, and some new warm milk. These temper together very slightly, and put the yeast or dough into several small wooden dishes to ferment and rise; which it will do, if the place is not too cold, in less than half an hour; then turn it out of the dishes into the oven. Bake them about three quarters of an hour, and they'll be fit to rasp.—Some put a pint or more of yeast to a peck of flower, and add a little sugar, but take particular care to keep the paste or dough warm under a cloth or blanket, till it rises almost as big again as it was at first.—Or you may make a mixture with only three eggs, half a pint of ale-yeast, four or five pounds of flower, and so much warm milk as will make a very light dough, which bake in penny loaves, that are to be rasped for eating.—Others add a piece of butter, and put the dough or paste on tin plates, to bake it in the shape of very little loaves that they rasp.—Or you may fry a quarter of a pound of veal kidney suet, and mix all with a peck of fine wheat flower, six eggs, half a pint of yeast, half a pound of butter, and with warm milk and water knead the whole into a dough, which let lie half an hour to rise; then make it into roles or loaves, and wash their tops over with eggs and milk beaten together, and bake all in a very hot oven.

Tea Breakfast Roles made by the House-keeper of John Copping, *Esq; of* Market-street *in* Hertfordshire.—SHE melted a slice or two of butter in warm milk, and with two eggs kneaded it into a quart of flower, then moulded it into roles or cakes, which she brush'd over with cream, or a mixture of milk and eggs. These roles she sometimes baked at the oven's mouth in about half an hour's time, as we bake our common dough cake before the oven is stopt up for good, for baking our family bread. At other times she heated a little oven on purpose. These roles, while hot, she butter'd for eating with a tea breakfast; or to eat with victuals, particularly with cheese, for supper, without being butter'd. Thus a cheap fine role may be had, that relishes liquor to delight.

To make Bread more substantial than ordinary.—THIS and the following one are two old printed receits handed down from one author to another; and as they seem to be valuable, I also here insert them.—Take the bran that has been boulted off, and put it into a kettle of water and boil it, then strain out the water, and it will be white, and of a thick strengthening substance, with this wet the meal wherewith you make the bread, then add yeast and a little salt, and so make it into loaves, and it will be more heartening, pleasanter in taste, and increased in substance, than otherwise it would have been.

To make Bread that will keep moist and good very long.— SLICE a pumpkin, and boil it in fair water, till the water grows clammy or somewhat thick; then drain it through a fine cloth or sieve, and with this make your bread, well kneading the dough, and it will not only increase the quantity, but keep it moist and sweet a month longer than bread wetted with water only. It is, says one author, an excellent sort of bread: Another says, it is more especially so for those who desire cooling, being good to loosen the belly. It is somewhat of a yellower colour and fatter than common bread.

Maxims relating to the making good Bread.—MR. *Houghton* says, that the ferment or yeast of cherry-wine is an excellent sort for making bread.—Water is a principal ingredient in bread, for its goodness much improves it. This has been evidently proved, where that bread which is made at one place, in imitation of the best sort at another place, though made by the same bakers, and with the same corn, never succeeds, either as to the colour or goodness, equal to that which is made upon the place itself. This is wholly imputed to the excellency of the water; and that water which weighs lighter is best, relish will recommend it. The heaviest corn makes the best bread.—The best flower makes the best bread.—The whiter the flower, the less goodness in taste.— That wheat which grows on light, not fat ground, whose stalk is big and strong, makes ever the best bread.—New corn for bread is better in colour, crimp and pleasant in taste, but yields more bran than the old, which by often stirring wears husky, and falls away into dust.—A mill newly repaired, provided there hath some corn passed through it before, will perform better, than when the stones are worn.—Grind as much as will serve a family a month, because it will yield you a greater quantity of flower, than when otherwise it comes new from the mill.—Keep your flower carefully cover'd in bins, to preserve it from air and vermine.—In summer keep it in a cool place; for great heats produce the nightingale maggot, that turns to a black wing'd insect, that feeds upon and corrupts the flower.—That all stale bread set anew into the oven will much recover it, and if it be eaten immediately, little difference will be between that and new bread; but if kept, and set in a third time, it will not be tolerable.—The closer bread is wrought, so it be not heavy, the more hearty and nourishing; and the newer it is, the better.

An Account of the Method said to be made use of by two Country common Bakers, to prepare Allum for improving their Sale Loaves of Bread with the same.—IN my first part of the *Country Family's Profitable Director*, I have given an account of what a common baker's servant-maid told me she was an eye-witness of, in seeing her new set-up master mix allum with the wheat-meal that made his bread. And here I have thought it not amiss to add a second account, that I have since been informed of relating to the same.—This second account was given me on the 19th day of *November* 1748, by a man's wife, who was daughter to a common baker in ——*shire*, and niece to another common baker in another shire: In both which places, she tells me, she had a full opportunity of being acquainted with their method of making their sale bread, without any suspicion that she would ever discover their trading secrets; accordingly, they would (she says) never suffer any servant-maid besides herself, to see how they made their bread; wherefore, as often as they used allum, by first burning it, and putting it amongst their flower, they sent the servant-maid on some errand, to prevent her knowing it; and although her father kept one above eight years, yet she was wholly ignorant of this matter. But the daughter many times saw both her father and mother burn allum in a fire-shovel, and beat the same in a leather-bag to a fine powder, which they strewed amongst their flower, instead of salt, for making the bread white, light, and relishing. And why they made use of burnt allum, and not raw allum, she believes was, because raw allum would be apt to give the bread a harsher taste, and be discover'd sooner than burnt allum: She further says, that in the many years time that she has bought common baker's bread for her family, she verily believes she never eat one such loaf but what had allum in it: But whether a loaf of bread is the worse for the burnt allum, I leave to the judgment of my reader. She says it makes the bread quickly stale, crumbling, harsh, and hungry, therefore does not satisfy like home-made bread.

Allum, an Advertisement of it.—In a *London* news paper, intitled *The Daily Advertiser*, dated *June* 13, 1749, the following words are inserted, *viz.* "Whereas the Act relating to the baking trade is expired, and it being notoriously known, that the use of allum in making bread by many bakers, in divers parts of this town and kingdom, is a detriment to the fair trader, and the destruction of many thousands of his Majesty's subjects, and of infants in particular; and as there is a clause in the Act of the 8th of Queen *ANNE*, to prohibit the mixing any other grain, than what is settled by the Assize, under the penalty of 20 *s*. It is therefore humbly hoped, that the legislature will insert a clause, with a penalty on every baker that shall use allum on any account whatever." If the qualities of allum would be known, they are described by Dr. *Quincy*, in his *Dispensatory*, 4th edition, page 111. "Allum is made with allum mineral mixed with urine and kali, is extreamly rough and astringent, apt to provoke vomitting, by vellicating the fibres of the stomach very much, upon which account it is not much used inwardly, and then not without some smooth aromatick ingredients in composition with it, &c.["]

How the London French *Bakers supply the Use of Yeast.*— YEAST or barm is a composition of a salt or sower matter, and therefore the *French* bakers in *London*, who make the nicest and finest of bread, to avoid the ill taste and bad quantity of yeast, use a mixture of first wort immediately from the malt, with some fine wheat flower and whites of eggs, for making *French* bread, and gingerbread.

The Cause of heavy Bread.—IT is the opinion of our country-women, that if wheat-meal is made into bread immediately after the wheat is grinded, it will be apt to cause the bread to be close and heavy; therefore such meal will make lighter bread, if it is kept a week, two, or more, before it is used.

To make Bread of Potatoes.—TO make potatoe bread, it should be done with those potatoes that are of the shorter nature and the whitest colour. Of this sort, I had some brought me from near *Stockport* in *Cheshire*, for propagating their species at *Gaddesden*; these, when boiled and mash'd, and then mix'd with its liquor, with the same quantity of wheat-meal, will, after the common method of kneading and baking, make loaves of bread; which has been done, in dear times of wheat, to the relief of many poor families.

To make Potatoe Cakes.—MR. *Bradley*, at page 55, in his *Essays* says—Pulp of potatoes made into a paste or dough, with a little milk and some salt, and then flatted into cakes and baked, is often used by some of the poorer sort of people, when corn is dear.

Barley-meal and Turneps boiled in Time of Famine.—A poor woman that lived a mile from my house, in time of famine having no victuals, made her eldest daughter follow the man that shovel'd away the snow in a sort of path, for the sheep to come at turneps; here she pull'd some up, and boiled them to a mash with some barley-meal, which she and her several children eat as pap-meat with only salt, and it sustained them much.

To make Barley-meal short Cakes.—Stir barley-meal with water, melted fat, a little yeast and salt, make this mixture into pancake-fashion, and as large; then cut it into pieces like little cakes, fry them in hogslard or other fat, and they'll eat extraordinary well in a poor man's family without any sauce.

Barley Dumplins with Bacon, &c.—Knead barley-meal with warm water and a little salt, till it is as stiff as common dough for bread; then cut bacon or pickled pork in thin slices, and put one or two of them at most in each dumplin, with a little pepper, salt and parsley. These, when boiled, will have all the gravey of the bacon in them, and be very good; but if milk and butter, or other fat is mixt with the barley-meal, they'll be the better: In the same manner any sort of meat may be made use of, and the gravey of it being thus confined, it will relish and much improve the crust part of the dumplin, whether it is made with barley or wheat meal.

The Method of making and baking Wheat and Barley Bread, as it is practised by most of the common People's Families in Devonshire.—In great part of this county, the common people eat hardly any other sort of bread than that made from barley. Their method of making this sort of bread is the same that others make use of for wheat bread, only they allow a greater quantity of yeast or barm, and knead it slighter than that of wheat, and instead of water, such as have it to spare, use scalded skim milk; by making their bread in this manner, it is little inferior to the second sort of wheat bread, it being sweet, hollow, and pretty hearty. Their method of baking adds to its goodness, as it gives it somewhat of an agreeable quality; which method is perform'd by baking a loaf under a large iron kettle, that is chiefly made use of for washing dishes in. As soon as the dough is ready, they make it into a loaf of about three parts the size of the kettle; a large kettle will cover a loaf of near half a bushel of flower, which being clean and dry, they sweep the hearth, and on the hottest part of it they lay down the loaf, and immediately cover it with the kettle, then put over it a good quantity of damp straw or horse litter, and upon this a few ashes: This done, they set fire to the straw, which will burn leisurely away, and cause the upper part of the loaf to be baked equal to the under part; and to this end they commonly allow four or five hours for baking it, if it is a loaf of a moderate size; but if very large, they frequently bake it thus all night. And thus some bake their best wheaten bread, pies, and puddings, because it saves the expence and trouble of heating an oven, and by many is accounted the sweeter method of baking.—This account, with some other serviceable ones, I received from a young man I sent to a gentleman in *Devonshire*, whose landed estate is reputed five hundred a year, for it is one branch of my business to help gentlemen to servants well skill'd in husbandry business. In this family the servants in general eat all barley bread, baked for the most part on a hearth, as the gentleman was a batchelor, and kept but few of them.

Wheat-meal damaged by Mites.—This article has escaped the pen of most or all authors, though it is of no little importance for housekeepers in particular to have a due knowledge of it, in order to avoid the mischiefs that may happen by these insects, they are in fewer or greater numbers in most wheat meals, occasion'd chiefly by the dampness of wheat before it is grinded, which causes their breed in the meal, wherein they mightily increase in a short time, and quickly swarm. The millers sacks and appurtenances are seldom free of mites, because here are all sorts of wheat grinded, and the same sacks made use of for years together; likewise the flower or kneading hutch, wherein the meal is kept till used. As this repository is seldom or never free of mites, how can the flower escape being infected by them? Also, as many persons (the poorer sort especially) buy their wheat-meal at shops by retail, their sacks that stand some time with flower in them, and even their wooden scales, must consequently have mites in them.

How to know when Wheat-meal is infected by Mites.—THERE is more than one sign or token that discovers it. First, when the meal appears on the outside of a sack, as if drove out in many parts of it, it is a true indication that mites work it through. Secondly, if a handful of flower is laid on a board, heap-like, and there be many mites in it, they will soon level it, or at least alter the shape of the heap, but a night's time will give a plainer proof. Thirdly, mity flower may (if much infected) be smelt, if some of it is put into a hand and held to the nose. Fourthly, mity wheat-meal makes a bread that will prove hottish in the mouth, and of a disagreeable taste, and why it is so, I have to add, that the dung and bodies of these insects are the cause of it, and in course gives the bread an unwholesome quality. This I have wrote in my first part, but for further explaining this important matter, I have renewed it here.

How to prevent the Breed and Increase of Mites in Wheat-meal, and kill Worms, Wevils, Maggots and Mites.—IT is very common for gentlemens, yeomens, farmers, and labourers families, to make use of the same sack or bag, the next time they want to have it furnished with flower, as they did the time before. Now if such sack or bag is infected by mites, and sweet sound meal should be put into it, it may be depended on, it will be damaged by mites that staid behind in the crevices of such sack or bag, and so on time after time. Wherefore such sack or bag should be served as a poor woman does hers once or twice every year; as soon as the bread is out of the oven, she puts her meal-bag into it, to kill all the mites that harbour in it, well knowing that nothing will kill these vermine like the oven. This the poor woman observes to do about the middle of every summer, when mites are in their greatest strength and increase; for if these are let alone, they will eat the finest flower first, and then the branny part.—Or in case your flower-hutch (which is a sort of wooden chest, that most farm houses keep their wheat-meal in, after it is brought from the mill) is infected by mites, wevils, or maggots, you may destroy them by Dr. *Hale's* invention.—Dip a rag in melted brimstone, and lay it on a little earthen chaffing-dish placed at the bottom of the hutch, which set on fire, and clap down the lid imme-diately for a minute, and the fume will kill all manner of insects in the same, without damaging the meal that afterwards is put into it.—The same if small holes are bored thro' the boards of a chamber or grainary, so little, that the corn cannot fall through them, and tow or rags dipt in melted brimstone are set on fire at a yard's depth under them, on sand, or other earth, eight or twelve inches thick, the fume will ascend, and destroy all wevils, maggots, worms, or mites, that have got into the same, and yet not in the least hurt the wheat, malt, or other grain; but then the place or room, where this is done, should have all air possible kept out of it, and no person in it from the moment the brimstone tow is set on fire.

The honest Miller, or the Profit of grinding Wheat.—A FARMER sent five bushels of pirky wheat to be ground, and it yielded four bushels and a half of flower, fit for his family uses, which at four shillings a bushel is eighteen shillings, and the bran worth two shillings; out of which deduct one shilling for grinding, and the neat worth of the whole was nineteen shillings. Whereas, when this sack of wheat was exposed to sale in the market, they bid the farmer no more than fourteen shillings; so that he got by the grinding five shillings, with the help of the miller's honesty. If a farmer carries and fetches his wheat, the miller, in our country, takes three pounds of flower for toll, rough as it comes from the stones; but if they fetch and carry it two or three miles, four pounds out of every bushel. If we pay ready money and carry it, it is only one shilling for grinding five bushels; if they fetch and bring it home, eighteen-pence.—If barley is carry'd to be ground by the farmer, they take one shilling ready money, and no toll; but if tolled, they take a pottle of the barley-meal out of every bushel, as it comes rough from the stones.

Horse-beans, their Uses for being eaten by Christians and Heathens, as Bread, &c.—HORSE-BEANS when old, dry'd, and boiled, are somewhat bitter and strong tasted, but very nutritious; and therefore made use of for feeding black slaves, during their voyage from *Africa* to the *American* plantations; and when they are in their growing green condition, are by some of the poor common people in *England* eaten as a hearty meal, boiled and mixed with butter; and by many pods and all are eaten. In several of the Northern counties these beans are dry'd on a kiln, and ground to flower, for mixing with wheat or barley meal, to make bread of them.—Others soak the dry horse-beans in water over night, and next day boil them, to eat with a piece of bacon or pickled pork, or with only milk.—These beans are also very serviceable to pack-horses and others, to keep them in heart, and from catching cold; but are rather too hot for their constant food.

The knavish Miller.—A PERSON that formerly was a miller's servant (but now follows another business) says, that where he lived, the master would sometimes take two or three shillings worth of the finest and heartiest of the flower out of a five bushel sack, and put in the room of it a coarse flower, pollard, or small bran; so that by this means there is no proving a miller's honesty by weight. And if it is asked, why there is no more bran, they have their excuse.

O A T M E A L, its Preservation and Uses.

*T*HE Cheshire *Method of preserving and using Oatmeal.*— As soon as it is ground very fine, they put it into earthen pots, or a large close tub, or into square wooden bins, or what they here call arks; and as one man puts in the oatmeal, a little at a time, another treads it into the bin, ark, or tub, with his shoes on; and thus they proceed till the whole quantity is filled in, and then they lock it down. Here it will keep sound one, two, or three years, and be as good at the end of that time as at the beginning, during which it must never be disturbed till the whole quantity is removed at once; for it is the farmers way here to thresh out their oats, and make them into the finest of oatmeal, even near as fine as wheat flower, and by keeping the oatmeal, thus close from the air, in large quantities, it improves in keeping, and becomes rather better than worse. A gentleman of five hundred pounds a year landed estate, that kept only one of his farms in his own hands, of about fifty pounds a year, made use of two of these bins or arks, which contain'd each eleven or twelve sacks of such fine oatmeal, which he commonly fill'd every year, either with his own oatmeal, or with what he bought of his neighbours, to make up his quantity for filling up the bins; and in this manner he kept his oatmeal by way of store, sometimes a year, two or three, till a dear time happened, and then sold it to bakers or dealers; for most people in that part of *Cheshire*, near *Manchester* in *Lancashire*, eat oat-cakes, or oat-bread, and very little wheaten-bread; if they eat any, it is commonly of the very whitest sort, for making manchet to eat at a tea breakfast, or else the very coarsest of all at their meals; but very few indeed eat either the white or the brown wheaten bread in this country, because but little of their land will bear wheat, and therefore in most, as well as in their great market at *Manchester*, their sacks of fine oatmeal stand for sale, as our sacks of wheat do in the Southern parts. Again, as this gentleman thus kept much oatmeal, by way of store in bins, for the improving the penny, that must not be meddled with till sold altogether; he, for supplying his family uses, had a large cask, wherein he put so much oatmeal as he thought would last him all the year, and that was about sixteen bushels; for both this gentleman and his whole family lived much upon oat-cakes or oat-bread, which they preferred to ordinary wheat-bread. I am indeed sensible, that they have here much wet sandy land, that, if wheat was sown on it, would chill and kill it, or subject it to other fatal accidents, and therefore are discouraged from sowing it with wheat. But did they know the right method of draining such wet land by subterraneous cuts, I am persuaded that much more wheat might be got in these parts; especially if they would make use of my most excellent of all drill-plows, the four-wheel light plain one.

Why Oatmeal goes further in a Family that is ground very small, than that which is ground larger.—Oatmeal ground very small will sooner mix with water or milk than that which is ground coarse, and consequently will go the further, require less time to extract its virtue, and save fire, much labour, and time. Also, the finer any oatmeal is ground, the closer (as I said) it will lie in a tub, glazed earthen pot, or bin, and therefore may be thus kept sweet and sound longer than a coarse ground sort. It is my own case in the choice of ground oatmeal, to send for what I use in my family seven miles (to *Leighton*, in *Bedfordshire*) because there it is exceedingly smaller ground, than is commonly done in our part of *Hertfordshire*.

The Cheshire *Way of making Burgoo, in the best Manner.*—THEY first boil their milk, and then thicken it by degrees with fine oatmeal, hasty-pudding like, and after boiling it well they eat it with butter. In *Derbyshire* they call this thin pudding.

The Cheshire *Way of making Burgoo in a common worse Manner.*—HERE the farmers make a worse watry sort of burgoo with water, or water and milk mixed, which when boiled they stir their oatmeal into it by degrees, and eat it hot with some spoonfuls of milk now and then. Some few eat butter with it.

A rich Cheshire *oatmeal pudding*—Is here made with oatmeal grouts, minced herbs, suet chopped small, plumbs, and as much milk as will make it into a pudding consistence. This they put into a large bag and boil it very well.

A more common cheap Way of making a Cheshire *Oatmeal Pudding.*—THEY take the finest oatmeal, and mix it with milk and suet chopped small, till it is brought into a pudding consistence, which they boil in a bag, and eat it with a little butter. This in *Cheshire* is reckoned the sweetest of puddings, for it is so luscious, that a little satisfies.

The Hertfordshire *Oatmeal baked Pudding.*—WE first boil a pint of grouts or oatmeal, which is commonly sold for five-pence the pottle; when boiled tender, we mix it with a quart of milk, half a pound of chopt beef suet (but hogslard or flair is better) half a pound of plumbs, two eggs and some sugar, and bake it.

The Hertfordshire *Oatmeal boiled Pudding.*—TO boil it, we first soak the grouts in milk, then mix it with half a pound of chopt suet and half a pound of plumbs, and put all into a bag. But poor people, that have not milk, use water instead of it, and reckon that boiling such a pudding is a better way of preparing it than baking, because baking causes it to eat drier than boiling. However, it is accounted by all a wholesome, palatable, good pudding.

An excellent baked Oatmeal Pudding.—BOIL a quart or more of cream, and when it has boiled, add half a pound of beef suet, or (better) hog's fat chopt very small, half a pound of sweet butter, a quarter of a pound of sugar, a grated nutmeg, a little salt, and five eggs. Mix these with a pint of the finest oatmeal, and work all into a thin dough or paste. Bake it in a pewter or earthen glazed dish an hour and half, or longer, as you see occasion.

An ancient Author's Way of making a boiled Oatmeal Pudding.—TAKE a pint of milk (says he) and put to it a pint of large or middling oatmeal; let it stand upon the fire till it be scalding hot; then let it stand by and soak half an hour; pick a few sweet herbs, and shred them, and put in half a pound of currants, half a pound of suet, two spoonfuls of sugar, and three or four eggs: These boil in a bag.

An ancient Author's Way to make and bake an Oatmeal Pudding.—TAKE (says the same author) middling oatmeal and steep it all night in cream, half a pint of oatmeal to a quart of cream; make your cream scalding hot before you put in your oatmeal, so cover it close; then take a good handful of pennyroyal, and shred it very small, with a pound of beef suet. Put it to your cream with a pound of raisins of the sun, sugar, spice, four or five eggs, two whites cast away. So bake it three quarters of an hour.

His second Way to make and bake an Oatmeal Pudding. HE says, take two handfuls of great oatmeal, and beat it exceedingly small in a mortar, set on three pints of milk in a skillet, put into it three sticks of cinnamon and large mace, stir the oatmeal into your milk before it is hot, so much of it as will make it reasonably thick, fit to be eaten. Boil it for the space of half an hour, keeping it stirring. Put therein a good handful of beef suet shred small, th[e]n take it off the fire, and put it in an earthen pan, and let it stand till it is almost cold. If it grows thick, thin it with a little more milk. Beat in four eggs, with almost a handful of sugar, a grated nutmeg, and some rosewater. Butter the bottom of a dish, and pour in your pudding; it ought to be as thin as batter. Bake it softly half an hour, then scrape sugar on it for eating.

His third Way to make and bake an Oatmeal Pudding.—TAKE (says he) a porringer full of oatmeal, beaten to a flower, a pint of cream, one nutmeg, four eggs beaten, a quarter of a pound of flower, a pound of beef suet well minced. Mingle all together, and bake it an hour.—But to make an oatmeal pudding richer than this, you may make it either for boiling or baking thus. Soak a pint of whole oatmeal in a quart of warm milk two hours; mix it with a quarter of a pound of currants and as much plumbs, some sugar and salt, and a quarter of a pound or more of fresh butter; then boil or bake it.

A short Way to make and bake an Oatmeal Pudding.—STEEP oatmeal in warm milk four hours, then take the blood of a hog, sheep, or other beast, and mix it with cream, minced suet, parsley, spinage, and thyme, pepper, mace, and four eggs. Mingle all together, and bake it.

A short Way to make and boil an Oatmeal Pudding.—TAKE the biggest oatmeal, and mix it with such shred herbs you like best, with some pepper and salt. Then tie it up close in a bag, and boil and butter it.

An Oatmeal Pudding made constantly, as part of a Milk Diet, for a gouty Man.—THIS person lived at *Cambridge,* where he exercised the trade of a confectioner, *&c.* and served colleges with sweatmeats and other viands; besides which, he was owner of a landed estate, and thus he was enabled to live luxuriously in drinking, (claret especially) which he had the greater opportunity of enjoying, by being intimate with many of the students, but which brought him under severe and frequent fits of the gout in his hands and feet, and to that degree as obliged him to creep up and down stairs. This forced him to follow Doctor *Boerhaave's* directions for living on a milk diet, and as he must eat no flesh nor drink any malt-liquor, his common food was an oatmeal pudding, made once a day with only some fine oatmeal, an egg, and milk, that was mixed and boiled in a bag to the bigness of a penny-loaf. When enough, it was turned out on a plate, butter'd and eaten. *N. B.* More than one egg must not be used, because they will bind the pudding too much.

An Oatmeal Drink made use of by the same gouty Person.— THE same person's chiefest drink was water put on oatmeal in a pot, and when it had stood a little while, he would drink it, and then put more water on the oatmeal.

Rabisha's Receit for making Oatmeal Puddings with Fish or Blood of Flesh.—TAKE (says he) a quart of whole oatmeal, steep it in warm milk over night, then drain the grouts from it, and boil them in a quart or three pints of good cream; the oatmeal being boiled and cold, take thyme, pennyroyal, parsley, spinage, savory, endive, marjoram, sorrel, succory, and strawberry-leaves, of each a like quantity; chop them fine and put them to the oatmeal, with some fennel-seeds, pepper, cloves, mace, and salt, boil it in a napkin, or bake it in a dish, pye, or guts; sometimes of the former you may leave out some of the herbs, and add these, pennyroyal, savory, leeks, a good big onion, sage, ginger, nutmeg, pepper, salt, either for fish or flesh-days, with butter, or beef suet, boiled or baked in a dish, napkin, or pye.

To make Oatmeal Pap.—SOAK fine oatmeal an hour or two in milk, as you usually do oatmeal in water to make flummery. Then pass it through a strainer. If too thick, add more milk. Set it to boil, and stir it all the while to prevent its burning. An hour's boiling or less will be sufficient, for in this time it will grow pretty thick. Then stir in a piece of butter, with some sugar, and take it off the fire. Strew fine sugar over it, add salt, and eat it.

In Praise of Oatmeal.—OATS are so valuable a pulse, that their meal is made use of in many nations. But I presume most of all in the northern parts of *Europe*, where their excellence is proved by growing where wheat, rye, and some other sorts of grain will not. And by its becoming a cheap, sweet, nourishing, wholesome bread, preserves the lives of millions of people in sound health. Six several sorts of it may be made, every one finer than the other, as your anacks, janacks, and such like. There are also made of it both thick and thin oatcakes, which are pleasant in taste and much esteemed. But if it be mixt with very fine wheat-meal, it maketh a most delicate dainty oatcake; such that no prince in the world but may have them served at his table. And it is on this account that vast numbers of them are toasted and consumed in winter-time especially, for their agreeable eating, as a breakfast with tea. Great and small oatmeal mixed, with blood and the liver of either sheep, calf, or swine, maketh that black-pudding, which is well known and affected by most men. Likewise from small oatmeal is made that excellent, pleasant, cooling, wholesome dish called flummery: A food so agreeable to all constitutions, that physicians have praised it for the best of food to sick and well people, eaten with honey, which is reputed the best sauce, some wine, either sack, claret, or white wine, beer, ale, or milk. And for the bigger sort of oatmeal called greets or grouts, many sorts of puddings are made, as the black made with the blood of swine, sheep, geese, red or fallow deer, or the like, mixt with greets or whole oatmeal, suet, and wholesome herbs. Or else white puddings; when greets are mixed with cream, eggs, crums of bread, suet, currants, and wholesome spices stuft in guts. Of both which sorts many thousands are sold in links at market in a year, and accommodates poor people with a dinner at a cheap rate; and is a repast for the rich, when these white gut puddings have marrow mixed instead of suet. Again, if you roast a goose, and stop her belly with whole greets beaten together with eggs, and afterwards mixt with the gravey, there cannot be a more pleasant sauce. Nay, if a man be at sea in a long voyage, he cannot eat a wholesomer and pleasanter meal than these whole greets boiled in water till they burst, and then mixt with butter, and so eaten with spoons, which although formerly called loblolly (now burgoo) yet there is not any meat, how insignificant soever the name may be, that is more toothsome or wholesome; besides which, it will in a great measure supply the use of rice. In short, the right management of oatmeal ought to be one of the chiefest parts of our housewife's study and care, for indeed no family can be well thriftily maintained where this is either scanty or wanting, because both poor and rich generally boil it with meat, and make that broth we call porridge, and the poor throughout the kingdom seldom boil one without the other; for it is to us as rice is to the *Indians*, sago to the *Chinese*, and vermicelli to the inhabitants of the *Mediterranean* sea coast, and is a common food for the sick. The whole kernels of oats, called grotes (says Mr. *Houghton*) with milk, butter, spice, and pennyroyal, make oatmeal puddings; but some put to them suet, raisins, *&c.* With the flower of oatmeal, water, and yeast, are made oatcakes, which are baked on a stone, and at *London* are toasted, slit, butter'd, and eaten as rarities: With oatmeal, says he, is made flummery, with oatmeal is made caudle for lying-in women. In the mountainous parts of *Wales*, and elsewhere, most of the bread the ordinary people eat are oatcakes made in divers forms, and they thrive well and live long with them. With malted oats is made pale colour'd small pleasant ale, which pleases our gentry much. I have heard (continues Mr. *Houghton*) that the *Scots* use oats in a great degree in their wars; with a bag of oatmeal and a kettle they'll sustain themselves a great while, and indeed it is a fit corn for their country, for that oats may be sown and mow'd while the sun is hot, when harder corn requires a longer time. Oats are not only the best food for horses, but will also feed poultry, and make them lay good store of eggs. An ox (says Mr. *Markham*) has been fed with them till he was sold for thirty pounds, and sheep, goats, and swine, to great profit; the last in particular, he says, will fatten apace, if ground oats are given them with whey or butter-milk: But then, as he observes, their fat should be hardened with the feed of some pease besides; and in case the swine should be seized with sickness, some raddle, or what we call red-oker, should be mix'd now and then with their meat. He also commends ground oats thus served for sick dogs and poultry, and truly almost for every live creature, thinking the same as useful as salt.

Oatmeal made with black Oats and white Oats.—BLACK oats in loamy chiltern countries are the sort most sown, but in sandy chiltern countries the white oats are chiefly made use of. In *Hertfordshire* the black oats best agree with our land, and is mostly in request for its having but one skin and a down, the latter of which turns only to dust, and the former is of a softer substance than the skin of a white oat, whereas the white oat has two skins, and they so tough and sharp as to be compared to our nails; therefore by many thought not to be so good as black oats, and because the flower or meal of the black is accounted rather sweeter than that of the white. Others again like white oats for oatmeal, as thinking their meal the whiter.

What the Produce of a Bushel of Oats is. A BUSHEL of good black oats will make a peck and a pottle of oatmeal more or less, according to the goodness of the corn. We give three-pence a bushel for making them into oatmeal, and a half-penny for grinding every half peck.

An Oatmeal Bite.—I WAS informed by a maker of oatmeal, that it is too often a custom with ill persons, to mix barley-meal amongst oat-meal, to hitch out its quantity, that they may afford to sell it the cheaper.

A quick Way to make an Oatmeal Pudding.—TAKE whole oatmeal, and mix some hogs suet, milk, pennyroyal, onions, a little salt: Put these in a bag, and boil it two or three hours.

A second quick Way to make an Oatmeal Pudding.—WITH whole oatmeal mix hogs suet, sugar, plumbs and spice; stir all these with milk, tie it up in a bag, and boil it two or three hours. These two ways are much in use in hog-killing time.

A quick Way for preparing an Oatmeal Pudding for baking.—Mix grouts with suet, plumbs, and milk, and bake it in an oven.

Burgoo, its cheap Use in a poor Man's Family.—ONE of my day labourers wives, having four children, is often necessitated to find out the cheapest and best ways to make the daily shilling go the farthest. To this purpose she often feeds them with burgoo, by stirring some water and a little salt into a quart of ground oatmeal, that she boils about half an hour. The longer it boils, the thicker it comes; when she takes it up, she puts a little bit of butter amongst it, and eats it. This saves bread and milk, and is reckoned to go as far as a pottle of flower, as it is of a more satiating nature; for this quantity will give a hearty wholesome dinner to a man, his wife and four children, who eat it with a pleasing appetite.

A poor Woman's Way of managing Oatmeal.—WHEN she has had a bushel of her leased oats threshed, she carries them to the mill to be made into grouts, for which she gives two-pence; that is to say, for drying and hulling them. These, as she kept to use as she wanted them, she would now and then put into the oven after the bread to preserve them dry, and when wanted she would beat some in a wooden mortar with an iron pestle, and though not so fine as when grinded, she liked them better, saying this oatmeal was sweeter then sale oatmeal.

Of Milk-Porridge.

O F the Service that Milk-porridge is of to Families.*—THIS is such an agreeable wholesome liquid food, that it is of general service to almost all sorts of families both in town and country, and is much in use from the lord to the peasant. And although of late it has been supplanted in a great measure by the unwholesome breakfast of foreign teas, yet for the sake of its salubrious cheap qualities and ready preparation, it has recover'd much of its former reputation, and daily comes more and more into use, because it saves firing, labour, and prevents loss of time, as well as the consumption of cheese and butter, as also of sugar and tea, which in thousands of families is expensive indeed.

The common worse Way of making Milk-porridge.—THIS way is thought to save time and trouble; and therefore they mix oatmeal, water, and milk at once cold; then put it over the fire to boil, and thus is very apt to clot and burn to the pot, if not often stirred; and by being thus stirred over the fire, it is likewise apt to be smoak'd, and taken off before the virtue of the oatmeal is extracted by the liquor.

To make Milk-porridge a better Way.—MY maid-servant, if she makes use of new milk, mixes near half water with it, and puts it over the fire to boil. In the mean time she stirs her oatmeal into a little water, and lets it lie soaking till the milk and water boil; then she takes off the pot, and puts her oatmeal into it, which with little stirring will boil quickly: But if she uses skim milk, she mixes no water with it: A handful of oatmeal, provided it is very finely ground, will thus make two quarts of milk-porridge; if coarsely ground, near as much again is required. Skim milk makes better porridge than milk and water.

Mrs. Howard's *Way of making milk-porridge.*—SHE mixes her oatmeal with water, and lets it boil, before she puts in her skim milk, for thus it is not so apt to burn to the pot, as when milk is put in at the first: Skim milk will burn to the pot sooner than new milk, though the new milk is mixt with water.

To prevent Milk-porridge burning to the Pot.—WET the bottom of your pot or kettle, and dip it in ashes; this will prevent the milk-porridge burning to the pot.—Some rince the pot or kettle first with cold water.—Others put a little salt amongst the milk and water to do it.

Butter-milk Milk-porridge.—IN winter time, when butter-milk is in its sweetest condition, it will help to make a very good milk-porridge.

Milk-porridge improved by Bay-leaves. IT is the custom of one of my neighbours to boil a bay-leaf in it; it gives it a pretty flavour, and is medicinal against wind, &c.

Gentry's Method of making Milk-porridge.—SOME bruise grouts or whole oatmeal, and then boil it in milk and water for some time, putting a quart of milk to a pint of water, to boil away, and supplying the consumption by several additions of milk, so that the milk-porridge is almost a jelly: But the best way to do this, is to boil the grouts in water some time before the milk is put in, for preventing the waste of milk.

Various Accounts of Milk-porridge.—THE eating of the grouty part of oatmeal in milk-porridge is perfectly disagreeable to some persons, and therefore they have it all strained through a sieve.—Others boil *Jamaica* pepper in it, for preventing its breeding wind in the stomach; a few corns of it answer this end.—The more milk-porridge is boiled, the smoother it will taste, for then it will have the fuller virtue of the meal, which is the cause of this smoothness.—By boiling the oatmeal in water first, the goodness of it is extracted, and then putting in the new or skim milk, and giving it a warm or two, it occasions the saving of milk, for thus it is not much wasted.

Of Water-Gruel.

Savoury Water-gruel made by poor People.—Some put water, oatmeal, and shred onions or leeks, into a pot at discretion, and boil them till enough: The onion or leek gives the gruel a pleasing relish, and altogether supplies the place of meat-broth, milk, or other such liquid; this many poor labourers families are glad to make shift with, that have not an opportunity to come by milk, or because they can't afford a better breakfast or supper than such wholesome onion gruel stuft with bread. I call it wholesome, as having often observed the children that are fed with gruel, to shew the whitest of teeth, a ruddy-colour'd face, and a plump flesh, even those that very seldom eat any butcher's meat. In 1749, I hired a youngster about 16 years of age, who generally fed on such gruel from his infancy, and being so accustomed to it, refused sugar when it was offered to sweeten it; he proved a good horsekeeper to me.

To make Water-gruel taste somewhat like Meat-broth.—
OTHERS, to make water-gruel taste somewhat like meat-broth, and become the more nourishing, do thus: When the onion-gruel is boiled, they put into it the dripping of roast meat, or fat swimmings of pots, instead of butter, for cheapness sake, as being the produce of their own roasted, boiled, or baked meats; but the poorer sort of people, that have not this of their own, are forced to buy such fat at chandlers shops; to which purpose, these sort of shopkeepers generally buy fat of maid-servants, who in many places have it allowed them as a perquisite, and of this sort some are very good, and some are as much adulterated with worse kinds of fat.

To make plain Water-gruel.—SOME boil the water first, and then stir in their oatmeal; by this means the gruel boils presently with little stirring, which keeps it the clearer from smoak, than if the oatmeal was put into the water cold, and stirred often to keep it from burning to the pot.

A second Way to make plain Water-gruel.—My maid-servant sometimes first soaks her oatmeal in a little cold water, then after some water in a kettle is boiled, she stirs the cold oatmeal and water into the hot water, and boils it till it is enough: This way best prevents the oatmeal from clotting, and causes the gruel to be made the sooner, and with the least waste; add sugar and butter at discretion.

Rabisha's *Way to make Water-gruel.*—TAKE (says he) a pottle of water, and a handful of great oatmeal; pick and beat it in a mortar, and set it a boiling; when it is half enough, put to it two handfuls of currants washed, some sweet herbs, four or five blades of mace, a little grated nutmeg, and let a grain of musk (if you please) be infused a little while in it: Then season it with sugar and rose-water, and put to it a little butter.

A second Author's Way to make Water-gruel.—WHEN you set (says he) a pot of water on the fire to make water-gruel, let grouts be cut but once in two, and let them boil long till they are near enough, then boil it fiercely, and skim off all the top, which I suppose may be at times one third part of the whole, and is the cream of the oatmeal, because it has no gross visible oatmeal in it: Boil this a while by itself, with a little mace and nutmeg, and season it with salt: When it is enough take it off, and put sugar, butter, and a little red rose-water to it, with an egg and some white-wine, to make it the more palatable and nourishing. This skimmed part is much better than the body of the oatmeal at bottom, tho' this more grouty part will make good water-gruel for servants.—*N. B.* If you boil it more leisurely, you may skim off the cream as it riseth in boiling, else it will quickly sink down again to the rest of the gross oatmeal: And thus you may have a finer cream gruel, than with hasty boiling.

Smallage Gruel.—SAYS another, boil fine ground oatmeal three hours in spring water, to two or three quarts of water put about half a porringer of oatmeal, then chop a handful of smallage very small, and put it in a good half hour; before you are to take your gruel off the fire, season it with salt, nutmeg, and mace, and stir in some butter: This sort of gruel is said to purify the blood, open obstructions, beget an appetite, is good against shortness of breath, purges by urine, and is prevalent against jaundice, agues, and sore throats.—Thus you may make any herb gruel.

The Wholesomeness of plain Water-gruel.—HAVE in readiness, as I said before, some fine oatmeal temper'd with cold water, and when your water is just broke for boiling, put this mixture into it; stir them well together, and let it boil but a little while, and it is done: Then season it with salt, and let it stand till the oatmeal has settled, in order to pour off the fine part; of this drink more or less either before or after food, or in a morning, and fast till noon: It is excellent after labour, walking, sweating, or the like, to prevent surfeiting. It is much better than drinking wine or strong beer, which many times increases drought; but this is beneficial at all times of the year, for it allays heat and drought to a wonder.

Elder-bud Gruel, and Herb Gruel.—THIS will cleanse and open obstructions of the breast, and move by stool, and therefore good for fat gross people: Take what quantity of water you please, set it over a clear fire, and make it boiling hot; then have a spoonful of oatmeal (temper'd with cold water) and your elder-buds ready, put both into the boiling water, and keep it stirring, and boiling a little up; then take it off the fire, and let it stand five or six minutes; strain it, and add a little salt to it, or salt and butter if you like it; when cold, drink a pint or more, as your stomach can bear it.—Or make water just boil up, then put in either scurvy-grass, or corn-sallad, spinage, brooklime, elder-berries, smallage, nettle-tops, clivers, cresses, or the like; then take your water off the fire, and let it stand five or six minutes with the herbs in it, and having some oatmeal temper'd with cold water, put that into it, and brew it out of one pot into another many times with salt and butter, till it is fit to eat.—Notwithstanding the numbers of herbs proper for gruels, a certain author says, he gives the preference to those simple herbs that are thought most proper for that infirmity a person is most subject to; and declares, that he was delivered from a pain in making water (that afflicted him at times for forty years, proceeding from gravel) by gathering in the spring-time nettle-tops, elder-buds, groundsel, shepherd's-purse, plantane, cresses, clivers, *&c.* and using some of them in gruel for a month or two in the spring, putting butter and bread into the same.—Cold gruel is made by tempering a spoonful of good oatmeal with a little water, then take a quart of more cold water, and brew the mixed water and oatmeal well together in two pots, and it is done. This last is said to be a most excellent drink to be drank mornings and at meals, and at any time of the day and season of the year, for all sorts of people, healthy or unhealthy, especially in hot seasons, as being a friendly homogeneal liquor, quenching thirst and refreshing the spirits better than fermented drinks; it is not only profitable against the stone and gravel, but also against griping pains of the bowels, helps concoction, prevents fumes and vapours, scurvy and dropsy, by opening obstructions of the liver and spleen, and begets an appetite to admiration.

Of Furmity.

*T*O *make Family Furmity of Wheat.*—TAKE good wheat and sprinkle it well with water, then put it into a bag, and confine it pretty close; next, beat it with a rolling-pin, till its first skin or hull becomes loosened, then take it out and infuse it in a pan of water stirring it about for making the hulls part from the pure kernel; which skim off, and put the neat wheat into a pitcher with some water, not near full, because there must be room left for it to swell. In this manner, we put the pitcher into the oven, when we set our houshold bread in, and after it has stood there as long as the bread, we take it out, and keep it in the pitcher for using it as it is wanted. Then put about half a pint of this jelly wheat to three pints of milk, and boil it till it is more tender; when enough, we stir in some flower to thicken it, and boil it longer for ten or fifteen minutes, stirring it well now and then the while; but some boil the jelly wheat in water, and after it has boiled, add some milk and flower as aforesaid, then sweeten it with a little sugar, palate it with the powder of *Jamaica* spice, and it is fit to eat. Also in case you will have it further improved, you may boil some currants and raisins in water a few minutes, then throw away the water, and put the fruit into the furmity, when you stir in your flower. Some make it with skim milk mixt with water, and think it full good enough for their family.

To make Barley Furmity.—TAKE common barley, sprinkle it well with water, beat it in a bag, to make it part with its outward skin; then bake it in a pitcher, and manage it in the very same manner as you did your wheat furmity. This barley furmity by some is accounted a very healthful pleasant sort, and may be made a cheap hearty breakfast or supper for a family.

To butter Wheat or Barley.—THESE may be made to become a hearty family pleasant food, if ordered as done by those who cry about *London* streets —*Buy a Bowl of Wheat.*—You must sprinkle, beat, bake, and jelly your wheat or barley, and then keep it in store for use; when wanted, take a quantity of it out of your pitcher, and put it into a skillet or sauce-pan over a fire; then stir amongst it some butter, sugar, salt, and a little powder'd spice; when hot enough, it is fit to eat. Or to make it eat more smooth and delicate, you may instead of butter stir a little cream in it. Thus either hulled wheat or barley will keep a week or two, or more in water, if rightly jelly'd; and that it may do so, after it is baked it should be boiled in some water, till the water rises no more on it, and when cold it will be hard enough to be cut with a knife.

Of Barley-Broth, &c.

BARLEY-*Broth made with* English *Barley.*—THIS barley must be first baked, and then boiled in water till it is to a jelly consistence, as is before directed. The first water may be thrown away, but the second is here to remain with its boiled barley; then having beforehand boiled currants and plumbs in water some minutes, in order to take off their sharpness, and prepare them for less boiling amongst the barley-broth, they are to be boiled in it till full tender; then sweeten it with a little sugar, and a small quantity of spice, and it is fit to eat out of porringers for breakfast or supper.

French or Pearl Barley-Water for sick People.—IT is to be first only boiled till it is of a jelly consistence, and it will swell very much; when this is done, throw the first water away, and boil it again in fresh water; some will throw two waters away, till the last water shews a clear amber colour, before it is done for good; then boil orange or lemon peel in it, with currants if you please, because currants are cordial, cooling, loosening, hearty, and nourishing, especially to feverish persons, and to those that have a cough, and are asthmatical; and if their stomach is not strong enough to eat the barley, it may be strained off, and the liquor only drank sweetened with sugar, or better with syrup of lemons for a fever; some mix it with milk hot from the cow, but this is not common.

Pearl Barley-Broth with Meat.—THIS may be made with a knuckle or other joint of veal or mutton, that must be well boiled. Then having boiled four ounces of pearl barley in two or three waters, put the barley into the meat broth, with a pound of raisins, some cloves, mace, ginger, a little salt and lemon-peel; and a quarter of an hour before these are boiled enough put in also some onions, parsley, endive, spinage, lettice, purslane, or any other herbs.

A Dish of Barley.—BOIL a quarter of a pound of pearled barley till it begins to break, then strain the water from it, and set it on the fire in other fresh water; when it boils put in the barley, and boil it till it is soft, then strain this water likewise from it and reserve it; for now you are to beat four ounces of blaunched almonds in a mortar with the boiled barley, which done, put the reserved liquor to them with a little sack and rose-water, season with sugar, nutmeg and cinnamon, and boil them well all together on a stove-fire or chaffing-dish of coals, and sauce it with drawn butter and sugar.—If you please you may make use of milk in this composition.

Barley-gruel.—BOIL a quarter of a pound of pearl barley in three pints of water till tender, and after one water is thrown away, add to the barley three ounces of currants, two eggs, sugar, some white-wine, milk, and lemon-peel; stir all over a gentle fire and it is done.

A Barley Pudding baked.—BOIL half a pound of *French* barley or more (as you think fit) till tender, in milk, then add to it a pint or a quart of milk, four or five eggs well beaten, half a pound of butter, sugar, and nutmeg; put it in a butter'd dish, and set it in with your bread.

Of Rice-Milk.

TO make Rice-milk.—BOIL rice in water till it is soft, for it will boil better and sooner in water than in milk; and when it has boiled pretty soft, if there is too much water lessen it, and pour in milk upon it; then stir a little wheat flower among the rice, and boil it for about a quarter of an hour or more with some *Jamaica* pepper, at last add sugar, and it is done.—Some keep boiled rice by them by way of reserve, to boil it at several times in milk as they want it.—This is a ready breakfast or supper, is a very pleasant spoon meat, nourishes much, and stops looseness, and therefore is made use of in many families.

A boiled Rice-pudding.—BOIL a quarter of a pound of rice in milk till it becomes tender and thick, then mix with it some butter, a little powder'd cinnamon, cloves, mace, sugar, four eggs, and a quarter of a pound of currants; boil this in a pudding-bag an hour.

Butter'd Rice.—WHEN rice has been boiled in water, and then in milk, till tender, bruise it well with a ladle, then put milk and butter, or cream alone, to it; boil it with careful stirring; season it with a little salt, nutmeg and sugar, and eat it with sippets of toasted bread.— Or you may beat dry rice to almost a flower, then add some sugar, eggs, a little sack and some milk, or rather cream; stir these well over a fire till it is like hasty-pudding, and it is done.

Baked Rice-pudding two Ways.—WHEN half a pound or more of rice is boiled tender as abovesaid, then put to it a quart of milk, a jill of Canary, a little mace, cinnamon, grated nutmeg and salt, half a dozen eggs well beaten, half a pound of currants, and some white sugar: This mixture lay on a dish that has a paste first put over all its bottom, and cover the whole with a paste for baking it.—Or you may take a pint of cream, and mix it with a pint of new milk, and five spoonfuls or more of flower of rice; stir it over a fire till it is like hasty-pudding, then take it off, and put to it half a pound of fresh butter, some *Jamaica* spice, a grated nutmeg, a little salt, and six eggs well beaten with white-wine or Canary: All which lay over a puff-paste on the bottom of a dish, and bake it.

Rice and Oatmeal-gruel Diet for a Looseness.—It is recorded by Sir *Kenelm Digby*, that a lord had this diet prescribed for a looseness. Take two pints of fine oatmeal, and one part of flower of rice; boil these as a gruel with some cinnamon, then strain and sweeten it. Or an egg beaten with a little sack may be added to it, or butter.—It is, says he, palatable and nourishing.—Likewise to make a rich mess of rice, he says, mix a spoonful of rice-flower with a quart of cream, and boil it with cinnamon, mace, and nutmeg; when off the fire, mix beaten eggs, sugar, and crumbled bread.

Of White-Pot.

THE *Farmers cheap White-pot.*—TAKE three quarts of skim milk, or so much new milk, if the milk has been skim'd, make use of eight eggs (if new, but six) well beaten, half an ounce of *Jamaica* powder'd spice, a little salt, half a pound of coarse sugar, or more; then pare off the crust part, and cut the crumb part of two pounds of common baker's white bread in thin slices, soak them an hour or two in the milk, before you put the rest of the ingredients to it, and bake the whole in an upright glazed earthen pot, with houshold-bread, near three hours: This sort of cheap white-pot I have frequently made in my family, and it gives my plowman and other servants a pleasant dinner alone.

A better baked White-pot.—CUT thin slices of the crumb of a stale white loaf, and soak them first in three quarts of new milk or cream, then mix with it twelve beaten eggs, half a pound or more of white sugar, a nutmeg grated, some *Jamaica* powder'd spice, half a pound of plumbs first boiled a little tender, and bake the whole in a glazed pot.

A White-pot with Rice.—BOIL a pound and half of rice in a gallon of new milk till it is full tender, then take it off the fire, and stir into it some crumbled bread, seven beaten eggs, three quarters of a pound of white sugar, a grated nutmeg, cinnamon and mace, and bake it an hour.

Of Apple-Pudding.

*T*O make a Farmer's Family boiled cheap Apple-pudding.— TAKE a quart of flower to a pint of water and a spoonful of solid yeast; these stir together into a thick batter, then pare, core, and cut apples very small even to mincing, and mix them thoroughly well with the batter; then put it into a pudding bag or cloth tied up, leaving room enough for its swell: This boil an hour or an hour and half, and eat it with milk and sugar, or better with sugar and melted butter.—This makes a very cheap, wholesome, satiating, and pleasant dinner for a farmer's family; and as the apples are thus mixed with all the batter, they will not gripe any eater of them, which they are apt to do when boiled whole, or not mixt with paste, in the shape of dumplins.—But if this dish is to be made better, milk and eggs may be mixed with the flower instead of water and yeast.— Or the dough or crust may be made better with suet or other fat, instead of yeast; but for a farmer's family, I think yeast sufficient, as it makes the crust or dough eat somewhat hollow and palatable.

A second Way to make a Farmer's cheap boiled Apple-pudding.—MAKE a paste with hot milk and melted hogslard, dripping, or suet, and flower; which knead stiffish, and roll it into a moderate thinness; this done, take apples cut into small bits free of cores or skins, and inclose them in the paste after the round form of a pudding, so that water may not enter; tie it up in a linen cloth, and if about three pints of flower is made use of to a pint of milk or thereabouts, it may be boiled in an hour and a half's time; when taken out of the pot, eat it with milk and sugar, or with melted butter and sugar: This alone may suffice a family for a dinner.—Let your apples be a little sharp, else they will eat flattish.

An Apple-pudding to bake.—TO this purpose, scald your apples and pulp them through a cullender or otherways, then mix the pulp with crumbled fine bread, eggs, cream, and sugar; to which you may add some grated nutmeg, or *Jamaica* spice powder, and so bake it.

To make Apple-dumplins for a Farmer's Family.—MAKE a paste or dough with lard, butter, dripping, and milk; when the lard is melted in the hot milk, put it to the flower, and knead it; but where the lard or other fat is not to be had, knead the flower with yeast mixt in hot water: Then wrap a pared large apple in a piece of this paste, and thus as many more as you think fit, so that the water they are boiled in may not enter them.—These sort of apple-dumplins I have frequently made great part of the year, and eaten with sugar stirred in some milk for sauce, and they prove a very agreeable dinner with a piece of pickled pork or bacon.

A rich boiled Apple-pudding.—MAKE a puff-paste by rubbing butter into flower, and so on, rolling more bits of butter into the paste several times, till a true puff-paste is made; then grate a quince amongst some apples pared and cored, and cut into small bits, wrap it up in the puff-paste, and boil it as a pudding in a flower'd cloth. When it is enough, eat it with melted butter and sugar. This is a very palatable good pudding.

How a Lord's Family-Servants had Apple-Pudding made for them instead of Plumb-Pudding.—THE lord I mean here, was one that was a true œconomist, yet kept a good house both for eating and drinking, for I have known him keep two men cooks at a time. However, to save extraordinary expence, amongst his other management, he obliged his many common servants to eat no other pudding for seven weeks together than apple boil'd pudding, which with other victuals gave them a full pleasant meal; the apple-pudding was made thus:—The dough or crust was made with wheat-meal, and either butter, suet, or kitchen fat, rolled thick to wrap over apples chopt into small pieces. When this was done, the pudding was tied up in a cloth, and boiled three or four hours. Then they eat it with sugar in melted butter put over the apples. This was done to save the charge of plumbs, &c.

How to make various Sorts of compounded, profitable, Family Victuals.

*L*ittle bacon Pasties, to boil for a Farmer's Family.—MIX a pottle of wheat-flower with a sufficient quantity of warm water into a stiff paste, then roll it thinly out, for making 6, 8, or 10 little pasties. This done, take half a pound of bacon, and cut it into very small thin slices, and lay some of them on a piece of the paste, with good store of parsley and thyme shred very small, to which add a little black pepper, and make it up pasty-fashion; proceed thus till all the paste and bacon is made use of, and put them all into a pot of boiling water, keeping them boiling about three quarters of an hour with a quick fire.—If these boiled bacon pasties are to be made better, use new milk instead of water, with melted butter or lard. You may also, if you please, add some chopt onions or any other relishing herb or root.

Little Bacon Pasties to bake for a Farmer's Family.—MAKE these bacon pasties with bread-dough, out of the same kneading-kiver wherein the dough is kneaded for houshold bread, and in the very same manner as the boiled bacon pasties are done; then prick them, and set them in with common oven cakes. About half an hour bakes them at the oven's mouth, before the oven is stopt up for good with the bread.—These pasties are made by some labourers and farmers wives for the sake of their readiness, cheapness, and goodness; for as the gravey of the bacon is here intirely kept within the paste with the juice of the herbs, the mixture of them all renders these pasties a pleasant, wholesome, satiating victuals, and serves for a delightful change of diet amongst children and servants in particular.

The Hertfordshire *Way of dressing Eggs and Bacon.*—OUR housewife cuts her bacon into thin slices as if for frying, then puts them into a pot of water as it hangs over a fire, either when the water is cold or hot. If cold, it is to freshen the bacon, if when hot, it must be put in a little before the eggs, that they may be both ready together, for the eggs must not be broke into the water till it boils. When the eggs are done enough, put a little melted butter over them, and thus the bacon will eat fresher and pleasanter than if fry'd or broil'd, for frying or broiling makes it harder and hotter than when it is boiled.

A ready quick-made Dish, with Bits of pickled Pork and Eggs.—BEING on a journey, I put up my horse at a public house, and as I was in haste, I desired something to eat that might be quickly dressed; upon this the woman of the house cut some thin bits of pickled pork, and fry'd them in a pan, without any other fat than what the pork yielded: At the same time she had some water boiling, in which she broke three eggs, and all was done in a trice. This she said is a better way than frying the eggs, and putting grease over them, for that thus the eggs will be free from any tang, and of a pure white colour.

Mr. Houghton's *Way to bake or stew an Ox-Cheek.*—HE says, cut off the meat from the bones, and when pepper'd and salted lay it at the bottom of a pot, then lay the bones broken on the top, and pour on it a pint of claret and a pint of ale, over which put onions with sweet herbs, and the marrow will descend and keep all moist; some add verjuice, lemon-peel, salt, cloves, and nutmegs; stew it 4 or 5 hours, then sauce it with flower and butter.

Artificial Oisters.—A Cook told me, that as she was dressing a supper, and had got her oister-sauce ready to put to the fish, the footman spilt it. To remedy which, she sent for some sheeps-trotters, and taking out all the bones, she cut the flesh in little and bigger pieces, then dressed them up, and when added to the fish, they passed and were eaten for oisters.

To colour Savoys and Cucumbers green.—THE same cook said, that if savoys were boiled and afterwards turned yellow, she could recover them green again, by putting hot water on some ashes, and when they have tinctured the water enough, there will be a reddish scum: Of this take a spoonful, and put it into the water that scalds the savoys (or in cold liquor or pickle wherein cucumbers lie pickled) and it will make them of a fine green colour. To do this it is reported that some make use of vitriol, which is indeed of a poisonous nature. Or to boil things green, as savoys, pease, &c. put them into water boiling fast, don't cover, but as soon as they sink take them out.

Ox-Cheek baked the Farmers Way.—WE parboil one or two cheeks as they come from the butchers shops about two hours, till a little tender, then put the cheek into a deep glazed earthen pot, with as much water as covers it, some onions, parsley, thyme, winter-savory, and a little salt; then put it into the oven with our houshold bread. If the cheek is young and fat, and the bones of it well broken, it will yield a good sort of soup, in which we soak slices of bread, and then it gives us, our plowmen and other servants, a hearty pleasant meal.

Ox-Cheek-Pye.—BOIL a cheek till tenderish; when cold enough, hash the flesh by cutting it from the bones; season it with a little salt, pepper, mace, cloves, and nutmeg, and add to it what other sort of meat you please, with some onions and butter; then close it in pye-paste, and when baked put into the pye a mixture of claret, vinegar, and sugar, beat with yolks of eggs.

Dry'd or hung Beef.—THE *Dutch*, says Mr. *Houghton*, take a veiny piece of the largest heifer, which is best next the thick flank, the second best is the leg of mutton piece, then the first round of the buttock. Take one of these pieces, and lay it in brine thus made: Take four or five handfuls of common salt, three of bay-salt, salt-petre, and petre-salt, of each a handful; boil these in spring water to a full height that will bear eggs; when cold, put in half a pint of vinegar, which helps to make it short.—Now take one of the pieces of beef, lay it a fortnight in this brine, or ten days at least, as it is in bigness, then take it out and salt it well with equal quantities of bay-salt, salt-petre, and petre-salt, for a week or a fortnight; then roll it, and wrap it in three, four, or five sheets of brown paper, if you burn sea-coal, and hang it in a chimney, where it may be neither too hot nor too cold; turn it each day for a week, then once in two or three days, till it is well dried; then use it, or keep it in a dry place. If you hang it by a wood fire, it needs no paper; it may be dried with saw-dust, as neats-tongues are, but it won't be so white.—Or you may wash one of these pieces of beef, and then with six ounces of powder'd salt-petre, a pound and half of bay-salt dried and finely beaten, and a quarter of a pound of coarse sugar, rub the beef soundly, then keep it salting with common salt, turn it for a fortnight, and hang it to dry in or near a chimney; when it is wanted, boil it in water and hay, and it will keep good a month or two, or more.—But we in the southern parts of *England* do not prepare hung beef so well as they do in *Lancashire* and the North; because they dry it there with the smoak of turf, which gives the beef such a very pleasant tang, that it is much coveted and sent for to considerable distances.

To pot or otherwise to preserve Neats-Tongues—AT *Newcastle*, Mr. *Houghton* says, they are potted thus:—Salt them with common salt, petre-salt, and some salt-petre, which will make them look red. After ten days half boil them and skin them, then season them with spice, and bake them till they are very tender: Then dry, pot and close cover them with melted butter, and send them where you please. Or after they are thus salted, they may be preserved raw in pickle made with the salts, salting them now and then with common salt, and thus are ready to be boiled upon occasion. Or you may take them out of the pickle, and dry them for boiling afterwards.

The Use of Pease in Families.

A Hertfordshire *Farmer's Wife's Way to make her Family Pease-porridge, and afterwards Pease-soup of the same.* HER custom is, when they kill a hog for pickling pork, to leave the short ribs in it; for her notion is, that they keep the pork while boiling in less waste, and because the bones make the meat eat the pleasanter. Of such pork, she thinks, she makes the best pease-porridge, by putting a piece of it with some pease into cold water, which she boils so long, till the blue, white, or grey pease is hulled; and near the last of their boil[i]ng, she throws a little bunch of mint into the pot. This is the way she makes her family pease-porridge; but that for herself and husband she makes somewhat better, by boiling a small pease-pudding in a bag, amongst her pease-porridge, and when all is boiled enough, she breaks the pudding into some of the porridge, and boils it again, and thus makes a good pease-soup; accounting both right housewifery to the saving of much milk in a year. *N. B.* If the hog is killed in the summer, the bones must not be left in the meat, lest it taint.

Another Hertfordshire *Farmer's Wife's Way to make her Family Pease-Porridge.*—THIS woman thinks she makes the best pease-porridge when she boils a leg of pork, or other good piece of pork, with pease, till they are full tender; then she takes out the meat, and pours into the pot half the quantity or less of milk, as there is porridge, and boils it about a quarter of an hour, when she mixes two or three handfuls of wheat-meal with some water or milk, and stirs this into the porridge for thickening it, and making it the more hearty; this, when boiled up a very little while, will finish the pease-porridge.

A Poor Man's Family Pease-porridge.—MANY of these are glad to make pease-porridge of a bit of bacon or pickled pork. If the meat is in a small quantity, it need not be soaked to freshen it; but if it is in a large quantity, then it is necessary to soak it in luke-warm water, an hour or more, to lessen its saltness. This done, they boil it with pease, and afterwards thicken the porridge with some flower, which when boiled up is enough, for giving the family hearty breakfast and supper meals, crumb'd with bread, or without it; for some think the porridge thick and hearty enough without bread.

Pease-soup made by a Gentleman at Gaddesden.—THIS gentleman, my next neighbour, had frequently a leg of beef boiled with pease, for making pease-soup thus: After the beef had been almost boiled to rags, it was taken out and given to the poor, and then the pease hulled in a cullender; this done, there was put into the strained pease-liquor some whole pepper, mace, cinnamon, and sallary, and then boiled again.— Or instead of a leg of beef, you may boil any other piece of beef, and when the meat is strained off, you may put into the soup one or two, or more anchovies, onion, cloves, ginger, savory, thyme, and pepper, with some parsley, a bit of bacon and butter, and boil all half an hour, or rather less, then strain off and add bread, or not.—Or you may boil pease till they are fit to be hulled through a cullender, and as they are passing through mix some milk with them, which boil with the addition of some strong broth, parsley, onions, ginger, and what else you like best.—Or you may make soup with green pease in their pods by scalding them, and then beating them in a mortar, and when drained, boil in the liquor, onions, parsley, mint, sweet herbs, and crumbs of bread, in mutton-broth, season'd with salt and pepper. Or boil the green pease without their shells, when tender strain and hull them through a cullender, then boil the drain'd liquor with parsley, marygolds, lettice, sorrel, and mint, adding butter, some flower, a little pepper, salt, and bits of toasted bread.

The Mistake of a Farmer's Wife in boiling Pease.—SHE lives near *Dunstable*, and her father is a considerable farmer near me. The woman having no pease of her own, her father carry'd her some that were famed for boiling tender in a little time; but this woman complain'd she could not boil them tender; upon which her father ask'd, what water she boiled them in? she said, our well water. O, says he, you have a river near you, boil them in that water. She did, and then they were tender enough.

Hertfordshire *Way of making green Pease Porridge.*—WE boil green pease quickly after they are shelled, and when they are boiled a little tender, we put some milk into the pot, and boil them about a quarter of an hour, then stir in some flower, till the porridge is almost as thick as pap, and when all is boiled a little longer, with a bunch of mint, it is done enough. At last, some pepper and salt is put into each mess, and eaten generally without bread or butter, because in this way of preparing green pease porridge, it is thick enough without bread.

Hertfordshire *Farmer's Wife's Way to make a Family Pease-pudding.*—WHITE hard pease are commonly soaked in water all night, for making them boil the sooner tender; but for blue pease we seldom let them lie in water above two or three hours. After this, we put them into a pudding-bag, and boil them about three quarters way, till they are pretty tender, when we take the bag out of the pot and beat it well, for causing the pease to boil the sooner into a mash or pudding, and when we think they are beat enough, we return the bag into the pot, and boil it about a quarter or half an hour longer; at the end of which time, we turn the pudding out of the bag, and eat it with a piece of bacon or pickled pork. Some indeed put a little butter amongst the slices of the pudding; but our farmers seldom do any thing else than scatter a little pepper over the pudding. It will come out of the pot as firm as a bread-pudding.

The most proper Pease for making Pease-Porridge and Pease-Pudding.—I SOW the white dwarf marrow-fat pea, the nonpariel pea, the great union or blue pea, and the large hollow grey pea, in my inclosed fields, by sowing some broad cast and others out of my excellent four-wheel light drill-plow, that has two hoppers on it, one whereof sows pease out of it, and the other a powder'd manure, that falls on the pease, wheat, barley, or turnip-seed, the moment any of these are discharged out of the seed-hopper; and by a very little harrow of six tynes, fastened to the arse of the plow, it closes the drill as it is drawn along; and when the pease are four or more inches high, the most profitable two-wheel horse-break cleans the interval ground of weeds, as it is drawn thro' them two or three times in a summer, by which means we commonly have the best of crops of pease; but the readiest sort of pease for making pease-porridge or pease-pudding are the hulled, yellow, split pease, sold at many shops for this very purpose.

To pickle Mushroom Buttons.—As soon as milk is boiled put in your button, and when boiled 3 or 4 minutes take them out, and put them into a boiled brine, made with salt, water, mace, ginger, white pepper and bay-leaves. In this brine keep your mushrooms in wide-mouth'd glass bottles secure from air.

Potatoes, Carrots, Turnips, Cabbages, &c. preserved.

*P*Otatoes dressed by Farmers Wives.—As the readiest and cheapest ways of dressing and eating potatoes is the study of a good housewife, where these earth apples can be conveniently had, she often boils them with either a piece of bacon, pork, or salt-beef, or by themselves, and when boiled she takes off their skins, as believing this way is better than to pare them before boiling, because it better prevents the water getting into them, and makes them eat the firmer and sweeter. She also boils them (if she can get it) in hard spring water, and very gently, to prevent their cracking. Or if she first pares and then boils them, she ought to put some salt and *Jamaica* spice into the water, for the better hardening and relishing them, provided they are thus boiled for being eat with meat. But if they are to be used in puddings, or to eat with sweet milk, or in any other luscious way, the salt and spice must not be put into the water. Thus boiled, she lays them in a dish under meat to be eaten without butter or any other sauce, except pepper and salt, or in a dripping-pan under roast-beef, mutton, *&c.* for their being improved by the fat and gravey that drops on them while the meat is roasting, to the saving of butter; but where butter is to be made use of, the boiled potatoes are generally brought to table under the meat, and butter in a porringer by itself, for each person's choice: Always observing to put potatoes into the water cold; for if they are put into boiling water they will certainly crack. Or the boiled potatoes may be cut in thin pieces, and fry'd in good fat with onions or garlick.— Or stewed with a bit of meat, onions, pepper, and salt, in ale.—Or they may be baked with herrings or pilchers, by laying a row of potatoes and a row of herrings, and so on, adding salt, pepper, a very little vinegar or verjuice, and some sweet herbs.—Or when potatoes are boiled and mashed, they may be eaten in bacon, pork, or other meat broth, season'd with spice, salt, and herbs.—Or in milk alone, or sweeten'd with sugar.—Or if the potatoes are large, they may be roasted in embers, and eaten like an egg, with butter and salt.—Or so mashed, they may be used with currants, bits of a hog's flair, and other ingredients, in the making of skin white puddings.—Or raw potatoes may be baked in a pye with meat, or without it, seasoning it with spices and salt.—Or it may be made into a sweet pye, by adding to the potatoes alone, raisins of the sun, good suet, butter, or marrow, and sugar, with or without apples; when baked enough, beat the yolk of an egg in vinegar or verjuice, sugar, and salt, and pour it into the pye for sauce. Or when boiled, and eaten with salt-fish and butter, it will become a very good dish.—Some of our farmer's wives, when a hog is killed, will make a good family pye with the offald bits of meat and potatoes, otherwise with bits of the liver and crow and potatoes, by laying pared raw pieces of potatoes at the bottom of the pye, and next a layer of the meat season'd with salt and pepper, and so on, a layer of one and the other.—Potatoes may be so managed as to save much consumption of eggs, meat and bread, as is truly experienced every year by poor families in many parts of *Ireland* and *England*.—At *Manchester*, a great market in *Lancashire*, potatoes stand in many sacks as well as oatmeal for publick sale, for here they are in common use by both poor and rich; and as I have had potatoes brought me from that part, I think I may say they are the best sort in *England*, for whiteness, shortness, and sweetness. And therefore they are much eaten by the poor people, first boiled, then mashed, and the pulp boiled again in milk, in which they stir some flower, and eat it like hasty-pudding; but the richer sort mingle a little wine and sugar with it, and make sometimes a pudding with potatoes and other ingredients for the belly of a hare and other beasts.

To preserve Potatoes all the Year.—IT is not only obtaining a good crop of potatoes, but a farther knowledge is also perfectly necessary, and that is, how to preserve them sound all the year. 1*st*, Those potatatoes [*sic*] that are to be kept for eating all the year, must be kept from the frost and from moisture. Some of the *Irish*, as soon as they are taken out of the ground, dry them on an oat-oast or kiln, by laying them on it for about half an hour or more, immediately after the oats are off. Here they keep them turned several times, till dried enough for keeping all the year in a dry place; and thus they may be also dried after malt, when they are to be kept all the year; otherwise they eat them fresh as dug out of the ground. 2*dly*, Potatoes may be kept in the ground all the winter, if a thick covering of straw or horse-litter is laid over them where they grow. 3*dly*, Or a narrow long trench may be dug in a sandy or other dry soil, and after it is well lined with wheat straw on all its inside, it may be filled up with potatoes, and cover'd with more straw and a thick top of mould, to lie ridge fashion, in a field, or other place. 4*thly*, Potatoes may be kept above ground in a cellar or chamber between wheat-straw. 5*thly*, They may be dried in the sun sufficiently to be preserved sound, if kept in a dry place from the frost afterwards, and be ready for use till potatoes come in again. I have eat them good in the month of *June* in *Somerset-shire*, though a little sprouted: But they were first pared before they were put into the pot. Some gardeners put a bushel of them in a heap in dry sand in a barn, and cover them with straw, but put no mould over them.

Carrots, their Uses and Preservation.—THESE roots are a very pleasant and nourishing sort both for man and beasts; and if they are managed in a right manner, they may be enjoyed most part of the year; for their seed may be sown, so as to have several crops in that time. When made use of at about the thickness of a man's thumb, what is a more dainty root to eat with roasted or boiled flesh? And to preserve them for eating in winter and spring, they may be hoarded in pits of dry earth, or in other places, as potatoes are. They will cause a little meat to go the farther in a family; fatten horses, oxen, hogs, sheep, or rabbits; keep milch cows and other milch beasts in heart, and breed much milk. The trench or pit should not be above eighteen inches deep, and as much broad, but as long as you please. If you lay the carrots deeper and thicker, they will heat and grow. Others lay them in sand in a house.

Turnips and Parsnips.—MAY be preserved in the same manner, in the ground, or between wheat straw in a chamber or other convenient place, where there is no sandy ground to keep these or carrots in. But where there is sands, a certain gardener takes up his carrots about the first of *September*, and puts them in a pit six inches wide at bottom, eighteen at top, and covers with a ridge.

To preserve Onion, Garlick, or Shalots from one Season to another.—THESE roots are so necessary for family uses, that none should be without them. I am not a gardener, and therefore touch only upon a few particulars of it; one among the rest is, how to preserve onions, garlick, and shalots, by the natural heat of the sun, and by an artificial heat. By the sun, when they are ripe, and laid (and now and then turned) on the ground in sunshine weather till well dried: By artificial heat, when they are put into an oven after the bread is drawn out, with their bottom part downwards, there to lie till they sweat and become softish; for by such heat, vegetation is stop'd and utterly destroyed, and when the onions, garlick, or shalots are quite cold, they will be hard and keep sound. And now I am writing on onions, I take this opportunity to inform my reader of a most necessary cheap improvement that is to be made, by buying only one pennyworth of *Welch* onion seed at a *London* seed-shop, and sow it in a little square bed of earth about four foot long, and two or three foot wide. I did this, I think, in 1742, and at this time (1749) they are in a flourishing condition. They are of so hot a nature as to shoot out their flaggy stalks in *January*, always in *February*; and thus as grass onions, they may be cut (I am of opinion) twenty or more years together, but they must be duly weeded, now and then manured in the middle of winter, and never suffer'd to run seedy.—Or as these come sooner than any others, their seed may be sown annually to draw for young onions to be eaten in sallets, or with bread and butter in *May*, as the common gardeners do.—Some gardeners lay straw or mat over a rack in a house, and onions, garlicks, or shalots on it, but not to touch one another, for most of the winter.

To preserve Cabbages and Collyflowers.—CUT cabbages and collyflowers of their stalks at *Allhollantide*, with all their rough leaves on, and keep them under a cover of wheat straw from the frost; by which means they'll keep sound and sweet a long time, else the frost may take them, rot them, and make them stink.—Others only tie the upper leaves close on their top with bass-string, and if the frost be not too severe, the cabbage will be preserved sound from that and rain, almost if not quite a whole winter; or you may keep them hung up in a cellar with all their stalks and roots.

To preserve Kidney or French Beans.—STRING the beans and lay them in a glazed earthen pot, and between every layer of them lay salt, and they'll keep all the winter very green, eat fresh, and be near as good as when fresh gathered.—The white kidney bean or seed is preserved, by letting them be thoroughly ripe before gathering, and then well dried in the sun, for being afterwards conserved in their pods or without them, in a chamber or other dry place, secured from frost. These seed beans of late are cried about *London* streets in the winter and spring seasons, to sell for being boiled and eaten with melted butter, especially among the poorer sort.

Carrots preserved throughout the Winter and Spring by a Lord's Gardener.—HE makes a pile of them like a hay-cock in a ground-room, in which he sometimes puts six, eight, or ten bushels; and when it is thus finished, he has it surrounded with wheat straw, made into yelms as for thatching, on all its sides and top; then he has several wheel-barrows full of dry gravel laid all about them, so that the carrots are entirely cover'd with straw and gravel, and being confined in a very narrow place, the frost can't come at them, and thus they'll eat fresh and sweet. And as his lord's seat stands within a day's journey of *London*, carrots and other garden-ware are frequently sent up to the family in *London*; but to do this the seldomer, they uncover part of the pile, and take out about a bushel of carrots at a time, which they put into a hamper on a layer of dry straw, then a layer of carrots, and so on till full.

Potatoes preserved by a Lord's Gardener.—THEY are wash'd immediately after being taken out of the ground, and very well dried; then after laying a layer of straw in a hamper, a layer of potatoes on that, and so on till the hamper is full, it is kept all the winter and spring in a cellar, where neither frost nor moisture can come at them; and thus the potatoes may be securely kept in delicate sweet sound order in one or more hampers.

Onions and Garlick, &c. preserved by a Lord's Gardener.—HE has a large chest kept during the winter in a dry room even with the ground, wherein he first puts a layer of dry wheat straw, then a layer of onions on that, then straw, then onions, and so on till the chest is full.—Garlick he ties up in bunches, and keeps them in a dry room.

The preservation of Apples.—APPLES gathered ripe, dry, and free of bruising, if they are of the lasting sort, may be preserved almost till apples come again. My man in gathering apples puts them into a sack fastened before him from his left shoulder to his right hip, for if he gathered them into a wicker basket, it would be apt to bruise them; and to prevent the like damage happening to those apples that fall in gathering, he lays some straw, fern, or blankets under the tree: Some lay them thinly next the boards on a chamber-floor, and cover them with straw to prevent the damage of frosts, their heating, sweating, and rotting; and shift with fresh dry wheat-straw now and then, under or over them, or both. The famous early-ripe Parsnip apples will keep till *Christmas*; Golden-rennets, and some others, till *Candlemas*, and longer; Russettings, John-apples, Holland, Green, Kentish, Lemon Pippins, and Non-pareils, &c. till apples come again, therefore lay their several sorts by themselves. I have known some gentlemen so curious as to have their Golden-pippens gather'd before they were full ripe, to prevent the damage of frost, for by this means they will have the finest flavour, but are apt to shrivel a little. Be sure now and then to search for some decayed apples, for if any be rotten they will quickly infect sound ones; but forbear to do this in a frost, on a sudden thaw, or in very damp weather.—Holland pippins on the 17th of *May*, 1747, were cried to be sold for 4*d*. a peck; the woman that sold them said she cover'd them with nothing, only laid them on wheat-straw in a chamber; if they are not meddled with, the frost in such a place won't hurt them.

To preserve Pears.—WARDEN pears in particular deserve great care in their preservation for a family use, because they may be made to serve as part of their subsistence great part of the following year. The Pound pear, Black pear of *Worcester*, *Cadilliac*, and some other sorts that bear well every year, will agree with the same management of preservation as the apples.—Some direct to preserve apples in syrup, but this is rather too costly and troublesome, but both apples and pears may be preserved some time dry by baking them in an earthen glazed pot, or better in a flat pan; the apples should have first a skewer run through them from the eye to the stalk. Pears likewise may be preserved by being baked whole in the same manner, a peck with half a gallon of strong ale put amongst them, cover'd over with paper; then take them from the liquor, squeeze out their moisture, and dry them on sieves: The same way dries apples, after their baking, and being squeezed flattish from top to bottom, and put into an oven after bread is taken out; or the sieves may lie on a rack fixed to a ceiling near a fire. See *Evelyn's French Gardener*.

A Letter from a worthy Gentleman to this Author concerning the Improvement of baked Pears.

London, September 16th, 1745.

SIR,

SINCE no fruit is more wholesome, delicious, and gratefully cooling than a good baking pear, and as I take you to be an experienced judge of the agreeable quality of your own Orange pear of *Gaddesden*, let me recommend to you, as well as to all good housewives, who are not acquainted with the simple secret, that as the most inviting appearance and tempting dress this delicious part of a dessert can be cloathed in, is that of an agreeable red, so no simple and innocent art effects it so truly as that of baking them in a pewter-dish, or pewter-bason: I speak from the field of experience, as the following incident clearly shewed.—A relation of mine had some noted trees for baking-pears in his garden, and had also an admirable good cook, famous in the country for giving these pears a beautiful red in baking; but by accident being removed from the family, his successor quite failed in this particular point of baking the noted pears red: This put some of the family upon unsuspected means of applying to the old cook for his secret, which taking effect, behold it was nothing more than his having constantly baked them in deep pewter dishes, whereas upon examination the successor had always done it in earthen glazed vessels. Therefore after paring and coring, let them be only quarter'd or half'd, and laid on the naked bottom of the pewter dish or bason, with the proper quantity of best sugar according to the nature of the pear, and without any crust on the bottom or sides of the dish: Lastly, cover the sides of the dish or bason, when full, with a suitable pewter dish or large plate, so that this cover may even touch the top of the pears, then with a little dough or paste of coarse flower and water stop the edges of the cover, to retain the steam the better in baking. Some put a little water and such spice they like best; a thorough juicy right baking pear wants very little water, as much of it impoverishes it. I take these pears to be of the Warden kind, perhaps crossed, and (much improved by their fat loamy clay) fit to bake in *October*, but will hang on till *December*; they are great bearers like ropes of onions, being a middle-sized tree, inclinable to spread horizontally, and to be weighed down by its weight in fruit. It is also to be observed that no baking pear is so red as will turn after being cold, and the second or third day after baking they are at their clearest bright red, though they will hold a good full red colour some weeks in winter, if kept from freezing. Therefore to regard them with art, the crust should be broke from the cover before they are quite cool, then the cover taken off for an hour or two, and laid loosely on again, always observing to serve up the uppermost layers of pears as they rise, and pouring over them a spoonful or two of the clear crimson syrup. This I have instructions in from the ladies. A mouthful or two now and then may be given in burning fevers, to the great comfort and cheering of the patient; they are likewise good in dry hectical habits, especially as a light supper. They may also be given now and then with judgment in some stages of the small-pox, and very safely at most times in the meazles, especially when too plentiful a bleeding continues at the nose. They are admirable after great heats and fatigues, when the body is cool enough to receive them, because they gently cool, astringe, and corrugate the fibres of the stomach.—This was wrote before I went out of town, but forgot to be sent away. I have not time at present to answer your last favour of the 12th, but will soon.—I have undertaken to procure from you four choice plants of the black Kerroon cherry, for a worthy friend of mine in *Northamptonshire*, who has every thing very good about his house, but never heard of this famous cherry: He says he has no more room to spare in his garden for large standards, or I would have made him a present of more from you, as a Parsnip-apple-tree or two, and the Orange-pear. However, he is now marched against the Rebels, and if he comes back in time this season, or in the spring, I shall then give you directions about them; he has as strong and deep red mould as most in *England*, partaking more of the clay than sand, yet such as won't hold water, which added to his own ingenuity, good choice at first, and care afterwards, makes his fruit in general excellent, as well as his cyder, perry, and made wines.

I am, Sir,
Your assured Friend,

A. B.

To preserve Quinces.—A tree of these planted on the brink of a wet ditch is a constant bearer, and will thrive exceeding safe if its root-shoots are kept down. One of the right *Portugal* sort I have thus growing. Quinces will not keep long without good management, therefore gather them full dry and free of bruises, and rub them with a cloth; this done, lay them in wheat-straw, in a chamber, and in a row, then another row and straw, and so on: But they are better pack'd thus in a cask, for keeping the air from them.—Quinces may be also preserved in marmalade several ways; but to avoid too much cost, pare, core, and quarter the quinces, then put the quarters into a pitcher, with some sugar and water, enough to cover them, and paper tied over it's mouth: Let the pitcher be put into an oven with bread, and thus baked till the quinces are pretty tender, then take them out of the pitcher water and all, and add more sugar, and, if occasion, more water: Two pounds of quinces should have near a pound of sugar, and a pint and half of water, which boil all together till the whole is almost candied, for then it will be a red marmalade fit to be potted up, and cut out in slices, as it is wanted: You may make a sort of jelly liquor of the quince parings, cores, and kernels, by first beating them, and then soaking them 48 hours in cold water, which drain out, and put into a sauce-pan with the baked quarters of the quinces, and boil as aforesaid, or otherways.

To preserve the Golden-rennet and other such Apples till May *is over.*—I am credibly informed that a gentleman was so great a lover of the Golden-rennet apple, that to keep them sound till *May* was out, he made use of a butter-firkin, at the bottom of which he put a thin layer of dry wheat-straw, and then a layer of apples, then again another layer of straw, and a layer of apples, and so on till he filled the cask. This done, he put on the loose head, and buried the firkin under ground, where, by keeping out the weather, the apples kept sound and good till *May* was out; and by the same method may other apples be preserved in excellent order.

To preserve Walnuts, by a Lord's Gardener.—HE has a square tin chest or box that holds about two bushels, which he fills with walnuts, after the outward coat or husks of them are taken off, and they are well rubbed and dried in the sun. The tin box thus filled, he puts into a grave or foss in the earth, so deep, that about two foot of mould may lie on its top; here they commonly remain till *Candlemas*, when they are taken out in a fresh sweet condition; and for the family's enjoying walnuts in the mean time, some are laid in sand in a cellar, others under straw in a chamber.—One of my neighbours put a bushel of walnuts into a hole in the ground, and after they had lain till *Allhollantide*, they were taken up, and seemed to be as good as when first laid in.—Or you may put some dry sand at the bottom of an earthen pot, then a layer of walnuts at an inch distance from each other, and so on, till the pot is full. When they are to be eaten, soak them in warm water for an hour, and rub them dry, by which means they will peel, and taste sweet.

Cherries and Goosberries preserved a long Time.—IT is the practice of several of our *Hertfordshire* women to preserve some of our famous most excellent of all black cherries, the large black Kerroon sort, when they are dry, ripe, and sound, by filling stone or glass quart or bigger bottles with them, and as they are filling, to give the bottle a shake or pat on a cloth spread on a table to make them lie the closer, then cork very tight, and if you tie some leather over the cork it will be an additional security. About *Whitsuntide* they commonly make tarts of them, and as the cherries will in a little time after bottling yield juice enough to cover them, when any of their family is troubled with wind, or the wind cholic, they will pour out a tea-cup of the juice, and mixing a little sugar with it, it relieves them. By this method these sort of cherries have been kept serviceable above two years, and when they have been eaten with sugar, they have acquired a strength sufficient to warm the stomach.—If when you bottle the cherries, you add a little sugar to them, it is thought by some an improvement. Keep the bottles in a cool place, and from the air as much as you can.—So one of our housewives at *Gaddesden* preserves goosberries, by first scalding them, but not to break, and then corking them well up in a bottle. Or you may preserve cherries, goosberries, and currants, by filling quart large-mouth'd glass bottles with either, and putting them in an oven after bread, cork'd well.

To preserve black Cherries, Sloes, &c.—WE put either of these in a stone bottle that holds one, two, or three gallons, with some sugar, cork it well up, and bind leather over it. This we put into a hole in the ground and cover up, so that no weather can hurt it; in the spring time we take it up, and the liquor will be like claret: This is practised in *Hertfordshire*, where we abound with greater plenty of black cherries than any other county in *England*; but of this, more by and bye.— Or you may have cherries or sloes, *&c.* all the year, by laying a layer of hay and a layer of cherries, and so till a firkin is filled, to keep out all air, and under a bed, but the cherries must not be bruised.

To preserve Apples, Carrots, or Turnips, &c. *sound all the Winter.*—THIS is practised at a certain knight's seat in *Hertfordshire*, where they think bran is very serviceable on this account, by covering apples, carrots, or turnips, *&c.* in it, which will defend them against frost, dampness, and a quick decaying, and the better if they are thus placed in a dry room.—A Vale woman that lived about three miles from me took this method to preserve her apples: She laid them on wheat-straw on a floor above stairs, and when frosts were at hand, she would cover her apples with wheat-straw or blankets, and in open weather take them off to give the fruit air, but we take special care not to put one bruised apple amongst the gathered ones, for the bruised ones will certainly rot and infect the sound ones.

To preserve Goosberries, Strawberries, Bullace, Damsons, &c. *for Tarts or Pies.*—FOR this purpose the fruit must not be ripe, yet arrived to its full growth. Have ready quart glass bottles that are thoroughly dry, and when the fruits are well pick'd, put either of them into the bottles; and let your corks be of the best velvet sort, that they may keep water from entering, for the bottles must be put into a kettle of water up to their necks, but not to touch the corks. And when the water is hot enough, and the goosberries look white, take off the kettle, and let the bottles remain in it till cold. Then take them out and tie leather about them, or put wax or pitch on them, and keep them in a dry place for use.—Or you may preserve goosberries, mulberries, strawberries, and such like fruit, by putting them in large stone bottles close by a fire-side, for the heat to draw out the air; when full, cork up immediately, and keep the bottles in sand, to prevent air, in a cool place. White damsins are fine fruit to preserve. I sell the trees.

To preserve Nectarins, Peaches, Apricots, &c.—Wood ashes, finely sifted, are of a soft dry nature, and so impregnated with vegetable salts, that they are enemies to insects, and potently resist putrefaction. Therefore lay a layer of such ashes at the bottom of a wooden or tin box, and place your fruit on it at one inch distance from each other. Then sift ashes over all of them two inches thick. This done, lay more fruit in the same manner, and proceed on, ashes and fruit, till the box is full. thus laid, the ashes and box will keep out the air, and preserve the fruit fresh and sound some time, be they nectarins, peaches, apricots, plumbs, or others. Seeds also of any kind may be thus preserved; and if occasion be, they may be safely carry'd hundreds of miles unhurt. Or instead of wood-ashes, you may make use of dry'd sand; but I think the ashes best for keeping any stone fruit in good order till towards *Whitsun-tide.*—Or you may, according to *Evelyn's French Gardener,* page 294, preserve stone or other fruit in the must of new wine, cyder, perry, or honey-drink, provided two thirds of it are first boiled away. But this last way and by drying are costly and troublesome.

To preserve Grapes.—THESE, according to *Evelyn*, may be preserved by ranging them on straw, or hanging or laying them on sieves or racks placed near the ceiling, but not far from a fire-side; covering them over with paper, to keep them from dust.—Or they may lie in a barrel amongst wheat or oat-chaff, or wood-ashes.—Or they may be hung by the stalks of their bunches in a dry place.—Or they may be dried on a sieve, by being put into an oven after bread, and turned once or twice in the time. Thus in an oven may plumbs, peaches, apricots, cherries, *&c.* be dried; but the stones of the large sort must be first taken out when they are full ripe. Or you may preserve grapes in a syrup. Take white grapes, stone them, and boil them up with syrup of sugar on a quick fire; three quarters of a pound of sugar to 3 pound of grapes; and as they boil, strew a quarter of a pound of more sugar on them: When clear, take them off the fire, cover them, and at last take off the scum-part, and keep them in cover'd glasses. Thus they may be made a most excellent sweet-meat.—Thus currants, cherries, and several sorts of fruits may be preserved in syrup.

To forward the ripening of Apples, Pears, &c.—LAY them in heaps as soon as gathered (the larger the heap, the sooner they will sweat) and by thus sweating they will ripen and be fit to eat; or otherwise, to use the sooner, you may shake them in a sack, and by their being rubbed against one another, it will forward their ripening.

To preserve Broad-Beans and Pease dry.—TAKE them out of their pods before they are ripe and while their skin is green; strip them of their skin, and dry them thoroughly in the sun; rub them all over with winter-savory, and barrel them up in straw or chaff, or without either, provided you keep the air from them. In winter or spring, or when they are wanted, soak them six hours in warm water, and then boil them for eating. Pease also shell'd young out of their pods may be thus served.

To preserve Mushrooms dry.—STRING them on a thread, hang them up over an oven or other dry place, and keep them for use.

(307)

To make a very rich Family Cordial with Black-Cherries, Mulberries, Blackberries, &c.—PACK ripe pick'd black Kerroon cherries in a jar, or earthen glazed pot, with white sugar, by first putting a layer of sugar about half an inch thick, then a layer of cherries, next a thinner layer of sugar, then cherries, and so on till the pot is full: Then put half a pint of clean old molosses brandy, or better *French* brandy, into a gallon pot of them; cover them close, and bury them deep enough in the ground from the power of the frost. After three or more months time, you may take up the pot, and I will answer for it you will find an excellent rich cordial indeed, surpassing most others.

A Syrup to preserve white and black Damsins, Bullace, Plumbs, Cherries, Currants, &c. &c.—FOR this purpose, these must not be quite ripe. Boil up a pound and a quarter of white sugar in two pints and half of water to a syrup, and as it boils scum it till clear. Let the syrup be cold, and then put in either of these fruits, and over a soft fire keep stirring them till near scalding hot, and no longer. When cold, put all up in one or more glazed pots, so that the syrup may lie above the fruit. Cover all very close, for air prevents their preservation any long time. And thus cherries and currants may be preserved. If cherries, they should be large red *Kentish*, or Maydukes, not full ripe; these stoned, stalked, mashed with currants, and boiled with sugar, may be kept in cover'd pots. So rasberries and currants may be done in a mixture.—Or you may boil ten quarter'd small pippins in a pint of water, till the water is near half wasted; this strain through a fine sieve, and boil it with sugar to a jelly, and put in your white or red currants, boiling them till they are tender, which keep in pots or glasses. Or you may preserve damsins, bullace, *&c.* by baking them in a pot after the bread is taken out of the oven, and when cold cover them with melted fresh butter, or better with melted suet, in little pots, to use all at once.

Syrup of Cowslips given away by a Gentleman.—A GENTLE-MAN of a good estate, living near *Ivinghoe* in *Bucks*, used to boil the flowers in water about 20 minutes, then strained out the liquor and boiled it with sugar to a syrup. This syrup he mixed with elderberries, and gave it to sick persons to make them repose.

Cowslip-tea by the same Gentleman.—THE same gentleman would gather and dry the flowers in the sun, which he afterwards kept in a paper-bag, for making tea of them, which he did many nights to make him sleep, others for this purpose make a wine of them.

Elder and Black-berry Syrups made by the same Gentleman. THE same gentleman would put a pot of either of these berries into an oven with half a pint of water, and the liquid part that came from them he boiled up with sugar to a syrup. Some think syrup of blackberries the best of syrups.—In *London* they mix their elder syrup, in particular, with drams of gin or brandy.

Rob of Elder, Cherries, &c.—IT is made by boiling the juice of elderberries over a gentle fire, with a moderate quantity of sugar, till it is as thick as treacle.—Or when you have put your elder-juice into a copper or brass kettle, or pan, when it begins to boil put two whites of eggs well beaten up into it, which will raise a scum that you must take off as it rises; when well scum'd, put a pound and half of sugar to a quart and half a pint of juice, and boil all gently till it is a syrup. When cold, bottle it up, but do not cork it till winter; only tie prick'd paper over the cork-hole.—So for making a rob or syrup of the black kerroon cherries; it is only straining a quart of their juice through a fine sieve or common straining cloth, and boil it up with a pound and half of sugar into a syrup.—Currants the same.—If you will preserve the juice of elderberries a good while, be they the white or black sort, put them into a hair bag in a screw-press, and mix two quarts of brandy with 10 gallons of the juice.

Rabisha's *Way to make Syrup of Clove-july-flowers, or any other Flowers.*—TAKE a peck of their red flowers, cut them from their white part, and bruise them a little. Then boil a pint of water, and when it is a little cooled, put it to the flowers, which keep close cover'd a day and night. Then put a pound and half of clarified sugar to them, and let them all stand together one night. Next day put them into a gallipot, and set it in a kettle of water over a fire, and boil it till the sugar is melted into a syrup.—But to explain this receit the better, cut off the flowers with a pair of scissars, and put them into a high gallipot, with their weight of sugar mixt amongst them with a little water, till they are up to the top of it. Tie a cloth over it, and boil the gallipot in a kettle of water over a moderate fire for several hours, till the virtue of the flowers is extracted. Then strain out the liquid part through a fine sieve or coarse flannel, and bottle when cold.—Or to make this syrup the richer, you may a little bruise a pound of the flowers, and boil them in a quart of water, mixed with half a pint of white wine, for about thirty minutes; then strain out the liquid part, and boil and skim it till clear. This done, boil it again with some bruised cloves and other spice, and to a quart of the liquor put three quarters of a pound of sugar, or thereabouts. When boiled to a syrup, strain, and bottle when cold.—This syrup in my humble opinion exceeds all other sorts.

Syrup of Sloes.—THREE pottles of them baked yield something above a pint of juice: To this put one pound of coarse sugar, and boil a quarter of an hour, and by scumming it, it will become a clear syrup.

Rabisha's *Way to preserve green Walnuts in Syrup.*—BOIL them till the water is bitter, then take them off the fire, and put them into cold water; then peel their bark off, and weigh them; add to them their weight in sugar, with a little more water than will wet the sugar. Set them on the fire again, and when they boil up, take them off. Let them stand two days, and then boil them again; so keep them for your use.—These are a noble stomachick, and so much in esteem with the *French* gentry, that one or more of them are, with a dram after them, commonly made a breakfast of.

The following Receits, with many others, came to me by the Post, from a young Man well qualified in Husbandry Affairs, whom I sent into Devonshire *to a Gentleman of a landed Estate there, as his Servant or Bailiff, who made it his Business, as often as he had Time, for several Years, to collect for me those Curiosities, which he thought might be serviceable to me in this and other Works.*

Elfordleigh, near *Plympton*, Oct. 29, 1748.

Honoured Sir,

I have herewith sent you some receits as they are practised in our family, which I hope will be acceptable to you.

How to make a boiled Beef-steak Pie.—CUT the meat into steaks of a moderate size, beat them, and season them to your palate, then having dough made, with or without suet, make the pye in a pewter-bason, laying first a bottom of dough, and when the steaks are put in lay a close thick cover of dough on the top, and over that fasten a thick cloth to prevent the water getting in. This boil in the same manner a pudding is done; being a method that is frequently practised in our house, as it saves the trouble and expence of heating an oven. But mind always that in this way a cloth be well tied over the top. Our broken meat is often dressed in this manner, sometimes improved when mixed with some onions and apples.

To boil a Pye of squab Pigeons, &c.—THIS is often done with us, and so is an apple-pye, in the same manner as the beef-steak-pye is done.

To broil a Pigeon, or any other small Fowl.—WHEN it is well pick'd and clean'd, make up a seasoning in butter, and put it into the body of the fowl; then sow each end very close, and broil it whole over a moderate fire. This method is little or nothing inferior to roasting, as it preserves its full goodness, whereas by the common way of slitting them it is in a great measure lost.

To make Elder Syrup.—WHEN the berries are full ripe and dry, gather them, pick them very clean, and put them in a glazed earthen pot into an oven, and bake them in a moderate heat of it, then squeeze out the juice, and add to every quart a pound of sugar, which boil together. When cold, bottle it. This far exceeds the wine in virtue, and is excellent for a cold, taking a tea spoonful of it boiled in half a pint of ale going to bed, or in a morning fasting; and it is what no good housekeeper should be without. If enough of this syrup is preserved, an elder-wine may be presently made of it at any time. Cowslip-wine is a good liquor in a family, especially when made bitter with lemon-peel, which renders it very wholesome. So far this correspondent.

Elder-berries distilled.—IT was the practice of one of our country-women to distill elder-berries for a cordial water. She broke the berries with her hand, and in nine days they would ferment enough to distill a strong water or brandy from; and if that was distilled a second time, it would be extraordinary good. But for a farther improvement of it, she would with the elder-berries mix balm, mint, carduus, pennyroyal, or green wormwood instead of carduus, and distill it on saffron and loaf sugar first put into a bottle.—Or this, bruise the ripe berries well, and put them into warm water. Put yeast to them, cover them warm, and let them work three days, as beer does. Then distill them, and they will yield their spirit easily.—Or press out the juice of ripe elder-berries, and put it into a tub: To each gallon put three pounds of sugar and some yeast, to work it into a fermentation.—Or boil the juice and sugar, and when bloodwarm, put yeast to it. When the fermentation is over distill in an alembick by a gentle fire, till it taste sourish. Keep this for a fortnight close stopt in a vessel, and rectify it by a second distillation. This rectify'd spirit of elder cannot be taken alone, therefore must be mixed with a proper vehicle. It is an excellent antihydropick and antiscorbutick medicine, and works, as an author observes, both by urine and sweat. The spirit of elder may (of this sort) be made use of to mend *English* wines. And some have endeavour'd to distill a spirit from elder-berries strong enough to burn in a lamp.

To make Family Vinegar.—TAKE stalks of raisins, and pour boiling water on them; let this stand in a tub, earthen pot, or otherwise open to the sun, or the heat of a fire, for about fifteen days; then bottle it and it will prove good vinegar. The pressings of raisins will answer the same; but in either case there must not be too much water made use of, lest the vinegar want a sufficient body.—Sugar has been distilled, and I was credibly inform'd a person had liquor from it almost as sour again as common vinegar.

Vinegar made with rotten Apples.—TAKE rotten apples that are not mouldy, and squeeze them; put their juice in a vessel to stand in the sun or near a fire; with a cover to keep the rain from it, if exposed abroad.

Goosberry Vinegar.—PUT a quart of berries just turning ripe into four quarts of boiling water, and let them stand 14 days, stirring them well every day. Then strain through a flannel, and set the clear liquor with one pound of coarse sugar mixed in a painted iron-bound cask in the sun, with a piece of linen-rag pasted over the bung-hole, to keep out earwigs, *&c.* and a tile over that, when it will make a great hissing noise. Here let it stand till the fermentation is over, and it will thus get a large head or scum (which will be in about 3 weeks, or time enough to be fit to pickle with the same season) then draw it off clear, and reserve it in a dry close vessel for use. *N. B.* This is extraordinary sharp, and pickles any thing exceeding well. In this condition it never mothers, and therefore no family, who has a conveniency of making it, should be without it.

Vinegar made with green Apples and Pears.—TAKE green apples and pears that fall from trees by the wind. When you have got a good parcel, stamp and press them, and to every gallon of the clear juice add a pound or a pound and half of sugar, and a little bit of allum just boiled up together; then strain it into a clear vessel, and set it in the sun with a rag and tile over the bung-hole, and in about three weeks or a month's time it will be good vinegar; but be sure draw it off thoroughly fine.—Or you may put boiling water over the stampings, as directed for goosberries.

To make Vinegar with Malt Liquor.—TAKE some of the best table-beer wort, little or nothing hop'd; work it very high with yeast; when the ferment is over, fine it down with isinglass, and draw it off the grounds or settlement. If you have crabs or sour apples, cut them in pieces and put them into a painted cask, and let it stand in the sun or other heat till perfectly sour.— But the following receit is the more common practical one.

Second Receit to make a good Vinegar with Malt Drink. BREW a wort from malt, but do not boil it. Let it be fermented several days, then draw it off as fine as you can into a cask. Let it stand in the sun, and put into it chopt crabs, and also some rape-seed, to improve the taste of it. Keep a tile on the bung-hole.

Verjuice made by this Author.—IN *September* I have been used to stamp and press out the juice of crabs mostly of my own growth, which I kept in a cask by itself in my cellar. This done, I wetted the stampings, and after they had stood three days in a tub I pressed them again, and got out a water verjuice, that served my family a little while for vinegar. This done, I dug the crab stampings into a bed of earth, and from them raised many crab-stocks for grafting the best apples on.—Crab-juice is so necessary for abundance of uses, both for man and beast, that none ought to be without it. Two bushels of crabs generally produce five gallons of verjuice. Always keep old verjuice by you, it keeps back humours, is a fine wash for the eyes, and serviceable in many shapes for man and beast.

To make Crab Pies.—KEEP crabs sound till *Christmas*, and with sugar enough they may be made into good pies. *N. B.* These crabs bake thus with the reddest colour.

The profitable Uses of Scald or Black-berries in Farmers and labouring Mens Families.—THE value of this despised fruit is little known to the world, although there be those virtues contained in it, that if rightly made use of would tend very much to a family's profit. For example:

How to make Scald-berry Pies and Pasties to bake.—TAKE ripe scald-berries and put them into dough-crust, pie or pasty fashion, about the breadth of two hands, with some sugar; bake them at the oven's mouth before the bread goes in, as the common oven-cake is done; half an hour's time bakes them.

Scald-berry Pies or Pasties to boil.—BY the same way make turn-over pasties or pies, and lay them easily in a kettle or pot, and boil them a little; about half an hour does it.

Scald-berry Puddings.—WE stir them in batter as we do plumbs, and boil them in a bag or cloth.—These ways of improving scald-berries are in such common practice with many of our *Hertfordshire* housewives, that in some families they are thus prepared during almost the scald-berry season. For sauce to such a pudding, they strew a little sugar over it when out of the oven, and then it becomes so palatable that the children especially greedily eat it.—There is also an excellent wine may be made of them, that is very little inferior in taste and goodness to true claret, as I shall make appear in my designed next treatise on fruit-trees, cyder, &c.

To make a Goosberry boiled Pudding. THIS is a pretty contrivance to save much of the expence of plumbs, and yet to give a family a pleasant repast, by mixing green goosberries in batter, as we do raisins for making a plumb-pudding; when boiled, eat it with sugar and butter, or sugar alone.

Onion Pye made by labouring Mens Wives.—THEY mix chopt apples and onions in equal quantities, and with some sugar put them into dough-crust and bake them: This by some is thought to make as good a pie as pumkins do. It is a *Hertfordshire* contrivance.

Pumkin Pye.—WE pare and cut the pumkins in slices, then lay the slices in a glazed ea[r]then pot with salt between each layer of them, all night, for extracting out their watry juice: Then chop them with the like quantity or less of apples, and with sugar put them into a crust and bake. The pumkins save apples, and by some are liked better than apples alone.

Diseases and Medicines.

PLEURISY cured with Camomile. —To do this our country women, before they bleed, try camomile, by boiling a boy's handful of it in a pint of middling ale a little while; then strain, and sweeten it with half a half-pennyworth of treacle, and as soon as it is drank, go to bed, laying the boiled camomile to the side where the pain is, which if violent, some will make use of a whole half-pennyworth of treacle.

Hoarseness cured by Figs and Brandy.—TAKE three figs, split them and toast them, and then put them into half a quartern of *French* or old molosses brandy; eat the figs going to bed, and in about eight minutes after drink up the brandy.—Or bruise four ounces of figs, eight ounces of prunes, and four large cloves of garlic, boil in three pints of milk, strain and sweeten with candy or sugar, take some hot going to bed, and continue it for a cough[.]

Hoarseness cured by Treacle and Water.—TAKE three or four knife-points of treacle in your mouth, and then directly drink a draught of cold water after it, and go immediately to bed. It will sweat you, and is by some thought to be the best of medicines for this purpose.—Another wraps up a piece of butter as big as a walnut in sugar.

A Tympany cured.—MR. *Caser,* whom I knew, was a famous surgeon-apothecary and man-midwife at *Stroud* in *Kent,* whose wife having a tympany, or very large swell'd belly, it failed her husband and all the skill of his acquaintance to cure her, till happily a beggar-woman advised her to apply camomile dipt in spirits of wine, which effected a cure, and she out-lived her husband.

Vomitting stopt.—BOIL mint and camomile in water, sweeten the strained liquor with treacle and drink it, but apply the herbs hot to the belly; it cured my servant when other things failed.

Cough and Asthma.

*T*O *cure a Cough.*—MY landlord, the late Mr. *Colemare*, rector of *Little-Gaddesden* assured me, that the following receit is an infallible cure for a cough.—Boil two ounces of *Spanish* liquorice with three cloves of garlick, in a quart of spring water, till it comes to a pint; take a spoonful of it now and then as the fit happens. *For an asthma.*—A man was kept many years alive by drinking (as his common drink) rum, water, and sugar. Whey is good, and beer almost poison.— One *Daniel Watkins*, of *Long Marson*, near *Aylesbury*, declared to me, that he was cured of an asthma by swallowing young frogs.

A second Receit.—Mr. Justice *Duncomb*, of *Barley-End* in *Bucks*, laid much stress on this remedy for a cough: Boil, says he, bran in water, strain; and sweeten with sugar-candy.

A third Receit.—A farmer's wife used to put pepper into a pint of ale, and drink it going into bed. It has cured in one night's time.—Or swallow a pint of cold spring water going to bed; it will cause you to sweat.

A fourth Receit for Cough and Asthma.—TAKE five or six figs, as many cloves of garlick, and eight or ten prunes stoned and bruised; infuse all in a pint of rum, and fill up if occasion with another pint, taking now and then some of it.—The landlord at the *Bear-Inn* at *Southampton* told me nothing exceeds it.

Sir Hans Sloan's *Medicine for an Asthma.*—TAKE the yolk of an egg in a dram of rum now and then; it is a most excellent remedy.

The famous Cure for a Cough and spitting of Blood by Balsam of Sulphur.—DROP ten drops of balsam of sulphur on a piece of loaf sugar and swallow it; it will cause a cold to begin breaking directly, make you spit, and heal the lungs. My farrier, that is the Duke of *Bridg[e]water*'s farrier, tells me, that in ———— , 1749, he had such a violent cough, as to bring up much blood in clots, which he thinks must have terminated in an ulcer on his lungs and a consumption, had he not been cured; but he cured himself by taking twenty drops of balsam of sulphur in a tea spoonful of treacle twice a day, for several days, which directly stopt his spitting of blood, and cured him; but it was not the same with the following person.—*Tho. Cely*, a servant at *Barley-End*, having a cough that made him spit blood, was ordered by Dr. *Woodhouse* of *Berkhamstead* to take balsam of sulphur, but it did not answer; upon this he applied himself to one Surgeon *Rowland* of *Aylesbury*, and his remedy did not do; at last there happened to be two physical professors at *Tring*, who said one to the other, Come we shall lose this good pot-companion, if we don't do something better for him. Upon which, they ordered him to boil raisins, figs, coltsfoot-flowers, sassafras, liquorice-powder, and one spoonful of anniseed, in three quarts of spring-water, till it came to three pints, and drink it at discretion; *Cely* said, he found much benefit at the first taking of it, and was thoroughly cured by it afterwards.—It was thought the balsam was too hot for his constitution in the quantity it was given him.

For a common Cough.—Boil one ounce of butter, one ounce of honey; and a sprig of rosemary, in half a pint of milk, and drink going to bed; but treacle is thought by some to be better than honey.

Another Receit for a Cough.—Boil a spoonful of honey, and a spoonful of mustard, in less than half a pint of white-wine vinegar; let it but just boil up, and when cold enough, take it going to bed; it has cured when other things have failed, by giving a breathing sweat.

Another.—Make a tea of horehound and ground-ivy. Dr. *Woodhouse.*

A Smith cured of a consumptive Cough.—This smith lived near me, when he told me the following medicine cured him of a cough of two years standing: He put a handful of rue and a sprig of wormwood into a two quart large-nosed glass bottle

(319)

of ale, and after they had been soaked a day and night, he drank half a pint at a time, in the morning and at going to bed; when out, he filled up the bottle with more ale, and afterwards he put in fresh herbs and more ale, and thus cured himself; otherwise he thought the cough would have brought him into a consumption.

A Family Syrup to cure Coughs.—COLTSFOOT yellow flowers blow in *March* and *April*, and one of our country housewives makes a syrup of them to keep all the year by her, for curing her family of coughs.—Or boil a quarter of a pound of raisins stoned, with some horehound, in a quart of ale, and a quarter of a pound of sugar-candy, till a third part is wasted; take a coffee-cup full night and morning.

A fine Remedy for a Cough or Cold.—PUT twenty-four cloves of garlick into a pint and half of coltsfoot, mint, and hysop-water; boil the cloves till they are tender, then lay them on a plate. This done, take the liquid part, and add to it half a pint of the very best white-wine vinegar, and one pound of sugar-candy, which boil gently till it comes to a syrup; when cold, let the garlick lie in it.—Directions for taking it.—Take two cloves in a spoonful of the syrup every morning, and fast till dinner; at night only one spoonful of the syrup; continue at discretion: It is said, that nothing is better to cure a cough or cold, or to preserve the lungs, and create an appetite. Another boils a whole head of garlick in two quarts of water to a quart, then puts in a pound of sugar-candy, and boils it to a pint: Take a tea-spoonful frequently.

A poor Family's Remedy for a Cough.—THEY take brandy thicken'd with sugar, or (better) brandy, coarse sugar, and sweet oil mixt.—A hooping-cough has been cured in children, by putting coarse sugar between sliced turnips; or sugar-candy in the liquor.

Sore Throat.—OUR country housewives mix honey and pepper together; or turn a fig inside outward, and put powder'd race-ginger on it; or boil rosemary and sugar in milk.—Or you may make a good gargle for a sore throat, by adding pepper or powder'd ginger to the above cough medicine, consisting of honey, mustard, and vinegar. This warm'd, should be frequently used to gargle the sore part of a throat, and applied now and then with a liquorice stick.— Another of my neighbours drops *Hungary* water on loaf-sugar and swallows it.—Esquire *Williams*, of *Devonshire*, mixes best brandy with a little water, and swallowing it several times a day cures him.—Another for a cough or sore throat holds a large pewter spoonful of honey over some embers, till it is melted thoroughly hot, and takes it very hot going to bed; this is much practised in *Hertfordshire*.—When the palate of the mouth is down, boil pepper in milk with butter and rosemary; take some now and then very hot, and stroke under your jaws at the same time.—Or as soon as the throat begins to be sore, wrap pepper in a piece of fresh butter about the bigness of a small walnut, and when the butter is cover'd all over with the pepper, swallow it: This has proved a present cure.

Jaundice.

JAundice cured.—My next neighbour the widow *Howard*, who lives on her landed estate, and has more experience in medicines than thousands of others, says, old women cure this distemper better than doctors.—That she knew a woman gather a bushel of chickweed for getting and saving the juice of it, purely for having (she thought) the best remedy in the world by her ready to cure the jaundice at any time of the year, I suppose by making a syrup of it. In 1747, Mrs *Howard* had a niece, naturally of a ruddy complection, and of a sound constitution, but the mother of it having indulged the girl (almost six years old) in drinking tea every morning, and sometimes in the afternoon, she fell into the jaundice, but was cured by Mrs. *Howard*, who only gave her a spoonful of chickweed-juice fasting, and another spoonful at four of the clock in the afternoon in a little ale; but it would not be amiss, if a little saffron was mixt with the juice. This was continued till perfectly cured, and she tells me that this has done, when all other remedies have failed. The saffron by tincturing the juice makes it excellent. *N. B.* The juice of chickweed has cured several grown persons about *Market-street* in *Hertfordshire.*

To cure the Jaundice by Lice.—It has often succeeded by giving the patient nine live lice every morning for a week, in a little ale.—Or take half a dram of cochineal, the same of cream of tartar; mix them with two drams of Venetian soap, which incorporate well together, and take half a dram three times a day, till the patient is well, which will soon be: This receit is said by Dr. *Fuller* to be a most excellent one, refraining from salt meats and strong drink.

To cure the Jaundice in Children by Mr. Boyle's *Receit.*— Mix half an ounce of powder'd rhubarb with three ounces of currants, and beat the whole into an electuary; give the quantity of a hasel-nut every morning for several days.

The original Receit for curing the Jaundice in old or young, by the Juice of Chickweed, runs thus.—Take pimpernel and chickweed, stamp and strain them into posset-ale, and let the party drink thereof morning and evening; but our country housewives have found by many experiments, that the juice of chickweed alone never fails curing a yellow jaundice, if given in time.—Mr. *Boyle* says, a lady cured herself twice by boiling an egg hard in her urine; and then pricking holes all over in it, she buried it in an ant-hill, and as the egg wasted, so did her distemper.

Black Jaundice.—It is said, that if shell snails be roasted and dried at the fire, or in an oven, and made into powder, and a spoonful thereof drank in ale at a time, and so taken nine days together, it perfectly cures the black jaundice.

Dropsy.

HOW Mr. Axtell, *a Surgeon and Apothecary at* Leighton *in* Bedfordshire, *preserved himself many years, while his Legs were spotted and swell'd with the Dropsy.*—THIS person I knew to be well skill'd in his profession. He drank no malt liquor, but bought old *Jamaica* rum of Mr. *Ladbury,* a distiller, near *Doctors-Commons* in *London,* for eight shillings a gallon. To one quart of it, he put two quarts of water, two lemons, two oranges, and four ounces of double-refined sugar; the peels he cut small, and to them and their juice he pour'd on boiling water, and so let them stand cover'd; when cold, he put in the rum, and when he would drink of it, he warm'd a coffee-dish full. This was his constant drink, with another made of Rhenish-wine and green tea, in which he would pour some drops of spirit of vitriol.—These liquors preserved him many years from being overcome by his dropsy, till at last he died in 1727. *N. B.* I am well acquainted with a physician in *London,* that undertakes to cure the dropsy without tapping, where another would tap for it. He did a surprising cure of this kind at *Gaddesden,* as is well known in the parish.

Dropsy cured by a Country Housewife.—IN the first place she advises to take a purge or two of pilla-cochia. Then take two besoms made not with birch but broom, and two handfuls of sweet cisley, by some called maid-sweet, that grows like a kecks in wet meadows; boil these in six gallons of the best wort drawn from five or six bushels of malt; let it boil an hour gently, then strain, work it, and barrel it; this must be a common drink, for every thing should be avoided that creates thirst in meats and drinks. Both the receits are excellent, and will undoubtedly answer expectation, if duly followed.—Or which is better, take five spoonfuls of broom ashes, the ashes of eight burnt nutmegs, one ounce of mustard seed, two ounces of scraped horse-radish, and some sage of virtue: These infuse in a gallon of white-wine for four or five days, and drink a jill in the morning fasting, and another at night:—Or infuse or boil them in the wort.

The Gout.

THIS obstinate malady is much easier prevented then cured.—Gum guaiacum is certainly the greatest remedy known by man for the gout; but the several ways of making a right use of it, is the main thing to be known.

The first Way to relieve a Fit of the Gout.—As soon as ever the fit is come on a person, let him take a short half quartern of the following mixture going to bed, on an empty stomach. Infuse half an ounce of gum guaiacum powder in a pint of good rum, shake it well, and it is fit to use directly; you may take the rum and powder in a mixture alone, or in a quarter of a pint of ale or mountain-wine; cover close in bed and lie till nine next morning, for it will cause a gentle sweat, and perhaps a stool or two. This has discharged the pain entirely in one night's time, and if you think fit you may take it again, letting one night pass between; but it has been observed of this excellent medicine, that the oftener you take it, the less effect it has.

A second Way to relieve a fit of the Gout.—I knew a person of my intimate acquaintance, that as soon as he had taken the gum guaiacum dose, rubbed the gouty part with some spirit of lavender, and when he had done this, he claps a rag over the same besmear'd with treacle, and it answered.—But as for making use of an application of mustard for this purpose, I am against it, for I knew a person by this means draw a blister on his gouty foot that cost him five shillings curing, notwithstanding it was laid on in a rag, and although it is said the rag should be twice or thrice doubled to prevent the blistering; yet if any of the mustard in the bed should get beside the rag, it may do mischief.

How a Higler cured himself of a Fit of the Gout.—I am informed that one Mr. *Gould*, a higler, being seized on a journey with the gout in his foot, so that he could not walk, stopt at *Busby* near *Watford*, and poured some spirit of lavender into his shoe, and by the time he rode fourteen miles to London, he was thoroughly cured.

Sweat for the Gout.—I have been informed that a person of note took of hartshorn one scruple, powder of snakeroot the same quantity, mithridate half a dram, drinking it in any cordial water.—It is a violent sweat, such a one that I should not care to take, unless it was at the last extremity.

A Medicine for the Gout put in Practice by a robust Tradesman.—HE says he mixt spirit of saffron, spirit of turpentine, and spirit of hartshorn together, half an ounce of each, and took twenty drops at a time in ale, and found it an excellent remedy for gout or rheumatism.

A Preventive for the Gout.—A gentleman at *Watford* in *Hertfordshire* put half a dram of the powder of gum guaiacum into half a pint of warm ale, and drank the same dose fasting eight mornings successively, and forbore seven mornings, then took it again, and so on.—This I think to be an excellent preservative against the gout; but we have a country apothecary that takes a dram and a half of gum guaiacum and alloes each, and makes it into pills with balsam of Peru: Dose half a dram before supper.

A Gentleman cured of the Gout for four Years.—As soon as the gout began, he took a spoonful of flower of brimstone in some spring water going to bed, with a glass of mountain wine after it, and the same next morning, and so on till it removed the fit, which it soon did, and he had no gout for four years after.—But if I am not mistaken, he at the same time applied on very fine flannel hot treacle, so that with these internal and external remedies he soon overcame his gout. The treacle, shifted twice a day, helps to sweat the part and extract the gouty matter.

Outward and inward Applications for the Gout.—SOME lay much stress on a little tar mixed with treacle, and applied on a doubled cloth hot to the gouty part.—Others say it is better done, if the tar is mixed with mutton-dripping, and cry this up for the very best of outward cures; for both these draw out the humour.—My farrier, who has now and then the gout in a violent manner, takes a little spoonful of flower of brimstone mixt with treacle three mornings fasting, as the quickest inside relief of all others; and for an outward relief he heats a brick very hot, and applies it in folds of cloth as hot as can be endured; it draws much, and holds its heat a long time; but if used too much, it is apt to leave a weakness in the part.— A gouty correspondent writes to me, that he knew a person wear a piece of common allum, cut into the shape of a middling oystershell, to weigh a quarter of a pound; that this is the same remedy prescribed or made use of by the famous Jew, Mr. *Moses Hart*, as an easy preventive one, and so cheap, as to cost but one penny, and that it must be constantly wore in a breeches pocket.—Another prefers a piece of roll brimstone for the same purpose.—Where the gout is settled, mix Barbadoes liquid tar with olive-oil, and apply it plaister-wise.

The Gout said to be relieved by one or more Issues.—I HAVE heard it as the opinion of several learned gentlemen, that if a person has an issue in each leg, or better above the knee, it will deliver him from having the gout. But I think this is not infallible, because I knew two persons that have had two issues at once on them for this purpose, and yet were not cured. The late Mr. *Meadows*, living near *Hempstead*, had an issue in one arm and one leg, as I have been informed; it is true he had great relief by it, yet by the gouty pains and rheumatism he died in *February*, 1748, at the age of about forty-seven. Another person now alive, a gentleman's park-keeper in *Hertfordshire*, the most troubled with the gout that I ever knew any one of a young man, found the greatest relief by having an issue in each leg; but not a total cure. Another, his companion, now alive (in *May* 1749) of considerable worth, had a place lanced on the joint near his great toe, where the surgeon took out chalk stones that would mark, notwithstanding he has an issue in one leg, and is now but about forty years of age.

How the Duke of Bridgewater's *Farrier cured himself of the Gout in his Stomach.*—Here I shall bring to the test an action performed on my farrier by his own management. He generally keeps Venice-treacle by him for horses distempers, and being so much afflicted with the gout, that he had it in his legs, feet, hands, and shoulder at once (and at last it got into his stomach) finding his case desperate, he directly had recourse to Venice-treacle, and took a piece of it about the bigness of a small walnut dissolved in ale, going to bed. And sure enough, it drove the gout out of his stomach, as he assured me. And to prevent its return, he next day took a large dose of gin to keep his stomach warm for the purpose, after he had by the treacle gone through a deep sweat.

A second Receit to cure the Gout in the Stomach.—A correspondent of the *Esculapian* tribe writes to me, that to prevent the fatal effects of the gout in the stomach, when it has seized this part, take elixir salutis one ounce, tincture of rhubarb made in wine a quarter of an ounce, tincture of gum guaiacum made in spirit of sal volatile, aloes, and spirit of lavender, of each half a dram, *Sydenham's* liquid laudanum fifteen drops, to be directly taken when the fit seizes.

Doctor Quincy's *(and another's) Ale for the Gout.*—In his *Dispensatory*, page 484, he says, Take guaiacum and sassafras each one ounce, leaves of germander and ground-pine dry'd each two ounces; boil in wort instead of hops, in five or six gallons of it, then strain and work it with yeast as usual. When it is put in a barrel, take roots of avens, half a pound; hermodactyls, four ounces; agrimony, sage, betony, dodder of thyme, stœchas-flowers, each two ounces; raisins stoned, half a pound; and hang them in the vessel.—Or take one pound of raisins; four ounces of sassafras chips or shaveings; the same quantity of hartshorn shavings; candy'd eringo-roots, six ounces; angelico roots, three ounces; guaiacum chips, two ounces; dry'd orange-peel, two ounces. Hang these in five gallons of small ale when it is tun'd. Tap at a fortnight's end, and drink constantly of it.

An experienced serviceable Account how to manage and relieve the Gout.—EXPERIENCE is the best doctor; a merry life and short one is too often the wrong choice of imprudent persons, but a sober life and a long one is a true choice; however, as many by the unthinking folly of youth unwarily, by drinking, lay the foundation of a gout, which they can never be cured of, without submitting to Dr. *Boerhaave*'s milk-diet—Therefore drink half a pint of the quicksilver-water every morning throughout the year, and towards *April* take now and then a dose of the preventing gum guaiacum pills, and when you have the gout rub your foot with human urine a little warm'd. This done, rub also over the same hogslard, or rather adders-tongue neat ointment, and immediately lay on the part one or more bruised colewort or cabbage leaves a little heated; draw your stocking over the same, and lie in it; this do till the pain and swelling are gone. This outward management I knew an ancient gentleman, very subject to frequent fits of the gout, always to make use of, to his quick relief.

An outward Application to relieve the gouty Pain.—A MIXTURE of common tar with mutton dripping, laid on a gouty foot, has been affirmed to be an excellent remedy. Others say, that to mix *Barbadoes* tar with olive oil, apply'd for the same purpose, is better. But by what I understand of an outward application for the gout, I advise to mix this liquid excellent *Barbadoes* tar with treacle; a fourth part tar, and three parts common treacle; and lay it plaisterwise on the gouty part, as a most excellent remedy. And withall take this caution, that you employ no outward application which may force in the gouty humour, lest it drive it back to the stomach or head; but only such as those that are drawers, and not repellers.

New way of relieving the Gout by inward and outward Applications, sent to this Author by his ingenious Correspondent

(328)

in London.—SIR, agreeable to my promise, I have now sent you the following receits: And first an internal remedy against the gout.

As soon as you find the pain attack you, take three fine fresh rocamboles (which are sold in *Covent-Garden* for one shilling and six-pence per pound) in a glass of mountain wine going to rest.—The next night take six, and so every night advance three, till you take fifteen for the last dose. Then omit for five nights, and begin the same course again, and you may expect the happy effect.—A gentleman that was laid up with the gout in his feet, so that he was forced to use crutches, was able, after he had taken two doses (number 15 each night) to get on his boots, and ride from hence to *Oxford* races.

Another gentleman takes five rocamboles in a glass of mountain at the tavern, at any time, and frequently whenever he finds the least symptoms of the gout; and likewise uses himself to it now and then by way of prevention, when he is free from it.

An external Application.—A CERTAIN apothecary advised a gentleman to apply a large piece of green oilcloth (such as is commonly used for issues) over his foot swell'd with the gout, and wrap flannel about it, which gave him great ease in about half an hour, and drew the part so, without fretting the skin, that the cloth was almost as wet as if a blistering plaister had been applied: Then it was dried and put on again, and the patient was well in about three days, who before used to be confined much longer.—*N. B.* This apothecary was much afflicted with this distemper, and used the same means himself.

This last was told me as a great secret, therefore I think it would not be adviseable to divulge it, but to yourself; because could we find it answer but in four cases in six, with the use of some medicine inwardly at the same time, that would not purge so violently as the gum guaiacum does in some constitutions, but as potently promote insensible perspiration;

or even with the use of the rocamboles as above. But I believe many would object against them as being nauseous and offensive, tho' they certainly must be very good in this case, being hotter than garlick.—A rocambole is of the onion and garlick tribe, about the bigness of a large pill.

Rheumatism.

IT is the notion of many, that the gout proceeds from a hot cause, and the rheumatism from a cold cause. If the rheumatism is not cured in its infancy, it is apt to grow very painful and stubborn, often times making cripples of both old and young. The poorer sort of people are mostly afflicted with it.

Two Persons cured of the Rheumatism.—THESE had it in their legs, and were lamed by it; but cured in about a fortnight by the following drink: Take a handful or more of dwarf-elder, being what some call Dane-weed; bruise and steep it in water, or better in ale, a night and a day, and at the same time put in some bruised mustard-seed, strain, and drink it at discretion.—This is said to have been sold for half a crown a quart, a long time, by a professor of physic in *Hertfordshire*.—Another advises to rub the afflicted part with *Hungary* water.—Another declares, that the rheumatism may be cured by boiling the roots of blackthorn in water, and drank sweeten'd. A farmer by me, though young, was almost a cripple with the rheumatism, but cured several times by boiling a handful of elder-buds, a handful of rosemary, and a handful of rue all together in verjuice, and bathing the afflicted part as hot as possible.—Some bind the greens on after bathing.

What a Person said in Praise of a Remedy for the Rheumatism.—THE late Mr. *Dodgson*, minister of *Edlesborough* in *Bucks*, told me, that he was informed nothing exceeds spirit of hartshorn for curing the rheumatism, if a tea spoonful of it is taken once or twice a day in white-wine and water, for that it thins the blood and causes a free circulation. Hence it is thought that cold and sour juices occasion this distemper. My day-labourer being almost dead with the rheumatism and a great cold in his stomach, his wife gave him a tea spoonful of this spirit in water twice, which sweated and cured him.

Nettle-Tea good for the Rheumatism.—A PERSON said, that nettle-tea, drank half a pint in a morning fasting, if continued long enough will cure any rheumatism.

Infusion of Rue cures a Rheumatism.—STEEP a small handful of rue in a quart of rum or gin, and take half a quartern at night, and the same next morning, for a month.

Boar Stones extraordinary good for the Rheumatism.—A POOR man told me, he had try'd several things for his rheumatism, but nothing did him so much good as the powder of boar stones dry'd in a slow oven, taking as much of the powder in warm ale, every night and morning, as would lie on a six-pence; he said, it moved the cause at once, and gave him present ease.

A young Man, seized with the Rheumatism, was relieved by taking Mustard-seed in Treacle.—HE was so bad in our neighbourhood, that he wore hat shoes, and said he took a whole bottle of *Bateman*'s drops, but it did not cure him, so that he was a cripple. In *May*, 1745, a beggar woman bid him mix some mustard-seed, and take it with treacle on the point of a knife, night and morning, which did him the most service of any thing, and when he left it off he grew worse.

Rheumatism relieved by an outward Application.—A young man, after being in a *London* hospital, and discharged uncured of the rheumatism, made use (as an outward application) of old verjuice, in which was dissolved some allum; this being heated, and froted well in his joints, proved (it was thought) his chief cure, with the help of an internal medicine.

Rheumatism cured by Dwarf-Elder and Buckbean Tea.—A woman, almost ruin'd by the charge of doctors, for she was so bad of the rheumatism, that she could not help herself, was told by a beggar to make a tea of Dane-weed and buckbean, and it cured her. Buckbean grows by the river-side, and has a top like a bean; in *May* gather and dry it in the shade in a room, but never in the open air or sun, for these extract their virtue. Some have found buckbean tea alone the best of medicines for the rheumatism. A young woman that had been in an hospital was relieved by this tea.

White-Elder Wine for the Rheumatism.—THE late physician of *Hempstead*, Mr. *Wigg*, advised a woman of worth to drink white-elder instead of red-elder wine, saying the white sort is much better for a rheumatism than the red.

A young Man cured by the cold Bath of a dangerous Rheumatism.—HE was troubled with it a year together, and was forced to be often carried to bed. He found some benefit by drinking milk hot from the cow, with a little balm in it every morning, and at last was intirely cured by going into a cold bath, for he had the rheumatism sometimes all over him; sometimes it shifted into and swelled his fingers, and once he had it in the hinder part of his head, when he thought it would have made him mad.

Rheumatism cured by Gum Guaiacum.—THIS is a hot gum, the powder of which infused in rum, and the same dose taken of it as aforesaid for the gout, is perhaps the best of remedies for the rheumatism. Clothe well, and eat and drink well.

St. Anthony's Fire.

IT generally proceeds from excessive heat in the blood occasioned after surfeits, or by too free a use of spiritous or other strong liquors, and commonly causes great pain in the part it comes out in. In this case use bleeding and purging.

A Widow Woman's Remedy for St. Anthony's Fire.—THIS woman, living at *Little Gaddesden*, finds the greatest relief to her inflamed face, that sometimes has a scarlet red-hot place in her cheek, even almost all over it, by beating in the first place white lead in a rag, and after it is thus beaten, she grinds it small between the bottoms of two pewter plates, then mixes it with sweet oil, and lays a plaister of it over the part: And for an internal remedy, she makes a tea of sena leaves, which proves a cool purge, and thus overcomes the St. Anthony's fire.

A second Remedy for St. Anthony's Fire.—ANOTHER woman used to drink without sugar a tea made with elderberries and dandelion, and sometimes infused these in a small malt-wort for her common drink.

Adders-tongue Ointment good for St. Anthony's Fire.—IN the month of *May* gather adders-tongue, that grows in its top-part like an adder's tongue in meadows; bruise the herb, and squeeze out as much juice as will answer one pound of un-salted butter; boil both a quarter of an hour, and let stand in a pan to cool; when cold, take away the liquid part, and reserve only the fat part for an ointment for the St. Anthony's fire, or any inflammation in man or beast.—See the receit at large in my *Shepherd's sure Guide* (at page III.) sold at the *Rose*, in *Pater-noster-row, London*.

If you can't get adders-tongue, make use of the green leaves of elder in the room of it, and if you add a dram of fine powder'd camphire in its making, it will improve the poultice.—Some say cow dung applied is good to ease the pain of St. Anthony's fire.—I knew a woman my neighbour take two or three spoonfuls of the juice of elder leaves, for the St. Anthony's fire in her face; it is somewhat nauseous in taste, and purging.

Of the Imperfectness of a Receit.—The imperfectness of a receit has occasioned many mistakes in the composition; to go no farther than that I have just mentioned of making adders-tongue ointment, I have to say, that by only boiling the juice of the herb with butter, and when cold, to put it all together into the pot it is to be kept all the year in, is wrong; because then the juice will separate from the butter, and in this condition breed a rank mouldiness: Therefore, when the herb juice is boiled up with the butter, our housewife puts all into a broad pan, and when cold, the watry part she leaves behind, and just melts down the fat part in the earthen glazed pot it is to be kept all the year in, and then it will keep sound a year or two.

Of the Itch, Leprosy, and Scald-Head.

*H*OW to prevent catching the Itch by making a Bed.—Innkeepers, farmers, and travellers are more exposed to this cruel malady than all others: At a certain great market-town in *Bedfordshire*, where many of the northern passengers used to lie, the maid-servants, whenever they suspected any had lain in a bed that had the itch, would always in the first place lay the sheets open upon the spread, for an hour, to air and cool, before they made the bed for good; by this means they feared no infection, for it is the warm linen, not the woollen that does it.

How a Horsekeeper and a Servant-maid gave the Itch to several Families in Hertfordshire.—It is an ill custom in this county to hire servants without character, a thing chiefly owing to their being hired at statutes at all hazards; so that if he or she gets a new service two or three miles distance from the last, they are commonly safe from having their faults known. A horsekeeper, between a man and a boy, by this means gave four several farmers families the itch in a little time. At *Gaddesden* he lived about a month before he was found out, then discharged and went to another, and so on, till he thus mightily spread this horrid disease in *Hertfordshire*, because they neither inquired his character, nor search'd his body; if they had done the last, they had found his legs grievously scabbed, for he kept the itch out of his hands by now and then anointing them. The servant-maid was one that thus brought the itch into my family, for she was in as bad a pickle as the boy, having her arms and hands clear, but her legs sadly scabbed.

A Person like to have been killed by a Mercurial Ointment for the Itch, &c.—A man, living near me, used to make an ointment of quicksilver and hogslard, by beating and mixing them with spittle three hours together. Many pots of this were sold at markets for curing the itch, scald-head, and kibe-heels; but one person, applying the ointment plaister-wise, had like to have been killed, had he not been timely anointed with sweet oil.—A young woman servant, having been supplied with a pot of mercurial bluish-colour'd ointment from a famous country surgeon and apothecary, applied it till she was raw about her waste; at last the surgeon ordered her to put some (I suppose medicinal) paper over all, which relieved, but did not cure, till she got a remedy from a person that did not profess surgery.

The Itch cured by Advice of an Exciseman, who also acted as a Surgeon at Ivinghoe.—HE bid a poor woman of the same parish mix common soap and flower of brimstone together, and after taking flower of brimstone in some treacle three mornings before-hand, to anoint only twice with the ointment (that is to say, after the first time, a week after) wearing the same linen all the time, and it cured.

A strong Ointment for the Itch.—ANOTHER person, to make the same remedy stronger and surer, added black pepper and hogslard to the soap and sulphur, and boiled all into an ointment, with which, after taking brimstone in some treacle three mornings, he anointed himself by a fire-side three nights together, and was cured.

A very strong Ointment for the Itch.—BEAT stone brimstone, then mix it with soap, hogslard, tobacco, and pepper, boil and strain all through a cloth, after taking sulphur inwardly; anoint with this three nights.

How a Smith in Hertfordshire *cured his Family of the Itch, without Mercury or Sulphur.*—THIS man's family was dreadfully infected with the itch, brought to him by a journeyman, but cured by first taking flower of brimstone inwardly three times, and then anointing twice with a liquor made thus: He boiled two ounces of tobacco in three pints of strong beer, till a third part was consumed, with a piece of allum in the same; and others have since been cured by the same remedy, wearing the same linen for a week.—This remedy I am sure is a very good one, and as it has no mixture of mercury is not dangerous, nor offensive, as it is free of the smell of brimstone.

Itch cured by white Hellebore-root.—A beggar woman told a family that had the itch near me, that it had cost another family ten pounds to be cured of the itch, and it was not done, till she told them to buy two ounces of white hellebore-root powder at the apothecary's, and boil it in a quart of milk mixt with water to a pint, with some hogslard. This ointment, after taking sulphur in treacle three times, was made use of a few nights, and cured them all, for it is a very strong powder, and will make the body smart, as if stung with nettles.

Itch said to be cured in a certain Workhouse.—THEY boil an ounce of camphire, an ounce of long pepper, and a little hogslard in water, and anoint.

A most potent Remedy for curing the Itch. TAKE tobacco stalks, allum, hogslard, and powder'd salt-petre, the three first must be put into a full quart of strong beer, and when it is warm, the salt-petre must be put into it by degrees, for if it is put in cold, it will lump; the whole must be boiled well into an ointment.—If sulphur in treacle is first taken, I think no itch can resist the remedy; but for a more cleanly one, the following is made use of by some.

Author's Plowman cured by Dr. Dover's *Mercurial Water.*— MY plowman, wanting a plowboy to drive my plow team, took one that had the itch in his legs, which being unperceived, he let the boy lie with him, who gave him the itch heartily, and the fellow desiring to be cured by a cleanly medicine, I made use of Dr. *Dover's*, thus—Take one dram of white sublimate mercury in powder, and mix it with half an ounce of cream of tartar; these infuse in a quart of spring water, then take sulphur in treacle on the point of a knife three times, and wash the body before the fire with this water three nights together, change your linen, and the Doctor says it is a sure cure, and a safe one.—If you don't wash before a fire, the cure will be the longer, for then the wash must be continued longer.—It is said, that many persons about *London* get a tolerable livelihood by this water.—But although I have here published a mercurial water, yet I am entirely against all other mercurial medicines, both in ointments and in a quicksilver girdle, because of the many damages that have happened by their uses.

A Leprosy cured by the Herb Fumitory.—FUMITORY grows with a red flower in *May* and *June* amongst wheat, and about *Michaelmas* in our turnep fields. A yeoman's wife, living at *Ringsell*, a village lying about a mile distant from *Gaddesden*, having a leprosy, made use of a capital surgeon and apothecary's diet-drink for three months together, but in vain; till she was advised to infuse the herb fumitory in whey, and by drinking the same for some weeks she was cured of her leprosy.

A sure Cure for the Itch without Sulphur or Mercury, by which a poor Man cured his own Family and others.—TAKE a root of elecampane; in some grounds, as in an orchard, I have known it grow almost as big as a parsnip; cut three slices of this root short ways, and make a tea of it, which drink three mornings and nights, then take the rest of the root, and boil it in water till it is soft like a turnep; boil the thinnest part of this again with hogslard and soap, anoint the body every night for three nights together, and it is a sure cure. My day-labourer says he has cured several others with the same.

A Scald-Head cured by a Beggar Woman.—THIS happened to my wheelwright's son, who having a scald-head, at about twelve years of age, his parents applied for a cure to the late physician Mr. *Wigg* of *Hempstead*, who told them, there was no cure but by a pitch plaister. Quickly after this, a beggar woman hearing of it, bid them roast a shoulder of mutton, and let it drip on tar, and when mixed, to rub it all over the head well. This they did twice, and it proved a cure, not only to the son, but to another in *Albury* parish near *Gaddesden*; but it is said, if the shoulder of mutton was basted with tar, it would be rather more efficacious.

The Traveller's Remedy for curing the Itch.—As most of the begging travellers have now and then the itch, they that know the following medicine say nothing exceeds it.—After taking as much flower of brimstone as will lie on half a crown, in a spoonful of treacle, three mornings fasting, they boil salt and tobacco in urine, and rub their bodies over with the same three times in all, and wear the same shirt a week, two, or more.

To cure Wounds, Swellings, and Burns, and how to make Ointments and Salves.

A Quick Cure for a green Wound.—First with a feather apply tincture of myrrh, for this is one chief means to prevent a gangreen.—Or do it with brandy or spirit of wine.—Or wash the wound first with warm milk; then beat the yolk of an egg into two ounces of Venice turpentine, and apply a lint dipt in it, or otherwise. If dangerous, dress twice a day: It is a strong digestive, and so efficacious, that if a bone is crackt, it will heal it, being a remedy much in use with surgeons at this time, tho' the receit of it has been in print near a hundred years ago.

To heal a green Wound with Copper Oar.—Wash the wound as aforesaid, then infuse some copper oar as it comes out of the mine in a quart of spring water. It cures all green wounds, and skins beyond all other things; as a gentleman at *Glassenbury* in *Somersetshire* assured me, who was concerned in a copper mine in *Devonshire*.

To cure a Wound with Leaves.—Apply the rough part of the leaf bearbind to a green wound or running sore. It has cured when a surgeon's skill failed.

A Swelling in a Man's Leg attended with great Pain cured.—

My neighbour had a swelling in his leg attended with great pain, if he walked but a little way; a stranger, being in his company, bid him mix the marrow of a bacon-bone with spirits of wine, and rub it well in. This he did two or three times, and was quickly cured.

A ready cheap Way to cure a green Wound.—Mix water and salt with soap, beat up all into a lather, soak the cut in it, and apply the settlement to the part, which renew at discretion.

A Doctress's cure for a green Wound.—She always for the first dressing uses tincture of myrrh, because she says it prevents soreness and festering; as soon as she has besmeared the wound with this, she applies a plaister of black basilicon; at the second dressing, she washes with spirit of wine, and renews her basilicon plaister. Dr. *Quincey* says (at page 303 of his *Dispensatory*) that this tincture of myrrh is in great esteem amongst surgeons for cleansing ulcers, and for exfoliating carious bones.

A good Housewife's Salve for curing Wounds.—Take mutton suet, bees-wax, frankincense, resin, and Venice turpentine, each four ounces; some linseed and train oils. Melt all these over a fire, and stir in powder'd camphire and Roman vitriol, a dram of each; when cold, roll it up in oiled paper for use.— If a wound is deep, first wash it as aforesaid, then melt some of the salve, and dip a tent in it; if shallow, spread a little of it on lint, and apply it with a plaister of the same salve over it; or if the wound is slight, a plaister alone may do.

A ready, cheap, good Balsam for curing green Wounds.—Mix over a gentle fire Venice turpentine with oil of the herb St. John's-wort, of each a like quantity; when they are well incorporated, put them into a glazed gallipot for use.—This herb has many excellent qualities in it for curing wounds or bruises, it dissolves swellings, and strengthens feeble members, *&c. &c.* And such a liquid is sometimes more proper than salve, where veins, nerves, or tendons are cut, and which also for the same purpose makes a mixture to be preferred to all

THE COUNTRY HOUSEWIFE'S FAMILY COMPANION

other applications, that is composed of a little spirit of wine, a little camphire, and more oil of turpentine, laid on the wound warm; and afterwards a plaister must be laid on the same.—But the following balsam is said to exceed all others whatsoever, and which has never failed my expectation in curing many wounds in my family.

The most excellent of all Balsams, Salves, or Ointments, for curing Wounds, Bruises, Strains, Burns, Bleeding, &c. &c.— IT is a balsamick tincture, that not only cures all bruises, strains, burns, scalds, and common green wounds, but also (which with difficulty will be believed) stops the most obstinate bleeding at the nose, and any arteries wounded or cut quite in two, although the largest branches of the body, without any ligature. If the brain is wounded quite thro', either length-ways or breadthways, or the eye pierced in the very pupil or sight; and if the chief tendons are wounded, or cut quite asunder, the wound will not inflame, be sore, or run matter, or require digesting, deterging, incarning, or cicatrizing, as the common method is, which takes much time to do; but this medicine so agglutinates the parts, and defends them from corruption, that sometimes in one or else in a few days, according as the case is, it effects a cure. It is a balsam that may be taken inwardly, being as harmless as the food we eat; it gives almost immediate ease in fits of the gout, being applied with soft rags to the inflamed part, and in the stone does the same as Mrs. *Stephens's* medicines, but in a more compendious manner, as has been fully proved to be true before many apothecaries, surgeons, and physicians, in and about *London*.

This balsam is made by my friend, a most ingenious chymist, from whom I have it in bottles sealed up, price one shilling each; a remedy of such importance, that no family ought to be without it, because it may not only save great expences, but even life itself; for as we are all liable to accidents, a person may receive a mortal damage, or bleed to death,

(340)

before a surgeon can be had. I therefore have just reason to observe, that a farmer especially ought never to be without this balsam, because in the use of scythes, chaff-engine knives, reaping and other cutting hooks and sickles, hedge-bills, and axes, &c. &c. men are more than ordinarily liable to cut and bruise themselves, and also to be hurt by the kicks of horses, falls from carts, waggons, cocks and mows of corn and hay, trees, &c. &c. Which most excellent liquid balsam I furnish any person with, in bottles sealed up, at one shilling each, with printed directions for its uses.

A Poultice to disperse a Swelling.—STAMP the inner rind of elder and boil it in chamberlye, of which make a poultice and apply it. This is not to break but disperse and reduce a swelling.

A Brine Ointment to reduce Swellings.—IN beef brine, boil the green bark of elder, some nettles, wormwood, and rue; strain, and boil up the liquid part with lard.

To make a cooling Elder Ointment.—PUT the flowers of elder into a pitcher, and stop the mouth of it; then set it in a pot or kettle of water, and boil it two or three hours, and as the flowers sink, add more. Some put in mashmallows of the garden, not wild mallows; then separate the juice, and boil it up with hogslard or unsalted butter for use. It is a great cooler, asswager of pain, and disperser of humours.

A Turnep Poultice to reduce a Swelling.—ROAST a turnep in the embers, and when enough, take out the pulp and leave the shell; with this pulp mix hogslard, and apply it while hot to a swelling; it will either break or disperse, if repeated.

A Woman's sore Breast cured by herself.—THERE being a fiery red inflammation settled in it, she first anointed with elderflower ointment, and then applied roasted cabbage leaves (the first asswaged the pain, and the last drew out the feverish inflamed quality) and by due applications was cured.

A Country Housewife cured her Neighbour of a sore Breast.— She reduced a swell'd breast, by anointing it with tobacco ointment; and no wonder, since it is generally allow'd to be a great discusser of scrophulous tumours. A woman had three holes in her breast, for which she boiled the inner rind of elder stampt, white bread, and hogslard, in milk; this is healing, cooling, and a little drawing.—Adders-tongue is also good for this.

To keep back a Humour from falling into a Wound.—BOIL a piece of allum about the bigness of a walnut in somewhat more than half a pint of milk, separate the curd from the whey, and dip a linen rag in this drained whey, and bind it above the wound, but let none of it touch the wound. It will keep a humour back.

To prevent and cure proud Flesh.—POWDER of precipitate is a good mercurial powder for this purpose; but if not understood, it is next to the putting a sword in a mad man's hand. Therefore rather make use of a wound water, by boiling a pound of powder'd allum, in three pints of spring water, till it comes to a quart, then put in one ounce of Roman vitriol— Or with powder of burnt allum—Or with powder'd double refined sugar.

Burns and Scalds cured by a Country Housewife.—THIS woman's way is—Break the blisters, because they contain a hot fiery water in them, and clip the skin off if you can; then burn fresh butter in a broad stew-pan, and pour it into a large bason of water, and work it well therein, for from a blackish brown it will become whitish. Spread it on rags, and lay them on the wound; it is an excellent way of curing a burn or scald, by fetching out the fire and healing the wound.

Burns and scalds cured by another Country Housewife.— AFTER she has clipt away the blistery skin, she washes the wound with a mixture of vinegar and water; then she stamps some onions and salt together, which she applies as a poultice for a night and a day, then lays over it a plaister of burnt salve, after the onions and salt have drawn out the fire. And if proud flesh arise, she puts powder of burnt allum.

To cure Burns or Scalds by a third Country Housewife.—THIS woman mixes linseed oil with bruised onions, and (by shifting it now and then) says it is the best of things to draw out the fire.—Or to fetch fire out, you may beat up powder'd allum with whites of eggs, and apply it.

An excellent Ointment for curing Burns, Scalds, &c.—TAKE elder leaves, St. John's-wort, garden mallows, ivy leaves, and adders-tongue, of each two handfuls. These are in their perfection in the month of *May*. The wort and tongue grows in meadows. If you can't get all, make use of some, and take housleek in the room. Stamp and squeeze out their juice, and boil it up with a pound or more of butter fresh out of the churn, that has no salt in it, for a quarter of an hour; then pour all into a glazed broad earthen pan; when cold, take off only the hard buttery part, and leave the liquid part behind, to be thrown away. Next, you are to put this butter part into a glazed earthen pot, and set it just within the heat of the fire, enough only to melt it into a close body; then keep it well cover'd for use.—This ointment is a most excellent sort for dispersing humours, and allaying swellings in man or beast, healing green wounds, St. Anthony's fire, burns, scalds, hot tumours, spreading sores, impostumes, and ruptures.

An excellent Salve for Burns or Scalds.—YOU may make the above ointment into an excellent salve for dressing burns and scalds, wounds made by the bite of venomous beasts, green wounds, dispersing of humours, and allaying of swellings, *&c.*—Take what quantity you please of the above ointment, supposing it to be about half a pound, to which put a large spoonful of Venice turpentine, one ounce of bees-wax, and as much white powder'd lead as will lie on half a crown. Just boil these up, and keep it as a salve in particular for dressing a wound made by burning or scalding, *&c.* to be spread on a rag, and applied now and then till it is cured.—The herb adders-tongue I have growing in my meadows, and make an ointment of it every year for reducing the swell'd bags of my cows, and for diseases in the human body as aforesaid.

To break a Swelling by a Country Housewife.—SHE wraps sorrel in a wet paper, and covers it with embers; and thus it will be reduced to a pappy consistence; she says, nothing breaks a swelling sooner nor better. But another country housewife does it rather better, by laying the sorrel between two tiles, which she covers with embers.

A swelled Leg cured.—A young woman, about nineteen years of age, in her lying-in month, in *September* 1748, had her left leg swell'd to a great degree, insomuch that she could not walk cross a room without help. Some persons in the neighbourhood bid her boil some rosemary, rue, and elder-leaves in old verjuice, and bathe her leg with the strained liquor, as hot as she could endure it. This see did several times, and it cured her.

To stop Bleeding inwardly and outwardly.

A Woman cured of spitting of Blood.—THIS was a poor widow and a chair-woman living near me, who applying herself to a physician, he out of charity bid her stamp the leaves of plantane and nettles together, and take a tea-cup of their juice three mornings; which she did, and was cured. The same juice, he said, will stop bleeding at the nose if snupt up, and also that of cuts. In the month of *May*, the juice may be boiled up with sugar for a reserve.—Or bruise common nettles, and thrust it into the bleeding nostril.

How a Girl's Arm was stopt bleeding by a Surgeon's Advice.— A girl in *Gaddesden* parish, having had a nail run into her arm, neither her parents nor neighbours could stop its bleeding. Upon which, the girl cried mightily as she stood at the door of her mother's house, when a *Hempstead* surgeon, coming accidentally by, said, What ails you my girl? She told him. Take, says he, some hogs-dung and lay to it; and it was done accordingly, to the entire stopping of it: For this dung is said to abound with a very pungent and nitrous salt.

A Labourer's Finger stopt bleeding by Tobacco.—ONE of our day-labourers, that was plashing a hedge, happened to cut his finger with a bill, and was at a loss how to stop its bleeding, till another labourer, working with him, took a chew of tobacco out of his mouth, and by applying thereof stopt the bleeding at once.

Bleeding at the Nose stopt by a Woman.—A MAN bled so at the nose by a small blow given him, that none of the surgeons could stop it: A woman coming by, she desired leave for an application, which was, it is thought, oil of vitriol (somewhat weakened) rubbed on the forehead of the man; which, by no more than once using, made his skin peel, but stopt the bleeding.

Bleeding at the Nose stopt by Frogs.—A young man, the son of a yeoman living near *Gaddesden*, bled so violently at the nose, that all applications proved in vain, till frogs were made use of; and then, by their being bound to his neck, their cold nature intirely stopt it.

Bleeding stopt by Vinegar.—IT is a good old remedy to stop bleeding by washing, or better by soaking the testicles in the sharpest vinegar.—Or if a cloth is dipt in it, and applied to the nape of the neck—Or against the heart, but then it must be new dipt, as soon as it is warm.—Or if allum and salt-petre are dissolved in vinegar, and applied by a rag dipt in it to the breast, or by a tent to the bleeding nostril, and renewed now and then.—Clay mixt up with vinegar, and applied to the testicles, stops bleeding.

Of making an Issue, and of several Cases relating to the same.

THE Case of a Woman that lost her Life, partly by having an Issue made with Spanish *Flies.*—THIS woman, about forty years of age, having a humour fell into her thigh or leg, employed a sort of country doctress to make her an issue for curing the same; but it happened quite otherwise: For by her application to make the issue with Spanish flies, the part became inflamed, and the humours much increased; so that a surgeon was sent for, who lanced the part, and applied remedies; but in vain, for a mortification ensued. To cure which, it is said he used little else than camphorated spirit of wine, and oil of turpentine; at last, after several times cutting away the flesh, till her thigh bone was near bare, he dress'd the wounds with lye as hot as possible, but she died in 1740, and her husband was arrested for and paid ten pounds to the surgeon.

How an Issue presently after cutting became inflamed, but cured by Vine-Leaves.—A man having had an issue cut at *London*, after he had been at home in *Hertfordshire* a day, the part became much inflamed and very sore. The issue was made by the surgeon's forcing the point of a lancet into the inside of his leg a little below the knee, and then he put in a pea, with a plaister of basilicon over it; notwithstanding which, it was thought the inflammation would have brought on a mortification, had not a farmer's wife advised to lay on the issue a parcel of vine-leaves thick, one upon another, which cooled the part, brought on a fine digestion, and made a cure. The same person, some time after desiring to be rid of his issue, dried it up, but was quickly obliged to have another cut, because for want of it he could not walk. The second cutting was much better performed than the first, for in making this, the country surgeon gathered up a little skin, and cut it quite off, so that there was a round pea-hole at once, that succeeded much better than making an incision with a lancet.—In case vine-leaves can't be had, cabbage-leaves may supply them; for this, as well as the other, is a cooler and drawer.

Of Plaisters and Peas, &c. *for Issues.*—THESE are fine sticking plaisters sold for promoting the discharge of issues in the neck, leg, arm, and back; but the good old common issue plaister is made of oil-cloth.—There are also sold several sorts of medicated peas, some greenish, and some blackish, for making an issue run the better. Many of our country people prefer carrot cut into pea shape, but I have the following direction on this account given me by a surgeon—After you have taken off (says he) any fungous or proud flesh, if any there be, with the mercurial ointment I prescribed you, get a large piece of Florentine arrach-root, soak it in water till it is a little soft, then cut it out in small bits, which lay in the sun upon paper to dry; then cut them roundish with a penknife, and constantly use these instead of the common peas, a fresh one every day, and your green oil-cloth over it, and you'll find the issue will discharge better.—But no mercurial ointment for me, the blue vitriol stone rub'd over any proud issue flesh will take it off safely.

To make an Issue or a Seaton run.—MIX thick Venice turpentine with the yolk of an egg, and anoint the silk rowel for a seaton.—For an issue, one of my labourers gets two or three roots at a time (by way of store) from a moorish ground of the broad flags, and dries them, about the bigness of a man's thumb; when the issue in his leg will not run, he cuts a bit like a pea, and in a day, or a day and a night's time, it will cause it to run, when he takes it out and puts in a pea; the root will tingle the flesh, and is apt to inflame it.

Sprains and Bruises.

*T*O *cure a sprained Wrist in Harvest.*—IT is common for men to sprain their wrists the first or second day, by reaping, in harvest, before they are much used to it; some dip a red cloth in verjuice, and wrap it going to bed about the wrist.

A second Receit for the same.—A man was cured in one night's time, by wetting a rag with tincture of amber, and binding it on the wrist.

A third.—DIP a flannel in some warm brine.—Or in want thereof in urine mixt with salt.—Or urine alone.

A fourth.—APPLY camphorated spirit of wine on a rag.

A fifth, or for a Bruise.—BOIL soap and vinegar in strong beer grounds, dip a cloth and apply it.—Or boil bran in vinegar, and apply as a poultice.

A sixth.—STAMP a burdock-leaf, and bind it on the wrist; by morning it has cured.—Or mix the white of an egg with oil of turpentine and vinegar, and apply on a rag.

Inward Bruise.—THE common remedy is to bleed and take two drams of powder'd *Irish* slate in half a pint of spruce beer, now and then repeating the same.

A Woman bruised and cured.—HAVING by a fall been much hurted, she bruised parsley, and beat it up with fresh butter; so mixt, she applied it, and it fetch'd the bruised quality out of the flesh; then she applied adders-tongue ointment, which reduced and cured the swelling.

Sprain.—BEAT Venice-turpentine and brandy together, and rub it in three times in three days before a hot fire-shovel.— Or, if red cloth soaked in brine and applied will not do, clap after it a plaister of *Paracelsus*.

Bruise.—A SURGEON directed a man at *Aylesbury*, if he was bruised, to drink cold water immediately, for it will cause the blood to circulate and prevent stagnation.

A Man almost bruised to Death cured.—MY collarmaker was thought dead, by a fall from a horse, but by bleeding him, and giving him half a pint of salt water he was cured. The same at sea; they give salt water for a bruise, because it makes the blood circulate presently, and therein lies the cure. He says, he takes the same two or three times a year in his best health.—Some say, to scald urine, and put it on bran, if applied presently, as hot as possible will hinder a swelling and cure the bruise. Renew if there be occasion.

Consumption and Inflammation of the Lungs.

A Person, given over by two Physicians, cured of a Consumption.—Mr. *Hume*, who was then servant to the Earl of —— ——, assured me, he was cured of a consumption (being far gone, and given over by Sir *Hans Sloane* and Dr. *Stewart*, and directed by them to be sent home to his native air, as the best thing they could advise) by paring some fresh-gathered turnips, cutting them in thin slices, and strewing some powder of brown sugar-candy over each layer in a cullender, and letting them stand a few hours to drain into a dish; of which liquor he drank three or four cups in a day, and without taking any thing else by way of medicine was cured in three weeks, to the great surprise of the doctors and his friends.

A Woman cured of a Consumption.—ONE of my neighbours informs me, that her near kinswoman being given over by the doctors in a consumption, was cured by making use of conserve of red-roses and a mixture of mithridate, taking a little at a time of it.

A Remedy for a Consumption.—TAKE half a pound of raisins of the sun stoned, a quarter of a pound of figs, a quarter of a pound of honey, half an ounce of *Lucatellus* balsam, half an ounce of powder of steel, half an ounce of flower of elecampane, a grated nutmeg, one pound of double refined sugar pounded; shred and pound all together in stone mortar, pouring into it, by degrees, a pint of sallad oil, of which eat the bigness of a nutmeg four times a day; every morning drink a glass of old Malaga sack, with the yolk of a new-laid egg in it, and as much flower of brimstone as will lie upon a sixpence, and next morning as much flower of elecampane.

A second Remedy.—TAKE two gallons of small beer, 2 handfuls of oak-leaves, and 2 handfuls of fern-roots (let the oak-leaves be gathered two or three days before you use them) wash the fern-roots, and split them; then put them into the small beer, and boil them all together, till about two quarts are wasted out of the two gallons. Then have half a pound of brown sugar-candy ready, and strain it off upon the candy boiling hot. When cold, put it into bottles. Drink a pint first in a morning, and another going to bed last at night.

A Gentlewoman prodigiously relieved in a deep Consumption, if not cured.—THIS was a maiden gentlewoman, sister to — W——t, of *Derbyshire*, Esq; who was in a deep consumption, and so weak that she could hardly lift her hand to her head, for which there were eight sheeps-trotters boiled five hours in spring water, then strained off and kept as a jelly; when used, she put a spoonful or more of it in warm or hot milk, and supt it. She took this half a year together, being of a most strengthening nature, far beyond the jelly of hartshorn or calves-feet, and will restore, it is said, when nothing else will. The same after a fever has weaken'd a person. It is a great healer of the lungs and stomach, damaged by any means, but must be continued some time, for it will not have effect presently.

Inflammation of the Lungs cured.—THIS stubborn and too often fatal malady, that generally is acquired by hard drinking, I am informed, by a very creditable person, was cured in a gentleman by the following medicine: A spoonful of beech-oil was mixt with a spoonful of the juice of ground-ivy, and taken going to bed. This repeated several times had the desired effect.

A young Man cured of a Consumption in a very particular Manner.—IT is reported, that a young man was absolutely cured of a consumption, by baking turnips with a piece of rusty bacon, which produced a very disagreeable liquor, but cured the person.

A Drink for a Consumption.—BOIL two handfuls of small bran, in two quarts of spring water, till a pint is consumed. Sweeten it with honey, and it will drink like mead.

A G U E.

A Young Man cured of an Ague.—THIS person lives now at Gaddesden, of wealthy parents, who having an ague (by advice) put pepper into his beer every time he drank, and was cured; being told that it was the best of remedies for this disease.

A young Woman cured of an Ague.—THIS was done by Dr. *Dover*'s receit, in his book intitled *The Physician's Last Legacy*, page 93, where he has these words:—"Take two ounces of fine bark grosly powder'd; infuse it cold in a quart of red-port for twenty-four hours, then filtre it off as you use it, taking six spoonfuls every third or fourth hour, beginning just as the fit is off, till you have taken the whole quart. Thus repeat it four times, and it will not return. This must be observed, that if it purges, it will do no service. In this case put two or three drops of liquid laudanum into each dose, till the purging is stopt."— A daughter of mine, having a second-day ague, was partly cured by this receit; for I put one ounce of gross bark into a pint of claret, and she was cured before the pint was out, though she purged the day before the ague left her, but I quickly stopt it by bruising cinnamon in milk.—I remember, when I was about 20 years of age, that I was cured of an ague I had had nine months (for ten shillings) by a person who said, I should not have my ague any more. And he made his word good (not only to me, but, as it was said, to all he undertook) by giving them three sorts of colour'd powders at once in a half-pint glass of small-beer, twice the day I was to have the ague, and once a day for a fortnight after. This medicine neither purged, nor vomitted, nor made sick (I only suck'd a bit of orange after taking it) which makes me believe it was only bark disguised.

A Woman cured of an Ague by a Country Apothecary's Advice.—THE apothecary (Mr. *Goodwyn*) then lived at *Barkhamstead*, and advised a near neighbour of mine to beat two yolks of eggs, their whites and all, into half a pint of brandy, just as the fit was coming on, and take it going to bed; which she did and was cured.—Never drink small-beer in an ague, it is apt to bring on a dropsy, and cause knots in several parts of the body that cannot be cured.

A Schoolmaster in Ivinghoe *cured of an Ague*—by boiling honey in a quart of old strong-beer and drinking a little at a time as hot as could be endured, just as the cold fit was coming on.—Another person was cured by burning a quart of claret with honey in it, and drinking it hot, some at a time, leisurely.—Another was cured by drinking a quarter of a pint of the juice of rue just before the cold fit came on.

My Collar-maker's Boy cured of an Ague.—HE put his son into a tub of cold water while the fit was on him.

Ague cured by Dr. Quincy.—HE says, in his *Dispensatory*, page 99, "That he had it from a worthy person, that he had cured a great many poor people in the country of agues, with a large nutmeg, and its equal weight of allum, powdered and divided into three doses, giving one every morning fasting."—Others have given bay-leaves dry'd, and the powder mixt in a quart of the strongest old beer, of which take three spoonfuls every two hours, a little before the fit comes on.—Another takes a spoonful of flower of brimstone in honey or treacle.—A most excellent remedy, after brimstone is taken, is to boil half a pound of sugar, a piece of allum as big as a marble, and a quarter of a pint of the juice of rue in a pint of white-wine vinegar, and give a quarter of a pint just before the fit comes on. I learnt this of a traveller, on the 19th of *May*, 1749.

A very excellent Receit for an Ague.—TAKE a handful of wormwood and a handful of rue; steep them all night in a quart or two of strong beer, and drink some of the strained liquor a little before the fit comes on. This, tho' somewhat nauseous, commonly cures at once, if not, the dose must be renewed; and it has this property beyond the bark, that it generally prevents the return of the ague; because it not only warms, but sweetens and thins the blood.—An old woman cures the ague by giving gun-powder in half a pint of ale.— A surgeon cures it by boiling an ounce of bark in three pints of water to a quart, to which add half a pint of claret, strain off with a little loaf sugar. After a vomit, take a quarter of a pint three times a day.

Stone and Wind Cholick.

A Woman troubled with the Stone-Cholick lived to a great Age, by an excellent Remedy.—SHE usually scraped as much Castile-soap as would lie on a shilling, and drank it in half a pint of warm ale. This was the only medicine she made use of, and it did her exceeding great service, so that she lived to above eighty years of age.

Stone and Gravel.—I KNEW a certain woman who took the juice of leeks and honey mixt up like a conserve, which did her great service.

How a young Woman was cured of the Stone-Cholick.—I AM credibly informed she was cured by taking balsam of capivi; but in what manner she took it, I cannot say.

Wind-Cholick relieved and cured.—A CREDITABLE person near me, very subject to the cholick, put a handful of rue and as much camomile into a quart bottle that had a large nose, and on them he pour'd a quart of ale. Next morning, he drank a quarter of a pint of the liquor, and continued it three mornings; then rested some time, and took it again. This, he says, secures against the cholick; but if you have it, drink half a pint, and it is an immediate cure, though of a hot nature and nauseous.—Another person boiled nettle-seeds and sprigs of box in water, which, when sweeten'd, he would drink for the wind-cholick.—Others boiled daucus or wild carrot-seed with bay-leaves in water, which they sweeten'd and drank for the wind-cholick, and therefore kept them dry'd by them all the year.—Colonel —— found the greatest benefit in taking some syrup of poppies in double anniseed-water, which would sometimes make him sleep; at another time he would take a dram of brandy, in which snake-root was infused.—Another drinks a tea for the cholick, made with wild thyme growing on the top of mole or ant hills.—A gentleman, going over to *Calais* in a ship wherein was Dr. *Garth*, was taken with a violent cholick, and desired the doctor's advice, wishing himself on shore; says the doctor it is all one for that, and order'd a tea-kettle on. When the water was hot, he drenched him with it, till it went upwards or downwards, and cured him of a wind cholick.—Another, one of my labourers, used to cure himself of a wind-cholick, by boiling the herb centory in ale or water. As much of it as the quantity of an egg, if the liquor is drank, will cure if the stomach is swelled. See its virtues in *Quincy*, page 101.—I myself was cured intirely of a wind-cholick, by drinking half a pint of water in a morning fasting, and so every morning by way of prevention; by which means you will not be troubled with this tormenting disease.—Or steep as many onions bruised as will lie in a quart of white-wine, and take a glass of it.

For a Stone-Cholick.—ONE Mr. *Fennel* of *Leighton* says, That he has taken 40 drops of balsam of sulphur for the stone-cholick, by dropping them in the middle of a glass of white-wine, which made it look like the yolk of an egg, and then went to bed. This he did once a week for some time, and it made him piss stones on the ground as big as a thetch, after being troubled with the gravel 20 years. Dr. *Quincy* allows from 4 to 12 drops for a dose, page 450.—A woman boiled parsley-roots, burdock-roots, and fennel-roots, in water, which when strained, she sweeten'd with syrup of marshmallows.— Another woman took as much sal prunella in powder, in a spoonful of white-wine, as would lie on a penny, for easing the stone-cholick.—Another found nothing answer better than daucus-seed for his stone-cholick. Its seeds are like carraway seeds, of which make a tea. A person vastly troubled with the gravel, being treated by a Lord in *Hertfordshire* with a seven-year old bottle of perry, voided almost a handful of small stones.

Wind-Cholick.—TAKE as many grains of paradise, powder'd, as will lie on a shilling, in a glass of ale or brandy. It has cured when a doctor could not.—A gentlewoman, by advice, took as much turmerick as would lie on a shilling in a small glass of gin, for her wind-cholick.—Another burnt a large piece of the bottom of a common glass-bottle, and while it was fiery hot, quench'd it in gin, which he drank and was cured, though (as he said) he struggled for life, when all other means failed.—Another boiled winter savory in ale, then sweeten'd it with sugar, and drank it with some pepper mixt in it.—Another, a woman, my neighbour, boils wild thyme and St. John's-wort, together with carraway-seeds, and drinks it with or without sugar, as an excellent remedy for the wind-cholick and other diseases.—Another boils balm and mint in half a pint of gin, strains and sweetens: This has cured, though raw gin will not.

Promiscuous Receits for various Diseases.

*P*AIN *in a Man's Legs and other Parts cured.*—THIS man had great pains, particularly in his thighs and knees, and was cured by drinking now and then two years old verjuice, mixt in a glass with some brandy. If it binds you, take a little lenitive electuary, or other loosening thing.—A young woman, living in *Acton* parish, *Middlesex*, was cured of a pain in her legs, by beating oil of roses with vinegar, and bathing it in before a fire for three days together, twice each day; she cover'd them with flannel.—A wealthy person in our parish having a violent pain in his back, he tried sear-cloths and other things to no purpose, till one told him, he would pawn his life, if grains of paradise, taken in powder in a spoonful of ale, as much as would lie on a six-pence or shilling, several mornings fasting, did not cure him; and it answer'd the end.—A young fellow living near me, about 17 years of age, had a pain which was called a sciatica in his knees, to that degree as forced him to crawl about, for he could not walk, nor could hardly have any rest. This induced his parents to consult our country surgeons, who gave it as their opinion, that he was incurable; yet he was cured by his mother, who practises as a sort of doctress. She boiled wooden dishes which held about a pint, and while they were very hot, she clap'd them on camomile first laid on the knees, where they remained an hour and half; this she did every day for a fortnight, and removed the pain into his hip; here also she made the same application, and entirely cured her son.— Others rub in goosegrease on the pained part, and find a cure.—Oil of petre has cured an old ach or pain, by anointing once in two days, and keeping a flannel on the part.

For curing a Fever.—A FEVER attended with a cough went about the country, but was generally cured with a quart of honey mix'd with a quart of spring-water, which was to be taken a little at a time.—For a common fever, our country housewife advises to give a treacle-posset going to bed, where it sweats the party; next day she binds, under a broad rag, on each wrist, some beaten lettice and currants mixt together; or wood-sorrel, plantane-leaves, and the dry blue currants beat together; and for a drink, she gives a liquor made with wood-sorrel-leaves, five-leaf-grass, strawberry-leaves, housleek, blackberry-briary-leaves, dandelion, primrose-leaves, sage, and mint; these she makes a tea of, and so much that several bottles were filled with the same, and kept cork'd ready for drinking as wanted.—Others add to this liquor juice of lemons. This is a most cheap and efficacious method of curing a fever, for it seldom misses, even when they are light-headed, as is frequently experienced in our country.—A gentleman in *Derbyshire*, when he finds himself feverish, takes of pearl-barley a quarter of a pound, marshmallow-roots, liquorice, and half a pound of raisins of the sun, which he boils in a gallon of water, and makes a drink of it, for malt drink is not good in this case. This is his liquor after hard drinking; as being serviceable against cholick, fever, gout, stone, and scurvy.— For an epidemical fever, as published in a common news-paper; when the patient begins to be disorder'd, let blood immediately, and provided there be no violent pain in the head, give a vomit forthwith; during the disorder the patient must be kept warm, and lie in bed as much as possible. The drink that should be administer'd very plentifully, should be tartar-whey made thus: Let a quart of milk just boil, and then throw a quarter of an ounce of cream of tartar into it, strain it, and give it to the patient blood-warm; two quarts, at least, should be drank in a morning, and the like quantity of balm-tea in the afternoon: Beware of taking cold. If the patient is restless, syrup of poppies, and three or four drops of syrup of saffron may be added to the balm-tea; it should be the last thing taken going to bed. This has preserved many hundreds from a long sickness if not from death.—Others stamp blue currants and hops together, and apply them to the wrists as an excellent remedy.

A Man cured of a Scarlet-Fever by his Wife.—IN *March*, 1747-8, many men, women, and children had the scarlet fever in and about *Gaddesden*; my next neighbour, a man in good circumstances, looked frightfully red with this malady, and to cure him his wife gave him a weak treacle-posset, and treacle and sometimes honey in his drink. This drove out the fever, by a gentle sweating, into a rash or scurf, and in time he recovered without bleeding, for this woman's notion is, that the disease cannot so well be drove out, if they take the strength of the blood away. But this is contrary to the notions and practice of the famous Dr. *Boerhaave* and Dr. *Dover*, who are recorded for bleeding plentifully in all fevers, for giving air immediately to their patients; for tearing off all blisters, and for indulging the sick person with all manner of cooling and diluting liquors, see *page* 107, in Dr. *Dover's Last Legacy*, where is shewn the cure of Sir *John Dinely Goodyere*, who, though under a most violent fever, was presently thus cured.—Some lay beef steaks or sheeps lights to the feet, for drawing down the fever.—*N. B.* Some of our country women think nothing exceeds a tea made of the aforesaid leaves, and binding powder of white resin about each wrist for curing any fever. It is used even to lying-in women.

Cramp.—THIS malady causes exquisite pain, especially to persons in years. My neighbour, having a fractured leg that confined him to his bed, tells me, he suffered more pain from the cramp than from the fracture. It is thought to be wind in the blood, and for immediate relief some jump out of bed to walk on the floor.—Others rub their foot, leg, or thigh as hard and as fast as they can with their hand, for the cramp generally begins in the great toe, and runs up to the calf of the leg, and sometimes higher.—Others tie their garter about their foot or leg going to bed, to prevent it.—Some report, that wearing roll-brimstone in the breeches pocket is good for the cramp; but I think there is little or nothing in it.—The next seems valuable, which is, to tie an eel-skin pretty tight about a leg or arm, for it is said to be an excellent remedy for the cramp.—And so is *Hungary* water, rub'd on the part subject to the cramp, at going to bed.

Pain in the Stomach.—A woman, my neighbour, had it two days together, so that her stomach swell'd, but was cured by mixing three spoonfuls of gin with three spoonfuls of mint water, and burning it; when the flame was extinguished, she sweeten'd it, drank it, and was cured by three doses of it.—Another woman, my neighbour, that had been many years troubled with a great pain at her stomach, was advised by my brother-in-law, the late Captain *Henry Dodson*, who had been Governor of *Cape-Coast-Castle* in *Africa*, to take as much gun-powder as would lie on a shilling in a spoonful of brandy, which she did three mornings running, and it answer'd.—A correspondent wrote to me, that an acquaintance took a tea spoonful of gunpowder in a glass of white-wine, which work'd gently and quickly, and carried off a great deal of watry humour.

Loss of Appetite.—Mr. *C—h*, a wealthy person, at *Dunstable*, being sick, so that he could hardly eat any thing, was advised to steep a handful of camomile, a handful of wormwood, and a handful of rue, in two quarts of ale, a night and a day, and to drink a quarter or half a pint at a time of the liquor. He did so, and received a perfect cure. The same drink he takes now and then in his health, by way of prevention.—I know a young surgeon in *London*, who brought an old gentleman to eat two mutton steaks for supper, that has lost his appetite before, and took several six shillings of him for quart bottles of a liquor, wherein to my knowledge rue was a chief ingredient.

Rising of the Lights.—IF you put a little flower into water, and drink it in common, it will keep them down, else they are apt to rise and cause fits.

To stop Looseness.—BOIL deal shavings in milk, and take half a pint at a time, made strong of the shavings, three or four times a day; it is a leisure cure.—Or boil a sheet of writing paper in three pints of milk, which will make it thick; strain, and eat it with loaf-sugar and it is an excellent cure.—Or mix salt with water, and drink, if you can bear it, half a pint at a time; and if it offers vomitting, hold the vinegar bottle to the nose.—A woman in our neighbourhood tells me a certain person used to gather sloes about a week after *Michaelmas*, when they are just fit for it, before the frost takes them: These he put into quart bottles, and buried them under ground for half a year, then took them out, and drained out their juice, which was bottled with lump sugar, and thus became like claret for stopping a looseness, and for other occasions.—Or mix verjuice and brandy in equal parts; heat it, and take two or three spoonfuls at a time, which will effect a cure.

Scurvy.—A person having the nettle-spring or scurvy, which comes out in the skin, as if stung with nettles, being a high degree of the scurvy, a surgeon at *Hempstead* advised the party to take three spoonfuls in one day of nettle juice naked in a spoon at morning, noon, and night, for some time.—Or take the same quantity of juice of scurvy-grass naked, a spoonful at a time, in a glass of cyder or other liquor. The scurvy-grass juice is more pleasant than the nettle juice.—Dr. *Morton*, a famous physician of *Greenwich-Hospital*, used to do wonders by making men swallow a spoonful of this naked juice at a time. Our late parson Mr. *Dodgson* would scratch till his arms almost bled, and said, nothing relieved him more at forty-five years of age, than steeping scurvy-grass in table-beer, and sometimes eating it on bread and butter, and when he was bound (being of a costive constitution) he was relieved by lenitive electuary.

Another Receit.—BOIL two handfuls of fumitory and two handfuls of elder-flowers with sugar for a common drink; this with an issue is said to be serviceable. Bruise twenty millepedes or hoglice in a mortar, and moisten them with white-wine, which squeeze through a muslin rag. Take half a quarter of a pint every morning for a month of this juice or liquor; it is not only excellent for all scrophulous tumours and inveterate ulcers, but also for palsies, epilepsies, and all nervous distempers, and therefore strengthens the optick nerves of the eyes.

An antiscorbutick Cordial Elixir.—TAKE of the best nutmeg-grained rhubarb (not *Indian*) grosly bruised and a little toasted, one ounce, of the best *English* saffron and cinnamon each a quarter of an ounce, plain spirit of scurvy-grass six ounces, cut the saffron small, beat the spice to a gross powder, and put the whole into a bottle with a glass-stopple; after it has stood a week, shake the bottle now and then, and begin to take a tea-spoonful or two (pour'd off clear) in a dish of tea every morning. *N. B.* In this medicine you enjoy all the virtues of the rhubarb and those in an exalted degree; inasmuch as its purgative quality is somewhat restrained, and by the assistance of the scurvy-grass spirit does the easier insinuate itself into the blood, and thereby becomes a more powerful alterative and sweetener of the juices.—If you pour boiling water on coltsfoot-flowers in an earthen pot, and cover them, then let them stand till cold, strain off, and boil the liquor with sugar to a syrup, it is deemed a good antiscorbutick.

An excellent Receit for scorbutick Humours.—TAKE Æthiops mineral prepared without fire, native cinnabar finely levigated half an ounce, fine loaf sugar and gum guaiacum of each two drams, fine Turkey rhubarb and crabs eyes prepared each one dram, oil of sassafras-wood twelve drops; mix according to art, and divide the powder into twelve equal parts, of which take one in a little white-wine daily two hours before dinner, and likewise before supper. This is an excellent remedy indeed for destroying the scurvy, given me by my intimate acquaintance, a *London* physician.—A woman's legs broke out in blotches and scabs, so that she could hardly go, but was perfectly cured by steeping scurvy-grass in ale, and taking a little more than half a quartern fasting.

An Antiscorbutick Electuary.—TAKE medicinal antimony six drams, Æthiops mineral one ounce, rhubarb in powder one dram, conserve of the yellow rind of Seville oranges and lenitive electuary each one ounce; mix with syrup of cloves, and take two drams three times a day.

A sharp scorbutick Humour in the Skin.—DR. —— ordered a man Æthiops mineral and *Northaw* water, but an apothecary at *Enfield* put it by, and gave him cinnabar of antimony, sugar, and powder of crabs eyes and claws.

A Wen cured.—MRS. *Roberts*, of *Shedham*, about two miles from *Gaddesden*, having a wen many years almost under her chin, and as big as a boy's fist, could never get it reduced, till by advice she smoaked tobacco, and from time to time rubbed the wen with the spittle of it; this by degrees wasted the wen, and entirely cured it.

A swelled Arm that wasted, cured.—AFTER a fever, a man's arm swell'd, upon which the late Serjeant-Surgeon *Green* advised to quench some lime twenty-four hours in water, and apply it as a poultice, and when dried to wet it again, or apply new; it shrivelled the skin at first, but it reduced the swelling. Yet such a lime poultice must not be put to any sore; but lime-water is often applied to keep back humours from flowing to the part of a broken shin, or other wound. This man is my neighbour who received this benefit.

To draw out a Thorn.—HANG up the gall of a barrow-hog, and it will drop some of it out; that which remains and dries, spread on a linen rag, and apply it; it seldom fails.—Or apply a piece of adder's-skin.

To cure Shingles.—TAKE the black coom that is made by oiling or greasing bells in a steeple, and anoint with it.—A young woman of good fortune at *Gaddesden* had the shingles, so as to have blisters half round her body, but was cured by mixing the blood of a black cat's tail with juice of housleek and cream, and anointing warm three times a day.

Sore Mouth.—TAKE burnt allum powder, and mix it with honey; rub a little now and then on the part, and it will cure.—Or take honey of roses, a little tincture of myrrh, some strong sage tea, and red wine; mix and rub the mouth, and now and then use syrup of mulberries.—A woman my neighbour, troubled with a sore mouth, could not get it cured, till a surgeon told her it proceeded from the heat of her stomach, and that nothing would cure but a tea made of cooling herbs, and it answer'd accordingly.

Chilblains and Kibeheels—Mr. *Boyle* says have been cured by strewing on the sore part, powder of dried sliced quincies,—Or rub hogslard before the fire on the chilblain or kibe; then lay over the same a piece of bladder, or (better) the skin of a hog's flair. But some boil chickweed, and first wash the part with the strained water, for which reason they gather and keep chickweed dried by them.—A man and his children near me are much troubled with kibe-heels, but are always cured by rubbing oil of turpentine on them, before a fire, just before they go to bed, whether the kibes be broke or not broke.—But the kibe-ointment, mentioned in *Quincy's Dispensatory*, page 458, seems to be a most excellent sort for this purpose.

Canker.—A GIRL, about twelve years of age, that being daily employed to sew straw hats (which is most of the womens work in our part of *Hertfordshire*) used to put her brass thimble into her mouth, which bred many white cankering blisters on her tongue, gums, and lips, was cured by anointing the outside of her jaws, chin, and lips, three days together, with stale goose-grease, and binding a rag of the same over the parts.— Or stamp rue, sorrel, briar-leaves, and sage, and boil their juice with allum and a little honey, clear it of the scum, and wash with it the canker'd places now and then.

To fasten Teeth.—DROP five or six drops of tincture of myrrh into a tea-cup of water, and wash the teeth with it, for fastening them.—Or make use of allum, as one of the best of things to kill the scurvy in the gums and fallen teeth; make a wash of it, by dissolving a bit of it in water with a little brandy in it.—Or first wash with a tea-cup of water, wherein is mixt a little brandy and a few drops of tincture of myrrh; then roll in the mouth a bit of allum. This I do, and it ought to be done, every morning.—Or put two grains of salt of vitriol, a quarter of an ounce of tincture of myrrh, a bit of allum as big as a horse-bean, and half an ounce of honey of roses, into half a pint of claret; put a teaspoonful of this into a spoonful of water, and wash the teeth; the vitriol whitens, and with the rest fastens.

To cure the Tooth-ach.—DIP a little lint in tincture of myrrh, and put it in or upon the tooth; it is an excellent remedy.—Or stamp a little rue, as much as can be put into the ear, on that side the tooth achs, it will cause a noise, but makes a cure in an hour's time.—Tobacco ashes will clean and whiten teeth well.—A certain cooper burns the rind of ashes, wets them, puts them on leather, and lays it behind his ear, to raise a blister; which cures the tooth-ach, or other pain in the head.

How a young Woman lost several of her Teeth.—SHE tells me, that for curing her tooth-ach she smoaked henbane-seed; secondly, a mixture of tobacco and brimstone; thirdly, gunpowder and salt, in a rag held on the tooth; fourthly, salt and pepper; fifthly, spirits of wine; sixthly, spirit of hartshorn: These at times she smoaked, and applied, to the loss of several of her teeth. Some say, spirit of soot used once a month cures the scurvy in the gums.

Madam Howard's *Diet-Drink.*—THIS gentlewoman lived in *London*, and for preventing the breed of the scurvy and other diseases took an excellent method, by making a diet-drink in the following manner, *viz.*—She used to have a pin of brown ale brought to her house from a brewhouse, that held four gallons and a half; the ale she emptied into an earthen upright steen, and then soaked in the same, scurvy-grass leaves, gentian-root, snake-root, and wormwood. These she now and then squeezed, and after three days she strained off, and put the ale into the vessel again; then she cut some Seville oranges, and squeezed their juice into it, and after putting in some guaiacum chips she bung'd up the cask, for drinking this medicated ale at discretion. She sometimes only pared the oranges, and put them in whole. This is an excellent diet-drink for all degrees and shapes of the scurvy whatsoever.—Another of our farmers wives says the following is an excellent cheap diet-drink for the scurvy, which is made by boiling figs, liquorice, scurvy-grass, and water-cresses in ale.—Another says, take one ounce of sliced liquorice, two ounces of juniper-berries, and two scruples of salt of tartar, steeped in a quart of ale; then take four spoonfuls in a pint of ale.—A diet-drink is made and sold by a country doctress for the scurvy, rheumatism, and other diseases; she steeps mountain-flax, dwarf-elder, and buckbean, in ale, a night and a day.

The travelling Beggars Way of clearing their Bodies of Nits, Lice, and Fleas.—I believe I may affirm it for truth, that no county in *England* is so much frequented by beggars as

Hertfordshire; and upon asking them of their method of curing the several diseases they are incident to more than others, they tell me that, for clearing their bodies of lice, they boil copperas in water with hogslard, and by rubbing it over their bodies, no lice have power to bite them; on the contrary, it will make them forsake the cloaths they wear, and not damage their skin.—Another says, he is clear of lice by anointing the waist-band of his breeches with oil of russel, but this I doubt.—To clear the head of lice, first open and part the hair here and there, then cover the bole of a lighted pipe of tobacco with a linen rag, and blow the smoak into the places, which will make the lice crawl to the outmost parts of the hair, where they may be easily combed out.—To prevent and destroy fleas, boil brooklime, or arsmart, or wormwood, in water, and wash the room.—Or lay the herbs in several parts of the room.

To destroy Worms in the human Body.—A man cured of little white maw-worms. This man lived near me, and being much troubled with these worms, he took near half a pint at a time of salt water for four mornings together fasting, and it made him void great quantities of these worms, to the curing of him for some years.—Give to a girl twelve years old, that has worms, a teaspoonful and half of elixir proprietatis in water-gruel: It kills worms, and cures the green-sickness.—Bruise green tansy, and give a spoonful of its juice every day to a boy or girl: It is excellent to kill worms.—One of our labourers, having the small white worms, took a spoonful of sugar fasting, and in a few minutes after he took seven drops of oil of vitriol in half a pint of small beer, and in an hour or two's time, vomited worms to the quantity of a handful; then he drank half a pint of strong beer and vomited more worms, and so a third time; at last half a pint staid with him, and in three days after he took nine drops of the oil, which did not move him; three years after he was cured by the same.

To destroy Worms.—GIVE to a boy or girl a spoonful of the juice of rue now and then.—It is certainly true, that a dram of gin has cured several men, women, and others, of worms, in our parish, by taking it three mornings fasting.

To stop a Looseness or Flux.—A man given over for death, was cured of a violent looseness by eating an egg (boiled or roasted very hard) shell and all.—Another recovered by drinking now and then half a quarter of a pint of old verjuice.—Another stops a looseness by boiling blackberry leaves in small beer.

The Evil cured by Advice of a Beggar.—A girl at *Gaddesden*, having the evil in her feet from her infancy, at eleven years old lost one of her toes by it, and was so bad that she could hardly walk, therefore was to be sent to a London hospital in a little time: But a beggarwoman coming to the door, and hearing of it, said, that if they would cut off the hind leg, and the fore leg on the contrary side of that, of a toad, and wear them in a silken bag about her neck, it would certainly cure her; but it was to be observed, that on the toad's losing its legs, it was to be turned loose abroad, and as it pined, wasted, and died, the distemper would likewise waste and die; which happened accordingly, for the girl was intirely cured by it, never having had the evil afterwards.

The Evil in a Girl's Eye helped.—ANOTHER *Gaddesden* girl having an hereditary evil from her father in her eyes, her parents dried a toad in the sun, and put it in a silken bag, which they hung on the back part of her neck; and although it was thus dried, it drawed so much as to raise little blisters, but did the girl a great deal of service, till she carelessly lost it.—But I am humbly of opinion, no medicine known by man exceeds that of quicksilver water for curing the King's-evil. The cure of which I think likewise would be made very short, if the patient would exercise his body with some labour, and live on a milk diet, while he or she is drinking the water.

Pain in the Head cured.—MR. *Gadbury*, of *Dunstable*, kept his bed almost a year for it, and got a wry neck in the time; at last, by the advice of Dr. *Freeman* of *Amptill*, he was cured by the use of the following powder given in ale: He baked red sage and egg-shells together, of which he made the powder. Mr. *Gadbury* was alive in 1739.—Another, who is my particular acquaintance, took lavender drops every night he went to bed, to the number of sixty, in water, ale, or wine; but best of all dropt on loaf sugar, letting it gradually dissolve in the mouth, because by that means it soaks more immediately into the nerves, and gives a more sudden supply to the spirits.— Another takes thirty drops in water several times a day. In the decays of age, and convulsive or apoplectic shocks, such as bring on palseys and loss of memory, this is a most excellent medicine, as Dr. *Quincy* very well observes at page 363 of his *Dispensatory.*—I know a woman, who for the pain of her head snuffs some of these spirits up her nose very frequently.

Sneezing.—IT comes by cold taken in the head or other parts, and is very troublesome, and the more so, when it lasts some time: A good cure is, to dose the body with a hearty drink of wine, or other strong liquor, till it is thoroughly heated, but not with naked spiritous liquor, nor to the excess of drunkenness.—Or rub your head now and then with Hungary-water, and drink nothing that keeps your body open.— Or wash always your head with cold water in a morning.

Small-Pox.—They at first are generally taken with a pain in the head and back, coldness of feet, or vomitting.—The case of Miss *Howard* of *London,* under the care of a most eminent doctor of physick: At first she was thought to have only a cold, and so they gave her a raisin posset made to sweat her, but in three days the small-pox came out, after bleeding for a fever as they thought.—The doctor said, it is best to bleed on the apprehension of the small-pox, because it prevents their being vastly full, and prevents a fever joining them. She was kept always full of drink, either panado or gruel, and sometimes a little Sack and toast, with saffron steep'd in it, to drive the small-pox from the heart, or a Naple-bisket sopt in it; but no meat was allow'd till the pox was turned, which commonly is in nine or twelve days; then she had a little fish, or boiled chicken; and during all this time she had cordial powders in juleps given her every four hours, till they were turned and she out of danger. She was kept warm almost like as in a bagnio, and did not keep out of bed longer than till the bed was made; at last they wash'd her face with warm Sack and butter [or anoint with chopt rue boiled in hogslard] to shoal off the pocks, and prevent their pitting.

To prevent catching the Small-Pox.—DRINK, if you are going into any danger, a quarter or half a pint of rue tea without sugar; or hold a piece of rue in your mouth. This is an excellent antidote, and of infinite service to man and beast, in many shapes; particularly for cleansing the blood, and thinning it, for the better preparing the body to be easily cured of the small-pox. A piece in the mouth defends against the damage of any ill scents.

Deafness.—A tinker was cured by fleaing a hedgehog, taking out the guts, roasting the body without basting, and saving the dripping or fat, of which he dropt three drops into his ear at night, the same in the morning, and so for two days, when it cured him.—Or boil one or more adders in a small pot, save the grease, which will be almost as thin as oil, and drop one or two drops into the ear going to bed, repeating the same several times.—The late —— *How*, Esq; Recorder of *St. Albans*, being exceeding deaf, he shaved his head every day, and every night and morning rubbed it with Hungary-water, till he was perfectly cured by it.—Another is said to take oil of almonds, water in a jack-hare's bladder, and swan's grease, beating up 15 drops of each of these together, and dropping 15 drops into each ear going to bed, and so every night for a week. In the mean while, put white melilot on two bits of leather, and lay fresh ones to the ears every night.

Sore Eyes.—A woman having sore eyes dissolved fine loaf sugar in water, and it did her vast service.—Another did better by dissolving some white vitriol in spring water with loaf sugar, because the thickness of the sugar-water guards against the sharp vitriol: A little of this water dropt into the eye, or besmear'd by a feather with it, does great service.—The juice of green wheat takes spots out of the eyes.—Milk hot from the cow is a sovereign remedy for blood-shot or other sore eyes.— If you put the vitriol in sugar'd water, a bit as big as a large pea is sufficient for a two ounce bottle. It is an excellent water.

To take away Wrinkles from the Face.—MIX fine wheat meal in hot bean-flower water.

A Wine good for the Palsey.—TAKE woodlice or millepedes bruised, half a pint; vipers just killed, skinned, and freed from their entrails and fat, two, three, or more; horse-radish sliced and bruised, one ounce and a half; sharp-pointed dock-root, half a pound; juniper berries whole, four ounces; gentian sliced, six drams: Infuse these in a gallon of mountain wine, and take two ounces twice a day. This is the prescription of a professor of physick in *London.*—One of our country-men tells me, that he has the yellow flowers of the lady-finger grass distill'd for the palsey, and finds a great benefit by washing his face and hands with the distilled liquor, and by drinking a tea made with rosemary and lavender.—Spirit of lavender taken on loaf sugar, to the quantity from twenty to one hundred drops, is of such efficacy for this purpose, that by some they are called palsey drops.

Teas.—BOHEA and green are generally allowed to be unwholesome herbs; if drank to excess, they hurt the nerves (bohea especially) and cause various distempers, as tremors, palseys, vapours, fits, &c. And as lime and allum are employed in making loaf sugar, their corroding natures are likewise of very ill consequence when used immoderately; therefore cream, &c. is very necessary to qualify these bad properties. I know a gentlewoman who in her last dish of tea puts six or more lavender drops, to prevent the rise of vapours. Others boil archangel or nettle flowers in milk, to drink with their tea.—Some very judiciously make use of quicksilver-water instead of raw water for their tea.—A gentleman of my acquaintance, for avoiding the pernicious effects of loaf sugar, made use of white sugar-candy.—Another used all powder'd sugar.—A gentlewoman, a great lover of green-tea, drank it morning and afternoon, but was forced to leave it off, because it raked her stomach, and bred the cholick, being (as she thought) of a feeding nature; and therefore betook herself to ale-hoof or ground-ivy tea.—A surgeon of *Barkhamstead*, taking me into his garden, pointed to his balm and his sage, telling me these were his tea.—Another surgeon, named *Keston*, of *Hempstead*, said that green tea is the worst of things for the cholick and dead palsey. And I remember, the *Barkhamstead* surgeon said, that both bohea and green grow on one tree, are of a poisonous nature, and that the men who work on them have their hands blister'd by the oil, which is very hot.—Artificial tea may be made with saintfoin leaves, honeysuckle, the leaves of the white and black thorn and new hay.

Tea Caudle.—Sir *Kenelm Digby*, in his book called the *Closet*, tells us, that a Jesuit who came from *China*, in 1664, told Mr. *Waller*, that there they make an infusion or caudle of tea (green, I suppose) by putting a pint of scalding water on a drachm of tea, with two yolks of eggs beat up with fine sugar; the tea being first made, must be poured on the eggs and sugar, which being well stirred together should be drank hot. He says, that this infusion presently satisfies all rawness and indigence of stomach. In *England*, the Jesuit said, we let the hot water stand too long soaking on the tea, which makes it extract into itself the earthy parts of the herb; but by letting it remain a smaller time, you have only the spiritous part of the tea, that is much more active, penetrative, and friendly to nature.—Sir *Kenelm* says, Mr. *Waller* found the Jesuit's character of tea exactly answer.—And I say, I was in hopes I had sufficiently laid open the same hint on account of brewing malt liquors, in my treatise intituled *The London and Country Brewer*; but notwithstanding the great importance the same is of to men's health and pleasure, I find it passes, with too many, as if it was a tale of a cock and a bull.—Or you may mix the eggs with some white-wine and grated nutmeg, and heat and stir it over a fire, with the tea, as the right way.—Again, as tea is of such a pernicious nature to health, the stronger it is made, the greater damage it does. For my own part, as I drink near half a pint of quicksilver-water almost every morning, when I am to drink bohea or green tea I put into the quicksilver water some drops of spirit of hartshorn, or of lavender, as a defence against the ill effects of tea.—A young woman, seemingly about thirty-five years of age, whom I saw at *Otters-Pool*, near *Watford*, on her crutches, told me she boarded there for a month, to try if plunging once a day in this excellent natural cold bath would cure her of a dead palsey, that took her on one side; which she imputed to drinking tea in excess, that she was tempted to, as she lived in a service where she was not debar'd from it.—Another, that lived with a merchant in *London*, had tea in such plenty, that she thereby fell into a consumption and died.—A girl of seven years old, in my neighbourhood, fell into the jaundice, by drinking daily a large quantity of tea.—A gentlewoman said, if she drinks bohea tea, it gives her a trembling and head-ach; therefore she drinks green.—A gentleman, a hard drinker of spiritous liquors, was forced (because he must not leave them off all at once) to mix brandy with his tea.—An apothecary said, if green tea is laid on raw liver, it will eat into it.—Drinking too much tea breeds an asthma and stoppage at the stomach.

Diabetes.—THE late *Nath. Bent*, who kept the great *Bull-Inn* at *Redburne* in *Hertfordshire*, by tippling punch and six-penny stale strong beer, although a man of the largest size, fell into that lamentable disease a diabetes; and declared to me, that he thought none of the doctor's medicines did him so much service as smith's forge-water. I ask'd him, why he did not make use of *Bristol* or some other astringent well-waters; he answer'd, that it was his opinion, nothing exceeded the smith's water and isinglass. He lived several years after this malady seized him, and told me he thought himself well of it. He died I think in *April*, 1749, of a complication of distempers, a man of considerable worth, and deserving of a good character.—Diabetes cured by acidulated chalybeate waters, as related in Dr. *Hales's Philosophical Experiments, p.* 154.—Or see an excellent receit for it, at page 511, in *Quincy's Dispensatory.*—I remember a yeoman of a middle age was so often blooded for some distemper, that it brought him under a diabetes, and killed him.—One that is a surgeon and physician in *London* tells me, that the Hot-Well water of *Bristol*, and that of *Islington*, cures this distemper; but he says, to supply this, and make a liquor superior to either of them for this distemper—To two quarts of water put a scruple of salt of steel, and a little lump of lime, which is to settle a night, and then to be pour'd off; of this, drink half a pint two or three times a day.—But besides this, a diet-drink ought to be made use of; for which, boil guaiacum chips to a strong decoction, and add to the same a gallon of water, wherein two pounds of lime are infused; let it stand 24 hours and pour off; then add two ounces of sassafras chips, a nutmeg sliced, a quarter of an ounce of cinnamon, two ounces of liquorice, and half an ounce of coriander seeds; bruise them, and steep them in the liquor four or five days, and drink of it two or three times a day.

The Healthfulness of warm Drink.—THE late Dr. *Crawley*, of *Dunstable*, gave a strict charge to his cook-maid never to drink cold small beer when she was hot, be it in summer or winter; for that as her business greatly exposed her to heats, it would much endanger her health to drink cold small beer when she was hot. Warm drinks are by physicians said to be most beneficial to health; and although beasts drink cold water, yet it does them no good, till warm'd in their stomach. Warm drink allays thirst better than cold, and distributes, and better helps the digestion of our food; which leads me to present my reader (as a warning on this account) with the following case.—A very industrious honest farmer, named *John Gurney*, having taken a farm at *Nor-Marston* in *Buckinghamshire*, that was left in a most foul weedy condition by the last tenant, laboured almost incessantly to plow and get it clean and sweet, to that degree, as obliged him often to drink cold small beer when he was hot, which made him grow sickish, lose his appetite, and was so faint that he could not hold his work. Upon this, his wife carried his water to Dr. *Crawley* aforesaid, who said to her, Woman are you willing to be a widow? No sir, says she. But I tell you (says he) you will be one, for no man can cure him; for I find by his water, he has drank too much cold small beer when he was hot, and thereby so mixed his grease with his blood, that there is no remedy for him. Accordingly the doctor's saying proved true, for he afterwards pined away by degrees, not being able to retain his water (notwithstanding he consulted several physicians) which caused him to slink much, and after languishing a year, two, or more, he died, leaving a widow and five children, with a stock thought to be worth 500 *l.* to the great grief of all his relations and acquaintance.

Earwig, how one got into a Girl's Ear, and cured.—MY chairwoman told me, that when she was a girl about twelve years of age, riding in a cart to field in harvest-time, she laid herself down to dose, when an earwig crept into her ear, and presently caused it to swell, making her deaf to every thing but a terrible noise in it, and was in great pain by its stinging the part; being had in about an hour's time to Dr. *Crawley* of *Dunstable*, he syringed her ear, and by that means got out the earwig, saying, that if she had stay'd a little longer, he could not have done it, because the ear would have swell'd up; also that in twenty-four hours time it would have bred. When it came out, it was alive, and he said it bites at mouth and stings at tail; her ear was afterwards much swell'd.—It is said, that the juice of rue put into the ear will kill an earwig in it, if the party goes to sleep and lies on the contrary ear, and that when it has killed the earwig, the juice will come out.

A Cat cured Pain.—IT is said, that a gentlewoman having a swelled tumid hand, put her finger into a cat's ear, and within two hours was delivered of her pain; but the cat was so pained, that two men could hardly hold her.

A Purge.—A COUNTRY capital physician takes one ounce of manna several mornings together, as the best purge to keep him in health, in water-gruel.—Another says, dissolve half an ounce of the best manna in thin water-gruel, strain it through a fine rag, and add of the best tincture of rhubarb made in white wine, an ounce or two; tincture of cardamom-seeds, made according to *Bates*, twenty drops; mix them, and take what you think may answer your constitution.—The hiera picra purge is endued with such excellent qualities, that it is wrote of in several books, and therefore I cannot well help doing the same here, and the rather, because I know a physician that makes it the chief physick for his own body. They sell it at the apothecaries, druggists, and chymists, in powder. One says it may be taken from two to three drachms in Rhenish-wine, with an ounce of the syrup of mugwort, at night going to bed.—Another, I think, directs better, to put an ounce and a half of this powder into a quart of *Madeira* wine; and after it has been steeped three or four days, to pour off the fine part for use; then to take three, four, or five spoonfuls going to bed, or in the morning. A strong constitution wants no confinement nor alteration of diet, nor does it gripe like most other physicks. For a purge, the tincture of hiera picra is said to be the best that can be taken; it is an agreeable bitter, and never gripes. One ounce will carry off all the foulness of humours, and prevent a great many disorders.

For a Vomit.—IF you have a heaviness and foulness of stomach, and that you are more costive than usual, drink plentifully of green-tea, till all the slime be got off your stomach. It is a fine gentle vomit, and greatly relieves all scorbutick diseases.

Bite of a mad Dog.—MR. *Daniel Puttinham*, of *Gainsford*, near *Harrow*, in *Middlesex*, told me, *December* 9, 1746, that several persons were bit about him, as supposed by dogs that had run from *London*. The cure, he says, is absolute, if a person will every morning plunge himself over head and ears in a pond for a month together, and every other day for a fortnight after.—A man bit by a mad dog, about a week after, was had to the salt water; when he saw it, he snapt with his teeth, and started, which made the boatman say, it was too late; however, being dipt heartily it stopt the malady just where it was; but whenever at water, he started and snapt with his teeth.

To cure a Dog bit by mad Dog.—TIE up and bleed him in the neck-vein, pin and tie it about with thread, and give the dog as much white hellebore powder as will lie on a six-pence or a shilling in milk, but next time in flesh.—It is a sure cure.

Measles.—ONE of my neighbours had three of his children down at once of the measles; they came out very red in the face, upon which he gave his boy the quantity of a nutmeg of Venice treacle.

Whitloe cured.—A PERSON having a whitloe on the top of the thumb, when it was towards a ripeness, soap mixt with chalk was put to draw it to a head, and when it was broke, melilot salve was applied; and after that, the cure was finished with an old woman's healing salve.

Coffee —Is said to dry up crudities of the stomach and to comfort the brain, is very serviceable after a debauch of strong liquors, and so it is for those persons troubled with defluxions of rheum from the head to the stomach; but it is hurtful to dry constitutions, and is apt to hinder sleep. There are two sorts of coffee sold by grocers and druggists in *London*, and at shops in the country: The first are generally so honest, as to declare their difference, and sell the *Turkey* for 4 *s.* 6 *d. per* pound, and the *West-India* for 3 *s.* 6 *d.* I have therefore reason to warn my reader against this coffee imposition, that I may assuredly say is carried on by too many, especially in the country, where people are most ignorant; I mean for selling the *West-India* coffee for *Turkey* coffee, either alone or in a mixture.—The right way to make coffee, is to heat the berries in a fire-shovel, till they sweat a little; then grind them, and put the coffee-pot over the fire with water; when hot, throw the water away, and dry the pot by the fire, then put the powder into it, and boiling water immediately over the same; let it stand three or four minutes, and pour off the clear. By this means the hot water meets the spirit of the coffee, and will therefore be stronger than any boiled coffee; whereas if you boil coffee as the common way is, the spirit goes away, so that it will not be so strong nor quick to the taste; for, obtaining the spirit is the main thing to be desired. To experience the truth of this, boil the coffee half an hour, or a little more, and let it stand a while, it will be of a vinegar taste, and the stronger you make it of the coffee, the sourer it will be, because the spirit evaporates away in the boiling so long, and if the spirit of any liquor is gone, it soon becomes acid.

To make artificial Coffee.—BAKE a piece of bread in an oven to a burnt crust, afterwards scrape it to a powder, and it will have a taste very near true coffee. Or take wheat and parch it in a fire-shovel, or better on a tin plate over a clear fire, till it is black, then grind it, and it will imitate coffee both in smell and taste. The best way to keep roasted coffee-berries, is in some warm place. The powder ram'd well in a tin pot, and kept in a warm place, will keep well above a month.—Coffee poured on one or two yolks of eggs, and then just boiled up over a fire, will, with sugar, drink a little like chocolate.

Cutting and curing Corns.—I KNOW a man and his wife who when they cut their corns so to the quick, as to make them almost or quite bleed, always rub some spirit of wine on them, which prevents their festering, or bringing on a mortification.

Chopt Hands.—WASH them in chamberlye, and when dried by the fire rub them with hogslard, and wear gloves going to bed.

To relieve a Traveller's Feet.—LET him heat his feet every night before a fire very well, and it will draw out the fiery heat which they have contracted by walking in the day.—Or wash your feet with white-wine vinegar at night.—Or put an egg in each shoe when you walk.

Tobacco —Is an herb by some accounted wholesome, by others unwholesome. Tobacco, says Dr. *Archer*, physician in ordinary to King *Charles*, smoaked in a pipe, is very attractive of moist and crude humours, as water and phlegm out of the head and stomach; and thus it makes a pump of the mouth, for the benefit of some few, and detriment to the health of many others.—It is not good (says he) for those that are of a hot, dry, and cholerick constitution, nor for sanguine people, who are not troubled with rheums distilling upon the lungs. It is bad for the teeth for two causes, from its own heat from a burning oil with the smoak convey'd to the mouth, and from the frequent flux of rheum from the head to the teeth.—It is (says he) bad for the eyes, because the smoak carries such a hot oil with it, that weakens the eyes by its force upon the brain, drawing from the optick nerve.—It is good where cold and famine cannot otherwise be helped, for it heats the body, and defrauds the stomach by offending it, and so there may be the less appetite or craving for food. If chewing it is good for any, it is for those that have cold rheums distilling from the head; on this account I heard a physician say it is excellent, because it alters its cold nature into a hot one, and thus prevents its damaging the stomach and lungs; it is also by its smoak very serviceable in preventing contagious distempers, and therefore is commonly thus made use of by surgeons and others in hospitals, *&c.* Now to improve this narcotick herb, drop a few drops of oil of anniseeds into an ounce of it, it gives it a pleasant taste, and endues the smoak with several wholesome properties.

Too much Physick does Harm.—A physician said, It washes off the mucus of the guts, and then the meat passes too quick through them, because they are deprived of their retentive quality. I am credibly informed, that a gentlewoman in *Staffordshire* took the *Scotch* pills so frequently, that they occasioned this misfortune and killed her.

The Case of a Child of three Years old, which had liked to have died by catching cold in the Measles.—THE measles in this child appeared very full, but by the indiscretion of the nurse he had like to have died; for in the height of the distemper she let the child go to the door with a few of its garments on, which gave the air a power to strike the measles in, so that for two days and a half it was doubted whether the child would live, till a gentlewoman of *Dunstable* advised to give it now and then some strong drink wherein some marygold-flowers had been boiled, and after boiling, to sweeten it with treacle. This was done accordingly, and it brought the measles out again, to the recovery of the child.

Sir Hans Sloan*'s Eye-Salve.*—A MOST effectual medicine for soreness, weakness, and other distempers of the eyes, is faithfully prepared according to Sir *Hans Sloan*'s receit, printed in his sixpenny pamphlet, *p.* 4, where he says, he found it so surprisingly beneficial, that by the right use of it not one in five hundred missed of a cure.—And again, *p.* 7, he says, it has cured many whose eyes were covered with opake films and cicatrices left by inflammations and apostumes of the cornea, many of whom were so totally deprived of sight, as to be under a necessity of being led to him; yet after some time could perfectly find their way without a guide. This liquid or thin salve is to be applied with a small hair pencil, the eye winking or a little open'd. A bottle of Sir *Hans Sloan*'s salve is from one shilling to two shillings each.—A certain elderly man, in *London*, was so dark sighted, that he could not distinguish persons in the street, yet recover'd his sight by sewing a thin piece of lead, about the bigness of a crown-piece, to his perriwig.—Another, by washing his head daily, held his sight to a great age.

The Character of a Lord's great and unparallel'd Charity. Not a great many miles from *Gaddesden* now lives a nobleman, who although he was not bred a physician, extends his charity in a very uncommon manner; for he not only visits the sick in the most contagious illness, but supplies them with medicines at his own cost. He has condescended to walk through a workhouse, out of his own parish, to assist the distressed diseased people, and where he will not venture on his own judgment, he consults a physician at his own expence. Another instance of his charity happened to my knowledge; a poor woman lying ill of a desperate fever, her husband could get no nurse to attend her, for fear of catching the distemper, yet this excellent nobleman went to her in the greatest extremity, and gave her medicines at his own cost: An example, I hope, that will induce some others to imitate.

ADVERTISEMENT.

THIS is to give notice to all gentlemen and others, that I furnish them, on a proper order, with the new invented, light, four-wheel, plain drill-plough, either the single or the double sort, that carries two fixed hoppers on it, a seed hopper, and a manure hopper, being an improvement made on all other drill-ploughs whatsoever; for by its uses, with the assistance of a new invented horsebreak, that is drawn on two wheels by only one horse, and a very fertilizing compound manure, poor land (by the blessing of Heaven) may be made to produce rich crops of grain, turnips, rapes, or artificial grasses. The double drill-plough sows two drills at once, drawing along by only one horse, and the break being made to hoe and clean two intervals of drill ground at once drawing along, it will thus do more work in one day than twenty men can. I likewise sell the two-wheel *Hertfordshire* double plough, the two-wheel single fallow plough, the two-wheel bob-tail plough, the tarnrise plough, which is a proper one to lay all the ground even where it lies not too wet, by preparing it for the four-wheel drill-plough. Also the drain-foot plough for cutting water-furrows, which it does so well, as to throw out earth a spit deep, and a foot square, at once drawing along with a team of horses, and thus does more of this work, in one day, than twenty or thirty men can: The mole-bank-plough, that I sell but for one guinea at my house if single, or two if double, will likewise do more of this work in one day than forty men can: The late patent little light plough, that goes without wheels, is an excellent sort for working in soft earth, and turning a furrow the best of any plough: And chaff-cutting engines. I sell the famous Orange Bell pear-tree, not to be had in any of the nurseries near *London*, as I could find, upon inquiry: The Parsnip apple-tree, whose fruit, with that of the Orange pear-tree, is always ripe in harvest; being a most serviceable, pleasant apple, for eating raw or in pies and pasties, and for making cyder: White damsin and white elder trees: The excellent black Kerroon cherry-tree: Tame pheasants, guinea hens, and Poland dunghill fowls: The lady-finger and three other sorts of the very best of natural grass-seeds; the first comes up the second year, but the three last come up the first year, the seed of which produces the sweetest of milk, butter, cheese, and flesh, free of many dangerous noxious seeds of weeds that are generally sown when hay-seeds are taken out of hay-lofts. I sell receits for compounding various sorts of manures for the garden or field; also those for preventing assuredly the damage of flies on turnips or rapes in the field, or lice and caterpillars on cabbages, or on wall fruit trees: Likewise receits for preventing rats of any kind harbouring the thatch of barns or grainaries, cielings of dwelling-houses, or in the ground, or in malt or mill-houses, by several ways, without giving them any thing to eat; or I kill them and polecats, weasels, *&c.* several ways, by laying something for them to eat, which is no way poisonous or dangerous; with many other receits never yet published. I have further to observe, that on the 12th of *June*, 1749, I brought to *London*, in order to be sent further, three four-wheel drill-ploughs, one fallow plough, a sowing plough, a chaff-cutting engine, and several other instruments in husbandry; the whole number for those foresighted gentlemen, whose industry deserves high praise, because they endeavour to introduce the greatest of riches into their country, even the foundation of all trade and commerce, *viz.* the latest improvements in the art of agriculture. If therefore I say these instruments of husbandry, *viz.* the four-wheel drill-plough, with its two little harrows of six teeth each, and its two little iron gatherers, that gather up the mould, and leave it over the drilled corn; the horse-break likewise, with its two larger iron gatherers, that surprisingly deep gathers up the mould of two interval grounds, as the break is drawn along, and leaves it against the stalks of corn, without bruising them; were to be bought by some persons, who occupy much land, proper for their uses, for hundreds of pounds, I question whether they would buy them too dear. To which I add, that by the work of this plough and break, and proper manure that is to be sow'd out of the manure-hopper on the drilled seed; no worm, slug, snail, fly, or grub, can live near the drilled corn. And I wish our *English* gentlemen were as forward as foreigners, in thus promoting the interest of their landed estates. And for proof of what I here write of the drill-plough and horsebreak, *&c.* their operations may be seen at my farm in *Little-Gaddesden* aforesaid.

N. B. As the four wheel drill-plough sows corn, the horse-break almost finishes hoing the interval ground. Also that these instruments will save great expences in large gardens, and in manuring of land: For that quantity of manure, usually employed to dress five acres of land the common old way, will dress fifty acres in the new drill way.—This is the break that exceeds all other horse-breaks whatsoever, or any hoe-plough of any sort; for after it has hoed the interval ground between the drills of corn twice in a summer, and thereby killed all manner of weeds, the hoes are taken off, and the gatherers are put on for two men to hold and guide, because it cleans three interval lands, as it is drawn along by only one horse, at once, and throws up mould to the drilled corn, as aforesaid. And thus a field may be sown every year with grain, turnips, cole, or artificial grass, fifty years together, without any occasion to let it lie in the usual way to fallow it at all, and this with the least expence possible: For by these excellent instruments the land is kept in the finest tilth, free of weeds, and manured in the sweetest and richest manner; so that the poorest, chalky, hurlucky, sandy, and other shallow, lean earths, may be fertilized to a very great degree, and thereby made to bear large crops of these vegetables, to the greatest advantage of the owner; to the parson, by the increase of his tythes; to the labouring men, and to the nation in general.—I also recommend my treatise on sheep and lambs, that I published last year, as the most useful book that ever was wrote of the kind (for preserving them from the rot, red-water, wood-evil, and all other maladies, and for feeding them fat in a short time, with the least charge, and in the sweetest manner) which is sold by R. *Baldwin*, Jun. at the *Rose* in *Pater-noster-Row*, *London*.

OF THE

Butter and Cheese DAIRY.

IN many parts of *England* a fresh butter-dairy is thought to return the greatest profit, when it is carry'd on within forty miles, or something better of *London*, because at this distance of it, the carrier or higler can convey it timely and sweet enough for a beneficial market; but a much farther distance from the metropolis obliges the dairy farmer to salt down his butter in earthen pots, tubs, or barrels, against a proper sale time; for which *Suffolk* and *Yorkshire* are famous. And it is thought by some, that making of butter is more profitable than either making of cheese or suckling of calves (unless the two last are carried on by the feed of artificial grass) because in making of butter, there is skim milk for the service of a family, which will in some cases supply the use of new milk, especially if oatmeal or some other right ingredient is mix'd with it.

Of a Vale Butter Dairy.—THERE is no great difference between some Vale dairy farms, and some Chiltern dairy farms. In vales they seldom feed their horned cattle on any but natural grass and its hay, because most of their land is unfit for clover, ray grass, saintfoin, trefoil, lucern, turneps, *&c.* But although they want these profitable conveniencies, which most Chiltern farmers enjoy, yet are these deficiencies much compensated by the richness of their pasture and meadow ground; for as it is generally of a fat blackish marly nature, and lies low near the warm springs, they have a bite of grass, when that on hilly land is cut off by frosts or by heats, which has such an excellent feeding quality in it, that if a cow can but have enough for a bite, and plenty of water with it, she will milk well, which is what cannot be said of the upland meadow. But where their low wet ground produces rushy or coarse flashy grass, it causes a cow to give a poor watry milk, and that a pale rankish butter: For it is a true maxim, that as the feed is, so is the milk, butter, and cheese.

Furniture necessary for carrying on a Butter Dairy in Vale or Chiltern Countries.—THESE are a churn, leaden coolers, ashen tubs and pails, brass or earthen glazed pans, sieves, straining-cloths, butter trenchers, wooden shaping dishes, trays, baskets, weights and scales, *&c.* The churn may be either of the barrel or the upright sort. I use both; the barrel, when I churn a large quantity; the upright, when I churn less. The barrel is certainly the best sort, because it is work'd with the least labour, with the least waste of cream, and with a much more regular motion. By the barrel churn, one man alone can sometimes churn four or five dozen pounds without the least loss of cream, when one dozen pounds will sometimes make it hard work for him to churn it in an upright one, with the loss of some cream that unavoidably will plash up and waste in the top part. And what likewise much contributes to the making of good butter is, if a dairy with a sufficient number of cows belonging to it be furnished with leaden coolers, which are always made in a square form, from two foot square, to two foot one way and four another. These are first made boarded frames, and then lined with mill'd lead, that are to stand unremoved; for here the milk lying shallow and wide, the cream may be commodiously taken off, by letting the skim milk or under milk easily out by a cork-hole, and the lead readily washed and cleaned. In short, these profitable square leaden receivers or coolers are the very best contrivance of all others for a dairy farmer's interest, especially throughout the summer season, for in hot weather they will cast up the most cream and as these were first made in *Buckinghamshire* and *Bedfordshire*, near me, I send them to gentlemen at any distance, on a proper order. The next is the shallow tub, which is preferred to lead by some for its cheapness, and for keeping milk in a less compass, and warmer in winter, and thereby raising the more cream. But these have also their inconveniencies, for by their being sooner apt to fur and sour the cream than lead, they are with more difficulty clean'd and dry'd. And why I mention them to be made with ash (as well as milking pails) is, because this wood is white, and easily kept so, to the delight of the dairy-maid. The next sort of dairy utensils, for holding milk and raising cream, are brass pans: These in former days were much more in use than at this time, though by many they are still thought more proper for a hot dairy than earthen glazed pans. Others are of opinion, they are unfit for either a cold or hot dairy. Some again say, they are the best sort for both, because they are light in hand, and more easily and safely cleaned than tubs or earthen pans, provided they have a right management bestowed upon them, as they will then give the cream no ill taste; for which purpose they must be presently clean'd after the milk is out of them, and always made thoroughly dry before more is put in; nor must the milk remain too long in them. The sixth sort of dairy utensil is the earthen glazed pan: These in small dairies are in general use, because they are cheap, handy, cool, easily clean'd, and soon dry'd, but are very subject to be crack'd by scalding water, and to be broke by accident; however, they are serviceable both in hot and cold dairies. And as to their cracking by scalding water, I will by and bye shew a way to prevent it. The seventh dairy utensil is a hair straining-sieve: This is a very serviceable one, and must be had of a proportionable size to the dairy. A large sieve is about 18 inches wide, and the hoop six inches deep; for by this bigness it readily receives and discharges a large quantity of milk through it, leaving all hairs and other filth behind.

The Improvement of Milk and Cream.—THE improvement of milk and cream is chiefly to be obtained by cleanliness, timely skimmings, and preserving the cream sweet, which three articles I shall make my observations on. And first of cleanliness, which I here mention as a preliminary one, for being the foundation of making good butter. A company of farmers discoursing on this subject said—Such a one is an excellent dairy-maid, for she always in summer and winter boils the water she washes her dairy things with.—For which purpose, no farm-house, where six or more milch cows are kept, should be without a fixt copper in it, to heat a good quantity of water at once, not only for washing the milky utensils, but also for scalding pails, and those other smaller things that are not too large for being boiled in it. The square, shallow, leaden vessels indeed need not be scower'd with hot water in winter, but in summer it is absolutely necessary, and should always be scower'd with soft soap-boilers white ashes, or with fine sifted wood ashes, or with white salt, or with very soft sand; and this with either soft leather, straw, or hay; for hard coal-ashes, hard pearl-ashes, or hard sand, would be apt to give the smooth mill'd thin lead or tub a rough or furring coat. In the next place, no servant man or boy ought to have freeness into the dairy-room, because they are apt to take a lick of the cream, or a cut of the butter, and leave some dirt of their feet behind them, which turning to dust, may damage the milk and cream. In short, a dairy floor ought to lie on a pretty sharp descent, for carrying off all spilt milk or water often employed in washing it; for without a dairy-room is kept cool and sweet in summer, little good butter is to be expected. A dairy-room being thus kept clean and in good order, the milk should have twelve hours in hot weather before it is skimmed the first time, but in cold weather as long again, for making the best and most prime butter. In some dairies they let their milk remain more than two days and two nights, for skimming off two or three creams, till it looks of a whitish blue colour, and then they think this skim milk good enough for hogs. And to keep a parcel of cream in a sweet condition, till enough is got together for churning, there must be both care and art employed; for although cream may be skimmed in right order, yet it may be damaged if not spoiled in keeping.

To prevent which, the most common practice in hot seasons is to empty the cream out of one scalded glazed earthen pot every day into another, till cold weather comes in, and then once doing this in two or three days time will be sufficient. Others are of opinion, that if cream is set in a very cool place, it need not be shifted but once in two days in summer, and but once in four days in winter, stirring it about at every shifting; yet there are some farmers who are obliged to churn but once a week, and keep their cream accordingly: In this case they are forced to boil now and then a parcel of cream, for putting it to more raw cream to preserve it sound, or to put some hot milk from the cow to it, or add some salt to it.

The Use of the new-invented Barrel Churn in Winter.—A barrel churn is so late an invention, that the uses of it are known but in few counties in *England. Buckinghamshire* and *Bedfordshire* justly claim the first practice of this most serviceable dairy utensil, that every year comes more and more into fashion, for its being easily and quickly clean'd, as well as its being work'd with much facility and least waste of cream, and expeditiously producing the sweetest butter. I know of no author besides myself that has wrote on the profitable uses of this excellent barrel churn. And as there is a late improvement found out, and added to it, more than I have taken notice of in this or in any of my former works, I intend hereafter amongst many others to insert a cut of it in my book to be intituled *New Discoveries of Improvements in Husbandry.*—In winter time, a little before this barrel churn is used, my dairy-maid pours boiling water into it, and after giving it two or three turns in a quarter of an hour, the water is discharged, and the common straining-cloth is placed over the bung-hole, for straining the cream thro' it into the churn. When the wooden bung is fasten'd in, the work begins near the fire-side to preserve the heat the hot water left behind it; for if the cream gets colder, the butter will be the longer coming; therefore a quick turning of the handle, like that of a grindstone, to beat and keep the cream warm, is perfectly necessary in cold weather especially. And such turning should be perform'd with a constant as well as even stroke, for the better separating the oily or buttery part from the thinner part of the cream; for if the cream is turn'd too slow in winter, you may perhaps churn a day together and not get butter. Hence it is, that for preventing any intermission in working the barrel churn, when one is tired, another continues the same quick stroke, till they find the cream slops more lumpy than before. Now in churning with a barrel churn, the maid is obliged every now and then to pluck out the vent peg, for letting out the wind that the barrel contracts in beating the cream into a fermentation and this she does mostly in the beginning of her work, perhaps five or six times in all; and when she thinks the butter is come, she turns slowly, for causing it to gather into a body sooner, and by taking out the peg she can better tell is it is so; for if the butter is a little come, there will be an appearance of it like little pins heads: When it is fully come, she lets out the butter-milk, and gathers the butter into parcels or lumps.

The Use of the Barrel Churn in Summer.—THERE must be different methods made use of in churning butter in summer than in winter, and the same in several other branches of the dairy. In summer, contrary to the winter practice, we rince the barrel churn with cold water just before we put in our cream, and begin and continue churning an even slow stroke, in order to prevent beating the cream into too great a heat, for in sultry hot weather, notwithstanding the churn is so rinced with cold water, butter has come in less than half an hour's time, which in frosty weather would not perhaps under an hour, two, or more. And herein lies much of a dairy-maid's care and art; for if this churn is turned too fast, the violence of the motion will be apt to overheat the cream, and then the butter comes irregular, is very difficult to gather into lumps, looks pale like grease, has a very rank taste, and will not keep.

The Use of the Upright Churn, &c.—THIS is the most ancient and most common churn now in use, chiefly because the use of the barrel churn is not more known. If a large quantity of butter is to be made at once, it cannot be done in an upright churn, because it neither admits of room enough, nor strength enough to work it in the common way by one person. But as there is an improvement found out and made use of, to work this churn with more ease than in the common way, I intend to give a cut of it in one of my books as beforementioned. However, I will suppose butter made to the greatest advantage in this churn, yet it must be done in a far less quantity, in a more laborious, and in a more wasteful way than in a large barrel churn. It is true, that an upright churn gives a person an opportunity to place its bottom part in a tub of warm water, to keep the cream in such a heat as will expedite the coming of the butter; but then we account it almost an equivolent conveniency, when we rince the barrel churn with scalding water, and work it before a fire. There are wooden upright churns and earthen upright churns, both which in winter and summer causes the churner much labour, and especially so, if the cream is stale, for then the butter seldom comes under two hours working; therefore when these sorts are made use of, butter should be churned in them twice a week; for the newer the cream, and the oftner the churn is used, the sooner the butter will come.

How to make Butter from the Food of Clover, Trefoil, Ray-grass, or Lucern Grasses.—As I am owner of various sorts of earths; amongst the rest, I have some fields of a gravelly and chalky nature: These I have sown with ray-grass, trefoil, saintfoin, and lucern grasses, as I have done my stiff loams with clover, *&c.* Now to make good butter from the food of any of these grasses, is what very few know how to do; but I shall endeavour to shew how it may be done from my own practice, for I keep a dairy in a Chiltern country, and feed my cows with both artificial and natural grasses, and as a few of my fields lie at such a distance from my house, that it would hurt and make my cows feet sore to drive them daily to and from it, and thereby greatly lessen their due quantity of milk (for a little way driving a cow does much mischief in this respect) I oblige my servant to mow a parcel of artificial grass every day, or every second or third day, and bring it home in a cart, for laying and spreading it thinly over a covered floor, in order to give it my cows in racks under cover, undisturb'd from flies, and free from suffering by the scorching heats of the sun. Thus I feed them (this present summer, 1749) without danger of hoving or swelling them; a misfortune so incident to cows, when they feed on clover especially, and on lucern grass in the field, that thousands have been killed by it; but trefoil, saintfoin, and ray-grass, are the least subject to hove and swell the beast, and I am certain that a good butter may be made from any of these three grasses, if a right management attends the milk, the cream, and the making of the butter; to which I add, that where a very large dairy is carried on, and many acres of land are sown with artificial grass for this purpose, and where cow-houses are situated near the field, there I say it would be of great advantage to a farmer to mow any of these grasses every day, for giving it in due quantities to cows; because the fresher it is thus given, the more milk it will produce. And thus a person may go on mowing every day except *Sundays*, from the beginning of *May* to *Michaelmas*, and to provide for *Sundays*, it is only mowing a double quantity on *Saturdays*, which may be very conveniently done, where much ground is laid down with such grass, for by the time the mower gets to the end of it, he may begin again where he first began to cut. This therefore gives a farmer, that occupies large tracts of such grazing land, a far greater opportunity to make more of his dairy than a small farmer can, who for want of room is deprived of this valuable opportunity. Supposing then, that a farmer enjoys these conveniencies, one acre of good sowed artificial grass will keep two cows as well as two acres of meadow land can; and provided he has a good cellar and all necessaries, if he has not good butter, it is for want of skill and right management, which leads me to observe, that there are ways of making butter good from artificial grasses—First, that our housewife begins in *May* at furthest, and holds the same till *Michaelmas*, to skim her milk every twelve hours, that milk'd in the morning at night, and that milk'd at night in the morning; for if cream stands too long on this milk in summer, it will surely cause the butter to taste rank. And as a further security against this evil, a true housewife will boil her earthen cream pots well, and not use them before she has set them abroad, to make them thoroughly cold, for shifting the cream into them; and where a person keeps a sufficient number of cows for producing cream enough, to boil some to put to the raw cream, and churn once in two days. In short, to prevent any rankness of taste in butter made from foreign grasses, the sweeter the utensils are kept, the sooner the butter is churned. The more it is washed in different waters before it is made up into pounds, and the more it is beaten between two trenchers to clear it of the milk, the sweeter will be the butter, and the longer it will keep so: Which brings to my memory the loss that a gentleman sustain'd by having a bad dairy-maid.

The Loss that a Gentleman sustained by keeping a lazy sluttish Dairy-maid.—THIS gentleman was a bachelor well advanced in years, and owner of a very large farm, where sixteen cows and a bull had been kept on the grazing part of it, who (being obliged to take his farm into his own hands) was so opinionated in his ways, that it was very hard to convince him of his errors: Amongst which, one was his keeping an unskilful, lazy, sluttish dairy-maid, that frequently had very rank butter, by means of her ill management of her utensils, her milk, her cream, and her churning; insomuch that the common higler, that customarily bought it for selling it at a *London* market, refused it several times on account of its ill properties, which obliged the gentleman to send it about the neighbouring parts of the country, and get what price he could for it, to his loss, for that such damaged butter was sold for little more than half the price good butter would then fetch; which I think is hint enough to shew the value of a skilful diligent clean dairy-maid. For these reasons it is that I have been employed by gentlemen to send them dairy-maids out of the Vale of *Aylesbury*, as I live near the edge of it, and have an opportunity to hire those of a good character, and who are well qualified to make good butter and cheese. This therefore is to inform all gentlemen and ladies, that if they will give encouraging wages, I undertake to provide and send those that I hope will fully answer their expectation: I also on a proper order am ready to furnish them with any number of square leads, barrel churns, or any other dairy utensils.

The Nature and Value of After-Butter.—THIS sort of butter is more conveniently made in large dairies than in small ones: After-butter is that which is made from the second skimmings of milk; after the first cream is taken off, they let it stand till more cream arises, and there be enough to make another parcel of butter. By this they have a prime fine sort, and a second coarse sort. Now both these are sold in many markets as well as at chandlers shops in towns and in country, without many buyers knowing that one is made of the first cream, and the other of the second and worse. And it is this after-butter that serves many of the unconscionable sort to sell it as prime or first butter to two sorts of people, one that has money and no judgment to distinguish it, and the other that has judgment and not money, and therefore dares not dispute it with their creditor shop-keeper, because they can't pay for it on delivery: And thus poor people generally pay as much for this after-butter as for the first and better sort. Notwithstanding this, after-butter is commonly sold to the connoisseurs in a market for three half-pence a pound less than the prime or better sort. It is often the very same case in the sale of whey butter, of which much is made in cheese countries, where to preserve their whey cream they boil some to put to raw cream, and churn it twice a week; for by boiling some it lessens rankness of taste, and helps to keep it sweet the longer.

Artifices sometimes made use of to expedite the Churning of Butter.—WHEN necessity provokes the dairy-maid to make use of more than ordinary art for hastening the butter coming, it never is so good as when the cream is churn'd into butter by only a regular and timely working of the churn; for if hot water, hot milk, or hot cream, is added to the cream after it is begun churning, it is a sort of violence used upon its true nature: The same when pieces of money, or any other thing is put into the churn for the same purpose; yet to save time and labour, one or more of these remedies is sometimes made use of, but then this is commonly owing to some mismanagement of the milk or the cream, &c. As when the milk freezes in the leads or pans, or when cream is very stale by being too long on the milk, or kept in a pot too long before it is churn'd, or when the churn is too cold in winter time at putting the cream into it, or when too great an intermission is suffer'd in churning, &c.

How a certain Farmer manages his Milk and Cream, and churns his Butter.—THIS farmer makes altogether use of a barrel churn, and one of the largest sort; because he keeps twenty cows, and generally churns six dozen pounds of butter at a time, by turning its two handles with two mens labour. In winter they let a pail full of boiling water lie in the churn close stopt up for a little while, to heat the wood, and better prepare it for receiving the cream and bringing it into butter the sooner: But for a greater security of this, they boil a gallon of the cream taken from the same morning's skimmings; when it is ready, they put it into the churn to all their cold cream and churn away, and if it get cold, and is longer than ordinary in coming, they pour in some scalding water. Thus this farmer churns, and the better for preparing his milk and cream to produce the best and most butter in winter, he distributes some of the last and best milk or stroakings amongst his pans of milk, and in summer he applies cold spring water in like manner, designing by both to raise the most cream and keep it sweet the longest; and to make his barrel churn answer his expectation in hot weather, he puts boiling water into it at morning to scald it, and after it has lain in it a quarter of an hour, he empties it, and pours in cold water to stand two or three hours, which he empties, for putting in the cream directly to be churned.

How a neat Housewife had the sweetest of Butter.—SHE kept two large milch cows always on natural grass or hay, and during all the summer-time she used to skim every meal's milk, that is to say, she skim'd twice a day, and got three or four pints of cream each time which she boiled in a skillet, that she wash'd, but not scour'd, for if she scour'd her brass skillet, it would cause the milk or cream to taste of it; and as she churn'd but twice a week, she thus kept her cream sweet in the hottest weather, and had the very best of butter. Not like another, who, to make her butter have a yellowish cast, would at every cow's calving in winter-time, for the first two or three meals, put a dish or two of what we call beastings or beastning into her good cream.

Of several Sorts of Food, that occasion Cows Milk to make indifferent Butter, with Ways to help it.—OF these I shall take notice in particular, because no author has yet done it, as they relate to milk, butter, cheese, and flesh.—Turneps, cole or rape, green or dry thetches or vetches, are none of them so sweet and good as the feed of the most excellent natural lady-finger-grass seeds, tyne-grass seeds, honey-suckle seeds, and another. Turneps give milk so rank a taste, that it is easily perceived by the eater; cole or rape a worse, especially when it is old; somewhat of the like does green thetches and clover, but saintfoin, trefoil, and ray-grass are better: Thus also do the leaves of trees affect the milk in *September* and *October*, when they fall; likewise in *April* there is little good fresh butter to be had, because this month being between grass and hay, some farmers are necessitated still to give their milch cows dry thetches in straw, that are of a hot bitterish nature; or pea-straw, bean-straw, or indeed any straw where hay or better food is wanting. Grains alone produce but a watery insipid milk, but when mixt with chaff, bran, or malt dust, it does much better: Now as these sorts of food do not breed a delicate sweet milk, there are two ways to help it; one is by skimming such milk soon and only once, and with such cream to make butter, but the best way of all is to scald the milk in part, or in the whole; that is to say, if some of the cream is scalded and put to the raw cream, it will help to lessen the ill taste of butter, but much better if all the milk is scalded; and how to scald it, I shall presently shew. In the mean time, I think it necessary to acquaint my reader with the pleasant and healthy effects of four sorts of natural grass and their hay, as they relate to the making of the sweetest butter and flesh.

The Character of the Lady-finger Grass and its Hay, &c.— THIS is a true hardy natural grass of *English* growth, exceeding in sweetness and goodness all other grasses whatsoever. These qualities are truly warranted by even the cattle that feed in meadows where it grows, for they will eat this first and before all others; and whether it is given in grass or hay, it invites and feeds fawns, deer, lambs, sheep, and bullocks, and makes them fat with great expedition, producing the sweetest and wholsomest of flesh. When cows feed on it, they yield a milk that makes the finest of yellow-colour'd butter and cheese, and which is prefer'd for being drank from the cow, as conducing the more to the health of the drinker; and the same for its cream to mix with tea, for as a physician well observes, milk, tho' in its own nature healthy, is more or less so as the feeding of the cows and the disposition of the cattle are. This lady-finger grass I am the first discoverer of, for makeing it known in this publick manner. It will grow in the poorest or richest ground of any sort; and, if it be not mowed too soon, it will prove in a great degree corn and hay, for it is a podded grass. Hence I am led to observe, that it has been a reigning ill custom for persons to lay down their plow'd ground with a promiscuous mixture of common grass seed; by which means they may sow the seeds of plantane, hemlock, rennet-wort, crow-garlick, horse-mint, clivers, dog-parsley, penny-grass, couch or quitch grass, clob-weed, white-ash, sorrel, dock, and yellow and white daisy-flower sort, &c.— The plantane by its broad leaves hinders the growth of better grass. The penny or rattle grass has its faults. Quitch-grass is a sour and coarse sort, unfit to grow in any ground. The knot or clob-weed grass is a very great brancher, has high thick stalks and knobs at their ends like buttons, is a great increaser, and hinders the growth of better grass, therefore it provokes some to stock it up with a mattock. White-ash is much rejected by cattle, and so is the sour sorrel, for hardly any will eat it. The same may be said of the bitter yellow flower and daisy, &c.— The ladyfinger-grass seed I sell (as aforesaid) with three other sorts of the natural kind, and send them to any person on a proper order, with such directions for their management, that they need lose no time in obtaining a lasting meadow of the same. Two gallons of milk from the best grass that grows have produced as much cream as three gallons from flashy or weedy grass: This lady-finger grass, which (as I said) is the most excellent of all other grass, with the three others, gives a cow a milk that produces in the calf a bag of the most value for making the best of rennet, and consequently the best of cheese. And that persons may know how to come by these four sorts of natural grass-seed, if any will send me a letter, I will answer it, provided postage is paid to my house at *Little-Gaddesden*, near *Hempstead*, in *Hertfordshire*, which stands thirty miles to the northward of *London*.—The expence of laying down one acre will be as follows, *viz.* Three pounds of lady-finger grass-seed, seven shillings and six-pence; four pounds of tyne seed, four shillings; four of honeysuckle seed, four shillings; four of another grass-seed, four shillings; in all nineteen shillings and six-pence. And to sow the land effectually with these seeds, it must be first plowed till it is as fine almost as ashes; and after the seed is sown, there must be a particular cheap sort of manure sowed over the same that I can specify, to prevent the ill effects of too long drought, slugs, worms, flies, and frosts; and to fertilize the surface, so as to push forward the growth of the seed with expedition.

The exact Method of preparing Scalded Cream for making it into Butter the Devonshire Way, by a Correspondent at Stowford, near Ivy-bridge, Feb. 25, 1746-7.

SIR,

ACCORDING to your desire, I herewith send you our exact method of making butter from scalded cream. The morning's milk is commonly set over the embers about four o'clock in the afternoon; but this varies according as they have more or less of these embers in a right heat, for many will set their milk over them as soon as they have done dinner, as there is then commonly a good quantity of them free of smoak, and are ready without the trouble of making them on purpose. The evening's milk is commonly set over them about eight o'clock next morning, sooner or later; however, care must be taken not to do it before the cream is well settled on the milk, which will be in the beforementioned time. And as to the quantity of milk we scald at once, it is very different: From one gallon in a pan to three or more; and the measure of each pan of the biggest size is three gallons, or three and a half. There are pans of several sizes less, but the most common quantity is about two gallons, or two and a half in each brass pan; and brass pans are commonly used for this purpose, as they are certainly the best of all other inventions, because the milk will both heat and cool sooner, and far more safe than in the earthen sort; for these (especially in summer-time) are too long in cooling; and as the cream cannot be used before it is cold, these earthen pans are in disuse. I never saw any of them used in this manner but at Sir *John Rogers*'s: Their reason was, that they are something sweeter than brass pans; and I must confess they are so, if the brass ones are not kept in the nicest order possible. As to the height of the pans standing above the embers, it is according to the height of the iron trevit, which is commonly about six inches, with this difference; if on a stove six inches, if on a hearth eight inches, the latter being most in use. As to the exact time of scalding the milk, to have a full clouted cream on it, it is about one hour; yet this varies according to the heat of the embers, and therefore it is sometimes two or more hours, but seldom less than one. However, a moderate heat is best for raising the thickest cream; and you may easily discover when it is scalded enough, by a little swelling of the cream, and then it must be immediately taken off the fire. That which is scalded in the morning must be skim'd in the evening; and that in the evening or afternoon the next morning, with the hand only. When they have but little to scald at once, they save several meals together, and then scald it; but this does not make the best butter. When they have no embers, they use clean dry wood to burn under the pans, but they always refuse to burn rotten wood, because it is apt to give the butter an ill taste. The chimney must be kept very clean from soot, lest any drop into the milk. Sometimes, when the pans are not very clean, they rub them with bay-leaves (or in case they are very bad, they boil the leaves in the water they wash and scour the pans with) for these leaves are great sweeters and cleansers, and should be frequently used for this purpose, especially in the summer time.

The exact Method of churning scalded Cream into Butter, according to the Devonshire *Way.*

S I R,

I have further to add, that our method of churning scalded cream is the most expeditious of any I ever saw, and is done with the least trouble. The butter is made in a large wooden bowl, or shallow tub, according to the quantity; and this they do by keeping the hand with the fingers half bent in a constant stirring of the cream at the bottom of the wooden bowl or tub. Sometimes in less than a quarter of an hour the butter will come; at longest they seldom exceed half an hour. And this will be performed the sooner, by observing (when you begin to make the butter) to save out all the thinnest of the cream, untill the thicker harder sort begins to turn, and then add the thin cream; for the thicker part being of a harder consistence, is the chief cause of the butter being so expeditiously made. The quantity of butter made at once is from a quarter of a pound to ten pounds, but seldom more than ten. The greatest trouble in a large quantity of butter is in washing it, beating it, and making it up. Of the quantity of milk that will make so much butter I can't give you any exact account, for experience only must do this, because six quarts of some cows milk will produce as much butter as eight of others: Different pasture will cause it to vary much. But to give you the best account I can, I must add, that a pint of hard cream is reckon'd to produce one pound of butter; which I believe you may depend on, as I had it from one of our most credible dairy neighbours. As to the way of making up the butter, it is the same as your's. I think I need not enlarge further, because I hope this will give you satisfaction from, Sir, your most obedient servant.—This account came to me with several others from a servant I sent to live with *John Williams*, Esq; at *Stowford* aforesaid, who being a bachelor did not make butter, but bought it of his neighbours (I suppose his tenants.)

This young man, well skilled in husbandry affairs, lived in this country about three years, and collected for me several valuable improvements.

A Somersetshire Dairy-Maid's Account of making Butter with scalded Cream.—SHE says, they strain their milk directly from the cow in the evening into brass or earthen pans, and set them on iron-leg'd trevits, high enough for burning wood under them, which must be of the dry sort, that it may burn with the least smoak. But the burning of charcoal in stoves under the pans is the more regular and sweeter way of heating the milk. There are several signs to know (says she) when the milk is scalded enough; one is, by feeling it with the finger, for when you can but just bear it in the milk, it is in a right heat to take off; a second is, when the milk appears crinkly on the top; a third is, by the dull sounding of the brass pan: Then take off the pan, and set it by till next morning. But the milk must not boil, for if it does, it is spoiled for making butter; because the cream will then rise like skin, cut streaky and white, and waste away in little scales: Therefore if a pan of milk boils, they never make use of its cream to make butter. Next morning they take the cream off with a skimming-dish, or with the hand, and in cold weather put it by for one, two, or three days, till they have got enough together for churning; then they put all the cream into a tub, and stir it about with the hand or with a ladle, till butter comes. This is the way (she says) of churning and making butter. She also says, that the buttermilk by this management is very sweet, and (if mixt with skim milk and some new milk) will make good cheese. She also further says, that to make butter from clover, saintfoin, raygrass, or lucern-grass, so as to prevent its eating rank, the right way is to make the butter from this hot dairy, because the scalding of the milk in a great degree lessens the misfortune. This old experienced dairy-maid assured me, that she made butter two ways, when at home with her father, a considerable farmer; one by the cold, and the other by the hot dairy; and that they sold their scalded butter for more money than that made in the common old way of setting the milk cold.

The Somersetshire *Way to secure their earthen glazed Pans from cracking, that are to be used for scalding Milk.*—IN this county (the dairy-maid says) their way to prevent the fire from cracking their earthen pans, which they scald their milk in, is to grease them all over the outside with fresh hogslard, and when it is thoroughly dry'd into them by a fire-side, or by the wind or sun, they may then be safely made use of to scald milk in.

The Hertfordshire *Way to prevent earthen Pans from cracking.*—IN this county we make no more to do for preventing earthen pans from cracking by the fire, than to soak them before using in cold water a day or longer, after which they may be put into a very hot oven with a pye or pudding, or meat, without danger; nor will hardly one of them in twenty crack, if boiling water is put in, but will last perhaps as long again as if nothing was done to them.

The Welsh *Way of colouring Butter.*—SEVERAL dairy people in *Wales* take care to sow that sort of marigold-seed that produces double flowers, and as these in a rich earth and warm situation will grow almost throughout a mild winter, they seldom want wherewithal to colour their butter; in order thereto, they bruise the flowers in a mortar, then put them into a rag, to squeeze out their juice amongst the butter, which, on being work'd in, will give it a fine yellow colour and wholesome quality.—Others say a little bruised saffron in water will supply it; but as marigolds are readiest and cheapest, every dairy farmer in particular should have a bed of them, for as much as a quantity of their flowers will yield a quintessence little inferior to saffron for many uses.

Of salting, potting, and barrelling Butter, and how to know good Butter from that which is bad.—THE salting of butter is the more necessary to treat of, as there are several sorts of butter potted and barrel'd, and more than one way of doing it: There is an after-butter, a whey-butter, a damaged butter, and a new good butter, salted down. The after-butter is that fresh sort made from the second skimmings of milk. The whey fresh butter is that made from the skimmings of whey, which produces but a poor cream, rather worse than the last. The damaged butter may at first be a good sort of fresh butter, but for want of sale it becomes stale and rank, or it may be that butter that is damaged by some extream in making. The new fresh butter wants no explanation. The after or back butter generally begins to be made in *May*, and continues so till near *Lammas-day*, by which the dairy farmer has an opportunity to make the very best prime fresh butter, for which they skim their milk at twelve hours end, and likewise take the same time for skimming their after or second cream. Now to know such after or back butter, the first fresh butter is generally yellow coloured, from the flowers that the cow eats at this time of year; but the other tastes earthy, is whiter, and a little rankish. The whey they skim once in twenty-four hours, is whitish coloured, and has a little taste of the cloth and the cheese, and the same it is when these two sorts of worse butters are salted and potted, or barrel'd down, for they both will taste stronger than the finest first made butter, and be of a whiter colour, unless artificially coloured. However, if they are thus bad, the poor persons who are necessitated to labour hard for maintaining their families, are obliged sometimes to run into debt at a chandler's shop for bread, butter, cheese, and other necessaries, and thus forced to pay for bad butter at the best price, altho' the shopkeeper gives perhaps but little more than half what the prime butter costs.—A knowing woman being at *Dunstable* market, and cheapening some pounds weight of fresh butter, the woman seller ask'd the best price for it, but the woman buyer gave her to understand she knew it was bad butter, by saying the mice had run over it; as much as to say, Mrs. bad housewife let the cream stand so long on the milk before it was skimmed, that it was got thick enough for a mouse to run over it, and therefore made a bad butter.

Author's Method of salting down or potting Butter for his Family Uses.—To do this, my dairy-maid in the first place makes a brine strong enough to bear an egg, that it may be in a readiness to mix amongst fresh butter, for preserving it sweet and sound some time; when she has churn'd her butter, she beats some salt very fine, and salts it a little as they commonly do fresh butter; this done, she puts some brine at the bottom of a glazed pot, and on that a layer of butter, which she kneads close down, and by the impression of her knuckles she leaves hollow places sufficient to hold some brine; then she begins a second layer of butter, kneads it as before, and adds more brine: Thus she carries on this work of potting butter till the pot is near full, and when she has covered the whole with brine, enough to swim on the top of the butter, and the pot is well cover'd, the work is finished.

What an ancient Author writes of potting and barrelling Butter.—You shall by no means (says he) as in fresh butter, wash the butter-milk out with water, but only work it clear out with your hands, for water will make the butter rusty; this done, you shall open the butter, and salt it thoroughly, beating it in with your hand till it be generally dispersed through the whole butter; then take clean earthen pots, exceedingly well glazed, lest the brine should leak through the same, and cast salt into the bottom of it; then lay in your butter, and press it hard down within the same, and when your pot is filled, then cover the top thereof with salt, so as no butter be seen; then closing up the pot, let it stand where it may be cold and safe; but if your dairy be so little that you cannot at first fill up the pot, you shall then (when you have potted up so much as you have) cover it all over with salt, and pot the next quantity upon it, till the pot is full. Now there be housewives (says he) whose dairies being great, can by no means conveniently have their butter contained in pots, as in *Holland, Suffolk, Norfolk*, and such like; and therefore are forced to take barrels very safe and well made, and after they have salted the butter well, they fill their barrels therewith. Then they take a small clean stick, and therewith make divers holes down through the butter, even to the bottom of the barrel, and then make a strong brine of water and salt which will bear an egg, and after it is boiled well, skim'd and cooled, they pour it upon the top of the butter, till it swim above the same, and so let it settle. Some (says he) use to boil in this brine a branch or two of rosemary, and it is not amiss, but pleasant and wholesome. This ancient author says further, that you may at any time betwixt *May* and *September* pot up butter, observing to do it in the coolest time of the morning; yet (says he) the most principal season of all is in the month of *May* only, for then the air is most temperate, and the butter will take salt the best, and be the least subject to rusting.

Remarks on the aforesaid ancient Author's potting of Butter.— THIS author, I think, is a little too slight in his advice, by saying it is enough only to beat out the butter-milk with the hands; for butter that is to be potted down, is by some put and confined in a press under weight, the better to drain out the butter-milk, but where this conveniency is wanted, hand-beating may do; next it is to be salted down in a pot or barrel, by laying it two or three inches thick, and strewing salt between every layer of butter; at last to salt or brine as he directs. And whether it be butter made in the cold or hot dairy, it may be potted or barrel'd to a good purpose, provided the butter-milk is entirely got out, salted rightly, and done in a cool air; for if butter is barrel'd in very hot weather, it will be apt to grow rank too soon: Therefore in such weather, where they have not a cellar or other good conveniencies, it is hazardous work; and so tender are some on this account, who are not under a necessity of potting or barrelling butter in the summer-time, that they forbear doing it till the latter end of *August*, when the nights are pretty long and cool.—Again, when the salt part of butter decays, so as to cause it to grow bad, let it be taken under care time enough. The cure is, to

(404)

wash it well in more than one water, then to salt and pot it down again; for this may recover it, and bring it to be good salt butter a second time.—So likewise may good salt butter be made to become good fresh butter, as many do to their great profit; else the *London* pastry-cooks, as well as some others, would be at a great charge indeed, to buy always fresh butter in winter-time, when butter is at the dearest. Therefore it is the practice in some dairies, where they churn cream enough to make six pounds of butter, to cut three pounds of salt butter into thin slices, and just as the new butter is coming, to put them into the churn, and churn away till the whole parcel of butter is come. And if the work is rightly carried on, both the salt butter and the fresh, being thus churned into a mixture, will all become good fresh butter; but take care you do not put the salt butter in too soon, for if you do, neither the fresh nor that will come. You may preserve fresh butter the longer, by keeping it in brine.

Butter-milk Porridge.—BUTTER-MILK, when mixt with oatmeal, may be made into good porridge.

Butter-milk Hasty-pudding.—IN the Vale of *Aylesbury*, where are many large dairies, the poor people go from house to house to beg butter-milk, and some, when they have it on the fire ready to boil, will stir wheat or barley flower into it, to make hasty-pudding of it, and thus live several days on the same sort of management.

Butter-milk with Apples and Toast.—SOME coddle, and others roast apples till they are soft, and put them into butter-milk, and then boil them a little. This will make it thick like custard, and when a toast is made and sop'd in it, it is good eating, especially in winter-time, when the butter-milk is sweet; but the same mess may be had in the spring and summer-time, where they make butter from the hot dairy, if they have apples, because here the butter-milk is always sweet. My butter-milk I frequently give away to my indigent neighbours, as a very acceptable relief to their families. Others make a toast as for ale, and put it (cut in bits) into butter-milk, then roast some apples, and mash them into it with sugar, and think it an excellent repast.

Butter-milk Pancakes and Puddings.—SWEET butter-milk makes better pancakes and puddings than skim-milk.

Butter-milk Curds.—THE whey of cheese must be put over the fire, and heated till it rises ready for boiling; at this juncture of time, some butter-milk must be put into it, and stir'd by degrees, as when posset is made. This will cause curds to arise. Then take the pot from off the fire, and skim off the curds from the whey for eating them. Now the way our country people eat them is, by crumbling bread, and mixing it with a little sugar, or without sugar; when they say, this is a dish for a king. Others may eat these curds with cream and sugar, or with wine, or with beer and ale, but be sure you do not stir in your butter-milk over the fire if it smoaks, for if you do, it will have an unsufferable taste. The whey that is left may serve for a cooling wholesome drink. But although I have hitherto wrote on butter-milk for raising curds, yet where butter-milk is too sour for this purpose, or is not to be had, some will make use of cold water, by putting it in along the sides of the kettle or pot by degrees, as soon as the whey rises for raising curds; and when they are skimmed off, and let to stand till the whey is drained from them, they are fit to be eat.—Whey if good has so much of a milk quality in it, that if it is boiled, it will, without any assistance of butter-milk or water, throw up a skim or cream; therefore some instead of letting their whey lie cold in pans to skim it once in twenty-four hours, will get a cream from it by boiling it, in order to make a butter of such cream.—A second way to make butter-milk curds, is to boil new milk, and while it is boiling hot, pour it upon cold buttermilk, which cover, and let stand till curd rises; then take out the curd, and let it stand on a fine straining sieve, or in a linen cloth, till no more whey drops out; then beat the curd with a spoon till it is finely broken, and sweeten it with cream to your palate.

Of the Repository or Dairy-Room.—THE sweetest butter is certainty best made in the month of *May*, when all sorts of grasses, whether of the *English* or foreign kind, are in their infant or purest growth; yet this is not the time for potting down butter, because the weather at this time of year increases so much in heat, as would cause it to grow rank and spoil before the winter. Now a cellar or any low room, that lies below or even with the surface of the earth, is situated to a northern aspect, and has a brick or stone floor, must be of great service towards carrying on a dairy; for by this valuable conveniency, milk and cream will keep longer sweet than if it stands in a warmer place. I have known much stress laid upon this, where a number of cows have been kept, that though a dairy has made great part of a large rent for many years, yet a tenant has suffered to such a degree for want of a very cool cellar or room, that he never left soliciting his landlord till he had one made to his mind; for what damage must it be to those many farmers who keep ten, twenty, or thirty milch cows, and cannot sell their butter oftener than once or twice at most in a week, by reason the *London* carrier goes but once or twice a week at most to *London* from *Oxfordshire, Buckinghamshire, Bedfordshire, &c.* Wherefore when milk is kept in a cellar or other cool place, it will not only keep longer sweet, but it causes it to throw up the greater quantity of cream, that will produce a butter in such perfection as to sell for more money than that made from a dairy where this conveniency is wanting, as the case is with many farmers, in vales especially; because here the springs are generally so nigh the surface of the earth, that unless the bricklayer makes use of tarrass, and he is a very good workman, he cannot make a cellar to keep out water. Yet I have known this deficiency in a great measure supplied, by digging only two or three foot into the ground, and by laying it with a brick floor, and building this dairy-room at the north side of the farm-house.

What an ancient Author writes of keeping Cream.—HE says that with a shallow thin wooden dish you take in the evening the cream from off that milk which was milk'd in the morning, and skim the evening's milk accordingly. The cream so taken off, you shall (says he) put into a sweet well leaded earthen pot (he means a glazed earthen pot) close cover'd, and set it in a cool place; and this cream so gather'd you shall not keep above two days in summer, and not above four in the winter, if you will have the sweetest and best butter, and that your dairy contain five kine or more; but how many or few soever you keep, you shall not by any means preserve your cream above three days in summer, and not above six in winter.

What an ancient Author writes of churning Butter in an upright Churn.—THIS author, who wrote on butter and many other subjects in husbandry about one hundred and twenty years ago, says thus:—Take your cream, and thorough a strong and clean cloth strain it into the churn, and then covering the churn close, and setting it in a place fit for the action in which you are employed (as in summer, in the coolest place of your dairy, and exceeding early in the morning, or very late in the evening, and in the winter in the warmest place of your dairy, and in the most temperate hours, as about noon or a little before or after) churn it with swift strokes, marking the noise of the same, which will be solid, heavy, and intire, untill you hear it alter, and the sound is light, sharp, and more spirity, and then you shall say that your butter breaks, which being perceived both by this sound, the lightness of the churn-staff, and the sparks and drops which will appear yellow about the lip of the churn, cleanse with your hand both the lid and inward sides of the churn, and having put all together, you shall cover the churn again, and then with easy strokes round, and not to the bottom, gather the butter together into one entire heap, lump, or body. Now forasmuch (says he) as there be many mischiefs and inconveniencies, which may happen to butter in the churning, because it is a body of much tenderness, and neither will endure much heat nor much cold (for if it be overheated it will look white, crumble, and be bitter in taste, and if it be over cold, it will not come at all, but make you waste much labour in vain) which faults to help, if you churn your butter in the heat of the summer, it shall not be amiss, if during the time of your churning you place your churn in a pail of cold water as deep as your cream riseth in the churn, and in the churning thereof let your strokes go slow, and be sure that your churn be cold when you put in your cream; but if you churn it in the coldest time of winter, you shall then put in your cream before the churn be cold, after it hath been scalded, and you shall place it within the air of the fire, and churn it with as swift strokes, and as fast as may be, for the much labouring thereof will keep it in a continual warmth; and thus you shall have your butter good, sweet, and according to your wish. After your butter is gathered well together in your churn, you shall open it, and with both your hands gather it well together, and take it from the buttermilk, and put it into a very clean bowl of wood that has water in it, and therein work the butter with your hand, turning and tossing it to and fro, till you have by that labour beaten and wash'd out all the butter-milk, and brought the butter to a firm substance of itself without any other moisture; which done, you shall take the butter from the water, and with the point of a knife scotch and slash the butter over and over every way as thick as is possible, leaving no part through which your knife must not pass; for this will cleanse and fetch out the smallest hair or mote, or rag of a strainer, or any other thing, which by casual means may happen to fall into it. After this you shall spread the butter in a bowl thin, and take so much salt as you shall think convenient, which must by no means be much for sweet butter, and sprinkle it thereupon; then with your hands work the butter and the salt exceedingly well together, and make it up either into dishes, pounds, or half pounds, at your pleasure.

Remarks on this ancient Author's Account of churning Butter.—As there was no barrel churn invented in his days, he was confined to write only on the upright churn, and this he does well on some accounts, but he takes no notice of beating the salt fine before it is mix'd with the butter, though it is a material article; nor that working fresh butter (by way of kneading it) with a very strong brine instead of salt improves it; nor that too long an intermission in churning is of ill consequence to the work, because this will make the churning (as we call it) to go backwards, and very hard to be renewed, if at all, especially in winter weather; and yet this is a fault that some ignorant or slothful dairy maids are guilty of, that do not consider that an intermission, though but while one can tell fifty, is enough to divide the thick from the thin part of the cream, and prevent the butter coming in due time.

The Practice of a Vale Dairy Farmer, that generally milk'd thirty Cows.—THIS man kept thirty cows generally under milk, and for making the most profit of his dairy, he furnished his cellar with such a number of square leads, that were placed almost all round it, for receiving the milk as it was brought from the cows; for these he prefer'd before tubs, or earthen or brass pans, because they keep milk coolest in summer, and not amiss in winter, are very smooth, and presently and easily clean'd. By this and other ways of his ingenious and careful management, he seldom failed of making thirty dozen pounds of delicate sweet butter every week during most of the summer, by churning it every third day, but in winter only once a week; and because earthen pans or pots are liable to be crack'd and broke in their removal, and too small for holding much milk, he always kept it in the leads, which answer'd his purpose; and for keeping his cream sweet he boiled some to put to the raw cream, which he duly shifted into fresh leads, and thus preserved it in good order.

The Nature and Conveniency of Chiltern Lands for sowing them with foreign Grass Seeds, &c. for carrying on a Dairy.—

As I have before wrote of a Vale dairy, I come now to write on a Chiltern dairy. According to the common acceptation of the word *Chiltern* in *Hertfordshire*, we understand it to signify a hilly inclosed country, consisting of various sorts of earths, which although they are not of so fertile a nature as Vale grounds generally are, yet they give us a far greater opportunity of putting them to different uses than what Vale farmers can theirs; because Vale lands commonly lie in open fields, and so in low and wet, that they are forced to plow them all one way, for raising and keeping them up dry in high ridges, which renders them incapable for the most part of being improved by sowing them with clover, trefoil, saintfoin, raygrass, lucern, turneps, or rapes. It is true, that their earth is of a blacker richer nature than Chiltern lands are, and therefore the natural grass is certainly of the best sort for making butter and cheese; but then as our fields are most of them inclosed, and our land lies more dry, we can plow them long-ways and cross-ways, and sow them with clover, trefoil, saintfoin, raygrass, lucern, turneps, or rapes, according to our conveniency, not only for enriching our grounds by feeding them with cattle, but also for making butter and cheese with the feed of several of them.

Of a Cheese Dairy.

A Cheshire *Maid's Account of her making Cheese, as she gave it me in* Hertfordshire *on the 25th of* November, 1746.— SHE says, that the milk of thirty of their cows makes a cheese of fifty pounds weight every day, and for well doing it, there must be three persons employed; they heat the night's milk, and put it to the morning's milk, till both are warm as it comes from the cow; then they put two or three spoonfuls of rennet into it, and stir and mix it well together, and in one hour's time, or two at most, the curd will come fit to be broke. Now their way of breaking it (she says) is over a tub, for the whey to run into it, and when the whey is thus discharged into one tub, they put the curd into another, for two or three persons to break it small; this done, they salt it, and work it into the form of a cheese, and in working it, they press all the whey they can out, then they put the curd into a cloth, and bind it about with broad filletting, and lay it in a press that has a great stone on it for lying here two hours, at the end of which they take it out, and shift it into a fresh dry cloth, which they put again into the cheese-press, for its lying here eight hours; then they turn the cheese in the same cloth, and let it lie in the press twelve hours, at the end of which they take it out and shift the cheese into a finer cloth and lighter press, and thus the pressing work is finished. After it is taken out, they scrape the cheese, rub it all over with brine, and then salt it; next they melt fresh butter, and pour it all over the cheese, and then lay it on a rack not far from a fire, and with giving the cheese timely turnings, the whole work is finished.—She also told me, that their cheese factors seldom buy any *Cheshire* cheese under a year old. And why they cannot make such good cheese out of *Cheshire*, is chiefly because their land is of a particular rich nature, some by the River *Weaver* (she says) letting for five pounds an acre, though a reddish sort of land; and here they are so nice, as not to make cheese till the fifth meal is taken from a new calved cow.

A Way that some take in Cheshire *to make large Cheeses with a few Cows.*—She says they press the curd once or twice to clear it from its whey, then they cut it into thin slices and throw them into water; next day they break them short, by tearing them like dough into bits, and work and salt them well into one mass; this being done, they put this salted curd in the middle of new prepared curd which incloses it, then they bind it up in a cloth, and press and turn it several times as in the last way; a method practised by only those that have not cows enough to make a large cheese at once, for they that have, refuse it.

The Somersetshire *Dairy-maid's Way of making their common Cheese.*—This country contains various sorts of lands and situations; it has marsh lands, dry stony lands, short earths, and stiff earths, hills and dales, grasing and plow'd grounds. About the latter end of *April* they begin to make their cheese, which for the greatest part are of the thin sort, like those of *Warwickshire* and *Leicestershire*. Here they first squeeze their curd in the press a quarter or half an hour, then they take it out, break it as small as possible, and salt it; next they work it into the form of a cheese, put it into a cloth and press it again, squeezing it very gently at first, and follow the pressing of it a day together; in which space of time, they give the cheese several turnings, shifting it into a cloth wetted in cold water each time, in order as they say to give it a thin rind: At last they turn it in a fine dry cloth, to cause the rind to appear the better.

A further Account from the same Somersetshire *Dairy-maid, how they make their Cheese from the Feed of marsh Grounds.*— MARSH grounds generally produce the longest and rankest of grass, wherefore it puts the dairy-man on ways and means to take off, or to lessen any disagreeable taste that such grass may cause the cheese to retain.—A farmer here, that keeps forty cows, works two cheese-presses, when he that keeps thirty or less, works but one. After a cheese has been once pressed, they throw it cloth and all into scalding water, and there let it lie an hour if it is of the thinner sort, but a thicker one they let lie longer; then they take it out, and press it leisurely again. It is true, that this way is apt to extract and run out some of the fat part of the cheese curd, but then it gives the cheese these two good qualities, that it will eat the milder, and keep the longer sound.

The Somersetshire *Dairy-maid's Way to make Cream Cheese.*—She says, that she skims off the cream of last night's milk the next morning, and puts it into the morning's milk as soon as it is got from the cow; with this they mix a spoonful of rennet, and when the curd is come, they put it into a shallow wooden vat or mould, and with a wooden cover over it they press it by the hand. After this they put it into a cloth, and press it very tenderly, and turn it several times in one day; then they salt its outsides, and press it lightly again; at last, they lay it in nettles, rushes, or grass, to ripen, shifting it every now and then.

The Somersetshire *Dairy-maid's Way to make Cheese from the Feed of Clover.*—IT is certainly such a difficult thing to make good cheese from the feed of clover-grass, that very few attempt it. If sheep feed with cows in a clover field, their pissing on this grass will cause the cheese to hove on the shelf; and if cows feed alone on it, especially when the clover is in high growth, it will hove and swell the cheese, and give it a rank taste. Now to prevent these ill qualities in a great measure, there are two ways of doing it; one is, by salting the cheese curd soundly; the other is to let it lie in a good quantity of scalding water or whey half an hour in the cheese cloth, at the end of which time to put it into the press, and press and turn it as another cheese is usually done. She says the salt may fail answering this end, but the scalding will not. She further says, that for making their cheese like *Gloucestershire* cheese, they put the curd, after it is once press'd, into hot, but not scalding water; and that when the lambs have been taken from the ewes, she has milk'd them, and put their milk amongst the cows milk, and made cheese of it.

Gloucestershire *Cheese.*—THIS *Somersetshire* dairy-maid tells me that *Gloucestershire* cheese is made with only one meal's milk as it comes hot from the cows, where they keep a sufficient number of them to do it, and when the rennet has brought the curd enough, they take it off with a dish, and directly put it into the wooden vat, or mould, and here press out the whey without a cloth; this done, they take out the cheese curd and put it into a cloth, and press it again and again, shifting the cloth two or three times between the pressings, and salt the cheese only on all its outsides.

Shropshire *Way of making Cheese.*—I am told they make their cheese curd into balls with salt, and keep them a day or two, then break them extreamly fine into new curd, else it will cause the cheese to crumble too much: But if the work is perform'd rightly, they say it makes good cheese.

To make a compound Cheese.—TAKE the cream you skim'd off last night, and put it to the morning's milk in a tub. Then make some water scalding hot, and pour it into the milk and cream, which stir and mix till all is only lukewarm, and put rennet to it. This done, let it stand cover'd with a cloth about half an hour, and if the curd does not come enough in that time, you may add more rennet, then with a dish in your hand break and mash the curd, and press it with your hand down to the bottom of the tub. After this, with a thin skimming dish, you are to take the whey from the curd, and directly break the curd small, and squeeze it into your wooden vat till it is quite full; then lay upon the top of your curd your round cheese-board, and upon that a weight for making the whey drop out of it, and when it has done dropping, take a cheese-cloth, and having wetted it in cold water, lay it on your cheese-board, and turn the cheese upon it. Then lay the cloth and cheese in the vat, and press it in the common cheese-press. And after it has been there half an hour, take it out, turn the cheese into a dry cloth, and put it into the press again. Thus you may turn it into dry cloths five or six times the first day, and then let it lie press'd twelve or more hours, and at last turn it into a dry vat without any cloth at all. When the cheese is so far made, rub it all over with salt, and next day do the same; and for two or three days following turn it in brine; after this rub it and lay it on a shelf to dry, and continue rubbing it every day with a dry clean cloth, till it is got thoroughly dry and fit to be laid in a cheese-loft: But observe that you dry it hastily in the beginning, and leisurely afterwards. Such a cheese, if rightly made, and a due age given it, will be as good one as any man need to eat.

To make soft or what they call Cream Cheese.—AS to the second appellation, it is for the most part a wrong one, because these cheeses are seldom made with any other than the new milk as it comes from the cow, and while it is thus warm, rennet is put into it for turning the milk into curd, which when sufficiently come, it must be taken out with a skimming-dish (for the hand must touch it but as little as possible throughout all the operation) and put into a hair sieve, to give the whey an opportunity to drain from it. Next, the curd must be put into a wooden vat or mould with the skimming-dish, for a gentle pressure of it, for if the hand was employed to do this, it would give the cheese a disagreeable toughness. Then press it for about three hours, turning it once in the time, and salting it a little. Now in great dairies they make these soft early cheeses twice a day with each meal's milk, and press four or five, or six at a time, by putting each cheese in a cloth one upon another, and thus pressing them all together. And after each cheese has been press'd, they lay them on boards, and turn them twice a day for three or four days together, then lay some rushes on each cheese, and turn them on it twice a day till they get pretty dry, and when they are so, three or four or more cheeses may be laid over one another with rushes between them, to keep them hollow, and dry them the faster. Which management from the press to the buyer will take ten or fourteen days time. And when in *April* they begin to make these soft thin cheeses, or as some call them cream cheeses, some will have a fire of embers made from wood or otherwise in the middle of the room, on purpose to forward the drying of these cheeses, that they may meet with the better market; tho' they are not so good as those made in the month of *May* or later, because in *April* they are obliged to help out the short bite of grass with some dry meat to feed their cows with. Some for making the most profit in a great cheese dairy will take off a cream from thin milk to mix with whey cream, to make the better whey-butter, and put the skim milk to new milk for making soft thin cheeses, which in a near county to *Hertfordshire* they call dozen cheeses, because they sell them by the dozen for four shillings or four shillings and sixpence a dozen; and for giving them a little gloss, they use red-saunders, which gives them a brightish colour, for though they are naturally pale, yet a shade of red adds a small lustre to them. It is also observable, that these thin soft cheeses have most of them marks of the green rushes on their rind, which are accounted for this use better than nettles or grass, because these have hardish round stalks, that cause the cheeses to lie hollower to dry than the leaves of nettles or grass will admit of; besides which, it is a dairy maxim, that unless cheese is press'd well, it won't dry well. And although I have mentioned this way of making soft thin cheese with only new milk, and with new milk and skim milk, yet better cheese is made by some, for I have heard it affirmed that a gentlewoman, who kept but ten cows, made sixty cheeses in a season, weighing twenty pounds each, so rich that she sold them for one shilling *per* pound.

To make Slipcoat Cheese.—PROPORTION your cheese curds to your moulds and vats, and to six quarts of milk (or better stroakings) put a pint of spring water. If the weather is hot, let the water be cold, and before you put it into the stroakings, let them stand a while to cool after they are milked, then stir in the water with a little salt, which let stand a little while, then put in two spoonfuls of rennet and stir all well together, to stand cover'd with a linen cloth. When the curd is become like a thick jelly, with a skimming-dish lay it gently into the moulds, and as it sinks down fill on more curd till all be in, which will require three or four hours time; then lay a fine clean cloth into another mould of the same size, and turn it into it, and then turn the skirts of the cloth over it, and lay upon that a thin board, and upon that as much weight as with the board may make two pounds or thereabouts, and about half an hour after lay another clean cloth into the other mould, and turn the cheese into that; then lay upon the board as much as will make it six or seven pounds weight, and thus continue turning it till night; then take away the weight, and lay it no more on it; this done, beat some salt very fine, and sprinkle the cheese all over with it as slightly as you can; next morning turn it into another dry cloth, and let it lie out of the mould upon a plain board, and change it as often as it wets the cloth, which must be three or four times a day. When it is so dry, that it wets the cloth no more, lay it upon a bed of green rushes, and lay a row of them upon it; but be sure to pick the bennet grass clean from them, and lay them even all one way. If you cannot get good rushes, take nettles or grass. If the weather is cold, cover them with a linen and woollen cloth. In case you cannot get stroakings, take five quarts of new milk and one of cream. If the weather is cold, heat the water that you put to the stroakings. Turn the cheese every day, and put to it fresh of whatsoever you keep it in. They are usually ripe in ten days.

A second Way of making Slipcoat Cheese.—To two quarts of cream, add six quarts of milk directly from the cow, mingle these together and let them stand till they are cold; then pour three pints of boiling water to it, which stir in, and let all stand till they are very near cold; then put to it a moderate quantity of rennet made with fair water (not whey, or any other thing than water, for this is an important point) and let stand till it come; have a care not to break the curds, nor even to touch them with your hands, but only with a skimming-dish. In due time lade the curds with the dish into a thin fine napkin, held up between two persons, that the whey may run from them through it, while they roll it about, that the curds may dry without breaking. When the whey is well drained out, put the curds as whole as you can into the cheese vat upon a napkin. Change the napkin, and turn the cheese every half hour for ten times, till it wets the napkin no more. Then press it with half a pound weight for two or three hours; add half a pound more for as long a time, and another half pound for as long; and lastly another half pound, which is two pounds in all, a weight that never must be exceeded. The next day, when about four and twenty hours are past in all, salt your cheese a little, and turn it three or four times a day, keeping it in a cotton cloth, which will make it mellow and sweet, and preserve it a smooth coat, ready for eating, in about twelve days time. Some lay it to ripen in dock-leaves, but they are apt to give and mould the cheese, others in flat boxes of wood, and turn them three or four times a day, but a cotton cloth is best. This quantity of milk and cream is for a round large cheese, a good finger's breadth thick. Long grass ripeneth them well and sucketh out the moisture. Rushes are good also; they are hot, but dry not the moisture so well.

A third Way of making Slipcoat Cheese.—TAKE 3 quarts of stroakings, and as they come from the cow, put a skimming-dish of spring water with two spoonfuls of rennet to them, and let it stand cover'd till it come hard. Take it up by degrees, but break it not. When you have laid all in the vat, work a fine cloth in about its sides with the back of a knife, then lay a board on it for half an hour, at the end of which set a half pound stone on it, and let it stand two hours; then turn it on that board, and let the cloth be under and over it, and put it into the vat again. Now lay a pound and half weight on it. Two hours after turn it again on a dry cloth, and salt it a little; then set on it two pounds weight, and let it stand till next morning, when you are to turn it out of the cheese vat on a dry board, and keep it turning on dry boards three days. If it spreads too much, set it up with wedges. When it begins to stiffen, lay green grass or rushes upon it; and when stiff enough, lay rushes over and under it. If this cheese is rightly made and the weather dry, it will be ready in eight days; but in case it does not dry well, lay it on a linen cloth and woollen upon it, to hasten its ripening.

A short Way to make a Cream Cheese.—MILK seven quarts from the cow, and as soon as it is got, mix it with a pint of cream and a spoonful of rennet. Cover it in a bowl or bucket, and when the curd is come enough, lay a cloth all over a cheese vat. Take the curd out with a skimming-dish, and put it on the cloth till the vat is full; then turn the cloth over the cheese, and as the curd sinks lay more on till there be enough. When thoroughly drained of the whey, turn the cheese in a fresh dry cloth in the vat, and lay a pound weight on it; at night turn it on another dry cloth, and salt it on the morrow morning but very little; then lay it on rushes or nettles, and cover with the same, and turn it twice a day. This cheese will be eatable in twelve days time or sooner. To improve this cheese, stamp a handful or two of marigold flowers, and add some of the juice to the rennet.

Fresh Cheese.—Sweeten a quart or three pints of cream well with sugar, and boil it, and while it is boiling, put in some damask rose-water; keep it stirring to prevent its burning to the pot, and when it is thicken'd enough and turned, take it off the fire, and wash the canvas strainer and cheese-vat with rose-water, and roll it to and fro in the strainer, to drain the whey from the curd; take up the curds with a spoon, and put them into the vat, let it stand till it is cold, and then put it into a dish with some of the whey for eating.

Rich fresh Cheese.—To 3 pints of new milk (or better stroakings) while it is warm from the cow, put half a spoonful of rennet for turning it to curds and whey; then beat a quarter of a pound of blanch'd almonds with two or three spoonfuls of cream and one spoonful of rose-water. Shape the curd in a cheese vat or pan, and eat it with cream and sugar; but lest such a fresh cheese prove too raw and cold for some stomachs, you may add some powder of cinnamon, mace or nutmeg, or all.

Winter Cream Cheese.—Boil a quart of cream, and put it to a gallon of new milk; when all is milk-warm, put a spoonful of rennet to it, and cover it with a cloth till the curd is come enough; then with a skimming-dish lay it into a canvas straining cloth, to discharge it of its whey. This done, lay a board on it, and a two pound weight on that; and after the curd has been under this pressure for three or four hours, put a wet cloth in a mould or vat, and your curd in that, with six pounds weight on it. Here it must be turned into fresh wet cloths every three hours for the first day. Let it stand pressed all night, and next morning take out the cheese and salt it a little; then press it again, and turn it every three or four times in fresh dry cloths at every two hours end, and it is ready for laying on rushes or leaves of nettles in a dry place. Observe to lay the cheese every morning amongst a thick parcel of fresh nettles or rushes; and if the outsides of the cheese be moister than ordinary, apply dry cloths for the first or second time. With careful management, this cheese will be ready in twelve or fourteen days time for eating.

To make a Cream Cheese in a Cabbage-Net.—THIS cream cheese has been made many times by a widow woman; and as she told me, she has sold them for a shilling a pound. To this purpose, she takes the cream off last night's milk, puts it into a pail the next morning, and then directly milks upon it her desired quantity, to which she puts a spoonful or two of rennet. When the curd is come enough, she squeezes the whey from it very softly with her hand; for if she squeezes it hard, much of the curds goodness will go off with the whey; then she salts the curd a little, and puts it into a cabbage-net. And in this manner she has had four or five at a time hung up in a dairy room, but took care now and then to wipe the outsides of the cheeses; and in about six weeks, or two months, they would be ready for eating as a most excellent sort. In this manner, she says, she has made marigold and sage cheese in chequer work. The chief reason for making this sort of cheese is, for its convenient drying, and the rarity of eating a cabbage-net cheese, which is about a foot long and three or four inches thick; but it must be carefully rubbed as it lies in the net, to keep off the black or blue mold. However, if such rubbing wont do, it must be taken out and rubbed.

Welch Cheese.—WHEN the small *Brecknockshire* sheep come into the rich Vale of *Glamorganshire*, they give much more milk than they do in that mountainous country, and then they milk them for making cheese. To this purpose some keep five or six score, which they always milk behind, and get about a pint from each sheep; and as their milk is of a very fat nature, they mix it with skim milk of cows; when a little is heated, they put in their rennet, and make cheese that is of a short tartish nature.

Cream Curds.—STRAIN your whey, and set it on the fire, making a clear and gentle fire under the kettle. As the curds arise put in whey, and continue it till they are ready to be skimmed off; then take a skimmer and put them on the bottom of a hair sieve; let them drain till they are cold, then take them off and put them into a bason, and beat them with three or four spoonfuls of cream and sugar for eating.

Of the Cheese or Rennet Bag, as wrote of by an ancient Author.—THE cheese or rennet bag (says he) is the stomach bag of a young suckling calf, which never tasted other food than milk, where the curd lieth undigested. Of these bags (says he) you shall in the beginning of the year provide yourself good store, and first open the bag and pour out into a clean vessel the curd and thick substance thereof, but the rest (which is not curdled) you shall put away; then open the curd, and pick out of it all manner of motes, chiers of grass, or other filth got into the same; then wash the curd in several cold waters till it be as white and clean from all sorts of motes as is possible; then lay it on a cloth that the water may drain from it; which done, lay it in another dry vessel, take a handful or two of salt, and rub the curd therewith exceedingly; then take your bag and wash it also in divers cold waters till it be very clean, and then put the curd with a good deal of salt into the bag again, and salt the bag all over very well; then close up the bag, and lay it in a glazed earthen pot, to keep a full year before using: For (continues he) the hanging of rennet bags up in a chimney corner (as coarse housewives do) is a sluttish way, and very unwholesome. The spending of your rennet while it is new makes your cheese hove and prove hollow. Observe also, that if such rennet baggs are kept in pots in a dry room, well salted, they will keep good nine or ten months or more. When the rennet is wanted, boil a quart of the stronger brine, and when it is cold put it into the bag, which prick with many holes, and keep it in this brine and pot ready for use. The stronger the brine is made, the less rennet will serve. One spoonful of this brine will turn ten gallons of milk, is put into it while the milk is warm; but if too hot, it will produce a hard curd: So likewise if too much rennet is put to the milk, it will make the cheese full of holes and taste rank. If you have a large dairy, you may keep ten or twenty rennet bags in one large glazed earthen pot: And this is to be observed, that when cheese-time is over, the rennet bags, as they lie in the pot, should have salt sprinkled every now and then over them, else they will be apt to stink and spoil.

A Buckinghamshire *Dairy Woman's Account for using her Rennet Bags and Rennet.*—THIS woman says, that she puts a handful of salt into two gallons of whey, and that after it has boiled so long, and so much curd has been skim'd off that no more will rise, she then boils the whey longer, with either some flowers of the white thorn, or its leaves, twigs or boughs, in order to give the rennet a pleasant taste, and preserve the cheese a long time sound. Now this whey must be drained from the thorn as fine as can be done, and when it is cold, take three rennet bags out of your brine pot, and steep them in this whey, till you think they have tinctured it enough with a rennet quality, which will be in a day or two's time, when you are to take them out and return them into the brine pot. Thus you have an excellent rennet made, that is kept in bottles well corked, in a cool place, will last a great while for your leisure uses.

When Cheese is best made.—CHEESE is best made in the months of *May, June,* and *July,* when grass is in most heart and the days are at a right length, for then the cheese have the best opportunity of drying; and when they have got dry, a right housewife will dip them in hot whey, scrub their outsides with a brush, and when dry again, will rub them over with whey or other butter, for giving the cheese a fine saleable yellow-colour'd coat, but whey butter is full good enough for this purpose; which to come by, they set the grey whey at night and skim next morning, and so the white whey. The grey whey is that made by the rennet, the white by pressure of the curd. And when they have got enough of such whey cream, they churn it into a butter that cheats thousands of the ignorant people, who know not to distinguish between new milk butter, after butter, and whey butter; although the two last are not worth so much as the first by a penny or three half pence a pound.

The Artifice of a Dairy-Maid to get rid of a slovenly Boy milking her Cows.—THIS maid I recommended to be dairy-maid to a gentleman's family in *Essex*, who wrote to me to send him one, as I live on the edge of *Aylesbury* Vale, where many clever ones are brought up: It was this maid servant that told me, she once lived with a master that kept about four or five cows for his family use, which she could well milk and manage herself, yet the gentleman her master would oblige her to let a slovenly boy servant always milk some of the cows for dispatch sake, contrary to the maid's and the boy's inclination; which put her upon inventing a stratagem, how to get rid of the boy. For this purpose, she bid him put a corking-pin through his hat, and as the master was wont now and then to see his cows milk'd, the boy in milking push'd the pin against the cow's side, and thus prevented her standing still. This induced the master to ask the maid, why the cow would not stand still? She told him, because she does not like the boy should milk her. Then said he milk them all yourself.

The sluttishness of a Dairy-Maid, who milk'd her Cows with foul Fingers.—A man that lives about a mile distant from *Gaddesden*, and now keeps a publick house, said, that when he was a single man, he lived a servant with a dairy farmer, at

Simson, near *Water-Crawley* in *Buckinghamshire*, where, seeing the maid servant milk a cow that had a very foul bag, occasion'd by her lying down in a nasty cow-house, she was so lazy, as not to be at the pains of first washing the cow's bag before milking, but milk'd with her fingers besmear'd with the dung of the cow to that degree, as alter'd the colour of the milk, which made such an impression on the mind of this man, that he declared to me he never since could eat milk, tho' this happened twenty years before. A case very different from the following one.

How a Gentleman obliged his Boy or Man Servant to clean his Cow-house every Morning and Evening before his Cows were milked.—THIS gentleman, who lived in *Cheshire*, and whom I know as my benefactor, kept four or five cows wholly for his family uses; and was so remarkably neat in the management of one of his farms, which he kept in his own hands, that he was admired for it both by strangers and neighbours. One of his cleanly actions was, that he obliged his boy or man servant every morning and evening to clean his cowhouse before the maid milked, in order to free her from the danger of a foul milk by the cows dirty bags. The same good management is carefully put in practice in the great cow-houses near *London*, as well as in many little ones elsewhere; else what a sad condition must the many things be in that are made with milk. These cases may plainly shew the value of a cleanly skilful dairy-maid servant; and such a one I send to any gentleman or lady, that thinks fit to write me a proper order, and they may depend on having none but a true Vale-bred one, that understands the making of butter and cheese, &c. &c.

The cleanly Kudnal *Dairy-maid's Account how she preserves her Cream sweet all the Summer.*—SHE says, that she boils her earthen glazed pots, and shifts the cream twice a day out of one into another; and after one pot has stood on the other to drain the cream, she wipes the remainder off with her fingers. And every time, if she goes ten times a day into the cellar, she stirs her cream to keep it from clotting and souring; which it generally does, if not served in this manner. She also says, that every now and then she flings water down the cellar to keep it cool, and where there is no well or current, she, to carry it off, mops it up.

The Character of a certain sluttish Maid-servant.—THIS servant-maid, who lived with a very rich farmer in a parish about four miles from *Gaddesden*, whose family consisted only of the master, the maid-servant, the plowman, and the boy horse-keeper, would brew three bushels of malt at a time for only small-beer; yet, being a slut, besides an ignorant brewer, the beer was generally fox'd and ropy: And the wheat dough being over-water'd in summer, the bread was commonly so ropy that it might be parted in strings, and mouldy; for she usually baked six or seven half-peck loaves at a time, to save her the trouble of often baking for her small family. Her pasties were made exceedingly large, with the same dough the bread was made of, and only a handful or two of chopt apples, rinds and all, in each pasty. Her bacon, which was their chief food, had no herbs nor roots boiled with it, because the master would not allow them, lest they should prove a sauce, and cause them to eat more of it than ordinary.

Cheese-making by a Widow in the County of Bucks.—THIS widow carries on the farming business, and keeps six cows besides horses and sheep. Of her cows milk she makes butter and cheese, which are sometimes good and sometimes bad. To account for this, I have to observe, that her grass ground lies very low, and is subject to be overflow'd with water in long and great rains, that naturally produces a rank sort of sour twitch or couch grass, and this the more for its being now and then dunged; which occasions her cheese curd sometimes to become so very soft as to make hove cheese; that is to say, cheese full of eyes or little hollows, that eats unpleasantly rank. Now to prevent these ill effects, when she finds her curd thus very soft, after it has been pressed about an hour or two, she takes it out and breaks it over again as small as she can; then new makes it into a cheese the second time, and puts it into the press, where she lets it remain a day or a day and a night. I am also further to observe, That when she makes a thin cheese in dry weather, the milk is then most free of the hoving quality, and therefore she does not break, make, and press it twice; for as her thin cheese weighs but about seven or eight pounds, the whey is soon dry'd out of it, and therefore less subject to be damaged by it. But when she makes a thicker cheese (as she sometimes does) she generally breaks, makes, and presses it twice, the better to clear it of the whey and prevent its hoving.—This case plainly shews, that it is the nature of the grass in a great degree, that governs the quality of the cheese. I therefore take this opportunity to acquaint any gentleman, whose grass ground lies very low, and is subject to these inconveniencies, that it may be improved by more than one way: It may be done by drawing off the water through subterraneous drains, or by sowing certain natural grass-seeds upon old grass ground, and throwing over it at the same time a particular compost of manure, that will certainly produce a most excellent sweet grass, and that a most excellent sweet butter and cheese. Which secret I am ready to communicate on a proper order.

To make a scalded Cheese.—PUT two quarts of cream to six gallons of new milk, then put rennet to it for winter cheese; let it stand till it comes even, then sink it as long as you can get any whey out; then put it into your vat, set it in the press, and let it stand half an hour: In this time turn it once. When you take it out of the press, set on the fire two gallons of the same whey; then put your cheese into a large bowl or bucket, and break the curd as small with your hand as you do for cheese-cakes. When your whey is scalding hot, take off the scum; lay your strainer over the curd, and put in your whey: Take a slice and stir up your curd that it may scald all alike, putting as much whey as will cover it well; when it is cold, put in more hot whey, and stir it as before; then cover it with a linen and woollen cloth: Then set some new whey on the fire, into which put in your cheese vat, suter and cloth; and after three quarters of an hour take up the curd, and put it into the cheese vat, as fast as two persons can work it in: Then put it into the hot cloth, and set it into the press; after a while turn the cheese, and keep it in the press with turning till the next day; then take it out and salt it.

To make toasted or melted Cheese eat savoury.—CUT pieces of quick, fat, rich, well-tasted *Cheshire* or other good cheese into a dish of thick beaten melted butter, that has served for asparagus, pease, boiled sallet, or gravy, and if you will, chop some of the asparagus among it, or slices of gammon of bacon, onions, or anchovies, and all these in a mixture melt upon a chaffing-dish of coals, with good stirring, to incorporate them. And when all are of an equal consistence, strew a little white pepper over it, and eat it with toasts or crusts of white bread. You may scorch it on the top with a hot fire-shovel.

Of Calves.

OF *suckling Calves for weaning, with a Case of the same.*—THIS article comes under the care of many farmers wives, maid-servants, and others, and therefore I have thought it material to write on it, and the rather, as this oftentimes proves a profitable branch in the farming business. There are two seasons in the year for weaning calves; one in *September* and *October*, and the other in *April* and *May*. In the first two months suckling calves require much attendance and cost, for they must be fed with milk-porridge good part of the *winter*, besides sucking the cow for a month or more, and with milk and water to drink. To this purpose they must first be learned to swallow it out of a bowl or little tub, by putting the fingers into its mouth, and forcing it into the liquor, which by a little custom it will take of itself. I knew a farmer's wife wean two calves after this manner; the last was begun with about *Michaelmas* 1746, and for maintaining it well, her husband sent four bushels of oats at a time to the mill, to be made into oatmeal for this last one calf, which made one of her neighbours say the toll was more than the grist. For my part, I don't practise winter weaning, but commonly begin it in *April* or *May*, when (if I don't wean my own calves) I can buy a couple of calves about a week old, at *Leighton* great market in *Bedfordshire*, for six, eight, or ten shillings; and as grass is then firm and growing apace, I can give them milk enough; and after I have suckl'd and brought them to drink milk, or milk and water out of a bowl, which they will do in a month or six weeks time, I turn them (if the weather is agreeable) out about noon into some grasing ground, and when they have been here three or four hours, I house them, and after three or four times serving them thus, I turn them out to grass for good and all, where plenty of water is. In this cheap manner I wean my calves without any cow near them; and once I did it without giving the calves any water at all, the juice of the grass sufficed to quench their drought, and they did well. Next winter they will live on oat straw, or better on clover, or natural hay, for good keeping is not lost here. The better a calf is kept, the sooner it will take bull, therefore some to make a calf the more forward in growth, will give it skim milk at its weaning, wherein is first stirred some wheatmeal, barleymeal or oatmeal, and for obliging the calf to eat it, they will keep its mouth a little open with their fingers of one hand, and by bending its head to the meat with the other hand, it will soon be brought to take it of itself, and thrive a great pace. And if horsebeans, pease or oats, and the best of hay, are bestowed upon it the next winter, it will be a year forwarder in bulk and height of body than a straw-fed one.

Weaning a Calf at Christmas.—A farmer's wife having a great desire to wean a calf from a favourite cow, though calved at *Christmas*, she weaned it at three days old, for it was her opinion a calf could not be weaned too young. First she put her fingers into its mouth, and forced its head into a bowl of new milk for sucking it the first fortnight; then she gave it milk-porridge for three weeks, at the end of which it would eat hay and drink itself. The milk was given warm from the cow, and the milk-porridge (which was made with skim milk) she gave it always blood-warm. By this management she saved cream to make butter, and brought up her calf besides; but take care not to buy a drove calf to wean, for these are generally so beaten and fatigued, that they are either runted or die, but always buy those that are never drove, and has its four teats stand well; neither let it be a heifer's calf, for this will make but a puny cow.—Some give whey to drink in weaning.

Weaning a Calf in April.—ANOTHER weaned his calf in *April*, by forcing its mouth into a bowl or tub of new milk for the first fortnight, and then turn'd it to grass with a trough of water by it, but every day for a fortnight longer he gave it skim milk morning and evening, after which it was left to shift for itself; and if it is a moist time, and there be grass enough, it will do well without water.—An old neighbour of mine, a tradesman, owner of a pretty large orchard, bought in two calves to wean, that were hardly a fortnight old, and turn'd them directly into his orchard, without setting any thing but water by them, and they did well.—Always wean calves forward in *March* or *April*, and they will stand the winter the better if no hay is given them, for they will live on good straw if it be of the oat sort, or indeed any other. The next summer they will live on a common, by feeding on the long sour grass that grows among the fern, which the sheep won't eat.

Weaning Calves in Cheshire *and* Lancashire.—IF a calf falls in *January, February,* or *March,* some wean at a week or twelve days old, at which time they begin to teach it to drink, by putting a finger in the calf's mouth, and with the left hand thrusting its head down into the pail, when the calf laps its tongue about the finger as if it would suck, and so fetches up the milk. And after a few times thus doing, the calf will drink of itself very eagerly in good new milk from the cow till a month old. Then they mix oatmeal with skim milk, and give it blood-warm, and as the calf grows older, more oatmeal and less milk; but in cheese time they give it whey instead of milk and oatmeal, and continue this two or three months, with good grass in the day, and fine hay at night, says Mr. *Houghton*.

Of suckling and fatting Calves for the Butcher.—THIS work likewise in many farms is carried on by farmers wives, or maid-servants, as well as the business of dairies is, and many times (when veal sells dear) to a greater advantage than making butter and cheese, especially if it happens to be in the reach of *London*, for sending their fatted calves dead or alive, and this for more reasons than one.—As first, where water is scarce and bad, a butter-dairy cannot be rightly managed, because on plenty of good water very much depends the sweetness of the utensils, cream, butter, and cheese. Secondly, where few cows and few hands are kept, suckling of calves may be easier managed than making of butter and cheese. Thirdly, where a person lives remote from a market town, and has not a ready conveniency of selling butter. If he lives within forty miles of *London*, he may perhaps suckle and fat calves in a cheaper manner, and be at no other trouble than buying them in, suckling them, and delivering them fat to the butcher, who generally buys and fetches them away from the gentleman's, the yeoman's, or the farmer's house, to kill for a *London* market. For my own part, after I have fatted and sold off the calves that fall from my own cows, I send to *Leighton* market, where they are every week exposed to sale on a *Tuesday* in great numbers throughout the year; and there I buy them as I want them. And it is to this market, farmers and others come above thirty miles an end, to carry cart loads of calves away to suckle for a *London* market. And for fatting them with the greater expedition, they have all necessary conveniency. For which reason, and for their skilful management, they are justly accounted in *Essex* the best suckling calf farmers in *England*: For here most of them have their calf apartments or penns made with oaken planks laid on joists with a little descent, with large holes in them, by which the piss runs presently off into a deep hollow place, so contrived as to receive much of it. And it is on this account, that they are not obliged to consume much straw; for in the summer time they use little or none, because the planks are presently clean'd from the dung, and they seldom put above three or four calves at most in one of these apartments at a time; each apartment having a rack in it for straw or hay, and a trough for holding powder of chalk or some agreeable food. Suckling calves must not be confined in too close a place, nor in too large a one. If they lie too close, they are apt to heat one another and breed lice, which will assuredly hinder their thriving: And if they have too much room, they will frisk about and play away their flesh; for which last reason some tie each calf to a ring in a post by a swivel collar, to prevent its roaming. But as few farmers have the conveniency of calf penns made with oaken planks, what must they do that have none? Why then they should lay a foundation of faggots, and upon these faggots wheat straw, a little at a time, once or twice a day; for such fresh straw will prove an additional help to the calves fatting, by preventing their breeding lice, and inviting them to eat its thrashed ears; but then such a calf penn should be thoroughly clean'd out at every week's end, by carrying away all the dung and litter, and laying fresh straw in its room. But besides all this, there should be two or three large pieces of chalk, as big as a man's head, hung by cords in each penn, for the calves to lick at their pleasure; and also a trough that should stand two feet from the ground and is three feet long, for holding in it powder'd chalk, or corn, as aforesaid; for this mineral we account is of a binding and whitening nature, therefore perfectly necessary to create an appetite and prevent their scouring. And for hitching out and saving milk, some hang now and then a wisp of hay

(432)

before them. Others give them oatmeal finely sifted, or wheat-flower mixt with a little salt, or barley meal, or white pease slitted. And now, supposing these necessary conveniencies to be in order, the next thing I have to offer is the method of suckling calves.

The Method of suckling Calves as practised by this Author.— THERE are two sorts of calves that I suckle, one sort that falls from my own cows, the other that I buy (as I said) at market. As to the first sort, as soon as it falls from the cow, we strew a handful of salt over all its body, to be taken by the cow as she licks her calf, which we think tends to her health, and causes her to glean the sooner. When the cow has calved, we generally let the calf suck what it will, and milk the cow besides, giving her the milk to drink, and for two days after water made luke-warm. As to the calf, we let it lie with the cow the first night and day, and while the maid is milking one side, she lets the calf suck on the other: For by this the cow gives down her milk the freer, and therefore the maid continues this practice all the first week, and throughout the next she allows the calf short of a bellyfull, because their nature is too weak to be gorged with a full quantity of milk till they are about a fortnight old, and then they should not want what they can suck. This management is strictly observed by nice suckling farmers, not so much for saving the milk to give the more of it to older calves, but because if a very young calf should be over-charged with milk, it would be in great danger of scouring, and that so violently, as can't be easily nor readily stopt, and then the calf grows lean and sometimes dies.— Others give the cow, for the first drink after calving, a pail of water, wherein a small shovel-full of hot ashes are put, for their taking off the rawness of it, and for giving it a due warmth to prevent the cow's catching cold. And for the better preventing it, I not only observe to do after one of these ways, but also throw a handful of barley or wheat-meal, or bran, over the first pailful of cold water that I give the cow, and do the same a second time if I see occasion: For many cows have been lost by letting them drink cold water too soon after calving.

To cure a suckling Calf of its scouring.—SOME to do this let the calf go into some grasing ground with the cow, and it sometimes stops the looseness, but this is what I never practise. I always cure it in the calf-penn. If we find a calf begin to scour, the next time of suckling we allow it very little milk, and mix a little powder'd chalk with some salt: Of salt, as much as will lie on a shilling: Of chalk, as much as will fill a small tea-cup. This my maid rubs on the roof of the calf's mouth, and leaves it. Others put it down the calf's throat as far as they can. Some do it before the calf sucks, others after; and if this is begun and repeated in time, if clean wheat straw is twice a day given it, and the calf is not too close confin'd in summer time, it seldom fails of a cure; but if this does not do, we have recourse to a stronger remedy, that is to be made thus:—Knead a little brandy, verjuice, wheat-flour, and powder'd chalk together, and give the calf two crams of it, each made about the bigness of a man's little finger, as soon as it is done suckling, and pour a little milk after them. Others therefore will give the crams before the calf sucks, that they may the better be wash'd down.—Calves can't lie too cool in summer, nor too warm in winter; but in both seasons be sure to allow them fresh wheat straw often enough, for this, with a convenient lying, tends very much to keep them from being louzy and scouring. Not but that a little scouring, if it last not too long, will contribute to whiten the calf's flesh; and to this end some put fuller's earth always before them to lick, as well as pieces of soft fat chalk. It would likewise be a good piece of husbandry, where a plank floor with holes in it is wanting, to lay a foundation of great pieces of chalk; for if the place is bare of straw, the calves will be apt to lick the ground, redden their flesh, and lose their appetite by it. Chalk prevents it.

Of bleeding suckling Calves.—OF this I the rather write, because of the different practice made use of on this account.

Some are right and some are in the wrong of it, and therefore many calves disappoint their owners hopes of fattening them, when they bleed them too often, or when they take too much blood at a time away; both these extremes lessen the calves appetite, and backward their fattening. On the contrary, when they are discreetly bled, the first time at five weeks old, and again at 7, and killed at 8, they will thrive the faster and die the whiter, particularly in their fat part.—Two neighbouring farmers, that sold their fat calves at *Smithfield* market, bled their calves at different times; one about a week before the calf went away, and again two days before its sale: The other bled his calf for the first time at a month's age, and again just before it was carried to market. A calf has such a large neck vein, that it may be blooded by a penknife or struck with a fleam, or a bit of his tail-end may be cut off. —A cow-calf having a smaller vein than a bull-calf, a less fleam will serve to bleed it, nor does a calf that is naturally white require so much bleeding as a redder one; which two qualities may be partly distinguish'd by the eyes and mouth.—Always cord before bleeding, and pin up.—Bleeding a calf in the neck makes a lean shoulder, which is prevented by cutting off a little bit of the tail, to take near half a pint away, and tie it afterwards with an end: Yet some tie it not, but let it go as it is.

Of cramming Calves.—THIS is what has been much in practice with some farmers, in winter time especially, when milk is scarce, in order to make a little go the further. But my notion is, that this necessitous way rather reddens the calf's flesh than whitens it, because no artificial feed comes up to the natural milk: However, as necessity may engage the practice, I have to say that there are many sorts of invented crams to be given fatting calves. But no author, that ever I read or heard of, makes any difference in the time of year of giving these crams, but I do; by saying, that a summer cram ought not to have any spirits mix'd in it, because they will be apt to heat and sweat the beast too much, when in winter they may be necessary. Therefore for a summer cram mix fine wheat flower with the finest flower of oatmeal, or with the finest flower of pale malt, and with milk knead it into crams about the bigness of a man's finger; and begin with only giving the calf two about an hour before suckling in a morning, and the same at night, increasing the number of crams as you see occasion. But for a winter cram, begin to make them for the first very weak, by putting very little brandy or gin in a mixture with the finer wheat flower and milk or cream, and give them as before; and as the age of the calf comes on, increase your quantity of ingredients.—Or you may grind white pease and sift their meal fine, which mix with fine flower of pale malt and fine powder of chalk: These three knead into a dough with milk, and make crams to be given as aforesaid in summer; but in winter mix anniseed water, gin or brandy with them, and observe not to begin cramming too soon; at a month old is better than a fortnight. If crams are judiciously prepared, and rightly given to a suckling calf, it is, in my opinion, possible to save half the quantity of milk that otherwise must have been suck'd by it. But instead of these mixt crams, my maid cracks an egg and thrusts it as deep down the throat as she can in the midst of its suckling, and then directly suckles it again; and sometimes, when eggs are cheap and milk scarce, she gives two or three eggs immediately after one another, shells and all, for these are a cool food and nourish much.

To make a Calf suck that has lost its Appetite.—FOR this we make no more to do, than to take a little salt between the two fore fingers and the thumb, rub the palate of the calf's mouth with it over night, and it seldom fails to suck heartily next morning.

How long Calves ought to be suckled for the Butcher.—ONE certain time for suckling all calves can't be rightly adjusted, because of the several incidents attending the undertaking. For example: Some farmers suckle calves of the butcher's providing, for two shillings and six pence a week in summer, and three shillings in winter. Others buy them in on their own account, to suckle for a chance market, either for a *London* or country one. If for a *London* one, then a calf should not be suckled less than nine, ten, or twelve weeks. If for a country one, six or seven often proves sufficient; for at *Smithfield* they give the largest price, and require the largest and whitest calves; but in the country markets lesser and coarser veal will go down at a lower price. This I write at the distance of thirty miles from *London*. But to go further, I have to say, that many calves are killed in the country at six weeks old, and sent to London by the higler, for as in that metropolis there are poor and rich, they must have meat accordingly; and this is the poorest and cheapest veal that is so sent, some calves going with the cow in the field from the time of its falling to its killing, others are suckled in a house, and both employ considerable numbers of butchers and higlers within forty or fifty miles of *London*, who get most of their livelihood by it: Which leads me to make some observations on veal.

Observations on the Goodness and Badness of Veal.—VEAL, says a physician, is temperate and tender, though sometimes waterish; if it is thoroughly roasted, it affords good juice, is of a pleasant taste, and yields a thicker juice than lamb or mutton: But there is more to be said on the account of veal than what this physician writes. I say, that it is the practice of many cow-keepers to suckle the largest and fattest of calves for a *London* market, even till they are twelve or more weeks old, and in this time to bleed them often, and the night before they are carried to *Smithfield* to bleed them excessively; insomuch that I have seen several in London streets that could not hold being drove to the butcher's, but fainted and fell down by the way. Now such old rank flesh in the first place must be very coarse-grained, as being part beef and part veal: And in the second place, it must eat very dry, for want of that gravey which was exhausted by frequent bleedings. A calf therefore that has been constantly housed, been bled but once or twice at most, and kill'd at six or seven weeks old full fat, will prove by far the sweetest veal. To which I add, that there are two other sorts of veal brought to some markets: One sort is, that from calves always let run in the field with its dam-cow for a month or more; this sort is red, coarse, and cheap. There is also another sort suckled in the house, but killed at five or six weeks old, to give the owner the greater benefit of his milk for making butter; of this last, as they are generally those calves that fall at thirty, forty, or fifty miles from *London*, the butcher is forced to employ many white cloths to wrap the quarters in, for absorbing the bloody moisture, that is apt to ouze out of the flesh in such a long confined carriage in hampers by the waggon. This, with first soaking the flesh in cold spring water before, to make it look white when it comes to London, extracts the gravey and hearty valuable part of the flesh in a great degree, and leaves it an insipid flabby veal. But no matter, says the suckler and butcher, what the flesh is, so we get the more money by it; which made one say, he never doubted being master of white calves flesh, provided he bled it at a fortnight old, and the same a fortnight after, and so on, till the creature has been blooded perhaps four or more times; and as the last bleeding is done the day before the calf is killed, it is bled till it pisses or dungs before it is pinned up, but then what must the flesh be?—In *Cheshire* and several other parts of the North, where they carry on large cheese and butter dairies, they get rid of a calf as soon as they can; and therefore sell some at a fortnight old for four or five shillings a piece to the butcher, and seldom ever keep one above three weeks; but whenever any calf is killed, the butcher seldom fails of blowing it, for making the flesh the larger and fairer to the buyer's eye, and to give it the whiter colour, when the calf is flayed, he will lay the whole carcase in cold water or in wet cloths for several hours, or a whole night; others only joints.

Of Cows hoving or what some call swelling, by their eating Clover-Grass, or Rapes, or Turnip Tops.

HOW the Care and Inspection of Cows belongs to the Country Housewife.—IT is certain, that great part of the inspection and management of cows belongs to the country housewife and her maid-servants, where they carry on a dairy, and commonly where they suckle calves to fat for the butcher; for as these milk them morning and evening, they have an opportunity to espy the cause and beginning of distempers, and in some cases to administer medicines for the cure of the same, while the master and men-servants seldom do more than give them provender and clean their stalls; besides which, when the master and his men are abroad, the dame and her maid are generally at home, ready to assist or get assistance, if any extraordinary event should happen to the cows, an example of which take as followeth.

Of preserving the Health of Cows, and of Remedies when they are sick or hurt.—IT is a maxim in physick, that diseases may be prevented when they cannot be cured; therefore the first thing I have to advance on this account is, that something be given to a cow by way of antidote for keeping her in health, preventing future diseases, and causing her to give pure milk, and a due quantity of it. This piece of good husbandry is so little regarded by most people, that very few have any notion of it, and therefore let their cows take their chance, as if there was no such thing to be done. Hence proceed those fatal distempers, the murrain, the garget, the blain, the yellows, and many other foul maladies incident to these most serviceable creatures, merely for want of timely applications and remedies. While I am writing this very account, I hear that one of my neighbours cows has got the garget in her bag to that degree, as obliges the owner to send for the same cow doctor he did once before from *Ivinghoe-Arson*, who by a well composed drink cured her, though she was then like to have died;

whereas, had a good drink been given her presently after calving, this misfortune had not happened.

A Drink to be given a Cow presently after Calving.—As soon as a cow has calved and lick'd her calf, we stay a little from milking her to see if she will glean, which some cows will do in an hour or two's time; but if she exceed this, we commonly milk her, and give her the milk to drink, as I said before, which some will take, and some will refuse. Some cows again that go to grass are so full of milk, that they must be milk'd a little before they calve, else their bag will be in danger. However, the water she has for the first two days we give milk-warm, with a handful of bran or barley-meal strew'd over it; and this we do, let it be summer or winter, for it has been the death of some cows to drink cold water presently after calving, except it be those that always lie at grass and calve in the field, for these are not in so much danger as a cow that is housed now and then. The third day after calving I give three pints of piss out of a horn to a cow, and about a week after repeat the same; for this cleanses her body and blood, creates an appetite, and prevents the breed of diseases, and is so cheap and safe an antidote that none can object against it; and for giving it, one man must gripe her nostril with one hand, and hold the horn with the other hand, while another opens her mouth with his hand, and pours down the drink with the horn. Or you may make use of the following drink.

A Soot Drink to preserve a Cow in Health all the Year.—Get half a pint of pure fine wood soot, and mix it with half an ounce of diapente and a quartern of fresh butter. The soot and diapente must be first boiled about a quarter of an hour in three pints of strong beer or ale, and when it is half cold, dissolve a quarter of a pound of fresh butter in it, and when the drink is blood-warm, give it the cow well mixed; and for the greater assurance, you may repeat this drink a week or fortnight after. *N. B.* The diapente is a cheap powder, and is sold at most apothecaries shops in town and country. There are several other compositions that might be made to answer somewhat of this purpose; but as I have proved both these several times, I recommend them, especially the last, as a most safe and efficacious drink.

A Drink to make a Cow glean.—IT was the practice of a Vale dairy-man to heat two quarts of buttermilk, and while it was heating, to stir into it one ounce of treacle, and one ounce of flower of brimstone, and give it out of a horn a little more than blood-warm.

A second Drink.—A cow-keeper near *London*, that keeps above two hundred cows, gives bruised parsley-seed in ale, to make a cow cast her glean.

A third Drink.—GIVE some flower of brimstone in wort, and some diapente in it; one ounce of each powder in this or ale.

A fourth Drink.—MAKE a quarter of a pound of soap into a lather in a quart of warm ale, and it will bring it away in one hour's time. But this receit to make a cow cast her glean must be cautiously made use of, for it is of so slippery a nature that it may cause her bearing to come out; and then this remedy will be far worse than the retention of her glean.

A fifth Drink.—MIX one ounce of flower of brimstone with a quart or three pints of warm ale, wort, or milk, and as much powder of white pepper as will lie on a half-crown, and give it out of a horn. This is a very good receit to make a cow glean, and is also very proper to give to all cows the same or the next day after calving.

Of the ill Effects that attend the gleaning of Cows.—AN author that writes a book of this kind, and never owned a cow, must be obliged to compose such a work either by collections from what others have wrote before, or by hear-say; in either case he is liable to lead persons into very detrimental errors. It is true, I have in this and former treatises presented my readers with several receits to expedite a cow's gleaning but I here give cautions with them, a strong cow and a weak cow are both subject to suffer in gleaning, by that fatal malady that some call withering, that is to say, her bearing comes out behind, and when this happens, the cow is near spoiling. Now this misfortune may be occasioned naturally or accidentally; naturally, when a cow has calved a larger calf than ordinary; accidentally, when she has got a cold, or by having too strong and forcing a drink given her to forward her gleaning, or by drinking cold water too soon after calving. But these are not all the ill effects that attend calving cows; for if a cow is not carefully watched when she has calved, she may eat her glean, as most cows are prone to do. When cows calve at grass and eat their glean, it is not of such ill consequence as when she eats it in a house; because the grass helps to purge it away; yet there is this evil attending it both at grass and in the house, that a cow may be choaked in eating it.—At *Eaton* in *Bedford-shire* there was a farmer's best cow at grass, that happened to calve in the field, and in eating her glean it choaked her; so that in the morning, when the owner came to see her, he had for his sight a dead cow, but a live calf: therefore we are sometimes obliged to sit up with a cow all night to watch, and take her glean away with a fork; and if part of her glean hangs down, as it often does, we put the stringy substance through the hole of a tile, to prevent its returning in again, and for bringing it leisurely away; for such substance must not be pull'd away hastily, if it is, it may cause the cow to suffer.

A safe Way make a Cow glean.—To avoid the ill effects that too strong forcing drinks may produce in causing a cow's bearing to come out, it is a common way to hold oats in straw over a fire; or in case you have no oats in straw, take clean oats and hold them in a sieve over a fire to be smoaked, and then give them to the cow to eat. This will oblige her to husk or cough, and strain, and thereby help to dislodge and bring away her glean in a safe manner.

How to cure a Cow that by straining has her Bearing come out behind.—When this is the case, it is to be returned into the cow's body by the help of moist warm bran, and warm cloths.

Others mix new milk with powder'd linseeds for putting it up. But these will not do without the help of other means, for when the cow lies down, the bearing is apt to come out again; therefore when it is returned in, we sling her, so that her feet bear very little on the ground, and always keep her hind part higher than her fore part; by this and comfortable meat, some cows have recovered.

A knavish Trick that has been made use of to sell a Cow that withers, or has had her Bearing come out.—WHEN this misfortune has happened to a cow that has a bulky body in tolerable flesh, it has put some knavish persons on a stratagem how to cheat a buyer at a fair or market, by selling him such a cow and calf; and to do it cleverly, they get a shoemaker's end, and stitch up her bearing behind, just before she enters the fair or market, and takes the first chap that bids money; for there are some so ignorant, as not to mistrust any such thing, and therefore make no inspection about the matter, but when the cow comes to stale, the bite too late is perceived.

The Case of a Buckinghamshire *Gentleman's two Cows, whose Bearings came out; one died of it by wrong Management, the other was saved by right Management.*—TO cure the first cow, they made several attempts, but could not make the bearing stay in but a very little while, before she strained and forced it out again, notwithstanding they were an hour each time in putting it up; this so fatigued and hurt the beast, as made her bleed to death. After this, another of the same gentleman's cows was taken in the very same manner, upon which they employed another cow doctor, who, upon hearing how they had treated the last cow, said they had acted wrong. The first thing therefore that this called for was a sack, part of which he cut off; and when he had soaked her bearing in warm water long enough to make it slippery, he easily put it in, and sewed both ends of the sackcloth to the cow's skin, which had the desired success, by making her forbear to strain; for if she strained, it hurt her, and thus the cow was cured:

Whereas the other sewed up her sheath with tape, but this did not prevent her bearing coming out again; not but that some cows have recovered of this malady by only moistening the bearing and returning it in, and have done well.—I knew a cow at calving twice had her bearing come down, and at last was fatted and sold to the butcher.

The Nature and Cause of a Cow's pissing bloody Water.—THIS disease is fatal if not stopt in a little time, because in a few days it turns to what we call the oak water, and then from being of a red colour it becomes of a blackish red, and generally kills. All authors have hitherto been deficient in assigning the causes and prevention of this malady, therefore many people are ignorant how to prevent it. It is chiefly caused by their feeding in the spring time on flashy grass, crop[p]ing the black thorn and some other shrubs. In some parts of Vales it is customary for cows not to be admitted grasing on commons till the 11th day of *May*; other grounds in *June*. Then if it is a wet spring, and grass grows apace high and flashy, the poorer sort of cows are apt to feed very greedily, so as to bring themselves under this distemper.

The Method that some take to prevent a Cow's pissing bloody Water.—THOSE persons that are aware of this evil take particular care to give their cows some hay, straw, or chaff, when they come off from a common or other ground in the spring time to be milked; for by giving her this dry meat, it absorbs moisture, and very much prevents the ill effects of flashy raw grass; and this some will practise in a dangerous season, to almost *Midsummer*.

The Cure for a Cow's pissing bloody Water.—MY neighbour had one so bad of this disorder, that after applying several remedies they did no good, till one advised him to make use of this:—They got some shepherd's-pouch and cut it very small, bole armoniac and vinegar (the latter was about a pint and a half) which being boiled a little while all together, when cold enough they gave it to the cow, and it cured her. The herb shepherd's-pouch has a white flower, and grows in gravelly ground; it is a strong stopper of fluxes.

A second Receit for the same.—SOME have put a live squab tame pigeon with its head foremost down the throat of a cow, and it has cured. Instead of her drinking cold water, give her but little, and that milk-warm, with ground malt or bran in it.—Some had rather see a cow piss blood, than a bloody water, as reckoning the first easier to cure than the last. A cow that has pissed bloody water has been cured in three hours time, by putting a large live frog down her throat.

A sure Cure for a Cow that scours.—TAKE half a pint of rennet for a strong cow; but if it is a weak one, give it only a quarter of a pint, mixt with some powder of chalk finely sifted, in a quart of ale or strong beer; and repeat if occasion.

How an ignorant Farmer, by suffering his Cow to drink Dunghill Water, had near kill'd her by the Scour.—THIS is the second farmer that I have known guilty of this error to their loss. Cows naturally affect to drink this black dunghill water, and to eat the long litter of a dunghill; and for this reason, I oblige my servants strictly to keep them from both, tho' when their common drink water is only a little tinctured with it, it is of no ill consequence, but on the contrary, in winter especially, it takes off the chilly raw nature of it, and prevents the belly-ach and gripes; but when their drink water is black, especially in summer-time, it generally swarms with lice, polipes, and other worms, water spiders, the spawn of frogs and water toads, and other monstrous insects that greatly breed and multiply in shallow and narrow receptacles of such foul filthy water, and which are unavoidably swallowed by cows that drink at it. Now as that may be prevented which cannot be cured, I here, by plainly shewing the case, tell my reader how that damage may not fall to his lot, which befell the farmer I am writing of, who was one that rented about sixty pounds a year, living not many miles from *Dunstable* in *Bedfordshire*, and who (not having the like misfortune before) did not take any precaution to avoid it, but let his cow drink of a nasty dunghill water till it scour'd, and bugs bred in her skin to that degree, that on hard squeezing of the knobs they bred in, they came out; others that were bigger they lanced, and took out many that were half as big as a caterpillar. In short, this black water had so corrupted and poison'd the blood of the cow, that they were forced to dry her at two months end after calving, in order to try for curing her.— Another farmer rotted a cow, by suffering her to drink mudgell-hole water; as did another by letting his cow have free access to the hogwash-tub.

How a Farmer presumptuously bought a scouring Cow, in Assurance of his curing and fattening her.—A farmer living near *Charley-Wood* by *Rickmansworth* was tempted to buy a cow that he knew run out, for the sake of the little money that he gave for her, with an intent to cure and fatten her; and he did both, by keeping her always in the house, and feeding her with oats, chaff, and hay.

To cure an inflamed snarl'd Bag or Udder of a Cow.—THIS for the most part happens presently after a cow has calved, when the bag will look red and angry, which if not cured may oblige the owner to have part of the bag cut off, or it may turn to the garget in the guts and kill the beast. For the cure of this, there are many receits; one is, to hold a piece of fat bacon between a pair of tongs made red hot, let it drop before the fire into cold water, and rub the cow's bag well with the grease that so drops out, which will cure, if the bag is gargetty.—This is the *Cheshire* method; but our *Hertfordshire* method is otherwise.

The Hertfordshire *Method to cure a gargetty or inflamed Bag of a Cow.*—THIS garget or inflammation commonly begins in one teat, which it swells and makes hard, then gets into another, and so to all the rest; next it takes the bag, which also becomes hard and swell'd: At last it takes the guts, and then the cow very likely dies; but this like other diseases, if a proper remedy is applied in time, may be easily cured. My maid every year makes a pot of adder's-tongue ointment, solely for this very use; it grows as before mentioned in my meadows, is known by its pecked stalk, somewhat in the shape of an adder's tongue, and is in its full virtue in *August*, when we gather it, cut it small, bruise it, and boil it with some butter as it is taken out of the churn, free of any salt; then we strain out the thin parts, and press out what remains in the thick herby part, and keep it in a glazed earthen pot all the year ready for our want; and when we want it, she rubs it soundly on the cow's teat or bag, which generally at once or twice using it disperses the humour, allays the swelling, and cures. For, thus made, it is a balsam that heals green wounds, bitings of venomous creatures, St. Anthony's fire, burns, scalds, hot tumours, apost-humes, spreading sores and ruptures, as a physician's character is of it.—Others take adder's tongue, melilot, and sellery stalks, and when they have been well bruised, they boil the juice up in fresh butter without salt.—Others boil the juice of rue and houseleek with that of adder's-tongue in butter; but the nicest way of all is, to stamp the adder's-tongue herb in a mortar, squeeze out its juice, and boil it up in butter or fresh lard, without any salt: But butter is best, because the lard may give an unpleasant tang to the milk, if it should be mixt with it as the cow is milking. Put the juice and butter into your saucepan together, and boil them for a quarter of an hour.

The Damage of suffering long Hairs to grow on a Cow's bag or Udder.—THIS article, as trifling as it may appear, is of no little consequence, because it is the ready way to cause a cow to become a kicker if neglected. A dairy-woman being with her husband on business at an inn in the town of *Bedford*, she saw the maid-servant in a sad confusion as she was milking her cow, as not being able to milk her quietly; upon this the woman said to the maid, go fetch me a pair of scissars, and I will engage you may milk your cow to your mind; the scissars being brought, the woman clips all the long hairs short that grew on her bag, and then the cow stood perfectly still.—This was never before taken notice of by any author whatsoever, yet how necessary it is, I leave my reader to consider, since this is the very cause why many cows are made desperate kickers, and if they are suffered to be accustomed to it, some will never leave it. It is therefore the part of a good country housewife to clip the hairs from off the cow's bag twice a year at least; that is to say, at spring and fall of the year. But without staying for time, it ought to be more especially done, when a cow has calved; for if the hairs are suffer'd to grow long (as sometimes they do if neglected, till they are as long as the cow's teats, and curl again) the calf cannot help lugging the hairs as well as the teats, and then the cow in course kicks the calf, and thus hinders it from getting a belly full of milk. Again, the cli[p]ping off hairs from a cow's bag is the more necessary to be done for preventing their lodging dirt, as some short-legged cows are obliged to travel in the dirt in coming home to be milked, because long hairs will take up and lodge much dirt, but whether such cows have long or short hairs on their bags, the milkmaid is obliged to wash them before they can be milked clean.

Various RECEITS.

TO roast a Pound of Butter or more the Irish *Way.*—TAKE a pound of butter, season it well with salt, and put it on a wooden spit; place it at a good distance from the fire, let it turn round, and as the butter moistens or begins to drip, drudge it well with fine oatmeal, continuing so to do till there is any moisture ready to drip, then baste it, and it will soon be enough. A certain *Irish* woman told me this eats vere nicely, insomuch that she has done on a *Christmas* eve twenty-seven different pounds so, at a farmer's house in her country, where it has been kept all the holidays, to accommodate a friend with a slice or two, as we do cakes or minced pies here.

Another Irish *Country Dish.*—BOIL potatoes and parsnips till they are soft, make them into a mash with some new milk, and add a cabbage boiled tender and cut very small; mix the whole well over the fire with store of good butter, some salt and pepper, and eat it hot.

To make a Herricane.—TAKE slices of turneps, carrots, and some young onions; boil them a little to make them somewhat tender, and after some mutton steaks are fry'd and taken up, put in the parboil'd roots and fry them brown; clear your pan, put in some butter, flower, water, and some gravey (if you have it) and brown it; then put in your meat, *&c.* to warm, and serve it up.

To collar a Breast of Mutton.—BONE and skin it; then prepare some seasoning of parsley, a little thyme, onion, pepper and salt, with some small slips of bacon laid cross-ways, and your seasoning spread along it; roll it up, and tie it, setting it up end-ways in the saucepan with some water; cover it close, letting it stew gently till it be very tender; when you think it about half done, turn it.

To dress a Loin of Mutton.—SKIN a loin of mutton, and thrust in long-ways some stuffing of parsley, a little onion, egg, bread, nutmeg, pepper, and salt, and then roast it.

The best Way to roast Pigeons —Is first to stuff them with parsley chopt very small, some butter, pepper, and salt; tie them close neck and vent, parboil them, and afterwards roast them. The parboiling makes them eat pleasanter, plumps them, and they eat not so dry as otherwise; and it takes off the usual strong tang.

Jugging Pigeons —Is to put one or more so stuft without liquor into a stone or other wide-mouthed earthen pot close tied over with bladder, and so boiled in water till enough.

To eat raw Cucumers in a wholesome pleasant Manner.— WHEN you have pared and sliced cucumers, put a little water

(449)

and some salt over them, and let them stand so about ten minutes; then drain that from them, and just wash them with a little vinegar, throwing that away likewise, before you put oil and vinegar upon them. This will make them eat much crisper and finer than without such management.— The addition of a few green nasturtian pods fresh gathered and eat with them, correct them, and make them much wholesomer as well as pleasanter, especially to such as do not chuse to eat onions with them.

The best Way to pickle Walnuts after the French *Method.*— TAKE fine fresh-gathered succulent walnuts about the latter end of *June* or beginning of *July*; wipe them well with flannel, and pour upon them rape vinegar enough to cover them. Let it be upon them nine or ten days, then pour it off into a jar or wide-mouth'd glass vessel, adding thereto a few bay-leaves, some horse-radish grosly scraped, some black pepper and salt at discretion; stop the vessel close, and put it by to be used for sauce as kechup, which it far exceeds. Then having put some pieces of horse-radish, a few bay-leaves, and some whole black pepper between every layer of the nuts, till the jar is near full, fill it up with the stoutest right white-wine vinegar cold, and cover it very close with bladder and leather, and they are done.—Be sure let no salt touch the nuts, and (thus managed) they will appear beautifully green, have their natural fine taste, and eat firm and good for five years or more.—This receit with the following one was given by Monsieur *Lebat*, who says this is the right way, and that in *England* they do not know how to pickle walnuts right.

To pickle Cucumers.—TAKE *girkin* cucumers fresh and dry gather'd, wipe them clean with flannel, and cover them with the best vinegar cold; let it lie upon them nine or ten days, then pour it off and cast it away. Just boil up some more best vinegar with some grosly scraped horse-radish, and whole black pepper; let it stand till it is cold, and having first put a little horse-radish thin sliced and whole pepper between every layer of the cucumers, pour over them the boiled cold vinegar; stop your jar very close with bladder and leather, and they are done.

To pickle Walnuts white.—TAKE your walnuts at the latter end of *June*, try them with a pin, *&c.* pare the green outside till you come to the white, and put them into cold water as you pare them. When done, fling them into a pot of boiling water, boil them till tender and as quick as you can; then take them out, and put them into cold water. A hundred and half will take up a quart of vinegar, one ounce of black pepper whole, half a quarter of an ounce of mace, and twelve cloves. Let them boil together, then fling in the nuts, and give them one boil; when cold, stop them close, and keep for use.

To pickle Oisters.—TAKE a quart of oisters and wash them in their own liquor from the gravel, then drain your liquor to them again, and set them over a fire to boil a quarter of an hour softly, to plump them; then take them out of the liquor and put them into the pot you keep them in, drain the liquor over again, and put to it four spoonfuls of white-wine vinegar, half a spoonful of whole pepper, a blade or two of mace, and a quarter of an ounce of cloves, with some lemon-peel and some salt. Let all these boil together a little while, pour it to the oisters and the spice with it, and when cold cover close.

Mrs. Hays's *Receit to make a Seed Cake.*—TAKE three pounds of flour, four ounces of fine sugar, half a pint of cream boiled, two pounds of melted butter, one pint of good ale yeast, eight eggs with two whites. Mix the sugar with the flour, make a hole in the flour, and put all these together into it. Let it stand by the fire half an hour, then mix it together, and strew in one pound of carraway-seed, then put it in a hoop and bake it an hour.

A notable Oxfordshire *Housewife's common Way of makeing Marrow Puddings.*—TAKE the crumb of a penny loaf, a pound of clean pick'd wash'd currants, the quantity of two London quarts of new milk boiled, the marrow of a common large bone, a pound of suet, nine yolks of eggs, half a pound of sugar, a nutmeg, and two pennyworth of mace powder'd, a little salt, and half a dozen large spoonfulls of flour. Mix, and fill your hog's guts but half full, tying each yard in four equal parts. After you have tye'd them up (that they are not above half-full) wash them in rather hotter than blood-warm new milk, and directly throw them into a kettle of boiling water, letting them only simmer therein for eight minutes, for if they continue longer they will burst: When boiled, lay them upon wheat straw on a sieve, and they will dry in seven or eight minutes; then you may broil them brown, and eat them. They will keep five or six days in warm weather, but at *Christmas* or in a hard frost thee weeks.

The Process of making Hogs large Gut white delicate Puddings.—TAKE a quarter of a peck of the best flour, three pounds of the hog's leaf cut small, two pounds of the best raisins of the sun, a quarter of an ounce of powder'd ginger, half a nutmeg, a blade of mace, a little stick of cinnamon, and three whole eggs well beat. Season the whole with salt and with new milk, blend these together almost as stiff as paste for pye-crust, fill your large guts moderately full, tie them at both ends about half a yard long, put them in boiling water, and let them boil a quarter of an hour upon a slow fire. Lay these upon straw as the other, and keep them so till used; then cut them in slices about half an inch thick, lay them upon the gridiron over a clear fire, broil them brown and eat them.— *N. B.* These last are praised much, as being exceeding fine, short, and well relished of the hog's meat.

To preserve the Chine, the Tongue, the Spare Ribs, short Ribs, But-Pieces, Hocks, and Head of a Porker or Baconer.—THE common way practised by our *Hertfordshire* farmers wives to do this is thus: When they salt down the fleshy pieces of pork for pickling them, I say after this is done, they salt the two but-pieces, the two hocks, the two spare ribs, the chine, the head, and the tongue. If the chine and spare ribs are to be sold,

I generally contrive to kill the hog a day or two before the market day, for the opportunity of selling them to the *London* higler, because these pieces fetch a better price than ordinary; in this case they only just sprinkle them with common salt. But if they are to be kept for spending them in the family, they salt the spare ribs, and hang them up where the blow-fly cannot come; and the chine, the hocks, the head, and the tongue, they salt and lay in an earthen glazed pot or tub, where they are to remain as they are put in, till they are dressed. In doing all which, they make use of no other than common salt; for as they are to be boil'd or roasted, or baked in a little time, they think there is no occasion for any other salt.—A second receit is how to salt a chine, spare ribs, and tongue, for drying them in a chimney: To do this, mix about a quarter of an ounce of powder'd salt-petre with a quart of common salt, and with this mixture salt the pieces all over; and when it is rubbed well in, let them lie under this salting two or three weeks; then wrap each of them in paper, and hang them up near but not too near a fire, and if this is cleverly done, the chine and spare ribs will keep good four, five, or six months; the spare ribs for roasting or baking, and the chine for boiling, provided they are (just before using) soaked in warm water a day and a night; and if they are not fresh enough, you may soak them in more warm water, and you need not fear their eating good and fresh: And I also add, that by this same method both pork and bacon offald may be preserved a great while sweet and sound, though kill'd and thus managed in summer; partly because salt-petre is a most powerful searcher and preventer of taints, and because it forces and drives in common salt, when they are mix'd and used together. But salting spare ribs thus is not agreeable to all, because the salt-petre colours them reddish, and hardens the thin meat of these bony pieces too much.— A farmer's wife, that lives near *Market-Street* in *Hertfordshire*, allows it to be a housewifely way, to put the short ribs of a porker into pickle, because, as she says, there is less waste of the flesh this way than in salting them; besides which, she thinks this bony meat eats the pleasanter for being thus pickled.—Another of our country housewives manages her offald pieces of pork in this manner: She makes pyes of her short bony pieces, and the coarse pieces she boils first; so that she salts down only her fat fleshy pieces of pork clear of all bone, for if the bony pieces of pork were salted down with the fleshy pieces, they would stink and corrupt the fleshy pieces.

To make a Mince-Pye costly and rich.—To one pound of the meat of a tongue, add two pounds of suet, six pippins, and a green lemon-peel shred small, with an ounce of *Jamaica* pepper, two pounds of currants, citron, lemon, and orange peels, candy'd and shred small. Mix all these with half a pint of sack, and fill your pye with it. And to make this richer still, add two spoonfuls of lemon juice or verjuice, stoned and sliced dates, with some chop'd raisins.—Another says: take an ox heart, or tongue, or meat of a surloin of beef, parboil it, and chop it with two pounds of suet to every pound of lean meat; this mix with a two-penny grated loaf and eight pippins minced fine. It makes excellent pyes, if spice, sack, and orange-peel are added, with two pounds of currants to every pound of meat. Also that this composition may be kept in an earthen pot in a dry place a month or more good, and to make the pyes eat moist, as soon as they are out of the oven, put in a glass of brandy or white-wine.—Another says, that savoury mince-pyes are best made with equal parts of mutton and veal, and other proper ingredients.—Another says, that double tripe boiled tender and minced small, with currants, sugar, and other materials, makes good mince-pyes.—Another, to make mince-pyes without flesh, says: Boil a dozen or more of eggs hard, then boil also a pound of rice very soft; mince the eggs, and beat the rice to a pap: Mix these with beef suet shred, currants, raisins, sugar, nutmeg, candy'd orange-peel, and put the whole into a pye with sack, and bake it in an oven moderately heated.

How a poor Woman makes palatable Mince-Pyes of stinking Meat.—THIS is a poor industrious woman that rents a little tenement by me of twenty shillings a year, who for the sake of her poverty is every week relieved, with many others, by the most noble lord of *Gaddesden* Manour; who killing a bullock almost every week for his very large family, he has the offald meat dressed, and is so good as to have it given away to the poorest people in the neighbourhood. But it sometimes happens, through the negligence of careless servants, that this charitable meat is apt to stink in hot weather, for want of its due cleaning, boiling, and laying it in a cool place: However, the poor are very glad of this dole, as it does their families considerable service. And to recover such tainted meat, this woman, after boiling and cleansing it well, chops and minces it very small, and when mixed with some pepper, salt, chop'd sage, thyme and onion, she bakes it: This for a savoury pye. At another time she makes a sweet pye of this flesh, by mixing a few currants and plumbs with it. But in either form the taint is so lessened that it is hardly to be perceived.

How to make Hertfordshire *Cakes, Nuts, and Pincushions.*—These are much used in *Hertfordshire*, for giving farmers servants a changeable dinner now and then to their satisfaction; for if they are made as they should be, the men are generally fond of them. To do which, our housewife puts skim milk and hogs-lard over the fire, and warms them only for mixing. Then she takes some flour, sugar, yeast, and an egg or two, with the powder of *Jamaica* spice, and makes a paste of these and the milk and fat, as if for pye-crust; and when it is work'd and rolled enough, to the thinness of about a quarter of an inch, she cuts it out in two-inch square pieces, and boils them in hogs-lard in a little kettle, or in a stew-pan or frying-pan. Others roll up this paste in the shape of walnuts, and dress them in the same manner the square pieces are.—*N. B.* No fat is so good for this as hogs-lard, because the lard hollows the cushions or nuts, and makes them look whiter than any other fat does; though some for want of this make them with dripping, &c.

How much the Guts of Chauldron of a Calf in Esteem with the People in and about the Town of Tring *in* Hertfordshire, *for making Pyes of them.*—IT is notoriously known, that *Tring* market has acquired no little reputation for the sale of the whitest and best of veal, because the ground of the adjacent country produces a most sweet grass and milk, and white calf's flesh. By which there are great numbers of calves fatted and kill'd in a year for the *London* markets, to which the flesh is carried by common higlers. This gives the people in and about *Tring* an opportunity to buy the guts or chauldrons of fatted calves, to make pyes with them as a very delicious food. And accordingly these guts are seldom put to any other use, especially throughout the summer time. And for those of one calf the price is generally six-pence, but the butchers are indifferent of selling them so, because the fat that is on them might be taken off and sold for near that money without the guts. Now the guts of one calf is enough for one pye but for a large family pye two have been made use of.

How the Guts or Chauldron of a Calf is to be clean'd and prepared for making Pyes with them, or to eat them otherwise.— THERE is no receit as I know of extant, that directs a person how to clean and prepare the guts of a calf for making them eatable in pyes or otherwise: The most that any author says on this account is, that the guts must be first parboil'd before they are made into a pye, without taking notice what is to be done before. Wherefore I have thought it necessary to tell my reader, that our country housewife's way is, to slit the guts along with a penknife that has a pea stuck at the end of it, to keep the knife's point from entering the gut, and making it the better slide through it. When guts are thus slit and opened, they must be well wash'd till cleansed of their filth; then they must be laid in a tub, and salt strewed over them, for their being well rubbed with it, to bring off all manner of slime and foulness:

This being neatly done, the guts are to be rinsed in spring water twice a day for two days together.

How the Guts or Chauldron of a Calf is to be made into a Pye.—THE guts being thoroughly cleaned, as before directed, are to be boiled a little while, or what may be called parboil'd; and when cold, if there be any kernels in them, they must be picked out, then chopt into small bits, which are to be season'd with pepper and salt and nutmeg, and mixed with minced sweet herbs and a piece of fresh butter. These (put into pye-crust) are to be closed up with some verjuice, and when baked, a caudle must be prepared and put into the pye, made with nutmeg, vinegar, butter, sugar, the yolks of two new laid eggs, a spoonful of sack; and if you think fit the juice of a *Seville* orange.

A Second Receit to make a Chauldron Pye, or to make a delicious sweet Chauldron Pye.—THE guts should be chop'd very small, and mixed with currants, sugar, and some butter; or with plumbs and no currants, with the addition of some of the ingredients of the other receit.

A third Receit to make a Chauldron Pye.—HALF boil a calf's chauldron, when cold mince it as small as grated bread, with half a pound of suet or better, and as much marrow. Season it with mace, nutmeg, and cloves beaten small; then wring out the juice of half a lemon, and add some of its rind minced small. This done, mix them all together; and when you have laid a piece of puff-paste at the bottom of a dish, put your mixture on it, cover all with another leaf of paste, and bake it. When baked, open the pye, and squeeze in the juice of three *Seville* oranges.

To make a Pudding of a Calf's Chauldron.—TAKE the parboil'd guts, and mince them as small as possible, with half a pound of beef suet. Season it with a little onion, parsley, thyme, and the rind of a lemon shred very small, with beaten nutmeg, cloves, and mace, all mixed together, with the yolks of five eggs and a little cream; then take sheeps guts thoroughly cleansed and cured, fill them with this meat in the shape of hogs puddings, and boil them after the same manner.

To fry a Calf's Chauldron.—AFTER the calf's guts are cleansed and cured, parboil them, and when cold cut it into little bits as big as walnuts. Season it with powder'd cloves, nutmeg, mace, an onion, parsley, and a little pepper. Then put this mixture into a frying-pan, with a ladle full of strong broth and a little piece of butter, and fry it. When fry'd enough, put over it a layer made with mutton gravey, the juice of a lemon and orange, the yolks of three or four eggs, and some grated nutmeg. Toss this in the pan two or three times, then dish and serve it up.

Of Brewing Malt Liquors.

WHY so little good Malt is made in England.—IT is to little purpose to hope for the enjoyment of wholesome pleasant beer and ale, unless the malt is good it is brewed from; and such malt is more difficult to come by than most people imagine, which made an expert common brewer say, he believed there was hardly one malster in twenty that made true malt; and I am really of the same opinion, as thousands I am sure would be, if they had a knowledge of the many incidents and contrivances that hinder it. Incidents, I say, because when barley is mowed in several degrees of ripeness, as when some is full ripe, some half ripe, and some only begun ripening, it is then impossible to make good malt of such barley; the occasion of which is owing to a long dry season of weather, that directly succeeds the sowing of it; by which means thousands of acres of barley in some years are thus damaged, although this great damage may be very cheaply and easily prevented by liquoring the seed before it is sown, as I have, and intend in my future works further to shew, when I publish my treatise to be entituled *New Discoveries in the Art of Agriculture.*

Secondly, another incident of damage is, when barley after it is mowed is rained on, so as to make it spire in the field. Thirdly, in the malt-house by wrong management in the cistern, floor or kiln; on the kiln, by drying brown malt too hastily, so as to cause the kernels to jump and snap, which is blowing of malt, to make the fewer kernels fill the bushel, and thus they are often dried to a bitterness; whereas to dry it leisurely as it ought to be, it should be ten hours on the kiln, instead of which many dry it in four hours time. The same fault is also committed by many malsters in making pale malts, who to save time, labour, and fewel, dry them in eight hours instead of sixteen; and to deceive the buyer will just crisp them without-side, when the inside is rawish: hence it is, that we have such great quantities of bad beer and ale. Fourthly, there are thousands of quarters of malt damaged every year by whools or wevils, bred by the rawness of pale malt. Many people find themselves sick after drinking, little thinking such sickness is occasioned by whools or wevils; but I say, wevilly malt will cause the beer to give its drinker a sickness, and when many of these stinking poisonous insects are among it, a very panick sickness indeed. The *Londoners* have no notion of this; and that in some country towns, where are several malt-kilns, they are never free from wevils all the year.

To know good Malt.—It is known by smell and taste, by smelling, if it smells sweet; by taste, if the kernel bites mellow and tastes sweet; for if the kernels are hard throughout, it is a sign of bad malt.—See more of this, and many other curious serviceable matters in brewing, in my treatise intituled *The London and Country Brewer*, sold by *Astley*, at the *Rose* in *Pater-Noster-Row*, London.

Hops.—THE bright hops of the last year's growth are best, the older the worser. Hops ripe, when gather'd free of the damage of insects and rains, and if rightly kiln-dried, will (by rubbing them between the finger and thumb) feel oily, yield a delicate scent, and taste thoroughly bitter.

Of Water for brewing.—THE best water to brew with is a soft river, pond, or rain-water, because these make stronger drink than hungry hard well-water, and agree best with malt of any kind, in opening its body, whereby the beer or ale wort receives its strength the sooner, and more gradually than it does from an astringent, sharp, hard, well-water; insomuch that it is allowed by good judges, that one or two bushels of malt may be saved in eight, if brewed with a river or pond water. I knew a nobleman (whose well-water is a bracky, hard, chalky sort) say he could never have such good beer at his house, as the keeper of his park had at his lodge. The reason was, because the keeper brewed with a pond-water, that had much more strength in it than the well-water, and gave the drink a better relish; and if such pond-water should be (as sometimes it is in summer) stagnated and foul, it is only throwing some salt into the copper, and it will not only raise a filthy scum, but entirely cure the water. This and many other matters in brewing I have the more knowledge of, as I was executor to my uncle's will, a brewer in *London*; which engaged me a little while in that business.

Of keeping brewing Utensils clean and sweet.—WITHOUT a roomly brewhouse, a sufficient number of tubs or other coolers, and without they are kept sweet and clean, there is no such thing as brewing right malt liquors. But if any taint of them is suspected, it may be cured at once by throwing scalding water into them, and upon that some bay-salt, which when dissolved, scrub and wash them well with a birch broom, or hard brush; and thus you will deliver yourself from that poisonous damage, called in great brewhouses the fox, which gives the drink a sickish nasty taste, and a very unwholesome quality.

A good plain Way to brew a Hogshead of October *or* March *stout Beer.*—THERE are many ways of doing this; but the plain common way is this I am going to direct, I will suppose a hogshead of strong beer was to be brewed.—In the first place, I would see if my malt was not eat at the end of the kernels

(460)

by wevils, that it was sweet, and bit mellow; then I would have it only just broke, and that's all, between the two stones of a mill, or else only bruised between two rollers of the shape of a mill that flats tobacco-leaves, or the plat that our country people weave for making straw-hats: Then having my soft water boiled a minute or two, I would put it into the mash tub, there to stand till I could see my face in it, or just bear my finger in it; then to put my ground malt directly into it by degrees, stirring it all the while it is running leisurely into the tub; when all is in, I would mash the whole for about twenty-five minutes, then cover it with a bushel of malt that I left out on purpose, and leave it so for two or three hours; at the end of which, I would turn the cock to let the wort run out, and return it back on the malt till it run fine upon some rubbed hops. When I had my full quantity, or rather before, I would be putting it into the copper with hops, and boil all as fast as I could, till the wort breaks into particles as big as lice; then I would take all out of the copper as fast as I could, for then it is boiled full enough, and better than if the wort and hops were boiled longer. But to be more nice, I would put my hops in a large canvas bag or fine meshed net, to be boiled in the wort only thirty minutes at most, but the wort should be boiled on longer, till it breaks as aforesaid; for by boiling the hops so little a while, the drink will be impregnated with only the fine spiritous, flowery, wholesome bitter of the hops, free of that nasty-tasted earthy unwholesome quality that is in all hops whatsoever, and which would be extracted if the wort was to boil much longer. As to the quantity of malt and hops to brew a hogshead of strong beer from, it is as a person thinks fit; for from ten to sixteen bushels or more of any sort of malt, a hogshead of good beer may be brewed; and as to the quantity of hops, they may be used from four to ten pounds or more. Be sure to lay your wort thin in the cooling tubs or backs, for if it is laid thick, it will be very apt to fox; and when almost cold, take about a gallon, and mix some yeast with it in a pan, tub, or pail; do this in time, that it may be incorporated with the rest of the wort before it is cold, and when it has work'd into a curled head turn it, but never beat the yeast into it above once or twice at most, before you put it into the cask.—Others brew by lading over boiling water after the first mash is over, and this from time to time without stirring the malt, till all the strong wort is got off; which is a good way, but is too tedious for some people's patience.—Others work their strong wort in a cask, and will not put any yeast into it before it is all in it, thinking the spirits will not waste here during the fermentation, as when openly work'd in a tub.—Ale is to be brewed in the same manner, only with less malt and fewer hops; and if a person has a mind to brew an ale that is excellent for the gout or gravel, he may put some treacle into the copper when he puts in his malt wort to boil; this opens the pores, and promotes perspiration, to the great relief of the body. *N. B.* If your first hot water is not too hot when the malt is put to it, you need not fear a miscarriage in the brewing afterwards.

A Proposal for putting a Stop to that pernicious, but too common Practice, of beating Yeast into strong Beer and Ale.

NOtwithstanding I have done my endeavour, in my aforesaid brewing-treatise, to detect this pernicious practice, yet I find to my surprise it increases, especially in the country, as it brings the greater profit to the brewer, who by this means can save two bushels of malt in eight. For if one brews eight bushels of malt and does not beat the yeast in above once or twice at most, his drink shall be no stronger than the same quantity brewed from six bushels, if the yeast is beaten in near or quite a week together, as many do in winter time; because by this the malt liquor is so impregnated with the sulphureous and saline spirit of the yeast (which is of a poisonous nature) that a quart of such yeasty ale has fuddled a very stout man: Which inebriating quality tempts the ignorant to spend their money, lose their time, ruin their health, and bring their family to the parish. Besides which, it greatly lessens the consumption of barley and malt, and consequently the king's duty. Now to prevent this horrid practice, if the excise officer was to make a narrow inspection, and find yeast beaten into any strong beer or ale above twice, it should by a strict law be made very penal.

CONTENTS

OF THE

Country Family's Profitable Director.

A.

A L L U M, made use of by country bakers   61 & 257
    Author's servant's way to make a plain pudding   81
Antidote for preventing a cow's hoving   239
Apple Pye, a poem   85
—pies and pasties for harvest, *&c.*   84
————(Author's) how made   93
—pudding boiled for a family   284
————a farmer's cheap one   284
————a better sort to bake   285
————a rich one to boil   285
————made instead of plumb pudding for a lord's servants   285
Apples to preserve   299, 303, 305
—and pears, to forward their ripening   307
—Parsnip, its famous character   87
Apricots, nectarines and peaches, to preserve   306
Ague, to cure   351, 352
Advertisement, of allum   257
Anthony's (St.) fire   332
Arm wasted, to cure   362
Artifice made use of in churning butter   393

B.

B R E A D of barley   251
    ————to make eat like wheaten bread   251
—for servants   252
—made in *Finland*   66
—of three sorts out of wheat-meal   250
—*French*   253
————a second way   253
————a third way   254
—substantial   255
—bread to keep moist   255
—maxims relating to it   255
—heavy, its cause   258
—of potatoes   258

—made in *Cheshire*   61
—barley, by a yeoman's wife   64
—crumbling, what occasions it   64
————to prevent it   64
—lying too long in an oven   65
—made of beans and pease   65
—made with oats and tills   65
—ropy and musty, its occasion   65
—wheaten, made by a housewife   62
—of wheat and barley-meal mix'd   63
—pudding   82
Barley-meal, its management, by a labourer's wife   66
————boiled pudding   69
————baked pudding   69
————palatable pan-cakes   70
————its uses in a hard frost   70
————bread   71
————boiled with turnips   259
Beef and mutton suet preserved   95
—the best way to salt it in harvest   96
Black hogs puddings   139
————thick skin   156
Bacon, its necessary uses   147
—the *Hertfordshire* way of curing it   148
—made in the *West*   149
—made by a *London* bacon-man   150
—cured in some country towns   151
—made white by a farmer's wife   151
—why a gentleman would not have it singed   152
—flitches cured by a country housewife   155
Bacon-mongers country way to cure bacon   157, 158
Bean fed bacon, its qualities   170
Brine, its power in preserving bacon and pork   166
Boar, almost spoiled by wrong feeding   171
—of another gentleman's damaged by wrong management   172
—observations on their cases   173
—drest for brawn   172
—'s flesh to roast   178
Brawn collar'd and soused by *Rabisha*   175
—writ of by *Bradley*   176
—to bake by an old receit   177
—baked to be eaten cold   179
—by Sir *K. Digby*   179
Barley broth   280
—a dish of it   281
—grewel   281
—pudding baked   281

—short cake, to make 259
—dumplins with bacon in them 259
—(pearl) broth with meat 281
Bacon pasty boiled for a farmer's family 286
————baked 286
—and eggs dress'd *Hertfordshire* way 287
Broad beans and pease, to preserve 307
Beef steak pye boiled 311
Blackberry pye, to bake 315
————to boil 315
—pudding 315
Black berries, their uses 315
Black-kerroon cherries, the character of 89
Bleeding inwardly and outwardly stopt 344–5
Butter, whey 231
—second, its nature 231
—food that occasions cows to make bad butter 394
—how a dairy woman had it sweetest 394
—made from scalded cream 397
—a further account of it 399
—*Somersetshire* account of it 400
—a pound of it roasted in *Ireland* 448
—another *Irish* dish 449
Barrelling butter 401
—a second way 403
—ancient author's way 403
—remarks on the same 404
Buttermilk porridge 405
—hasty pudding 405
—with apples and toast 405
—pancakes and pudding 406
—curds 406
Burgoo, Cheshire way 265
—a second way 265
—for a poor family 272
Butter, its nature 392
—made to come by art[ificial grasses] 389
—the *Welch* way of colouring it 401
—dairy, its furniture 384
Barrel churn 387
—the use of it 388
Breast of mutton collar'd 449

C.

COLLAR of pork to roast   109
    Collar of pig to souce, by *Rabisha*   109
Cheese, its valuable properties in harvest-time   123
Cake-seed for harvest   126
—good, to make   127
Chitterlins, to make   145
—pye   146
—to boil or fry   146
Country bacon-monger left off smoking tobacco   157
Cure best in the world for King's-evil, pox, leprosy, and scurvy, by a water   193
Cake of potatoes   258
Carrots preserved   296, 298, 305
Cabbage and collyflower preserved   297
Cherries and gooseberries preserved   304
—black and sloes to preserve   305
Cowslip tea   309
Crab pye   314
Cough to cure by 11 receits   318–20
Consumption and inflammation of the lungs cured   349
Cramp   358
Chilblains and kibe heels   362
Canker   363
Cat cured pain   374
Coffee   375
Corns   376
Chiltern butter dairy   410
Cheese, Cheshire   411
Cheshire large cheese   412
Cheese, Somersetshire   412
—to make it in marsh grounds   413
—from the feed of clover   414
—*Gloucestershire*   414
—*Shropshire*   414
—compound   415
—cream   415
—slipcoat, three ways   417–19
—fresh   420
———a rich one   420
—in winter   420
—a short way of making it   419
—made in a cabbage net   421
—*Welch*   421
—when best made   423
—made by a widow in *Bucks*   426
—to make a scalded one   427
—toasted or melted eats savoury   428

Cream curds   422
—to keep, what an ancient author says   408
Character of a sluttish maid   426
Churn upright   389
Churning butter, what an ancient author says   408
Cucumers raw, to eat safe   449
—to pickle   450
Cake seed, by Mrs. *Hays*   451
Cordial rich, of cherries and mulberries   308
Chickens, to fat   214
—Sir *Kenelm Digby's* way   215
—*Hertfordshire* way   216
Capons, to fat   216
Cow poison'd by laurel leaves   209
—'s bloody water to stop   233
—their good and bad properties   233
—unlucky, to milk   235
—kicking, to manage   237
—to prevent holding up her milk   238
—her life saved   238
—stab'd to save her life   240
—the best remedy for a murrain one   240
—how to prevent the murrain distemper spreading   241
—how the cure belongs to country houswives   439
Cows, of preserving the health of them   439
—a drink to give them after calving   440
—to preserve them in health all the year   440
—five drinks to make her glean   441
—the ill effects attending it   441
—a safe way to make her glean   442
—how to cure her when strained   442
—a knavish trick used in selling her   443
—the case of a *Buckingham* gentleman's two cows,
    in regard to the bearings   443
—the nature of pissing bloody water   444
—the method taken to prevent it   444
—the cure of the above, by two receits   444
—to cure when scours   445
—of an ignorant farmer like to be kill'd by it   445
—bought of a farmer and had a scouring   446
—to cure of a snarl'd bag or udder   446
—to cure a garget in her   446
—the damage of long hair on her bag or udder   447
Calves, of suckling them for weaning   428
—wean'd   429, 430
—of suckling and fattening them   431
—the method of suckling them   433

—to cure them of scouring 434
—of bleeding them 434
—of cramming them 435
—how long to be suckled for butchers 436
—to make suck when lost appetite 436
—their guts or chauldron in esteem 456
—how the guts or chauldron is to be made into a pye, by three receits 457
—how the guts or chauldron is prepared for pies 456
—chauldron to fry 458
Cakes, nuts, and pincushions, how to make them 455
Coffee artificial 376
Child, the case of one in the measles 378

D.

*D*ROPSY 323
Deafness 368
Diabetes 371
Diet-drink, by Madam *Howard*, &c. 364
Drink warm 372
Dog mad, to cure 375
Dairy maid's artifice to get rid of a boy 424
Darkin dunghill fowls, the character of 218
Ducks, their profit 222
—several sorts of 222
—to breed 222
Dunghill fowls to lay early 211
—by *Mortimer* 213
Duke of Bridgewater's character 245
Dumplins (apple) for a family 285

E.

*E*GGS to preserve sound 228
—a second way 229
—a third way 229
—a fourth way 229
—rotten, sold knowingly 230
———to know 230
—Hertfordshire 230
English hams, to make like *Westphalia* 164
Eye salve of Sir *Hans Sloane* 378
Eyes sore, to cure several ways 369
—of Mrs. *Knight* cured, and an inflammation in her face 197
Elder syrup 309, 312
—berries distilled 312
Earwig 373
Evil cured 366
Earthen dairy pans season'd 401

F.

*F*Armer's management of butter 393
—way of dressing liver and craw of a porker 118
—hasty pudding 79
—pudding of *Buckinghamshire* 81
—family and a hog poisoned by a herb 208
—wife's family pease porridge 290
————way to make paste 90
————mistake in boiling pease 292
—disgraced by apple-pye 92
—another credited by apple-pye 92
—how his apple-pyes were made 92
Fats, how to make them go far in pyes or
    pasty crust made with barley-meal 66
—the cheapest way to save their expence 68
—the benefit of saving them 129
—of bacon and porker hogs to try up 130
—offald, to try up 131
Fritters apple, a quick plain way to make 75
————of *Hertfordshire* 76
————a second receit 77
—better to make 77
—potatoe 77
Flitches of bacon to dry and keep from rust 160
————spoiled by a lord's butcher 161
Flower of brimstone, the character of it 201
Food that occasions cows to make bad butter 394
French beans, to preserve 298
Fevers cured 356, 357
Fuel, how much may be saved in heating an oven 249
Furmity for a family 279
—made with barley 279

G.

*G*UT puddings with hog's liver 143
————with hog's humbles 145
—puddings, by three receits 143–4
Gentleman obliges man to clear his cow-house every day 425
—'s loss by a lazy dairy-maid 391
Gammon of bacon to bake 169
—to boil and roast 170
Gravel, a remedy for it 201
Green pease-porridge the *Hertfordshire* way 290
Golden Rennets preserved by a gentleman 303
Grapes, to preserve 307
Gooseberry pudding 315
Girls, two poison'd by henbane root 208

Geese	223
—their sitting and hatching	223
—their loss and profit	224
Glandville, Mr. poisoned by muscles	207
Goslings, 18 killed by a pole-cat	226
Gout cured, by many receits	324–330

H.

HARVEST men victualled	94
———fed various ways	120
Herbs to provide against harvest	97
Harvest posset	124
Hog, to kill in harvest	99
—cutting it out for pickling	100
—singed for pickling pork	101
—'s ears, feet, &c. to bake	109
—'s haslet, to roast cheap	112
—how scalded for bacon	153
—fatted in *London* for bacon	154
—guts to prepare for puddings	203
—puddings, *Welch* way, black	203
———ditto, white	204
—doctor's attempt to cure a sow that ailed nothing	185
—several cured, though jogged under the throat	185
—died with rotten liver	186
—some killed by acorns and others cured	186
—to prevent being bound by acorns	186
—to keep in health	186
—damaged by eating hen-dung	188
—large guts to make into white puddings	452
—soon choaks	185
Hams, to cure by unboiled brine	163
—cured by boil'd pickles	163
—to roast	169
Hens, their sorts	211
—sitting chickens and ducks	212
—pullets, capons and turkeys, to fatten	213
Hands chopt, to cure	377
Horse beans, their use	263
Herrings, to pickle	206
Herricane, to make	449
Hoarseness, to cure	317
—a second way	317
Hops	459
Hung beef, to make	289

J.

J A U N D I C E to cure, by five receits   321, 322
    Itch, leprosy, scald-head   334–338
Issues, with cases of them   345–7

K.

K U D N A L dairy-maid's account of her cream   425

L.

L E A V E N and leavened bread   59
    ———to make for a private family   59
Laplanders, their bread   66
Leg of Pork to boil   116
    ———to broil, by *Rabisha*   116
Lard, to preserve   132
Letter concerning baked pears   300
Lord's charity, the character of   379
Loaf spice, to make for harvest   128
Loss of appetite   359
Looseness, to stop   359, 366
Lice and fleas, to kill   365
Ladyfinger-grass   395
Loin of mutton to dress   449

M.

M E A T to prepare for black hogs puddings   139
    ———white hogs puddings   140
—salt, to boil to the greatest profit   205
Man poisoned by eating a toad   209
Meals made use of in Northern Counties   53
Miller, the knavish one   263
Milk-porridge, its service   273
    ———various sorts   273, 274
    ———with bay leaves   274
    ———for gentry   274
Mushrooms dry'd   307
—pickled   293
Marrow puddings   451
Measles   375
Milk and cream, their improvement   385
Malt, little good made in *England*   458
—to know good   459

O.

O Atmeal, Cheshire way of improving it   264
—small ground, why best   265
—pudding, rich   266
    ———a cheap one   266

————baked *Hertfordshire* way   266
————a boiled one ditto   266
————a baked one excellent   266
————a baked one by an ancient author   267
————his boiled one   267
————two other ways to bake one   267
————a short way of baking and boiling it   268
————for a gouty man   268
————by *Rabisha*   269
—drink for a gouty man   268
—pap   269
—its praise   269
—made from black and white oats   272
—pudding, two quick ways   272
—bite   272
—pudding, a quick way to prepare it for baking   272
—managed by a poor woman   273
Oats, what the produce of a bushel is   272
October beer, to brew   460
—ale, to brew   460
Onions, garlick, and shallots, to preserve   297
Onion pye   315
Ox-cheek to stew, by *Houghton*   287
—baked the farmers way   288
—pye   288
Oysters, artificial   288
—to pickle   451

P.

*P*Udding, rice, by *Rabisha*, to bake   80
————plain to make   80
—apple, *Hertfordshire* way   82
—potatoe   83
—with black cherries   83
—flour, for a farmer's family   84
—flour, to bake   84
—plumb, to make in harvest   78
—a second and cheap way   78
—to bake or boil   78
—a second way   79
—in haste   79
—hasty, by Mr. *Houghton*   79
—for a poor family   79
—baked, a rich one   80
—plain, to boil   80
—hasty by *Rabisha*   80
—of hogs maw and sheeps maw, the *Welch* way   204

—of *Sussex*, to make   205
—of a calf's chauldron   457
Pancakes for rich people   74
—farmers interest in making   71
—their cheap uses   72
—three made to dine four people   72
—made with small beer   73
—water, made by poor people   73
—apple for gentry   75
—with pickled pork   75
—made with Dugdale flour   75
—fine without butter or lard   76
—rice to make   76
—with Bacon   76
Pork pies or pasties to make   114
————to be eaten cold   116
—steaks to roast   117
————to broil   117
—to roast in joints   117
—fresh, to salt at once for present use   117
————a second way   118
————to salt on the spit   118
—pickled, its use in harvest   98
—to pickle   102
————practice of an old country housewife   102
————a second way   103
————a third way   103
—damaged by too much salt-petre   105
—why its bloody part should be first soaked out before pickling   105
—to pickle in summer   106
—pickling, the *Kentish* and *Suffolk* way   107
————by a *Yorkshire* maid   112
————with eggs   287
—collar'd to fry   111
—balls to fry   111
Pickles, to make for bacon   163
Porker, too small for pickling, what to do with it   107
—particular way to salt down   106
—'s head, feet, and ears to dress, by a farmer's wife   111
Pyes mince, with hogs haslet to make   113
————*Hertfordshire* way   113
————costly and rich   454
————made of stinking meat   455
—pumpkin   316
—to boil of squab pigeons   311
Pig to bake, by *Rabisha*   110
——- to roast   111

Pigs of one sow sold for 4 *l.* in one year   180
—lost by a sow's eating sour apples   183
—suckling lost, by a sow's eating wash with hop in it   187
Pigs to wean   189
Plumb cake of *Hertfordshire*   128
————good   128
Pear Orange Bell, its fine character   89
Pears to preserve   300
Puff-paste   90
Persons poisoned by rat's-bane   210
Potatoes preserv'd by a lord's gardener   298
—dress'd by a farmer's wife   293
—preserv'd all the year   295
Pease porridge and pease soup made at once   290
————for a poor man's family   291
—soup, for a gentleman at *Gaddesden*   *291*
—proper for pease porridge   293
—pudding, *Hertfordshire* way   292
Pigeons, to broil   311
—the best way to roast them   449
—to jugg   449
Piles cured   200
Pimpled neck   201
Pleurisy cured by camomile   317
Pain in legs   355
—in stomach   358
—in head   367
Palsey, to cure   369
Purge   *374*
Physick, why too much does harm   378
Proposals to prevent beating yeast into beer and ale   463

Q.

QUAKER's way to cure bacon   157
Qualities different in pork and bacon   159
Quicksilver water, its superlative virtue for curing diseases   193
Quinces, to preserve   303

R.

REMARKS on ancient author's account of churning butter   408
Rolls to make for tea breakfast   254
Rice-milk, to make   282
—butter'd   282
—pudding boiled   282
————baked two ways   282
—oatmeal gruel   283
Rabbits poison'd by hemlock   210

Repository of dairy room   407
Rob of elder and cherry   309
Receit famous for pickling pork   104
Rheumatism cured by various receits   330–332
—a second receit   195
Rennet bag   422
Rising of the lights   359

S.

SUET, to provide against harvest   95
Servant maid, how she spoiled pork in pickling   104
Service of pickled pork in poor families   119
Sousing drink for preserving pork   119
————by *Rabisha*   120
Sousing hog's feet, ears, hocks and chitterlins   120
Sausages, to prepare guts for them   132
—to prepare pork meat to fill them   133
—compleat for a private family   134
—a person broke for want of knowing how to make them   134
—*Bologna*, to make   135
—without skins   136
—to preserve them   137
—to preserve them in links   137
—by an old receit   138
—to make with pork and fowl   138
Sows, why better made bacon of than pork pickled   155
Sow hogs for pickled pork, observations on it   101
—to manage before and after pigging   182
—and pigs, why their inspection belongs to country housewives   179
—bursted   184
—killed by accident   184
————by wrong medicines   184
—poisoned by broth   185
—killed by eating brandy cherries   185
—ready to pig, killed by eating yeasty wash   187
—that had twenty-four pigs, how sold for a feast   188
—breeding, how cheaply kept   188
—that eat chickens   189
—'s milk to dry away   189
—in pig or not in pig, when to kill   190
Sucking pigs had all the year   180
Skins to prepare for hogs black puddings   139
————for hogs white puddings   141
Servant by a false key opened a cellar   243
Salt-petre, bay-salt, sal-prunella   161
—a butcher's notion of it   162
Sprats, to pickle   206

School-boy poison'd by vitriol   209
Swans, their pleasure and profit   226
—to breed   227
—to fatten   228
—to pinion   228
Skimming-dish of brass   230
Sluttishness of a dairy-maid   426
Small-pox   367
—to prevent catching it   368
Savoys collar'd green   288
Strawberries and bullace preserved   305
Syrup to preserve damsins in   308
—of cowslips by a gentleman   308
—of clove-julyflowers   309
—of sloes   310
Sore throat   320
Sprain and bruise   347, 348
Stone and cholick   353, 354
Scurvy to cure, six cases   360, 361
Sore mouth to cure   362
Shingles   362
Sneezing   367

T.

*T*A Y L O R became a farmer, and how robbed   244
Tea caudle   370
Tooth-ach cured by henbane root   209
—cured   363
Turkeys, to breed   219
—young, to feed   219
—old, to fatten   220
—to breed and feed   220
Theft by servants   143
Threshers, two stole wheat   242
Tongue neat's, to pot   289
Tympany, to cure   317
Thorn, to draw out   362
Teeth, to fasten   363
—lost by a young woman   364
Teas, their nature   369
Traveller's feet relieved   377
Tobacco, its improvement   377
Turnips and parsnips, to preserve   296

V.

*V*A L E housewife, why she refuses saltpetre in curing pork and bacon 162
—butter dairy   383

Vale dairy, its management   232
Vomit   375
Vomiting stopt   317
Veal, observations on the goodness and badness of it   437
Vinegar for a family, to make   313
—of rotten apples   313
—of gooseberries   313
—of green apples   313
—of malt liquor   314
———a second way   314
Verjuice   314
Utensils kept clean   460

W.

*W*H E A T, several sorts in *England*   41
   Why farmers grind their wheat   42
Why some refuse it   42
Wheat-meal, to preserve sweet in sacks   44–46
—how it becomes damaged by insects   46
—to know good from bad   48
—damaged by mites   260
—to know when infected by them   261
Wheat, grown in barn, how it happens   50
———how its meal may be improved   53
———how to cure it   51
—its use   248
—the profit of grinding it   262
—and barley bread, the method of baking it   259
Wheaten bread made in a gentleman's family   249
Water barley, *French* or pearl, for sick people   280
—for brewing   460
—*gruel* for poor people   275
———to taste like meat broth   276
———second plain way   276
———*Rabisha*'s way   276
———by a second author   276
———the wholesomeness of, plain sort   277
———with smallage   277
———with elder buds   278
Whitepot cheap   283
—a better sort   283
—with rice   284
Walnuts, preserved by a lord's gardener   304
—to pickle, *French* way   450
———white   451
—green, to preserve in syrup   310
Woman poisoned by a duck   208

White hog's puddings, to make	139
Wigs to make for harvest-men	125
—by a country common baker	126
Worms, wevils, and maggots to destroy	261
—to destroy	365, 366
Wounds, burns and swellings to cure	338–344
Whitloe cured	375
Wen cured	361
Wrinkles, to take away	369

Y.

*Y*E A S T, its nature	54
—to make a little go far	55
—to preserve sound in hot weather	55
—a second way	55
—to preserve in cold weather [*recte* water]	56
—to preserve sweet in pitchers	56
———in bottles	56
—how an old woman increased it	57
—its cheapness and dearness	57
—how sold to great profit	57
—bitter to make fresh	58
—of good neighbours	58
—how *London French* bakers supply the use of it	258
Yeasty grounds of barrels, how to make them serviceable for bread	55

F I N I S.

Glossary

The books consulted in the preparation of this glossary included the glossaries of previous Prospect Books facsimiles and editions: Hannah Glasse, *The Art of Cookery Made Plain and Easy*; Robert May, *The Accomplisht Cook* (both compiled by Alan Davidson); Richard Bradley, *The Country Housewife and Lady's Director* (compiled by Caroline Davidson); *John Evelyn, Cook* and John Evelyn's *Acetaria* (compiled by Tom Jaine); and *The Closet of Sir Kenelme Digbie Kt. Opened* (compiled by Peter Davidson and Jane Stevenson). I have also used Alan Davidson, *The Oxford Companion to Food*; Jancis Robinson, *The Oxford Companion to Wine*; the glossary by Elizabeth David in the facsimile edition of John Nott, *Cooks and Confectioners Dictionary*; *Martha Washington's Booke of Cookery*, Karen Hess; *The Englishman's Flora*, Geoffrey Grigson; *Cultivated Fruits of Britain*, F.A. Roach; *The Book of Apples*, Joan Morgan and Alison Richards; *Traditional Foods of Britain*, Laura Mason with Catherine Brown; Thomas Mawe and John Abercrombie, *Every Man his own Gardener*; *Encyclopaedia Britannica*, 11th edition; *A Dictionary of the English Language*, Samuel Johnson; *The Oxford English Dictionary*, 2nd edition. It is fortunate that the compilers of the *OED* consulted the works of William Ellis in making their collections. Many of his usages are recorded and compared in their pages.

Tom Jaine

ADDERS-TONGUE is the popular name for the genus of ferns *Ophioglossum*, as well as many other plants, for example herb robert and some orchids.

ÆTHIOPS MINERAL is a combination of quicksilver and sulphur ground together to form a black powder, hence its name.

AGRIMONY: *Agrimonia eupatoria*, also called Aaron's rod and liverwort.

ALCALOUS: alkaline.

ALLHOLLANDTIDE, ALLHOLLANTIDE: All Hallows' Day, All Saints' Day, 1 November.

ALLUM, ALUM: an astringent mineral salt (sulphate of aluminium and potassium, used in baking, dyeing, tanning, paper making and medicine). It was extracted from earth or rock, the latter being sometimes defined as 'rock alum'.

ALTERATIVE is a type of medicine, a treatment which 'alters processes of nutrition, and reduces them to healthy action'. 'Alteratives…have a power of changing the constitution, without any sensible increase or decrease of the natural evacuations.'

ANACKS: a type of bread made from fine oatmeal. Not for the first time, though rarely acknowledged, Ellis is quoting Gervase Markham (*d.*1637), a further instance of his relying on books written during the previous century rather than current manuals.

ANIMALCULA: a small or tiny animal, a mite.

APPLES

> FRENCH PIPPIN: it is unclear which variety is meant by this description. Pippins were generically French in origin, in English eyes, and described as 'fine-flavoured, late-keeping'. Mawe & Abercrombie (1805) include French Pippin in their list of varieties.
>
> GOLD-RENNET, or Golden Reinette, an English variety – similar to Blenheim Orange – associated particularly with Hertfordshire.
>
> GOLDEN PIPPIN is first recorded by Parkinson in 1629, widely sold in the 18th century and used in tarts, cider and jelly.
>
> GREEN: it is not clear which variety is meant by this description.
>
> HOLLAND PIPPIN is noted by Morgan & Richards as being first recorded in Lincolnshire in 1729.
>
> JOHN-APPLE is described by Morgan & Richards as a 16th- and 17th-century variety that was said to 'last until apples come again', i.e. until St John's Day (29 August).
>
> KENTISH is the Kentish Pippin, or the Colonel Vaughan, an early type, much used for tarts and cider and for sale in the London markets.
>
> LEMON PIPPIN: Morgan & Richards identify its first naming in William Ellis though it was probably known earlier. Used for drying, for eating and in tarts. It may be of Norman origin.
>
> NON-PAREIL is an eating apple of high repute in the 18th century. First recorded in 1696, it was possibly imported from France in Tudor times.
>
> PARSNIP: Ellis' favourite variety is not listed in any of the standard authorities.
>
> RUSSETTINGS is a generic description of russet apples.

ARCHANGEL usually describes either dead-nettle or black stinking horehound.

ARSMART or arsesmart: water pepper (*Polygonum hydropiper*). It was so called as it would be laid in bed linen to repel fleas and would sting or make smart any bare flesh that came in contact with it.

AVENS: herb bennet or wood avens (*Geum urbanum*). It was used in brewing to impart the flavour of cloves.

BAGNIO is a Turkish bath as well as a place of doubtful resort.

BALSAM is, literally, natural oleo-resin from trees or plants. The meaning was extended to an oily or resinous preparation (often using turpentine) in which various substances were dissolved or combined, usually for external application or inhalation of its heated vapours.

BALSAM OF PERU was the resin of the tree *Myroxylon Pereirae* which grew in San Salvador. Though fragrant, it has no specifically medicinal virtues (says *Britannica*).

BARK is the bark of the cinchona tree, from Peru. It contains quinine.

BARROW-HOG is a castrated boar.

BASILICON, BLACK is a description of a family of 'sovereign' (from the Greek) healing ointments, ingredients not disclosed. Ellis' favourite doctor, John Quincy (*d.*1722) called it a tetra-pharmacon (four ingredients).

BAY-SALT is made by natural evaporation in the sun in southern Europe. It is large and coarse-grained and was thought stronger than common salt but in fact it is a better material for use in salting meats, etc., because it is slower in dissolving.

BEARBIND: Grigson records this as a Home Counties name for bindweed (*Calystegia sepium*), though it was also used to name other sorts of convolvulus.

BEARING: *OED* defines this as the external parts of animals which are involved in parturition, citing 'The teats and external female parts…called by farmers the bearing' (1779). Ellis, however, seems to be describing a prolapsed womb.

BEAVER or, more commonly bever, is a snack between meals. Ellis' description, repeated in his *Modern Husbandman*, is 'they eat wholly on this [cheese] and bread at one time of the day, which they call their beaver and this is commonly about four of the clock in the afternoon.'

BETONY: *Stachys officinalis*, believed to be diuretic and cleansing.

BITE: an imposition or deception.

BLAIN is a sore or pustule, as in chilblain. In cattle, it describes specifically a swelling that erupts on the base of the tongue, stopping the beast from breathing.

BLOW, TO: Ellis talks of butchers 'blowing' or inflating veal to make the meat seem white and fleshier, and soaking the joints in water. *OED* cites Balfour (*c.*1550) on the same practice, to 'cause it seme fat and fair'.

BLUE VITRIOL STONE is made of copper sulphate – copper heated with sulphuric acid, then moistened. It is a desiccating agent.

BOLE ARMONIAC or bole armeniac is an astringent clay-like earth formerly brought from Armenia, used as an antidote or styptic. Bole (from the Greek) meant clod of earth: another sort was brought from Lemnos. It behaved like fuller's earth.

BOLSTER: a surgical compress or pad of lint.

BOTTS: a parasitical worm or maggot.

BRAWN: brined pork set in jelly, see *Traditional Foods of Britain*.

BRIMMING-TIME: the time a pig is in season.

BRIMSTONE: vernacular name for sulphur.

BROOKLIME: speedwell (*Veronica beccabunga*), growing near water, eaten as a salad plant, hot in taste.

BUCKBEAN is a bog plant (*Menyanthes trifoliata*) with leaves that resemble a broad bean's. It had wide medicinal uses and could be substituted for hops in beer. The name is a 16th-century homophone of the Dutch, which means goat's bean.

BURGOO is a thick oatmeal porridge or gruel. Ellis thinks it identical to loblolly.

The name derives (*OED*) from the Turkish *burghul* or *bulgur*. In N. America the name described a meat and vegetable stew or soup.

BUSHEL: a dry measure equivalent to four pecks or eight gallons (of wheat).

CANDLEMAS: 2 February.

CAPIVI: balsam of capivi is a resinous extract from the copaiba tree of Brazil. It was used in making lacquers, and in treating urinary disorders. Its taste is not pleasant.

CARDUUS is the blessed thistle, *Carduus* (now *Cnidus*) *benedictus*, or it was the milk thistle (*Silybum maritimum*) which was more generally used as a food plant and to increase the flow of mothers' milk – its flavour was bitter, like the wormwood's.

CAUDLE: a warm drink of thin gruel mixed with ale or wine and sweetened, often for the sick-bed.

CHAMBERLYE is urine. It softened the water. Ellis suggested in his book on brewing that it was used as an additive in London pale or amber malt drinks. More generally, it was the waste water from the house reycled to economize on soap.

CHAULDRON or chawdron is the general term for the entrails of a beast, most often a calf.

CHERRIES

> KENTISH OR MAYDUKE: first mentioned, as the Duke, by John Rea in 1665. This variety, and its cousins, was an English hybrid of the sweet *Prunus avium* and the acid *Prunus cerasus*. In France they were called 'Anglais'.
>
> KERROON, or Caroon, widely grown in Hertfordshire and Norfolk.

CHIERS or chires are blades of grass or stamens of flowers. The word is used by Ellis in an unacknowledged quotation from Gervase Markham.

CICATRIZE, TO: Ellis writes of 'a wound that requires digesting, deterging, incarning or cicatrizing'. To cicatrize means to heal by forming a scar.

CLIVERS or (a later spelling) cleavers, is goosegrass – which cleaves or sticks to the clothing.

CLOB-WEED: Grigson records this as a Gloucestershire dialect name for knapweed; Ellis also suggests it might be knotgrass (*Polygonum aviculare*). He seems to be describing batchelor's buttons, i.e. knap-weed.

CLOVE JULY-FLOWER or clove gillyflower is the clove-scented pink, the original of the carnation.

COFFIN is a stout pastry case.

COLLAR is a boned, rolled, bound, and tied joint of meat or fish. Collaring was a universal method of controlling floppy joints, as well as allowing them to be stuffed, spiced, then boiled without dissolution.

COLLOP is a small slice.

COOM is the black stuff, comprising grease and dust, which works its way out of axles or bearings.

COPPERAS is really the same as vitriol. The term embraced blue, green and white copperas, the salts of copper, iron and zinc respectively. Where it was used without qualification is usually referred to a salt of iron, ferrous sulphate, used in dyeing, tanning and making ink.

CORKING PIN describes the largest size of pin. The epithet derives from the word calkin: either the turned-down edge of a horse-shoe so as to raise its heel from the ground, or the pins around the edge of the heel of a clog.

CRAM is a ball of compressed food for cramming. Linguistically, the verb preceded the noun.

CRINKLINGS are now better known as pork scratchings.

CROW is the mesentery or giblets.

CROW-GARLICK: a wild species of garlic (*Allium vineale*).

DANE-WEED is dwarf elder (*Sambucus ebulus*), an important medicinal plant.

DETERGE, TO: Ellis writes of 'a wound that requires digesting, deterging, incarning or cicatrizing'. To deterge means to wipe off or cleanse an ulcer or sore.

DIAPENTE is a medicament containing five ingredients. *OED*'s citations mostly concern farriery, the medication being used to purge horses.

DIGEST, TO: Ellis writes of 'a wound that requires digesting, deterging, incarning or cicatrizing'. To digest means to 'promote healthy suppuration'.

DISCUSSER is a medicine or substance that disperses humours.

DODDER OF THYME was also called hellbind in Hertfordshire (Grigson) and was a leafless parasite that grew on thyme and other plants (*Cuscuta epithymum*). It was good for the itch or scabies, 'spleenful headaches' and other ills.

DOG-PARSLEY (*Æthusa cynapium*), also called fool's parsley. This is not cow parsley, which is wild chervil.

DRAM, DRACHM is, for apothecaries, $^1/_8$ of an ounce; avoirdupois, $^1/_{16}$ of an ounce; as a fluid measure, $^1/_8$ of a fluid ounce.

DWARF-ELDER is also called dane-weed (*Sambucus ebulus*), an important medicinal plant.

ELECAMPANE or elicampane (*Inula helenium*) is an important medicinal root. Ellis advises it against the itch or scabies. Others recommend it against coughs and snake venom, convulsions, contusions and bad sight. It was also deemed effective against elves.

ELECTUARY is a medical conserve or paste of powder on a vehicle of honey, syrup, or treacle. Venice treacle (q.v.) was one of the most famous such electuaries.

ELIXIR SALUTIS was the invention of Dr John Daffy (*d.* 1680) and consisted, more or less, of elecampane, liquorice, coriander, anise, senna, guaiacum, carraway, raisins, aniseed water, rhubarb and manna (*The New Female Instructor*, *c.*1810).

ERINGO is sea holly (*Eryngium maritimum*). The roots were often candied and were esteemed as an aphrodisiac.

FASTING: 'every morning fasting' – Ellis often uses this word to indicate that you haven't eaten before doing whatever he advises.

FETCH is vetch.

FILLETTING was tape for binding collars and other joints of meat.

FIRKIN is a small barrel. Its size depends on the material stored.

FLAIR or flare, the leaf or fat about a pig's kidneys.

FLASHY means watery, frothy, unstable, sometimes insipid or tasteless.

FLAY, TO, or flea means to skin.

FLEAM is the lancet used in letting the blood of animals.

FLEET is another word for skimmed. The verb describes the act of skimming.

FLORENTINE ARRACH-ROOT seems here to refer to the orris root: the edible iris, cultivated particularly around Florence. His spelling, 'arrach', might indicate orach, the wild spinach, but that was known for its leaves, not its root; nor was it especially Florentine.

FLUMMERY is a confection whereby oatmeal or wheat bran is steeped in water, the liquid then boiled until it became a jelly.

FRANK: pen or sty, usually used for fattening.

FUMITORY is the plant *Fumaria officinalis*.

FURMITY, FRUMENTY: whole-husked grains, cooked in water, then often enriched with cream, eggs, spices, sugar and dried fruits, or a combination of these.

GALLIPOT is a glazed earthenware jar.

GARGET may describe a swelling in an animal's throat, but Ellis uses it to define a hard swelling in, or inflammation of a cow's udder.

GERMANDER can refer to several species of plant. It is most likely that here it is the speedwell or bird's eye (*Veronica chamaedrys*) – a rather sinister number, according to Grigson.

GILL OR JILL is a quarter of a pint.

GLEAN: the placenta or after-birth, especially of a cow. The verb denotes the act of shedding the after-birth.

GRAIN OF PARADISE or Melegueta pepper is the fragrant seed of an African fruit widely used in traditional medicine, or as a stimulant (in its home territories), as an ingredient of hippocras, or as a fraudulent boost to the strength of ales. It has something of the taste of cardamom.

GRASS

HONEYSUCKLE, is white clover.

LADYFINGER, is birds-foot trefoil (*Lotus corniculatus*).

RAY, is presumably rye grass.

TYNE, or tine, is a wild vetch or tare. Ellis likens it to the cliver as a strangling weed in the wheatfield, yet persists in naming it and ladyfinger grass as his two favourite meadow grasses (*Modern Husbandman*).

GRASS-ONIONS: *Avena elatior*, a species of wild oat, so called from the rounded nodes of the root-stock.

GRAVES are a by-product of making tallow, the meat or skin residue after melting animal fat, often used as animal feed.

GROUND-PINE is the plant *Ajuga Chamæpytis*, so called from its resinous smell.

GUM GUAIACUM is the resin obtained from the American tree *Guaiacum officinale*, often called lignum vitae.

HARTSHORN is deerhorn, used as a source of gelatine.

HASLET has come to mean a meat loaf or porky confection, especially in Lincolnshire. Ellis and his contemporaries, however, used it to describe the offal of a pig that might be roasted or cooked in one way or another.

HERMODACTYL is a medicinal root, usually of the crocus family.

HIERA PICRA is a purgative drug, usually made with aloes.

HIGLER or higgler is an itinerant dealer who buys in the country to sell at market.

HITCH, TO: to extend. Ellis' use of the word does not seem to accord with *OED*.

HOAR, TO, means to grow mould.

HOGOO is a variant spelling of *haut goût*, words which spawned a bewildering collection of alternatives.

HOOP is a wooden or tin hoop or ring used for baking cakes or pastry. Those made of tin often came apart, as they do today, being joined together by a hinge and removable pin.

HORNY: hardened.

HORSE-BEAN is the broad bean but unimproved, grown as a field crop for fodder.

HORSE-MINT is another name for water mint (*Mentha aquatica*). Gerard was eloquent about its smell (Grigson).

HOVE, TO, means to swell.

HUMBLES are innards – usually referring to deer, but Ellis concentrates on 'hog's humbles'.

HUNGARY WATER is named after a queen of Hungary, which one is never revealed. It is a distillation of wine and essence of rosemary.

IMPOSTUME is a nasty swelling, cyst or abscess.

INCARN, TO: Ellis writes of 'a wound that requires digesting, deterging, incarning or cicatrizing'. To incarn means to heal by allowing the flesh to grow over.

INNSHIP is a hamlet.

ITCH is now usually called scabies, but may encompass a host of skin complaints.

JACK-IN-THE-HEDGE that caused so much trouble to the lady that gathered it in error, was probably *Alliaria petiolata* or hedge garlic, its name deriving from 'jakes' on account of its offensive smell (said one botanist, see Grigson).

JACK-JUMP-ABOUT is a folk name for ground elder, as well as for wild angelica. But the most likely candidate for this lady's discomfiture (was she the same lady as picked jack-in-the-hedge?) is birdsfoot trefoil (*Lotus corniculata*).

JAMAICA SPICE, JAMAICA PEPPER is allspice.

JANACKS: a type of bread made from fine oatmeal. Not for the first time, though rarely acknowledged, Ellis is quoting Gervase Markham (*d.* 1637), a further instance of his relying on books written during the previous century rather than current manuals.

JOG is a protuberance or swelling. Ellis' use is the only citation in *OED* (though from *The Modern Husbandman*, not *The Country Housewife*, indicating how much the one book leaned on the other for text and information).

KECKS or kex (in *OED*) is the generic term for the hollow stem of any umbelliferous plant such as wild angelica or hogweed. Grigson gives it as a particular name of hogweed (cow parsley).

KIBE-HEEL: kibes are chilblains, especially on the heel. *OED* suggests the word may stem from the Welsh.

KIVER is a shallow trough or tub, often describing that used for kneading dough, or for storing milk before skimming.

LEAF is the layer of fat round the kidneys of a pig, but was then generalized to describe the internal fat of any animal.

LENITIVE means laxative. A lenitive electuary is a thick syrup that will ease the motions.

LEVIGATE, TO, means to pound in a mortar to a fine powder.

LIVERWORT can refer to several plants, all thought beneficial to the liver. Agrimony is one, stone liverwort (*Marchantia polymorpha*) is another, *Anemone triloba* is a third, dog lichen (*Peltigera canina*) a fourth. Ellis does not specify.

LOBLOLLY is the same as burgoo (q.v.).

LUCATELLUS BALSAM was a soothing, red-coloured ointment or syrup made of olive oil, wax and turpentine. It was used specifically in cases of coughs, bruising and wounds.

MAID-SWEET is sweet cicely.

MANCHET is the fine white enriched loaf of medieval and early modern bakery. Johnson defines it as 'a small loaf of fine bread'.

MANNA is the subject of a definition by Johnson. It is the exudation or juice (then solidified) of the manna-ash (*Fraxinus ornus*), grown in southern Italy – a variant, from the larch, came from France – it was mildly laxative.

MANTLE when describing beer, is the froth.

MARSH-TREFOIL-ROOT is buckbean (*OED*), although Ellis seems to be treating the two names as distinct plants.

MAUKIN or malkin, a mop for swabbing the oven floor. The word had more vulgar meanings too.

MAW is stomach.

MAYWEED, maidweed or maythe, is stinking camomile, *Anthemis Cotula*.

MELLILOT or melilot, is a plant of the clover family (*Melilotus altissima*). In some districts it grew in cornfields to such an extent as to impart a rank flavour to the bread (*OED*).

MITHRIDATE is an electuary effective against poisons and infections, named for the King of Pontus. It, like theriac, was a polypharmaceutical of classical origin, fast falling into disrepute by Ellis' time.

MOUNTAIN is mountain wine, fortified wine from Malaga grown in the mountains immediately to the north of that city.

MUDGELL-HOLE is not defined by *OED*, but perhaps means standing water in a yard that is 'muddled' by ducks and geese, or one that is an outlet for drains.

MUGGET is the intestines of a calf or sheep.

MUM is a kind of beer originally imported from Brunswick during the 17th and 18th centuries (*OED*). However, John Nott gives a recipe and refers to English mum-makers: it was aged and complex, full of aromatics and flavourings.

NAPLES-BISKETS are the original of sponge-fingers, sometimes also a small macaroon made with pine-nuts (E. David, glossing Nott, *Cooks and Confectioners Dictionary*, 1726). See also the glossary to *John Evelyn, Cook*.

ORT is a word to describe scraps or left-overs, be they for humans or for animals. Ellis is advising his housewife on the true economy of the kitchen.

PEAR

    BELL-ORANGE, is the variety most favoured by Ellis. Perhaps it was related to the Bergamot pears, of which there were several.

    BLACK WORCESTER, is a famed baking pear (see *Traditional Foods of Britain*).

    CADILLIAC, was also known as Cadillac or Catillac, and was a cooking variety originally, as were so many, from France.

    WARDEN, were a near-local type, named for the Bedfordshire abbey of Warden.

PECK: two gallons of wheat make a peck, four pecks a bushel. As a dry measure, it was 14 pounds.

PEGGINGS are defined in the *OED* only by reference to Ellis. In his *Modern Husbandman* he describes them as the chaff which is swept off the heap of corn after winnowing.

PENNY-GRASS is probably yellow rattle (*Rhinanthus minor*), a grassland weed.

PETRE-SALT is defined by Woodward (1728): 'Nitre, while...in its native state, is called petre-salt, when refin'd, salt-petre.' It is potassium nitrate.

PILLA-COCHIA is a medicine, a purge: its composition is unknown.

PINCUSHIONS: 'Hertfordshire pincushions' are squares of paste which puff like pincushions when boiled.

PLAISTER OF PARACELSUS: plaisters or plasters were an adhesive salve spread on muslin or skin. Paracelsus (*d.*1541) promoted mineral substances as healing agents and thought the body produced its own healing balsam.

POLLARD is bran.

POSSET is a hot drink made of milk curdled with an acid (wine, ale, citrus juice).

POTTLE measures two quarts.

PRECIPITATE is mercury reduced to a powder by solution in acid. Precipitation is the opposite of sublimation. The powder is corrosive.

QUICKSILVER is mercury.

QUINCE, PORTUGAL, is among the most important and most popular quince varieties, identified by John Gerard and still grown today.

RADDLE is red-ochre. Rams wear a raddle (ruddle, reddle) or harness of coloured earth strapped to their chests to mark any ewes that they have tupped.

RANDAN is the coarsest wheat flour. Other citations in the *OED* define it as bran ground as fine as flour.

RENNET-WORT is probably lady's bedstraw (*Galium verum*), used to curdle milk in the absence of calf's rennet. *OED*, following Richard Bradley (a regular source for Ellis too), suggests it is *Galium aparine*, goosegrass or clivers: unlikely here.

RIDDER SEIVE is the largest sort of wheat sieve.

ROCAMBOLE is *Allium scorodoprasum* or sand leek, a milder form of garlic.

ROLL BRIMSTONE is presumably a piece of brimstone formed into a ball or roll.

ROMAN VITRIOL is sulphate of copper. It is also called blue vitriol.

ROWEL is a circular piece of leather or other material, with a hole in the centre, placed between an animal's flesh and its skin to provoke and permit the discharge of humours or pus.

RUSSEL, OIL OF: it is not clear what this is. It is possibly a variant spelling of rosil which is rosin, solid resin after the distillation of turpentine.

RUST, TO, is the verb that describes turning rusty or resty, i.e. rancid.

SACK is a generic name for fortified wine from Spain or the Canaries: it might be Malaga, Sherry, Canary or Palma (Majorca). The word (Robinson) may derive from the Spanish for export (*sacas*), rather than from the French for dry (*sec*).

SAGE OF VIRTUE is the 'narrow hoary-leaved sage' (Mawe & Abercrombie), a variety of *Salvia officinalis*.

SAINTFOIN, or more properly, sainfoin, is the forage plant *Onobrychis sativa*. The word meant not 'holy' hay, but 'healthy' hay.

SAL VOLATILE is an aromatic solution of ammonium carbonate, smelling salts.

SALIVATE, TO: it was a tactic of early medicine to provoke excess salivation, as you might provoke a sweat. The usual agent was mercury and the process was part of the traditional cure for the venereal pox.

SALPRUNELLA is saltpetre burnt over charcoal, melted and cast into moulds.

STEEL, SALT OR POWDER OF, is 'usually' (*OED*) iron chloride but may be sulphate of iron. 'Flowers of steel' were obtained by heating iron with sal-ammoniac. It may also be called copperose of Mars or vitriol of Mars.

SALTPETRE is potassium nitrate. It may be obtained by mixing decaying nitrogenous matter with lime (alkali), air and water, adding to the solution woodash or potassium, then crystallizing the result.

SASSAFRAS is the bark of the sassafras laurel, native to America. The oil was made from the roots of the tree.

SCALD-BERRY is the blackberry.

SCALD-HEAD is a skin disease, usually ringworm, but it may cover a multitude of scalp conditions, from pustules to scurf.

SCOTCH PILL was, Ellis states, a physic which killed by frequent application. It was a mixture of aloes, jalap, gamboge and anise.

SCURVY-GRASS is *Cochlearia officinalis*.

SEAR-CLOTH or cerecloth was a cloth impregnated with wax or sticky salve. It might be used as a winding sheet, or as a medicinal plaster.

SEARSE or searce is sieve or strainer. The verb is the action of sieving or straining.

SEATON or seton (from the medieval Latin for bristle, and also silk) is a thread or tape drawn through the skin next to a wound or sore to keep open an issue, to stop it entirely healing over.

SENA or senna are the seeds of the cassia shrub, used as an emetic or laxative.

SHEPHERD'S-POUCH, SHEPHERD'S-PURSE are two names for the *Capsella bursa-pastoris*, a common weed also called 'Naughty Man's Plaything' (Grigson).

SHIELD is the thick skin on the flanks of a boar that makes up the outside of the joint called brawn.

SHOCK is a group of sheaves of wheat or corn stood up in the field before gathering and storing in the barn or rick. The word itself derives from medieval German and was a collective noun meaning sixty.

SLUTS-PENNIES are hard pieces in dough caused by imperfect kneading. The definition in *OED* is derived solely from this reference in Ellis.

SMALLAGE is *Apium graveolens*, wild or primitive celery.

SNAKE-ROOT is the root or rhizome of one of several American plants deemed fine antidotes to snake's venom.

SOUCING or sousing is pickling. Souce-drink is pickle or brine.

SPANISH FLY is cantharides, from the beetle also called blister beetle. It is dried to a powder and its active agent is cantharidin. Applied externally, it blisters; internally, it is an emetic, as well as promoting tumescence. A little goes far.

SPIRE, TO, describes the shooting upwards of corn or grain in a field in wet or adverse conditions.

STEEN or stean is an earthenware jar.

STŒCHAS or *Lavendula stœchas* is the French lavender. The Iles d'Hyères were called the Stœchades due to the quantities of the plant found there. It was an expectorant (among other things).

STONE is a measure, usually weighing 14 pounds. However, Ellis also refers to the eight-pound stone – which was the measure for sugar and spice (*OED*).

STROAKINGS or strokings are well defined by Ellis. They are the afterings, the last milk taken from the cow, and the richest. Smollett's Roderick Random was treated to choice bits from the cook and stroakings from the milkmaid.

SUBLIMATE MERCURY is mercury that has been heated, vapourized, then resolidified into a white powder.

SUCCORY is chicory (*Cichorium intybus*).

TARNRISE PLOUGH is the turnwrest or the Kentish plough where the mould-board is shifted from one side to the other at the end of a furrow (*OED*).

TARRASS is a waterproof mortar made of a sort of pumice imported from Germany.

TEA, BOHEA, is black tea, fermented before drying; and GREEN TEAS are made with leaves dried immediately after picking and not fermented (Davidson).

TENT: probe of soft material for cleaning or searching wounds.

THETCHES are vetches.

THRUM-THREAD describes short odds and ends of thread, specifically strong yarn as might be used for a warp: the thrums were the ends of the warp not actually woven, trimmed off after taking from the loom.

TILLS are lentils. Worlidge (1640) says that Hampshire people thought the word lentils indicated the season of Lent, so they left out the first syllable as 'not agreeing with the matter' (*OED*).

UNDERLINE or underling, meaning weak (of animals, people or plants).

UNLUCKY: Ellis' usage means not so much full of misfortune as mischievous and bad-tempered. *OED* cites the agricultural author John Mortimer (*d*.1707) who so describes a stallion.

VELLICATE, TO, means to irritate. Usually, as here, deployed to describe the action of an astringent medication.

VENICE TREACLE was an electuary on a honey (later, molasses) base, especially good against venom but with many other properties. First developed in Italy, then exported throughout Europe from Venice, hence its name.

VENICE TURPENTINE: common turpentine consisted of oleo-resins that exude from many types of conifers (the French cluster-pine in the Landes district the most important). Venice turpentine was the particular product of larch trees in the Tirol.

VERJUICE is the fermented juice (in England) of crabs or sour apples; elsewhere it was made of acid green or unripe grapes.

VITRIOL is a sulphate of metal, i.e. metal acted upon by acid. Unqualified, it usually refers to sulphate of iron (copperas) – green vitriol. Spirit of vitriol is a distilled essence of sulphuric acid.

WALLOPS describe the bubbling of water when coming to the boil, i.e. 'boiled a few wallops'. Ellis' use seems archaic, most of the citations by *OED* are early.

WASH is, generally, liquid food for animals, but usually it denotes refuse, kitchen or brewery swill, given especially to pigs (hogwash).

WATER-DOCK-ROOT is debatable. It may refer to the butterbur (*Petasites hybridus*), called the water-docken in Cumbria, and known as a plant whose leaves were good for wrapping butter (as was dock). The root was a febrifuge (Grigson).

WHITE-ASH HERB is probably ground elder.

WIG is a small cake of lightly spiced and sweetened bread dough, or more simply (for a harvest-man's beaver) just a small cake of dough.

YELM is a bundle of straw laid straight for thatching.

YELT is a young sow or gilt.

YETTED: Ellis speaks of 'yetted barley', he may mean barley infused or soaked in water or milk. There is no parallel for his employment of the word.